MONEY AND BANKING IN JAPAN

Other books by L. S. Pressnell

Country Banking in the Industrial Revolution

Studies in the Industrial Revolution (*editor*)

MONEY AND BANKING IN JAPAN

BY

THE BANK OF JAPAN
ECONOMIC RESEARCH
DEPARTMENT

Translated by

S. NISHIMURA

Edited by

L. S. PRESSNELL

ST. MARTIN'S PRESS NEW YORK

This book was originally published in Japanese in 1969 by The Credit Information Company of Japan Ltd by arrangement with the Bank of Japan.

 For information, write:
St. Martin's Press, Inc., 175 Fifth Avenue, New York, N.Y. 10010
Printed in Great Britain
Library of Congress Catalog Card Number: 72-93885
First published in the United States of America in 1973

AFFILIATED PUBLISHERS: Macmillan Limited, London–
also at Bombay, Calcutta, Madras and Melbourne

CONTENTS

PART FOUR
MONEY AND CAPITAL MARKETS

LIST OF TABLES

LIST OF FIGURES

PREFACE

Money and Banking in Japan explains the monetary and financial system which underlies the remarkable growth of the Japanese economy in recent years. That growth has become sufficiently familiar to require no elaboration here. Less familiar is the complex structure of Japan's financial institutions; the involvement of these institutions in the finance of various forms of economic activity is both closer and proportionately more striking than in many other developed countries.

Hitherto, there has been no comprehensive account in English of Japan's financial structure, although the Bank of Japan has been in the forefront of central banks in regularly disseminating detailed, up-to-date information about the monetary system.[1] *Money and Banking in Japan* offers an overall view of the monetary system, dealing with its evolution, its functioning, its detailed organisation and its relation to the economy as a whole. It is authoritative, having been prepared by the Bank's Economic Research Department.

Money and Banking in Japan has been translated from the Japanese by Professor S. Nishimura, of Hosei University, Japan.

L. S. P.

[1] For example, through its *Monthly Economic Review*, *Economic Statistics Monthly*, and its *Annual Report*.

Note on statistical information:

1. Statistics have in general been revised to mid-1971, or as near to that date as possible.
2. Recent changes necessitate modifications to the accounts of Japanese policies on Bank Rate and in the foreign exchange market. These are indicated by footnotes on page 151 and 425 respectively.
3. Symbols and conventions:
   - .. not available.
   - — nil or negligible.
4. The Fiscal Year runs from April of the year named to the following March.

INTRODUCTION

I

Twin keys to an understanding of Japan's monetary system may be found in its history, especially since 1949–53, and in the flow of funds in the economy. In a general sense the broad structure of the monetary system dates back a century (Chapter 1). Following the Meiji Restoration of 1868, which in the economic sphere symbolised Japan's determination to pursue modernisation, a period of experimentation and difficulty preceded the emergence of reasonably stable commercial banks by the late nineteenth century. They formed part of a system of financial institutions which was characterised by specialisation based on arbitrary distinctions between short-term and long-term capital, between types of money flows, and between the supposed end-uses of bank loans. Despite a drastic fall in numbers, especially during the severe economic pressures of the 1920s (Chapter 2) and some changes in functions, this specialisation persists.

In examining the flow of funds (Chapter 8) two particular points command attention. They comprise the complementary aspects of the limited development of the Japanese capital market. First, external funds provide a high percentage of the financial resources of industry when compared with, say, Britain or the U.S.A. A substantial proportion of these funds comes from the commercial banks. This means that business is considerably dependent upon the banks, and is therefore likely to be sensitive to ease or tightness in the credit situation. Second, the flow of funds registers the subordinate status of the non-bank private sector (i.e. the general public) in the finance of Japanese industry: it holds 'indirect' securities, such as bank deposits and claims on other financial intermediaries, rather than 'primary' securities such as equities. Thus, the counterpart of the industrial borrower's dependence upon the banks is the general public's dependence upon the banks for an outlet for their savings. Regarded from the banks' angle this latter situation invites elaborate arrangements to attract deposits. The variety of deposits contrast sharply with the simplicity of deposit facilities in Britain, which has a highly developed capital market, and resemble rather those found in countries in Continental Europe which, like Japan, have poorly developed capital markets.

The relationships between banks and industry have been strikingly transformed since the Second World War, and so has the relationship between a formerly weak Bank of Japan and the economy as a whole. Previously, the concentration of economic power in a few huge groups (the Zaibatsu) had involved the existence of virtually captive client banks to serve these groups. The end of the war brought an Occupation Administration anxious, in Japan as in West Germany, to eradicate or to weaken economic arrangements that were believed to have led to undesirable concentrations of power and influence, and to have been important elements in the country's war potential. As in West Germany so in Japan, American influence stressed the breaking-up of monopolistic arrangements and the opening up of the economy to greater competition.

The emergence of the 'cold war' in the late 1940s arrested these processes in Europe and Asia. Indeed in Japan, although considerable de-concentration was achieved in industry, the reorganisation of the financial structure had barely begun when the changed political situation diverted American concern to the conservation and building-up of Japan's economic and financial strength. Enough had been accomplished, however, to begin the transformation of the old balance in the financial system. Banks were no longer client banks of private economic empires; business firms were to turn increasingly to banks essentially as customers seeking finance.

For the monetary system as a whole these historic changes were consummated between 1949 and 1953. In 1949 the 'Dodge Line' policy of economic reform was inaugurated in Japan (Mr Joseph Dodge, a Detroit banker, was financial adviser to the Supreme Allied Commander, General MacArthur). The 'Dodge Line' checked the inflation which had disordered the Japanese economy since the end of the war in

1945. It also ended the easy financing by the government of industry, which now had to turn to other sources, including in particular the banks. In 1950 the outbreak of the Korean War provided a powerful stimulus to the Japanese economy as a supplier of goods and services to the American forces. If the war thus threatened to undermine the disinflationary purpose of the Dodge Line, the slowdown of American procurement in 1951 and above all the worldwide recession of 1952–3, following the virtual end of the war, were ultimately to reinforce it. A massively unfavourable swing in the balance of payments produced such monetary pressure that business firms were driven to seek help from the banks, and the banks in turn were driven to seek help from the Bank of Japan. The post-war power and influence of the Bank of Japan, and its confidence in monetary policy as an economic control, can effectively be dated from this period.

A particular manifestation of dependence upon the central bank is the phenomenon of 'over-loan'. Technically, this is borrowing by commercial banks from the Bank of Japan to restore their liquidity when they have 'over-lent' to their customers. In the first instance, the flavour of opprobrium for the banks in the name for the situation invites explanation by comparison with monetary customs in Britain and the U.S.A. There, although 'excessive' lending by banks may indeed attract the reprimand of the monetary authorities, the responsibility for the level of bank credit is usually attached to the actions of those authorities in expanding the supply of liquid assets to the banks, for example, in Britain through a public-sector deficit involving increased issues of Treasury bills, and/or extensive official purchases of government securities in the open market. In Japan the Dodge Line had required balanced or surplus budgets and had restricted the government's power to borrow and thereby to create monetary assets; and open-market operations are correspondingly limited. Hence, some other means must be found for the public sector to ensure an adequate supply of liquidity to smooth economic fluctuations, and to facilitate growth in the money supply commensurate with the economy's growth. As a claim on the public sector – in this case on the Bank of Japan – funds provided by the 'over-loan' system provide a partial solution. The all-important effect is to give the central bank immense potential influence over the banks through the terms on which it will provide this liquidity.

II

The broad structure of the banking system resembles neither the American multiplicity of 'unit' banks nor the intense concentration found in the British Commonwealth. Lying between these two extremes, it resembles rather that found in some Continental European countries, with a small number of large banks having wide networks of branches, and a number of more local banks. There are fifteen 'City Banks', of which only eight, however, have their head offices in Tokyo. Then there are sixty-one local banks. These two groups comprise the commercial banking system as normally understood, but there are also two main groups of specialist banks: these are the Long-Term Credit Banks (Chapter 14) and the Trust Banks (Chapter 15). Finance for special purposes (e.g. for small businesses, agriculture, fisheries, etc.) is provided through specialist institutions to an extent approaching that supplied by the commercial banks (Chapter 16–22).

The regulation of the various classes of financial institution rests initially on specific legislation in each case. On a day-to-day basis, however, the Bank of Japan's policy is predominant. Like central banks in most other countries, it is technically subordinate to a government ministry (the Ministry of Finance); it is officially controlled by a 'Policy Board' representing a range of interests, over which the Governor of the Bank of Japan has hitherto presided as Chairman. The Bank has made use of a wide variety of controls which are largely familiar, with local variations, to students of central banks elsewhere (Chapters 3, 10, 12). This has represented not simply a catholicity of taste, nor just a desire to learn from best practice abroad, nor merely the complexity of the problems that were likely to arise when a badly impoverished country (as Japan was at the end of the war) seeks rapid economic growth. They reflect, more perhaps than all these, a desire to 'normalise' the monetary system, that is to secure its efficient operation free or reasonably free from excessive swings in either direction, and likely to conduce to the most efficient use of economic resources.

III

If the very high levels of investment, and hence of saving, have lain at the heart of Japan's striking economic growth, much of the credit has been attributed to the active participation of the banking system in facilitating investment. This must provoke reflection, not only upon the lower ratios of investment to gross national product in Britain and the U.S.A. for instance, but also upon the possibility of a connection between industry's greater independence of external finance in those countries, and their slower growth rates. Equally, however, a question arises about Japan itself. Will the natural tendency of firms to seek to generate more funds internally contribute eventually to a slowing down of the Japanese growth rate?

No two countries have precisely similar economic systems and it is therefore not to be expected that their financial systems will be similar. There are well-tested dangers, indeed, in transplanting the analogies and supposed lessons of other countries' experiences. Nevertheless, the similarity between the economic problems of major countries in recent years cannot be gainsaid: internal inflation, external imbalance, the control of the money supply, the growth of the economy, and so on. Japanese experience in all these matters over two decades has displayed a richness that cannot lightly be disregarded.

L. S. P.

PART ONE

Development of the Modern Financial System

CHAPTER I

ESTABLISHMENT OF A MODERN BANKING AND MONETARY SYSTEM

I. NECESSITY FOR THE ESTABLISHMENT OF A MODERN BANKING AND MONETARY SYSTEM

Unquestionably the Meiji Restoration (1868) was a great turning-point in Japanese history. Not least, in the economic sphere it cleared the way for the development of a modern economy. Japan's economic development had hitherto been unspectacular. One cause for this had been the closing of the country after 1639 under the Tokugawa feudal regime. Admittedly there was a considerable growth of commerce along with the development of a monetary economy, but, as far as industry was concerned, there were only embryonic developments of modern productive methods. It was the incursion into the Asian scene of advanced European countries and of the United States which accelerated the dissolution of the Tokugawa feudal system and eventually led to the Meiji Restoration. With the conclusion of the treaties of commerce and friendship with Britain, the United States, France and other nations, the expansion of foreign trades exerted a powerful influence on the economy of Japan, which had been virtually dormant during the country's closure to the outside world. The result was the formation of a new government in 1868.

The most urgent task for the Meiji Restoration Government was to foster the growth of modern industries in order to build up sufficient economic and military strength to deal on equal terms with Europe and America. There was, however, little scope for spontaneous development of domestic industry. The government therefore had to play an important part if it wanted the task to be accomplished within a short space of time. Thus, the Meiji Government prepared the ground for the introduction of modern industries by measures such as the abolition of the feudal hierarchy, land reform and so on. At the same time it implanted in the economy some of the techniques and institutions of the advanced countries in the West, and it enforced a vigorous, positive policy of encouraging the development of modern industries. This was known as the 'Policy of Enrichment and Industrialisation' (Shokusan Kogyo Seisaku).

In order to accomplish these aims it was first of all necessary to bring order into the monetary system, which was in a state of utter chaos: a legacy from the Tokugawa era. The Meiji Government set up the Osaka Mint in 1871 and at the same time promulgated the New Currency Act; this envisaged the adoption of the gold standard, but bimetallism persisted until the establishment of decimal coinage with yen, sen, and rin as units. Thus, the first step – currency reform – was taken. It may be said, however, that it was beyond the capacity of the Meiji Government to pursue successfully the dual undertaking of currency reform and the policy of 'Enrichment and Industrialisation'. It was a newly established government with financial foundations that were still precarious. It put into effect a number of measures including the implanting of modern industries, the rationalisation of business management, the organisation of transport and communication, and the protection and fostering of private industries. Naturally funds were necessary for these purposes. The issue by the Government of notes – Gold Notes – was the first manifestation of its effort to secure a source of revenue. The result of issuing such inconvertible notes, however, was to endanger the foundation of the monetary system. To remedy this situation it was essential to establish the convertibility of the currency and at the same time to introduce and develop a modern banking system. Consequently, the early banking policy of the Meiji Government was devised with the twofold aim of securing funds for a policy of Enrichment and Industrialisation and of establishing a convertible currency.

Both a unified currency and convertibility were achieved in 1882 with the foundation of the Bank of Japan. After that prices fell, exports grew and specie began to flow in, stimulating the accumulation of loanable funds to some extent. Because of these favourable conditions interest rates tended to decline. This, together with stabilisation of the currency, enabled the stripling modern industries to take root. Especially from about 1886 development was spectacular despite a temporary setback from the economic crisis of 1890, and it received new impetus from the Sino-Japanese War of 1894–5. During the nine years from 1894 to 1902 the number of joint-stock companies quadrupled, while their total paid-up capital increased sixfold. The scale of the boom in the promotion of new firms after the Sino-Japanese War may be gauged from the fact that about 80 per cent of joint-stock companies existing in 1902 had been established since 1894. One cause of this company promotion boom was the development and consolidation of the financial system, due to the development of commercial banks after the 1893 Bank Act and due also to the establishment of special banks after the Sino-Japanese War. This modern banking system stimulated the growth of modern industries, which in turn enabled the banking system to develop further and to expand. By the first decade of the twentieth century, when modern industries had taken fairly firm root in Japan, the special banks had been established and the shape of the banking system was more or less complete.

2. ESTABLISHMENT OF NATIONAL BANKS

The Meiji Restoration Government's first measure to develop modern banking was the setting up of Exchange Companies in 1869. They were established with strong government support at eight places, including Tokyo, Yokohama and Osaka, and had the privilege of note-issue. Their name was said to have been a translation of the word 'bank', although in fact their resources consisted largely of inconvertible government notes lent to them by the government. The government lent the notes in order to stimulate their circulation and to assist the exchange companies. Thanks to this governmental support their lending to producers of export goods expanded considerably for a time, but before long unstable economic conditions and especially the general mistrust of inconvertible notes led to a decline in their business. All of them were liquidated except for the Yokohama Exchange Company, which reorganised itself into a national bank. The experience gained through the exchange companies, however, contributed considerably to the later development of banking.

After the failure of the exchange companies the Meiji Government decided to establish 'National Banks' following the example of the United States, which had established national banks to redeem inconvertible notes. Accordingly, the government promulgated the National Bank Act in 1872, and the Gold Notes Conversion Bonds Act in 1873. Banks formed in accordance with the National Bank Act were to receive automatic sanction. This Act stipulated that up to 60 per cent of the capital of national banks could be subscribed in inconvertible government notes, which were in turn paid to the government by the bank, to be exchanged for Gold Notes Conversion Bonds. On the security of these bonds the Ministry of Finance would supply the bank with a corresponding amount of notes to be issued by the bank. On the other hand, the remaining 40 per cent of the bank's capital was to be paid in specie which was to provide reserves for the conversion of the bank-notes. If this system had taken firm root inconvertible government notes would have been recalled, and instead a convertible currency would have been established.

The project failed, however. Only four national banks were established under the Act and all soon suffered from inadequate resources. The fundamental error had been to issue convertible bank-notes. First, the government continued to issue inconvertible notes, although at a slower rate than formerly, so that paper money remained at a discount against specie, and there was a flood of demands for the conversion of the bank-notes; on the other hand specie was hoarded and did not return to the banks. Second, because of the fall in world silver prices from about 1873, gold flowed out as Japan had a *de facto* system of bimetallism. The national banks, therefore, had largely to cease issuing bank-notes. In order to escape from this situation the national banks asked the government to release them from the obligation of convertibility. The government had, therefore, to revise the National Bank Act in 1876 to enable the national banks to issue notes without specie reserves.

With this step the original intention of establishing a sound currency was frustrated.

The amendment of the National Bank Act facilitated the establishment of banks and their number rapidly increased to 153 by 1879. At the time most were small with a capital of less than 200,000 yen. Their resources, however, gradually increased during the inflation caused by the South-Western War (1877).[1] At that time, however, personal savings were insignificant, and deposits came largely from the government and local authorities. Moreover, deposits fell far short of lending (at the end of 1882 deposits at national banks were 20 million yen, but advances amounted to 41 million yen). The issue of inconvertible bank-notes filled the gap. (Bank-notes outstanding amounted to 34 million yen.) Most of the lending was in the form of loans and advances, as bill-discounting was not common. Money was lent both to agriculture, which was then the dominant industry, and to small businesses which sprang up during the inflation after the South-Western War. It seems that this lending materially assisted the rise of small industries. Although unquestionably many of these small businesses were set up primarily to secure speculative profits from the inflation, it may at least be said that the national banks played an important part in 'the take-off' of the Japanese economy during the second decade of the Meiji era (1877–86), and that they helped to lay a firm base for the development of modern industry.

3. FOUNDATION OF THE CENTRAL BANK

As already noted, the Meiji Government's original intention to establish a sound currency received a setback with the amendment of the National Bank Act. For this the financial weakness of the government was a sufficient explanation but, in addition, the outbreak of the South-Western War in 1877 involved military expenditure, which was financed by the issue of inconvertible notes. This produced characteristic inflationary phenomena from 1877 to 1880, such as the depreciation of paper money, price increases, specie outflow and rising interest rates. The inflation brought to a head the financial difficulties of

[1] An insurrection in Kagoshima prefecture.

the Meiji Government and at the same time hampered the growth of modern industries. It was now appreciated that the inflation must be halted by redemption of the paper currency and by the establishment of a convertible currency. The key to this plan for the redemption of paper money was to be the founding of the Bank of Japan.

In September 1881 Masayoshi Matsukata, the then Minister of the Interior, submitted to the government a 'Memorandum on Finance', which urged the redemption of inconvertible notes and the establishment of a central bank. The novelty of the 'Memorandum' compared with other plans for paper redemption was that it combined the two measures. Matsukata became Minister of Finance in October 1881 and set out to implement his plan. Thus, in March 1882 the 'Proposal to Found the Bank of Japan' was approved by the Prime Minister. In June the Bank of Japan Act was promulgated and the Bank was opened in October.

In these circumstances the prime task of the new Bank of Japan might appear to have been the redemption of inconvertible notes. There are, however, five reasons offered for the necessity to found a central bank in an appendix to the 'Proposal to Found the Bank of Japan', entitled 'Explanation of the Reasons to Found the Bank of Japan'. This appendix explained the need as follows: (1) 'to facilitate finance'; (2) 'to increase the resources of national banks and other companies'; (3) 'to lower interest rates'; (4) 'to entrust to the Bank those functions of the Ministry of Finance that can be safely entrusted to it, after the Bank's operation is under way'; (5) 'to discount foreign bills of exchange'. These were doubtless enumerated simply as general objectives to be pursued after the modernisation of the currency system. They nevertheless emphasised that the redemption of inconvertible notes was not the sole purpose of the establishment of the Bank of Japan, but that the Bank was also to serve broader objectives: to consolidate the banking system, with the Bank of Japan as its core, and to promote industrialisation through the consolidated system.

The Meiji Government intended to make the Bank of Japan the 'bankers' bank', 'the principal business of which was to be the discounting of bills of exchange'. The intention manifests itself also in the following passage in the 'Explanation of the

Reasons to Found the Bank of Japan': 'The central bank which we are going to found and the national banks are in their nature commercial banks'. This intention is underlined in the restrictions listed in Article 12 of the Bank of Japan Act: the Bank of Japan was forbidden 'to lend on the security of real estate or on shares in various companies', 'to lend on the security of shares in the Bank of Japan or to repurchase these shares', to have interests in industries, and 'to own real estate', otherwise than was necessary for opening the head office, branches and sub-branches. It is unlikely that at that time the government regarded the national banks as true commercial banks. The establishment of the Bank of Japan was evidently intended to expedite, and the government evidently expected, their development into genuine commercial banks, although hopes were not always fulfilled, as is shown later.

With the founding of the Bank of Japan the National Bank Act was again amended, in 1883. It now stipulated that the licences of national banks were to expire twenty years after issue; to continue operations thereafter they would have to become private banks. An aim of the amendment was to give the Bank of Japan the monopoly of note-issue. This revision settled the fate of national banks as issuing banks, and was another step towards consolidation of the banking system.

Article 14 of the Bank of Japan Act gave the Bank the privilege of issuing convertible bank-notes. When the Bank opened, however, there was still a considerable premium on silver, so that a separate law specifying the details of intended note-issues was not enacted. Subsequently, when the premium on silver vanished as a result of the redemption of paper currency, the Convertible Bank Notes Act was passed in 1884. Under this Act the Bank of Japan issued notes convertible into silver coins for the first time in May 1885. These notes circulated smoothly and the amount issued rapidly increased. On the other hand, national bank-notes were being redeemed as a result of the amendment to the National Bank Act in 1883. Government notes were also being redeemed in accordance with the Cabinet Decree of 1885. These developments permitted an amendment to be made to the Convertible Bank Notes Act in 1888, 'the time having come to establish the foundation of our currency system': this led to the adoption of a fiduciary system of note-issue with a flexible limit.

The first step had thus been taken to establish a modern monetary system. Within a few years the large indemnity obtained after the Sino-Japanese War (1894–5) provided the reserves necessary for the adoption of the gold standard. In March 1897 the Monetary Law and an amendment to the Convertible Bank Notes Act were promulgated and the gold standard was established; it came into operation in October. Further, government notes and national bank-notes ceased to be legal tender from the end of 1899. From that date the convertible bank-notes of the Bank of Japan became the sole currency.

Thus, the founding of the Bank of Japan was the central feature in the consolidation of the monetary, banking and credit systems. It also had wider significance, as a cornerstone of the modernisation of the Japanese economy and of the development of modern industries. It must be recalled, however, that the Bank had been founded primarily as the major instrument for the redemption of inconvertible paper money and that, therefore, it was very much the state's own creature. Admittedly the government's influence over the Bank of Japan subsequently receded, as capital accumulated in the private sector, but it is undeniable that quite close relations with the government persisted.

The original expectation that the Bank would become the central source for trade finance, with its chief function being discount of commercial bills, was incompletely realised, because the backwardness of the Japanese economy led the commercial banks to engage in industrial finance at an early stage. For instance, during the economic crisis of 1890, and despite the restrictive clauses in Article 12 of the Bank of Japan Act, loans were made against the security of shares, including those of the Japan Railway Company. This was known as 'secured bill-discounting'. Subsequently in 1897 the Bank opened private accounts, through which business firms were enabled to borrow direct from the Bank. The objcctive was to enable commercial banks to attract sufficient deposits to enable them to supply funds to business firms without depending upon the Bank of Japan. The opening of private accounts was a factor helping to establish the deposit banking principle and commercial banks gradually extricated themselves from dependence on the Bank of Japan. 'Secured bill-discounting' was abolished with the opening of private accounts. At the same time, however, it was decided to discount bills against the collateral of certain first-class shares, including those which had been used as security for the 'secured bill-discounting'. This was known as the 'collateral security system', which continued as a temporary expedient until 1942, when an amendment to the Bank of Japan Act made it legal to lend on the security of shares and debentures.

4. DEVELOPMENT OF COMMERCIAL AND SAVINGS BANKS

From the early years of the Meiji era the government had sought to foster the growth of the banking system by measures such as the establishment of exchange companies. From about 1871 the government had received a steady flow of applications to open banks, but at first it was reluctant to grant permission since it would conflict with the spirit of the National Bank Act. Later it decided to adopt a *laissez-faire* attitude to this question if these banks did not appear to be detrimental to the public interest. Thereafter, banking companies were established one after another, until they exceeded a hundred in 1875–6. As the National Bank Act prohibited banking companies, other than those established under it, to style themselves banks, they were designated 'quasi-banks'. Subsequently, however, they were allowed to adopt the title of 'bank'. Thus, many former quasi-banks re-styled themselves and the number of so-called private banks increased. Subsequently – after 1879 – new national banks were not permitted, and private banks and quasi-banks rapidly multiplied. For example, the number of private banks increased from 39 in 1880 to 218 in 1889, while that of quasi-banks grew from 120 to 695 during the same period.

Some of the private banks were as big as the national banks, but most had a capital of less than 50,000 yen, while the average capital of quasi-banks was only about 20,000 yen. It seemed quite clear that there were too many small banks and banking companies. According to the Proposal to Establish the Banking Act of 1890, private banks engaged in transactions in goods, shares and real estate 'without any knowledge of the trades' and they 'meddled in any business which promised profits'. As might well be imagined, the quasi-banks, which were smaller than the private banks, were little more than usurious money-lenders. Such a state of affairs, however, was probably unavoidable in a transitional period. Moreover, as these private banks and quasi-banks were spread all over the country, they may well have contributed something to the development of traditional rural industries.

Because of these conditions the government was quick to appreciate the need to reorganise the banking laws. The need increased with the opening of the Bank of Japan and with the decision eventually to abolish the national banks. Thus, in 1890, the Banking Act was passed, and came into force in 1893. It defined the nature and the business of a bank, made provisions for licensing for supervision and for a maximum limit to lending on one account. This last restriction was imposed in order to prevent a bank being bankrupted by the failure of a single debtor; a bank was intended to serve the public as a whole and it was desired to avoid such calamities. Banks were, however, opposed to this provision and it was abolished in 1895. At a time when modern industries were developing, such a rigid restriction may have been out of place.

After the Banking Act came into force the commercial banks developed spectacularly. It had been stipulated that quasi-banks would not be allowed to continue unless they obtained licences to become banks under the provisions of the Act. Most of them, therefore, were either transformed into banks or were absorbed by existing banks. In addition, the national banks had to become ordinary banks. Thus, the number of banks increased markedly, exceeding 1000 in 1896 and reaching 1867 at the end of 1901. During these years advances and discounts increased greatly (in 1901 the amount was fourteen times that of 1893), while the growth of deposits lagged behind (they multiplied elevenfold during the same period), so that the ratio of deposits to advances and discounts fell to only about 70 per cent. The excess of advances and discounts over deposits was made good by borrowing from the Bank of Japan. From about the turn of the century, however, the ratio improved, and borrowing from the Bank became less important.

Parallel with the development of commercial banks, savings banks also progressed rapidly. Savings deposits had made a comparatively early start in Japan. In 1874 the government had issued a regulation concerning savings deposits which Post Offices began to receive. Before long, private institutions began to bid for these deposits, and in 1880 the first bank specialising in savings deposits was established. It was modelled on savings banks in Europe and in the United States. After 1881 more and more national banks offered savings accounts, while the number of specialised savings banks increased to twenty-one by 1883. At this time, however, most of the savings banks were usurious in character, and their business was unsound. The government therefore decided not to permit the establishment of further banks until it could prepare legislation on their status. In 1890 the Savings Bank Act was promulgated together with the Bank Act.

The purpose of the Act was to promote the sound development of savings banks by imposing strict limitations on the use of their resources and by requiring ample reserves against deposits. At that time, however, such was the condition of savings banks that they could not have continued in business if they had faithfully adhered to the provisions of the Act. In 1895, therefore, it was amended and the limitation on the employment of their resources was abolished, while the reserve ratio was lowered. After this amendment the number of savings banks rapidly increased until it reached 441 in 1901; a twentyfold increase in less than ten years. Admittedly unsound management was an inescapable corollary of this expansion, but it may be said that they served the useful purpose of absorbing small deposits.

5. INTRODUCTION OF THE SYSTEM OF SPECIAL BANKS

Special banks were those banks established under special laws for particular objectives, Most were institutions concerned with long-term industrial finance. They occupied an important place in the Japanese banking system. Their common feature is that they were under the protection of the government, which granted them unusual privileges and at the same time placed them under strict supervision.

From early years the Meiji Government had planned to establish special banks. Already in 1881 the Memorandum on Finance quoted above had stressed the need to establish a 'Kogyo Bank' (literally Industrial Bank, but what was meant at the time was the subsequent 'Hypothec Bank of Japan'). The establishment of the 'Kogyo Bank' in addition to a central bank was planned because the central bank was to be the nucleus of commercial finance, while industrial finance was to be entrusted to special banks. It seems that the government had at first intended to set up a bond-issuing bank for real-estate finance, but by 1890 the shape of the plan had been changed: such a bank was to be founded in the capital, but at the same time 'agricultural banks' were to be established in the provinces in order to assist the operation of the central organisation: moreover, a crédit mobilier was to be formed for making loans on securities.

The purpose of these proposed agricultural banks was to advance money at low interest rates to small peasants in order to fund their debts: they had been particularly hard hit by the redemption of paper after 1881, which impoverished them, and led to a reduction in the scale of their farms. This situation was reflected in the Credit Co-operatives Bill, which was presented to the Diet in 1891 'in order to provide financial facilities for people of smaller means'. (The Bill eventually emerged in 1900 as the Industrial Co-operatives Law.) The Hypothec Bank of Japan, Hokkaido Colonial Bank and Agricultural and Industrial Banks were the embodiments of this plan to set up banks for real estate finance.

The scheme to establish a crédit mobilier, on the other hand, was devised partly to relieve the Bank of Japan of industrial finance. The Bank had originally been intended to serve as the central organ for commercial finance, but it was involved in industrial finance because of the 'secured bill-discounting', to which reference has already been made. The setting up of a crédit mobilier, it was expected, would correct this situation, and would ensure the separate developments of long-term and short-term finance. In addition, the flotation of a number of joint-stock companies in 1887–96 revealed the insufficiency of capital accumulation, and underlined the need to establish a bank for making advances on securities. Thus, the original scheme to establish only a bank for real-estate finance appeared inadequate. The plan for a crédit mobilier materialised as the Industrial Bank of Japan.

Apart from the above banks, the Yokohama Specie Bank was established as the special bank for international finance. The Bank of Chosen (Korea) and the Bank of Taiwan were established as issuing banks in their respective areas and also to serve as special banks to promote local development.

Most of the special banks were founded in the fourth decade of the Meiji era (1897–1906) – that is, after the Sino-Japanese War. This was a period when modern industries took firm roots in Japan and therefore the character of these banks was deeply coloured by the policy of 'Enrichment and Industrialisation'.

(1) *The Yokohama Specie Bank*

The Yokohama Specie Bank was born under circumstances somewhat different from those surrounding the birth of other special banks: it was promoted by private citizens, but the government did not limit itself to blessing the scheme. In 1879 an application was made to establish a bank dealing with specie transactions. The objective was 'to act as an intermediary between foreign and domestic traders, to facilitate finance and to prevent the rise in premiums on silver'. The government wanted to challenge the supremacy of foreign banks and merchant firms in foreign trade financing. It therefore authorised the bank and at the same time gave it liberal assistance by subscribing to its capital and by depositing public funds with it. The Yokohama Specie Bank commenced business in 1880. In 1887 the Yokohama Specie Bank Act, which defined its character as a special bank, was promulgated in order to protect and to consolidate it.

At the wish of the government the Yokohama Specie Bank became an organisation specialised in international finance and the Bank of Japan assisted it by making it eligible to borrow at low interest rates. This came about in the following manner. Originally the government had been lending part of the Treasury 'reserves' to the Yokohama Specie Bank, which had used the money for foreign exchange transactions, but in 1889 the government discontinued lending these funds to the bank, using them instead to redeem government notes; the money was transferred to a special account. The Bank of Japan now instituted the rediscounting of foreign bills of exchange held by the Yokohama Specie Bank, the limit of rediscount being about 10 million yen and the discount rate being 2 per cent per annum. This enabled the bank to devote itself to international finance.

Thus, at first the government gave financial assistance to the bank and then the Bank of Japan provided it with cheap money. Thanks to such help the Yokohama Specie Bank's foreign exchange business developed spectacularly. For example, its lending in 1900, at 45 million yen, far exceeded the average outstanding advances and discounts of commercial banks, which were 3·5 million yen. Even the five biggest commercial banks were no match for the bank, for their average lending was 10 million yen.

(2) *The Hypothec Bank of Japan*

The Hypothec Bank of Japan was established in 1897 under The Hypothec Bank of Japan Law of 1896. It was an organisation for making long-term loans on real estate, and had the privilege of issuing debentures. Its purpose was to 'lend capital for the advancement and development of agriculture and industry'. Priority was given, however, to the promotion of agriculture; the original intention of the scheme of 1890 – the funding of peasants' debts – had receded into the background. The composition of the bank's lending shows that at first loans and advances to industry predominated: this was due chiefly to relief loans made to the cotton industry during the crisis of 1899. Thereafter agricultural loans increased until they formed the bulk of the bank's advances. The majority of these loans was for the finance of agricultural developments, such as reclamation of land, afforestation, readjustment of arable land and so on. Borrowers seem to have been limited to rich farmers and landlords, but as they played an important part in agricultural production, such lending may be presumed to have assisted the 'advancement and development of agriculture'.

(3) *Agricultural and Industrial Banks*

Agricultural and Industrial Banks were formed under the Agricultural and Industrial Banks Law of 1896 promulgated at the same time as The Hypothec Bank of Japan Law. They were founded in 1898–1900; there was one bank in each of the 46 prefectures. The government gave subsidies to the prefectures which then subscribed to the capital of the banks. These banks were organisations for making long-term loans on real estate in the same way as the Hypothec Bank of Japan. They could issue debentures and made loans for advancement and development of agriculture and industry. The difference was that they were local in character, the average amount of loans being smaller and the proportion of agricultural lending being higher. They were expected to act as 'parent banks' of industrial co-operative societies, for which legislation was being prepared. The issue of Agricultural and Industrial Debentures was, however, disappointing, so that the banks were short of funds. Thus, their development did not come up to expectation. The shortage of funds was partially alleviated by such expedients as the agency lending system, by which they became intermediaries in the lending business of the Hypothec Bank of Japan. The proportion of agency lending to their total lendings increased year by year, so that in the end the banks in agricultural prefectures came to resemble mere branches of the Hypothec Bank.

(4) *Hokkaido Colonial Bank*

Hokkaido, too, was to have an Agricultural and Industrial Bank according to the law, but because of the peculiar local circumstances a special law, Hokkaido Colonial Bank Law, was enacted in 1899. The main business of the bank, which was founded under the Law in 1900, was long-term lending on real estate. It could, however, engage in a far wider range of banking business than Agricultural and Industrial banks. It also supplied funds for the developemnt of Hokkaido. It was intended that deposits and debentures should provide it with funds, but until roughly the time of the Russo-Japanese War (1904–5) it depended largely upon its paid-up capital; subsequently debentures were successfully issued, and its loans and advances steadily increased.

(5) *The Industrial Bank of Japan*

Although the Industrial Bank of Japan Law was promulgated in 1900 the opening of the bank was delayed until 1902, because a series of runs on banks in 1900–1 created a disturbed atmosphere in banking. The bank was a debenture-issuing bank for long-term industrial finance. As noted above (p. 14) one of its aims was to ensure the separate development of long-term finance, but essentially the bank was established to provide for substantial loans at long-term, the demands for which markedly increased as a consequence of industrial development following the Sino-Japanese War. The bank was also intended to develop trust business, which at that time was highly developed in the United States. This was in order to facilitate the import of foreign capital and to expedite the supply of funds to industry.

At first, the bank's operations were limited and consisted chiefly of making loans on securities, which brought it into competition with similar lending by the commercial banks: the latter were enabled to make such loans because the Bank of Japan supported them by its collateral security system. With the development of heavy industries after the Russo-Japanese War, however, the bank's lending increased because it began to discount bills (with securities as collateral) and to make loans on the security of going concerns. A considerable part of the bank's advances were of a public-sector character as, for example, investments in gold and silver mines and loans to the Government of Korea. From the beginning, the bank sought to attract foreign capital and a sizeable volume had been imported by the end of the Meiji era (1912). It was authorised to become a trust company under the Debenture Mortgage Trust Law of 1905, and it played an important role in fostering the development of the business of trust of mortgages relative to debenture issues.

(6) *Bank of Chosen; Bank of Taiwan*

Japanese financial institutions were quick to establish themselves abroad. As early as 1878 the First National Bank (later the First Bank) had opened a branch in Pusan and it gradually became the issuing bank in Korea. With the establishment of the Japanese 'Residency-General' of Korea in 1909, following the Russo-Japanese War, however, the Bank of Korea was founded; the First Bank transferred its issuing functions to the new bank. A year later Korea was annexed to Japan and the Bank of Korea changed its title to the Bank of Chosen under the Bank of Chosen Law of 1911. In addition to being the country's note-issuing bank it was required to foster the development of the country's resources.

The Bank of Taiwan was established under the Bank of Taiwan Law in 1897; its purpose was the development of Formosa, which was annexed as a result of the Sino-Japanese War. This bank had the privilege of note-issue and played an important part in the reform of the currency system in Taiwan and in the development of its industries.

6. DEVELOPMENT OF OTHER FINANCIAL INSTITUTIONS AND ORGANISATIONS

Parallel with the establishment of the banking system other financial institutions were organised, notably insurance companies, trust companies and the Deposit Bureau of the Ministry of Finance; a bill-clearing system was established.

(1) *Insurance Companies and Trust Companies*

Insurance has a fairly long history in Japan. The first accident insurance company was started in 1879, while the first life assurance company began in 1881. Thereafter a succession of insurance companies was formed until there were 68 by 1900. Reckless management, over-competition and other abuses, however, were prevalent, leading the government to enact the Insurance Business Law in 1900 to provide supervision for the industry and to ensure its orderly conduct. After this, insurance companies made steady progress and their paid-up capital doubled between 1900 and 1911, while the amount of insurance contracts outstanding quadrupled in the same period. It was in the Taisho era (1912–26), however, that their position in the financial system was really consolidated.

The trust business, on the other hand, began with the establishment of the Industrial Bank of Japan, as already mentioned (p. 18). After 1906 trust companies multiplied; there were 70 in 1911. At that time, however, the meaning of the term 'trust' was obscure and the business of such companies was not clearly defined, many of them being essentially non-specialist finance companies.

(2) *The Deposit Bureau of the Ministry of Finance*

As noted earlier (p. 13), the postal savings deposit system was founded in the early years of the Meiji era to provide facilities for small deposits. Postal Savings Deposits (until 1887 Post-Horse Office Deposits) had at first been redeposited with the First National Bank, but from 1884 they were paid in to the National Debt Bureau of the Ministry of Finance. The National Debt Bureau had been handling the employment of the reserve fund of the government from 1876. Thus, with the redepositing of postal savings deposits with the Bureau, the Deposits Bureau (later the Trust Fund Bureau) of the Ministry of Finance came into being, not in name but in substance. In 1885 the Deposits Regulation was promulgated, by which the Deposits Bureau was established in the Ministry of Finance to take over the functions of the National Debt Bureau. The funds received by the Bureau – mainly postal savings deposits – were at first employed almost exclusively in the purchase of government stock, but from about the closing years of the Meiji era the deposits came to be employed in the underwriting of local bond issues and also in loans to local authorities. By these means it was aimed to return to the localities the funds collected in the provinces. Some of the deposits were also used in making loans to special accounts of the government.

(3) *Bill-Clearing*

The first clearing house in Japan was opened in Osaka in 1879. The second was founded in Tokyo in 1887. Settlement of clearing balances was effected by the transfer of current account balances of the clearing banks with the Bank of Japan, from 1891 in Tokyo and from 1896 in Osaka; this step brought the system close to perfection. After 1897 clearing houses were established in various localities until there were ten in 1912. The amount of clearings grew remarkably, increasing more than tenfold between 1897 and 1911. Compared with former years, credit creation by banks was greatly facilitated by the better organisation of the clearing system.

(4) *Credit Co-operatives*

From the second decade (1877–86) to the third decade (1887–96) of the Meiji era, sales co-operatives of silk, tea, etc., and purchase co-operatives of fertilisers were started in various districts, some of which had credit functions. The government recognised the need to aid and to supervise them in order to promote the village economies. Thus, in 1900 the Industrial Co-operatives Law was passed in order to foster the development of the associations, including credit co-operatives. This encouraged the rapid growth of credit co-operatives, of which more than 2200 were in existence by 1910. They played an important part in accommodating peasants, small manufacturers and traders.

(5) *Mutual Finance (Mujin)*

From ancient times ordinary people in Japan have adopted a method of financing called 'mujin' or 'tanomoshiko'. This is a system peculiar to the East, and in Japan it is said to date from as far back as the Kamakura period (thirteenth century). Originally it was a non-profit-making association for mutual help, but in 1901 the first commercial 'mujin' was started. Thereafter they developed as peculiarly Japanese financial institutions for ordinary people. Their number is said to have exceeded 1000 in 1913.

(6) *Short Loan Fund Market*

In 1901 the bill department of Moroi & Co. began to deal in call money and in the next year Fujimoto Bill-Brokers & Co.

was established. These events were crucial in the development of the short loan fund market; it seems to be no accident that they broadly coincided with the final phase of the organisation of the banking system although the major development of the market belongs to the Taisho era (1912–26).

(7) *Securities Markets*

The development of securities markets lagged far behind that of the banking system, even though various features of such markets, for instance, the joint-stock company, stock exchanges, and trading in debentures, had taken firm shape at an early stage. Stock exchanges had been authorised by the Stock Dealings Act of 1874, although it was not until a further Act, the Stock Exchange Act of 1878, had been passed, that exchanges were actually opened in Tokyo and Osaka. Even after the third decade of the Meiji era (1887–96), when the principal items traded in the market changed from government stock to shares, only a few popular shares, apart from bank shares, were listed. Moreover, most transactions were futures, so that the market was very speculative; this speculative character, together with the smallness of average savings, prevented the mass of the population from making direct investments in securities. As a result the market could not perform its proper functions, and business firms had to rely on bank lending, not only for working but also for fixed capital. It goes without saying, however, that there was a more fundamental reason for this phenomenon: in order to accomplish 'Enrichment and Industrialisation' in as short a time as possible, recourse to credit creation by banks and an effort to accelerate the accumulation of capital were inevitable. In any case, it must be borne in mind that a high degree of indirect finance, which continues to characterise the Japanese financial system, is a deeply rooted historical tradition.

CHAPTER 2

DEVELOPMENT OF THE FINANCIAL SYSTEM UP TO THE END OF THE SECOND WORLD WAR

THE thirty years from the outbreak of the First World War to the end of the Second World War was a period of violent vicissitudes: the unprecedented boom during the First World War, chronic depression and then war again. The period may be roughly divided into two, with 1936 as an approximate demarcation line.

I. FROM THE OUTBREAK OF THE FIRST WORLD WAR TO THE OUTBREAK OF THE SINO-JAPANESE INCIDENT (1914–36)

I. FINANCIAL CONDITIONS

After the Russo-Japanese War the Japanese economy suffered adverse balances of payments, which were worsened by the heavy burden of servicing the enormous volume of national debt issued abroad to finance war expenditure and other purposes. The outbreak of the First World War in 1914 provided the economy with an opportunity to get out of its impasse and to begin a fresh leap forward. Exports expanded and productive capacity increased, because orders from the belligerents and from other nations for war munitions and other goods, which had normally been supplied by the European countries, flooded into Japan. During the four years from 1915 to the armistice of 1918 the excess of exports over imports amounted to 1·4 billion yen, while invisible items showed a favourable balance of 1·3 billion yen. At the outbreak of the war Japan had been a debtor nation with obligations of over 1·9 billion yen, but she now became a creditor country. Moreover, the value of industrial production increased fivefold during 1914–19 (if we deflate this by the price rise during the years, production doubled). The progress of heavy and chemical industries and the electric power industry was particularly notable.

With the end of the war the economic strength of the belligerents recovered, international competition sharpened, and overseas markets, which had provided the basis of Japan's great development, gradually narrowed. A violent reaction in the Japanese economy was therefore unavoidable. After a brief post-war boom in 1919 there was a succession of blows: the sharp crisis of March 1920, the financial crisis of 1922, and the Great Earthquake of 1923. Immediately after the earthquake various emergency edicts were promulgated to allay the public's fears and to ensure the smooth supply of goods. In financial affairs two emergency edicts were issued after consultation with the Bank of Japan: a moratorium edict and an edict on the recompense for losses on earthquake bills. There was a temporary reconstruction boom, but the imports for reconstruction caused huge trade deficits and a substantial weakening of the foreign exchanges. In consequence there was considerable controversy about the desirability of lifting the ban on exports of gold, which had been imposed in 1917. The government had recommenced specie shipments and intended to lift the ban, but it first planned to liquidate the earthquake bills and to promote the reorganisation and strengthening of banks and business firms. While the Diet was debating the bill on earthquake paper in 1927, however, fears about banks which held such bills produced a financial panic, which subsided only when the Bank of Japan granted special accommodation to banks, the government promising to recompense the Bank for consequent losses up to 700 million yen. The depression, however, persisted.

The government wanted to revive the economy by lowering internal prices and by stimulating exports. To this end, the ban on gold exports was lifted in January 1930. The world depression had, however, already begun and was steadily worsening. The expected increase in exports could not materialise. Moreover the return to the gold standard had been made at the old parity; speculators who had purchased yen in anticipation now sold them, causing gold to flow out. All this contributed to the severe depression of the Japanese economy, and it was against this background that the Manchurian Incident broke out in September 1931. In the same month the United Kingdom went off the gold standard. These events gave tremendous shocks to the Japanese economy. At the end of the year the government prohibited gold export again and stopped the conversion of bank-notes into gold. It sought to stimulate economic recovery through reflation by the issue of government bonds via the Bank of Japan. In the middle of the following year (1932) the system of bank-note issues was revised so as to abolish in effect the limit hitherto imposed by the gold reserve. A managed currency system was thereby established. In order to restrict the depreciation of the exchanges the law to prevent capital flight was enacted in July 1932; it was replaced by the Foreign Exchange Controls Law of March 1933. The government also pursued a cheap money policy, partly as an anti-depression measure and partly to minimise the costs of the national debt, which was increasing as a result of 'the Incident'. From the latter half of 1932 there was a gradual recovery in industry, until full capacity was approached in 1935. 'The 26 February Incident'[1] of 1936, however, marked a turning-point: circumstances rapidly changed, and the economy was geared to war.

2. COMMERCIAL BANKS AND SAVINGS BANKS

The tendency for the amalgamation and concentration of commercial banks in Japan began comparatively early. The number of banks reached a peak of 1867 in 1901 and thereafter gradually decreased. The development of heavy industries during the First World War led to a growth in the size of firms and to a growth in the demand for finance, to meet which banks also had to be enlarged. Commercial banks, therefore,

[1] An attempted coup by young army officers.

tried to augment their resources by increases in paid-up capital and by attracting more deposits. Bank mergers progressed modestly at first, and the scale of banking gradually increased.

After 1920 there was a substantial acceleration of bank amalgamation. The chronic depression after the crisis of that year brought about a series of liquidations of banks connected with small businesses. Even big banks, such as the Fifteenth Bank and the Bank of Taiwan, were not necessarily secure. Accordingly the government tried to encourage amalgamation by amending the Bank Law in 1920 so as to simplify the merger procedure. As the business of the medium and small country banks differed from that of big banks in the cities, amalgamation was by no means easy. The government, therefore, sought to foster 'local amalgamations' – that is, amalgamations among these medium and small banks themselves. As a consequence, the number of banks decreased by about 100 per annum during 1921–6. In particular the number of banks with less than 100,000 yen of paid-up capital was halved. Since, however, there was scant hope of improving the position of business firms during the chronic depression, there was correspondingly little chance of improvement in the condition of the banks; on the contrary, the situation of medium and small banks steadily worsened, until the financial crisis of 1927 exposed their underlying weaknesses.

The government tried to facilitate bank amalgamations by abolishing the Bank Act in 1927 and by enacting a new Banking Law, which came into force from January 1928. Article 3 of the Banking Law stipulated a minimum amount for a bank's capital, the provision being applied to existing banks; of the 1400 banks existing at the end of 1926 more than half were thus to be disqualified. This is evidence of the government's strong desire to promote the concentration of banks, the number of which was drastically reduced to 683 by the end of 1931 and to 418 by the end of 1936. Furthermore, the Banking Law prohibited banks from engaging in trades other than banking; imposed a limit on the establishment of branches and sub-branches; and provided for closer governmental supervision. It was thereby hoped to eliminate the weaknesses of commercial banks.

Thus, the financial crisis of 1927 and the Banking Law accelerated the amalgamation of medium and small banks. On the other hand, big banks consolidated their dominant position. The relative shares of the five biggest banks rose as follows: deposits increased from 24 per cent of the total of all commercial banks in 1926 to 37 per cent in 1930; their lending rose from 20 to 30 per cent of the total and that of their investments from 26 to 41 per cent during the same period.

Let us now turn to the savings banks. The crisis of 1920 revealed that many of them were unsound. The government therefore abolished the Savings Bank Act in 1921 and enacted the Savings Bank Law which came into force in January 1922. This law sought to regularise their business by stipulating a minimum amount of capital and by restricting the range of their business and the employment of their resources. The smaller savings banks fell short of the new law's requirements; and the law prohibited banks from engaging in other businesses. Consequently many of them were converted into or absorbed by ordinary banks. There had been as many as 636 in 1921, but they were reduced to 124 by the end of the Taisho era (1912–26). With the new law, savings banks concentrated upon their proper function, and their soundness was assured for the time being. Their numbers continued to decline, reaching 72 in 1936.

3. THE BANK OF JAPAN

The Bank of Japan had endeavoured to achieve the purpose for which it had been founded, i.e. to facilitate commercial finance. In the chronic depression period, however, the Bank modified this 'commercial finance' principle. In the 1920 crisis the Bank's attitude was that, as there had been a rush of speculative firms, natural selection among them was both proper and necessary. The Bank, therefore, refrained from giving relief indiscriminately. It could not, however, avoid granting accommodation to commercial banks to enable them to maintain liquidity nor to the Stock Exchange which needed money to settle transactions. Further, in individual cases the Bank had to make loans to assist those who, they felt, had a reasonable claim to help, such as those who had expanded their productive capacity for legitimate purposes, for instance to meet overseas demand during the war. The Bank felt that, in the absence of such emergency loans, confusion in the economy would be aggravated and might lead to a catastrophic crisis. It is clear, however, that thereafter there was an impression that the Bank was a relief organisation for private firms, particularly financial institutions; people came to regard it as no shame to depend upon the Bank for help. Thus, the Bank had more than once to give emergency help: during the 1922 crisis, the Great Earthquake of 1923, and again during the 1927 crisis. These actions of the Bank enabled the Japanese economy to avert the worst catastrophes, but it must be admitted that the Bank lost sight of its ideal of giving priority to commercial finance and that its control over the market was weakened.

After the lifting of the ban on gold exports of 1930 such relief measures involving special accommodation by the Bank ceased. The outbreak of the Manchurian Incident in 1931, however, imposed a new duty on the Bank: to finance budget deficits. The hostilities made budgetary expansion and bond issues inevitable. In 1932, for the first time bonds were issued via absorption by the Bank. Formerly they had been issued for public subscription through bank underwriting syndicates, or they had been taken up by the Deposit Bureau. By those methods absorption of money from the private sector preceded expenditure by the government, so that not only was there no net change in the supply of money, but there was also temporary tightness while money was being absorbed by the government. When, however, the Bank of Japan took up the bonds, it created extra credit, easing the market and risking inflation through public finance. The Bank was well aware of this danger, and tried to unload such bonds in the market in order to absorb funds and thus to prevent the depreciation of money. The Bank's market purchases and sales of bonds had hitherto been exceptional, but they now became a regular instrument of monetary control along with Bank-rate policy. After 1932, when an easy money policy was adopted, it became virtually the sole weapon, displacing Bank-rate policy.

During the second half of 1935 business activity at last showed signs of revival; it was felt that if the government continued to issue bonds via absorption by the Bank, maintenance of the value of money would be difficult, even if the Bank undertook open-market operations. As the government had originally regarded the issuing of bonds via the Bank as 'a temporary expedient' to combat the depression, it now undertook gradually to reduce the national debt. In fact, however, government bond issues became, after 1937, the chief means of raising money for military expenditure, so that the Bank of Japan became an unlimited source of governmental finance.

4. SPECIAL BANKS

Although the Japanese economy suffered chronic depression from the crisis of 1920 to the lifting of the ban on gold exports in 1930, the business of special banks continued to expand. For instance, the lending of special banks, excluding the Bank of Taiwan, the Bank of Chosen and the Chosen Development Bank doubled between 1920 and 1931. (During this period the lending of commercial banks hardly increased.) The amount of their bonds outstanding increased; at the end of the period it was 2·7 times as great as at the beginning. The Hypothec Bank of Japan and the Industrial Bank of Japan made particularly notable progress. On the other hand, the number of Agricultural and Industrial banks was substantially reduced many of them amalgamating with the Hypothec Bank. As the scope of the Hypothec Bank and the Industrial Bank became clearer, credit co-operatives and their associate organisations and other private financial institutions acquired a new significance in the finance of agriculture and of small businesses.

In rural prefectures Agricultural and Industrial banks had become, in effect, lending agencies of the Hypothec Bank. During the 1920 crisis some of them sought amalgamation with the Hypothec Bank. In 1921, therefore, a law for the amalgamation of the Hypothec Bank and Agricultural and Industrial banks was passed. This was the last straw and the merger process accelerated: 17 Agricultural and Industrial banks were absorbed by the Hypothec Bank during 1921–2. After the 1927 financial crisis there was a revival of amalgamations and by 1930 only 19 of these banks survived. It goes without saying that these mergers enlarged the Hypothec Bank and enhanced its position in the banking world.

From about 1907 landlords were tending to abandon their active concern with agricultural production; absentee landlordism developed in the provinces. Parallel with this development the Hypothec Bank and Agricultural and Industrial banks in cities tended to lose their agricultural character, a tendency strengthened by amendments in 1911 to the Hypothec Bank of Japan Law and to the Agricultural and Industrial Banks Law (which abolished the provision in the laws restricting their lending to the improvement and development of agriculture and industry). These banks did not withdraw entirely from agricultural finance, but they were to be no more exempt than other banks from the need to observe sound principles of management; moreover, as mortgage banks concerned with loans on real property, they could not lend directly to propertyless small peasants. Thus, when the government decided to tackle the serious agricultural depression in the middle of the Taisho era (1912–26) with a policy of aiding small farmers, it had to look beyond the Hypothec Bank and the Agricultural and Industrial banks for agricultural finance. In 1923, therefore, new legislation made the Central Co-operative Bank of Industry (renamed in 1943 the Central Bank for Commercial and Industrial Co-operatives) the nucleus of the national network of industrial co-operatives and their prefectural associations.

Meanwhile, as modern industries developed, the Industrial Bank of Japan was lending more and more of its resources to them and became firmly established as their long-term finance organisation. Further, in the recession after the First World War it made relief loans to the chemical, silk and other industries; and following the Great Earthquake of 1923, and also during the 1927 financial crisis, it provided emergency finance for small businesses. It had been lending to small industries from the beginning of the Taisho era (1912–26), but the proportion of such advances to the Bank's total lending was not very large. (At the end of 1930 it was 5·3 per cent.) After the financial panic of 1927 medium and small banks closed one after another, so that deposits were transferred to big banks. This further intensified the financial difficulties of small businesses. To meet this difficulty mutual finance on co-operative principles gradually spread. Without some co-ordinating body, however, such a move was not very effective. To meet this need, a law of 1936 established the Central Co-operative Bank of Commerce and Industry, to be responsible for facilitating the finance of small business.

5. OTHER FINANCIAL INSTITUTIONS

(1) *Trust Companies and Insurance Companies*

Trust and insurance companies made marked progress from the latter half of the Taisho era (1912–26). As noted earlier there was a rush of trust companies after 1906, their number reaching 488 at the end of 1921. Most of them, however, were quite small, their business not being that normally associated with trusts. To deal with this situation, the Trust Law and the Trust Business Law were enacted in 1922. This provided an opportunity to weed out weak and small trust companies. Meanwhile, genuine trust companies emerged; there were 37 of these by the end of 1928. During these six years successive banking disturbances occurred because of the chronic depression, and led to the transfer of funds from bank accounts to trust companies. (During 1926–31 commercial bank deposits decreased by 10 per cent, while money in 'trust' at trust companies almost trebled.) With this substantial increase in their resources, trust companies achieved maturity and standing in the financial world, and they became important suppliers of funds to industry.

The number of insurance companies reached 90 in 1921. Some of them, however, were little more than outlets for the funds of their related undertakings. In spite of this, the volume of insurance contracts steadily grew, in contrast to the static or declining trend of bank deposits (during 1920–31 outstanding insurance contracts trebled). By 1935 their resources far surpassed those of trust companies and savings banks and were second only to those of commercial banks. The position of insurance companies as suppliers of long-term funds had been established.

(2) *Credit Co-operative System*

Credit co-operatives established under the Industrial Co-operatives Law had developed principally in rural districts, but an amendment to the law in 1917 facilitated the development of Urban District Credit Co-operatives. These differed from existing credit co-operatives in being forbidden to engage in ancillary business such as the purchase and sale of commodities: on the other hand, they could discount bills and receive deposits from non-members. They developed rapidly as financial institutions for small businesses in cities, a trend which the Urban District Credit Co-operatives Law of 1943 reinforced. In the meantime credit co-operatives governed by the Industrial Co-operatives Law also became more important in agricultural finance during the depression in the 1920s as channels for government funds lent to peasants and small businesses at low rates of interest.

(3) *Credit Guarantee System*

To promote the finance of small business, various devices were adopted to reinforce their creditworthiness and the elegibility of the security they could offer. For instance, after 1932 various systems were instituted by prefectures and by the six biggest cities to indemnify those lending money to small businesses. In 1937 the Credit Guarantee Association was established.

(4) *Mujin* (*Mutual Loans*)

The 'mujin' institutions came to be organised as joint-stock companies towards the end of the nineteenth century. Their excessively rapid growth led the government to enact the Mujin Business Law in 1915, which prohibited the promotion of unlicensed mujin companies and imposed restrictions on the employment of their resources. An extensive revision of the law in 1931 stipulated that 'mujin' could be conducted only by joint-stock companies. The number of such companies increased from 136 in 1916 to 259 in 1935.

(5) *Deposit Bureau of the Ministry of Finance*

The funds at the command of the Deposit Bureau continued to increase during the Taisho era (1912–26), chiefly through the growth of postal savings deposits. With the increasing significance of these funds the Deposit Bureau Deposits Law of 1925 laid down regulations for their employment. This laid a basis for the bureau's further development. Its funds came to be employed not only in long-term finance, such as in the purchase of securities including public bonds, loans to local authorities and special banks and special companies, but also in short-term finance, such as short-term holding of government bonds, purchase of short-term securities, bridging-loans to special banks and special companies anticipating their bond – or debenture – issues, and in call loans. In war-time, when the government acquired extra powers, the bureau's funds became a powerful influence in financial markets.

6. THE CALL MONEY MARKET

The development of the Japanese economy during the First World War stimulated the growth of the money market. Moreover, the establishment of new branches by the Bank of Japan and the extension of branch networks of banks through amalgamations facilitated the flow of funds between districts; the surplus funds of country banks came to be employed increasingly in Tokyo and Osaka through larger country banks which were parent organisations of smaller banks, and through the branches of big banks. This greatly fostered the development of the call money market.

Before the First World War call money was borrowed largely to settle clearing balances, but the war-time increase in exports brought a spectacular growth in the demand for money for exchange transactions; call money came to be borrowed for these purposes. Thus, the volume of dealings in call money increased, prompting the growth of dealers in call money. The number of joint-stock bill-broking banks increased and their resources multiplied. The market flourished until the 1927 financial crisis, although it must be recognised that inappropriate policies were far from uncommon, a typical example being the absorption of call money by the Bank of Taiwan.

The experiences of the financial crisis of 1927 led the big banks to seek ways to improve the market. Moreover, the Banking Law of 1928 prohibited banks from engaging in business outside the sphere of pure banking. For this reason the bill-broking banks had to be converted into specialist bill-brokers.

7. SECURITIES MARKET

It has been remarked already that the predominance of banks in financial markets and the limited development of securities markets have been distinctive features of Japan's financial structure, although their development has been encouraged since the Meiji era (1868–1912). With the development of heavy industry and the rise of big business in the boom during the First World War, however, it became necessary to mobilise capital from the general public, and this paved the way for the development of the securities market. In particular, the raising of capital by debentures increased after the First World War. At the end of the Taisho era (1912–26) the amount of debentures in issue exceeded that of shares. Such issues became so active in 1928 that people talked of the advent of the golden age of debentures, and a stable, free market for debentures was maintained until the outbreak of the Sino-Japanese Incident. It must be noted, however, that this expansion in debentures largely reflected two circumstances. First, financial institutions had considerable surplus funds, for which they sought investment outlets in debentures; until 1931 the depression had reduced the demand for bank loans, and between 1932 and 1936, with idle capacity persisting, the issue of government bonds via absorption by the Bank of Japan enabled the government to make large-scale disbursements. Second, as interest rates were declining, there was widespread conversion of existing debts and a lengthening of their maturities, while borrowings from banks were also funded. Hence, there was little change in the market for existing debentures, although considerable progress was made in its organisation from the end of the Taisho era (1912–26).

The new issue market in shares also showed signs of fresh development in the Showa era (1926–), when newly established big businesses made considerable progress. As these firms did not have affiliated banks, they had to raise capital by issuing shares for public subscription; new issues and the offering of shares in existing companies increased from 1933 to 1934, the demand for large sums of capital accompanying the full-scale development of the heavy industries after the Manchurian Incident. Admittedly, these public issues and offerings were still very small in comparison with the total amount of shares outstanding or even with the total amount of shares issued publicly and privately, but this might well have been the prelude to further development of the new issue market.

II. FROM THE OUTBREAK OF THE SINO-JAPANESE INCIDENT TO THE END OF THE PACIFIC WAR (1937–45)

I. FINANCIAL CONDITIONS

The Japanese economy was firmly geared to the war after the outbreak of the Sino-Japanese Incident in July 1937. In September the Emergency Military Expenditures Special Account was created; its successive budgets amounted to 22·3 billion yen by the outbreak of the Pacific War in 1941. This far exceeded the 0·2 billion for military expenditures of the Sino-Japanese War of 1894–5 or 1·5 billion for those of the Russo-Japanese War (1904–5). Practically the whole of the money was raised by the issue of government bonds taken up by the Bank of Japan, so that inflation was inevitable unless these bonds could be marketed satisfactorily. Hence, immediately after the outbreak of the Incident the Bank of Japan lowered the minimum rate of interest on loans against government bonds to the same level as the discount rate for commercial bills, in order to facilitate the marketing of bonds; the government endeavoured to create favourable conditions for the marketing of bonds by accelerating the amalgamation of country banks. Another and new duty was imposed upon the financial system, that of providing funds for the expansion of the productive capacity of the munitions industry. A series of laws to control the flow of funds was enacted. These included the Temporary Funds Adjustment Law of September 1937, the aim of which was to ensure the supply of funds for fixed investment in plant and equipment for priority industries, and the Bank Funds Utilisation Order of September 1940, which sought to control the supply of working capital. In May 1938 the National General Mobilisation Law provided for export and import controls, and for restrictions and prohibitions on the use of important raw materials for the manufacture of goods for domestic consumption. Then, in July 1941 was published the Synopsis of Fundamental Fiscal and Monetary Policies, according to which totalitarian controls were to be imposed in order to utilise the nation's economic potentialities to the full during the war. With the outbreak of the Pacific War in December 1941 this Synopsis was implemented. Measures in the financial sphere included the reform of the Bank of Japan, the acceleration of bank amalgamation by the Ordinance for the Consolidation of Financial Institutions, and the creation of various war-time financial institutions and of financial control associations.

In 1943 an amendment to the law on the issue of government bonds empowered the government to issue bonds without limit for the purpose of emergency military expenditures. The cumulative total of the budget for the Emergency Military Expenditure Special Account amounted to 195·8 billion yen during the Pacific War. Although the Bank of Japan made every effort to market the government bonds it had acquired, such sales were largely offset by the great increase in its lending to the munitions industries. Thus, the aggravation of inflation became inevitable. On the other hand, the military situation steadily deteriorated from the beginning of 1943. Accordingly, in January 1944, the system of designated financial institutions for the accommodation of the munitions industry was adopted; this aimed to provide easy finance for key industries, such as aircraft and shipbuilding. By this system munitions companies were assured of easy access to necessary funds. Furthermore, the Synopsis of War-time Emergency Monetary Policy and Re-adjustment of June 1944 provided for an extension of the Bank of Japan's guarantee of deposits, so that time deposits could now be drawn out before maturity. These nullified the anti-inflationary measures which had hitherto been applied, however imperfectly. The air-raids began from the end of 1944 and almost completely destroyed the munitions industries. The Pacific War at last came to an end in August 1945.

2. THE BANK OF JAPAN

Originally adopted in 1932 as a 'temporary expedient', the system of issuing government bonds through absorption by the Bank of Japan had become the chief method of raising money for military expenditure after the Sino-Japanese Incident. The Bank of Japan did its best to market bonds in an effort to avert inflation from such deficit-financing. The outstanding amount of bank-notes expanded every year, however, by a large margin. The issue of notes in excess of the fiduciary limit became permanent. The government, therefore, had repeatedly to increase the fiduciary issue. In March 1941 the law concerning the Temporary Amendment to the Convertible Bank-Notes Act abolished the distinction between the issue of notes against specie reserves and that against fiduciary reserves, and adopted the maximum issues limit system. By this step the adoption of a managed currency system was legally confirmed, although the law in question was a temporary one. By the Temporary Funds Adjustment Law of 1937 and the Bank Funds Utilisation Order of 1940, which instituted controls on the flow of funds, the Bank of Japan was the agent in implementing the control.

The reform of the Bank of Japan in 1942 fixed its national character. Until then the form of the Bank had remained virtually unchanged from that established at its foundation in 1882, except for the system of note-issue; an opportunity for a large-scale reform was provided in October 1942, with the expiry of the Bank's charter, which had been extended for 30 years in 1910.

The Bank of Japan Law of February 1942 was modelled on the 1939 Reichsbank Act of Nazi Germany. It declared that the Bank was a special corporation of strongly national nature. The Bank was 'to assume the task of controlling currency and finance and supporting and promoting the credit system in conformity with policies of the state to ensure the full use of the nation's potential'. Further, it was 'to be managed with the accomplishment of national aims as its sole guiding principle' (Article 2). As for the functions of the Bank, the law abolished the old principle of priority for commercial finance, empowering it to supervise facilities for industrial finance. The law also authorised the Bank to make unlimited advances to the government without security, and to subscribe for and to absorb government bonds. In respect of note-issues the law made permanent the system of the maximum issues limit; thus, the Bank could make unlimited issues to meet the requirements of munitions industries and of the government. On the other hand, government supervision of the Bank was markedly strengthened. The government could nominate, superintend and give orders to the president and the directors; there was also a clause giving the government more comprehensive powers to give so-called 'functional orders' to the Bank, to direct it to perform any function it deemed necessary for the attainment of the Bank's purpose. Moreover, the law made a wide range of the Bank's business subject to governmental approval, including such matters as the alteration of Bank rate, note-issues and accounts.

A noteworthy event in connection with the revision of the Bank of Japan Law was the formation of the Financial Control Association. The Synopsis of Fundamental Fiscal and Monetary Policies published in July 1941 made clear the government's intention to impose controls on financial institutions. The intention took shape in the Finance Control Organisations Ordinance of April 1942. By this ordinance the absorption and distribution of funds by various financial organisations became subject to the government's policy on financial control. Formally the Control Association was a separate entity from the Bank of Japan and was to co-operate with the government, but its administration was entrusted to the Bank.

3. COMMERCIAL BANKS AND SAVINGS BANKS

The amalgamation of commercial banks, as noted earlier (pp. 25–7), made considerable headway after the depression of the 1920s and the 1927 financial crisis. After 1936, when the economy was geared to war, amalgamations among country banks were pushed forward on the principle of one bank in one prefecture. The aim was not so much to consolidate the banks' business as to strengthen financial control, such as the promotion of the easy money policy, the improvement of government bond marketing and the provision of funds for munitions industries. The Ordinance for the Consolidation of Financial Institutions of 1942 gave legal sanction to this policy of bank amalgamation. In consequence the number of commercial banks fell drastically, from 377 in 1937 to 61 in 1945. Needless to say, the average size of commercial banks was considerably enlarged as a result. Moreover, during this period there were also amalgamations between big banks, for example, between the Mitsui and the Dai-ichi First banks, and between the Mitsubishi and the Daihyaku banks. Thereby, the relative importance of big banks was further enhanced.

Meanwhile, savings banks also were exhorted to amalgamate after the outbreak of the Pacific War, in order to improve the mobilisation of funds. Further, a law of March 1943 enabled commercial banks to do savings-bank business as well; this led to savings banks being rapidly absorbed by ordinary banks, their number decreasing sharply until only four remained at the end of the hostilities (there had been 69 in 1940).

Control over the flow of funds had been progressively tightened by the Temporary Funds Adjustment Law in September 1937, and by the Bank Funds Utilisation Order of October 1940. Big city banks gradually developed as sources of finance for munitions industries, while medium and small country banks tended to become sources of surplus funds. This was because big firms with close ties with banks had entered the munitions industries, while country banks, hitherto associated with local industries, had lost their lending customers because of the ban on lending outside the munitions and related industries. At the same time they were acquiring more funds as a result both of industrialisation and of the agricultural boom, phenomena which reflected the intensification of hostilities. Thus, the local banks had no alternative but to lend to the big city banks and to the special banks. This division of function between local and city banks was further underlined with the establishment of the system of designated financial institutions for the finance of the munitions industries in January 1944.

4. SPECIAL BANKS

During the war financial institutions were reorganised in order to facilitate the finance of the munitions industries and the marketing of government bonds. Special banks were no exception to this. In particular, the Industrial Bank of Japan became an important source of funds for the expansion of the munitions industries capacity, so that its lending increased enormously. From the end of 1936 to August 1945 the total lending of all commercial banks increased about eightfold, but that of the Industrial Bank was multiplied about 37 times. On the other hand, the Agricultural and Industrial banks, of which 16 still remained at the end of 1936, were strongly advised by the government to amalgamate with the Hypothec Bank. Their number was reduced to five in 1938; in September 1944 these were also absorbed by the Hypothec Bank. Thus, the Agricultural and Industrial banks disappeared completely from the Japanese banking system.

5. SPECIAL FINANCIAL INSTITUTIONS

As the demand from the munitions industries for advances was extremely large and the attendant risks were great, it was difficult to rely entirely on private financial institutions for the necessary funds, although efforts were made to mobilise them for the financing of the munitions industries. Consequently, under a special law of 1942, a new institution, the War-time Finance Bank, was formed. Its task was to provide 'funds necessary for the expansion of production and for reorganisation of industries', where such funds were 'difficult to obtain from other financial institutions'. Two-thirds of its capital was subscribed by the government, which also guaranteed it against any loss it might incur. Until the end of the war the bank was active in making loans, chiefly to priority industries; it also bought and sold shares, sometimes holding them in order to stabilise security prices. To serve the same objective the Joint Loans Bank was established under the Banking Law in April 1945 – that is, almost at the end of the war. This bank was formed by the joint subscription of country banks, which had been deprived of their normal outlets for their funds and which consequently sought to lend directly to the munitions industries. Such direct loans were, however, in conflict with the principle of centralised control of lending, so that the scheme had to be revised. Eventually the bank became an agency for pooling the surplus funds of country banks; there seemed little purpose in its continued existence, and it was absorbed by the Funds Unification Bank (an ordinary bank) which had been founded in May 1945, to concentrate the surplus funds of special banks, commercial banks, the Central Co-operative Bank of Agriculture and Forestry, trust companies, insurance companies, etc., and to make joint loans to the munitions industries. The bulk of this bank's capital had been subscribed by the Bank of Japan and the rest was allocated to the principal financial institutions. The bank's chief resources were its surplus funds and also borrowings from the Bank of Japan. Lending was chiefly to designated financial institutions, such as the Industrial Bank of Japan and other big banks. It also made direct loans to special corporations and control companies. This system encouraged the conversion of local banks into money-absorbing agencies, and of special and big banks into instruments for making advances to the munitions industries.

In overseas finance the Southern Development Bank was founded in 1942; in 1945 the External Capital Bank was established in order to protect the Japanese economy from inflation in overseas territories. These were established under special laws.

6. OTHER FINANCIAL INSTITUTIONS

Trust companies and insurance companies had been improving their positions in the financial world from the end of the Taisho era (1912–26). With the consolidation of the war economy, however, they came to be treated as mere money-collecting organisations. Although the funds under their control expanded, thanks partly to the national savings campaign, they were not free to employ these funds as they wished; they were turned into organs for the absorption of government bonds and for the supply of funds to the munitions industries. In this sphere, too, amalgamations continued during the war, so that by the end of 1945 the number of trust companies had fallen to 7, that of life insurance companies to 21, and that of non-life-insurance companies to 16. Moreover, the law of 1943 relating to the involvement of ordinary banks in savings bank business and trust business permitted the combination of banking and trust business, which had hitherto been strictly separated by the Trust Business Law. At that time banks absorbed 11 local trust companies, which became their trust departments. This law may be said to have cleared the way for the post-war conversion of trust companies into trust banks.

Industrial co-operatives were merged with agricultural societies, which had been organised under the Agricultural Societies Law of 1900 for the improvement and development of agriculture, to become agricultural associations. Their original functions were, however, overshadowed by their roles as terminal agencies for agricultural control.

As the economy became more closely geared to the war there was less and less scope for the call money market to function. The call rate was virtually pegged at a low level after 1942, when control associations were established under the ordinance for financial-control organisations. Controls were also tightened in the securities market: the Temporary Funds Adjustment Law regulated the establishment of companies and the increase of capital, and their issue of debentures; while the ordinance on the control of stock prices, and the market operations of the Wartime Finance Bank aimed at eliminating speculative factors from the market, stress being laid upon its function of mobilising funds for priority industries.

CHAPTER 3

THE POST-WAR FINANCIAL SITUATION AND CHANGES IN THE FINANCIAL SYSTEM

I. FINANCIAL CONDITIONS

The Pacific War ended with Japan's defeat in August 1945. The defeat led to unprecedented changes in many spheres, including the financial system.

In the background was the runaway inflation which more than anything else characterised the post-war economy. Inflation had been developing beneath the surface towards the end of the war, but it became open inflation in the confusion after the defeat. In addition, a huge volume of currency was issued through Treasury disbursements immediately after the war. This made for an even worse situation, in which there was a heavy demand upon financial institutions for money for speculative purposes; meanwhile deposits were rapidly run down, so that the Bank of Japan's lending continued to expand just as it had done during the war. The government therefore published emergency measures to deal with the economic crisis; and in February 1946 it promulgated the Emergency Financial Measures Ordinance and the Bank of Japan Notes Deposit Ordinance. These emergency actions sought to freeze cash and deposits in order to remove them from circulation, thereby blocking excess purchasing power. These monetary measures were to be co-ordinated with price control and other physical controls to form a coherent and systematic anti-inflationary policy.

These actions averted runs which might have bankrupted financial institutions, but inflation was halted only temporarily.

The reason was that these were merely half-measures, which froze existing deposits and bank-notes, but which placed no obstacles to fresh credit creation and note-issues. Moreover, apart from price control, no important physical control was instituted. Hence, by the end of September 1946 the amount of outstanding Bank of Japan notes exceeded that prevailing before the emergency measures. The government therefore tried to put the public finances on a more sound footing: various forms of war compensation, principally those to the munitions industries, were cancelled by an enactment of October 1946; in the following month a capital levy was imposed. Nevertheless, there were frightening budget deficits because of the costs of occupation forces. These deficits were financed by credit creation by the Bank of Japan; this steadily worsened the inflation.

To extricate the economy from its predicament a system of priority production was adopted, giving precedence to steel and coal. In finance there was a parallel measure in the full-scale control of lending. In March 1947 a regulation issued under the ordinance for emergency financial measures gave a legal basis to restrictions on lending. The purposes of this control were, first, to restrain as far as possible private financial institutions from borrowing from the Bank of Japan by limiting this, in principle, to their deposit liabilities. Second, to establish priorities among industries both for working capital and for fixed capital; those of high priority could borrow readily, while those low down were, in principle, to be denied accommodation. The crisis measures did not, however, strike at the source of inflation – that is, at the budget deficits. Moreover, the Reconstruction Finance Bank, which had been established in January 1947 to supply urgently needed funds to basic industries, made some unwise advances. Its resources derived from credit creation by the Bank of Japan, so that the bank was an engine of inflation.

Around 1947, there was, however, a shift in American occupation policy; substantial aid was provided to enable the Japanese economy to stand on its feet. Furthermore, improvements were gradually made in the fiscal situations and in the operations of the Reconstruction Finance Bank. At the same time controls on lendings became more effective. Thus, both fiscal and financial measures were taken to contain inflation. After 1948 the Japanese economy at long last showed signs of being stabilised.

It was against this background that in 1949 the 'Dodge Line' was adopted; its principal features were sound finance based upon a super-balanced budget and the establishment of a single exchange rate. This finally ended the prolonged inflation. As inflation ceased and as recovery developed economic controls were lifted one by one. Since then the Japanese economy has grown spectacularly; in this finance has played a prominent role.

With the restoration of a free economy the business cycle reappeared. From the collapse of the Korean War boom in 1952 to the present day there have been five periods of 'over-heating' in the economy, accompanied by adverse balances of payments in 1953–4, 1957, 1961, 1963 and 1967. Severe internal and external competition and the need to innovate have encouraged business firms to borrow money, even after reconstruction had been completed. A high rate of growth with instability may thus be said to characterise the post-war Japanese economy. The financial system faced difficult problems in this connection. In the long run, however, the value of money has been safeguarded, and it may indeed be said that a stable currency has made possible the great development of the financial system of Japan.

2. THE BANK OF JAPAN

In the post-war period of runaway inflation the Bank of Japan had to shoulder responsibilities more grave than formerly. The exceptional circumstances made it difficult to use orthodox monetary weapons, but in an effort to contain inflation the Bank employed quantitative controls by restoring 'the Higher Rates Application System', as well as resorting to qualitative controls and moral suasion. With the end of the inflation and the gradual lifting of economic controls, orthodox monetary control by the Bank once more became important. In particular, after 1952–3, when the business cycle could be clearly observed, use was made of monetary policy.

These circumstances fostered dissatisfaction with the Bank of Japan Law, the abnormal character of which was noted above. To date, however, only partial amendments have been made; overall revision has not been possible because of the complexity and gravity of the issues involved. Of the partial amendments the most important was that of 1949, which set up the Policy Board of the Bank of Japan. The Policy Board was established within the Bank as the supreme decision-making body. The Bank's autonomy was thus strengthened and at the same time it was democratised. Subsequently, in 1957, a separate Law on the Reserve Deposit System was enacted on the recommendation of the Investigation Committee of the Financial System which had been established in 1956 as an advisory body of the government. By this legislation the Bank acquired a new policy weapon. It should be noted, further, that the Investigation Committee subsequently took up the problem of the overall revision of the Bank of Japan Law (see Part Three, Chapter 12).

3. CHANGES IN COMMERCIAL BANKS

It goes without saying that the defeat also affected commercial banks adversely. Particularly hard hit were big banks which had been turned into instruments of finance for the munitions industries during the war. Furthermore, banks were severely affected by measures such as the dissolution of the Zaibatsu, the prohibition of monopoly, deconcentration and so on, which were part of the policy of democratisation in post-war Japan. Big firms were weakened by the dissolution of holding companies and by partition. This, together with the depressed condition of the capital market, strengthened the position of banks *vis-à-vis* business firms, with which banks came to have closer relationships. As there was persistent and strong demand for bank credit even after the reconstruction period, banks enlarged the scale of their business. Throughout the entire period, therefore, both during and after inflation, banks have played a central role in Japan's financial system.

At the same time the old special financial institutions had

been abolished. Some of them[1] made a fresh start as commercial banks; some were later further reorganised (see below, pp. 204–5). Trust companies and savings banks suffered a great deal in the post-war inflation because of the nature of their business. The former were turned into commercial banks with their trust business as a subsidiary function and the latter became ordinary commercial banks.

4. ABOLITION OF SPECIAL BANKS

Special banks had played an important role in the war economy. It was therefore natural that they should be targets for the democratisation policies of the occupation forces after the war. In September 1945 a directive of the General Headquarters of the Allied Forces closed overseas banks and special war-time institutions; accordingly, the Bank of Chosen, the Bank of Taiwan, the Funds Unification Bank, the War-time Finance Bank, the Southern Development Bank, the External Capital Bank among others were abolished. The Yokohama Specie Bank, too, was designated a 'closed institution' in 1947, and was transformed into a commercial bank as the Bank of Tokyo. In 1948 the General Headquarters of the Allied Forces instructed special banks either to become commercial banks, or to be reorganised as bond-issuing banks (subject to severe restrictions on taking deposits). The Hypothec Bank of Japan and Hokkaido Colonial Bank were therefore turned into commercial banks, but the Industrial Bank of Japan chose to become a bond-issuing bank. In 1948, however, the General Headquarters issued a recommendation on 'the overall reform of the banking system by new legislation'; this recommendation materialised in 1950 as the Law on Bond-issues of Banks and the Law Abolishing the Hypothec Bank of Japan Law, etc., which abolished the system of special banks. In consequence the Industrial Bank of Japan had temporarily to become a commercial bank. In June 1952, however, the Long-term Credit Banks Law was enacted to establish a division of labour among the various financial institutions; under this law the

[1] The Industrial Bank of Japan, the Hypothec Bank of Japan, the Hokkaido Colonial Bank and the Bank of Tokyo – formerly the Yokohama Specie Bank.

Industrial Bank became a long-term credit bank. Subsequently two new banks, the Long-term Credit Bank of Japan and the Real Estate Bank of Japan, have been established under this law. In 1954 the Foreign Exchange Banks Law was passed; under it the Bank of Tokyo became a specialised foreign exchange bank.

Before this flow of legislation, and in order to stimulate the reconstruction of the Japanese economy after its near-annihilation, the Reconstruction Finance Bank had been founded in 1947 to channel funds to the basic industries. Although this bank made some contribution to economic recovery, it unquestionably had a hand in accelarating inflation, because it raised its resources by the issue of Reconstruction Finance Bank Bonds, which were purchased by the Bank of Japan, and its lending was somewhat reckless. The original principle was that the bank's funds would come from governmental subscription of its capital, but the bank was permitted to issue Reconstruction Finance Bank Bonds to bridge the delay in payment by the government. This expedient degenerated into a lax policy of issuing bonds to be absorbed by the Bank of Japan. Ultimately the bank had to cease operation with the adoption of the 'Dodge Line' in 1949 and it was dissolved in 1952.

Specialised governmental financial institutions were re-established from about 1950, when reconstruction was nearly complete. They are designed to supplement the work of private institutions, in fields where these cannot function. They are:

- the People's Finance Corporation (1949);
- the Housing Loan Corporation (1950);
- the Export Bank of Japan (1950, renamed in 1952 the Export–Import Bank of Japan);
- the Japan Development Bank (1951);
- the Agriculture, Forestry and Fishery Finance Corporation (1952);
- the Small Business Finance Corporation (1953);
- the Hokkaido Development Corporation (1956, renamed in 1957 the Hokkaido and Tohoku Development Corporation);
- the Local Public Enterprise Finance Corporation (1957);
- the Small Business Credit Insurance Corporation (1958);

the Medical Care Facilities Finance Corporation (1960);
the Overseas Economic Corporation Fund (1960);
the Environmental Sanitation Business Finance Corporation (1967).

5. OTHER FINANCIAL INSTITUTIONS

There have also been considerable post-war changes in other kinds of private financial institutions. Changes affecting financial institutions for small businesses and co-operative financial institutions were as follows: under the Law for Co-operatives of Small Business of 1949 all the urban district credit co-operatives under the Urban District Credit Co-operatives Law and most industrial co-operatives performing financial functions under the Industrial Co-operatives Law, were reorganised into credit co-operatives. Two years later, the Credit Associations Law was enacted, and credit co-operatives akin to ordinary financial institutions became credit associations. In 1951 also, in order to modernise existing mujin companies, the Mutual Loans and Savings Banks Law provided for their conversion into mutual loans and savings banks.

The Agricultural Co-operatives Law of 1947 was directed to the financing of agriculture and forestry and in the next year the Central Co-operative Bank of Agriculture and Forestry was reorganised. During the war agricultural associations and the Central Co-operative Bank had been instruments of state control; the legislation of 1947–8 re-established democratic arrangements, with the Central Bank as the apex of a system of financial institutions operating on co-operative principles.

The call money market which had been inactive during and after the war revived from about 1950. Active transactions were resumed in the securities market, also, after the stock exchange had been reopened in May 1949.

Thus, with the passing of the abnormal conditions of the immediate post-war years, Japan's financial system has gradually been improved, although imperfections remain. It has contributed materially to post-war economic development.

At the same time economic development has itself revealed some disharmony between the financial system as constituted at present and the needs of the economy. Since 1965, moreover, continuing changes in both external and internal conditions have strengthened the belief that some reorganisation of the financial system is needed. (Details of the present position of the various financial institutions and markets are given in Parts Three and Four.)

FIG. 3.1 *Pedigree of Financial Institutions*

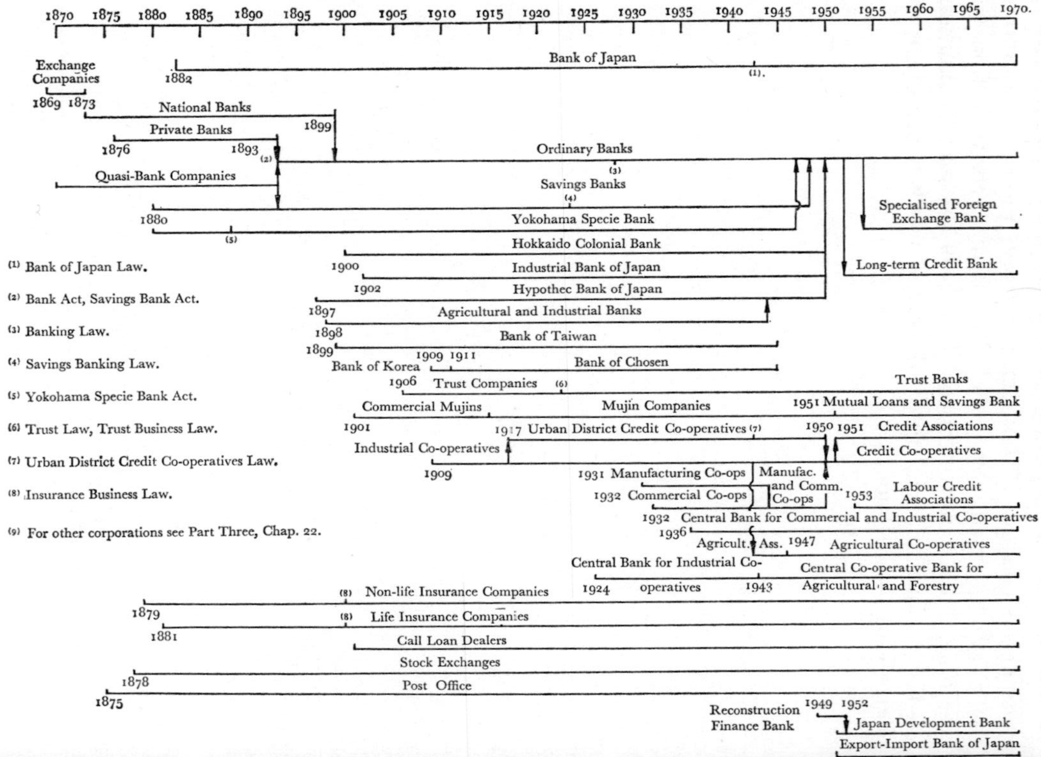

(1) Bank of Japan Law.

(2) Bank Act, Savings Bank Act.

(3) Banking Law.

(4) Savings Banking Law.

(5) Yokohama Specie Bank Act.

(6) Trust Law, Trust Business Law.

(7) Urban District Credit Co-operatives Law.

(8) Insurance Business Law.

(9) For other corporations see Part Three, Chap. 22.

PART TWO

The Japanese Financial Structure

CHAPTER 4

GENERAL SURVEY

I. GROWTH AND BUSINESS CYCLES IN THE JAPANESE ECONOMY

THE Japanese economy has achieved spectacular growth during the last decade or so. The average annual growth rate of gross national product (at constant prices) has been as high as 11 per cent during 1955–69. This rate is almost equal to the growth rate of 11 per cent in the post-war reconstruction period (1947–52), when the economy was recovering from an extremely low level at the end of the war. It far exceeds the pre-war annual growth rate of 4·5 per cent (1931–6). By way of comparison, the recent growth rates (average of 1958–67, at constant prices) of other major economies are: the United States, 4·1 per cent; the United Kingdom, 3·0 per cent; West Germany, 4·6 per cent; Italy, 5·5 per cent. Japan's recent growth rate, therefore, far outstrips those of other industrial countries.

The major factors underlying this spectacular development may be found in vigorous fixed investment, particularly by large firms, in plant and equipment; in the rapid expansion of exports; in the existence of an abundant, but high-quality, supply of labour; and in the stability of the value of money, which has been essential for this development. There was no easy road to such a high growth rate. Of the factors enumerated, that which provided the greatest impetus to growth was, needless to say, private fixed investment in plant and equipment. This repeatedly led to over-expansion of the economy, with violent economic fluctuations as the consequence. During some 15 years the Japanese economy has experienced five cycles – that is, booms in 1952–3, 1956–7, 1960–1, 1963 and 1966–7, which were respectively succeeded by recessions in 1954, 1957–8,

1961–2, 1964–5 and 1967–8. The booms invariably brought an adverse balance of payments and price rises; the Bank of Japan, which pursued a conscious, contra-cyclical policy, reacted by applying a severe credit squeeze.

The high growth rate brings its own problems. Moreover, in recent years both external and internal economic conditions have been changing markedly for Japan. Labour shortages have emerged as a consequence of growth so that wages have risen and differentials have been narrowed. This is reflected in the persistent rise in consumer prices especially in those of the products of small businesses and of agriculture. Furthermore, public expenditure has become relatively more important in recent years. Since January 1966, government bonds have been issued in large amounts for the first time since the war; public finance has therefore had a greater impact on the economy and on the monetary system. Externally, in April 1964, Japan joined the countries adopting Article 8 of the I.M.F. Agreement, and liberalised trade and foreign exchange dealings. Later Japan became a regular member of the O.E.C.D. and has undertaken to liberalise capital transactions entirely. Thus, the Japanese economy has directly or indirectly become much more 'open' than formerly. In sum, the conditions which originally favoured a high growth rate have been considerably modified in recent years. Consequently, steadier growth has become more desirable.

2. CHARACTERISTICS OF THE FINANCIAL STRUCTURE

A variety of factors has been noted as contributing to the growth and fluctuation of the economy, but the peculiarities of Japan's financial structure have had a significant influence. These may now be summarised as follows.

First, the biggest borrower in financial markets has been the corporate business sector, the centre of investment activity, while the biggest lender and the main saver has been the personal sector. A reflection of the pattern of economic growth as explained above, this borrower–lender relationship between the business and personal sectors is a phenomenon widespread beyond Japan, although it is more striking there because the corporate business sector's vigorous investment activity has been the main impetus behind the high growth rate. It must, however, be stressed that public investment and private residential building have recently increased, so that the public and personal sectors have become more important borrowers. Particularly because of its bond issues, the government has taken its place with the corporate business sector as a large market borrower.

A second characteristic of the financial structure is that the flow of funds from the personal to the corporate business sector has mostly been through financial institutions ('indirect financing'), while the flow via the securities market ('direct financing') has been relatively unimportant. This is because of the predominance of mixed banking since Meiji times, and also because of the limited development of the securities market.

The third, 'over-borrowing', characterises corporate businesses. As 'indirect financing' has been predominant, business firms with a strong demand for funds have come to borrow heavily from financial institutions. Because of this the capital structure of corporate businesses is decidedly unbalanced, with too little net worth and with too high a proportion of external liabilities.

Fourth, during the high growth period of 1955–64 money for economic expansion was supplied mainly through loans from the Bank of Japan. This characteristic is in truth a reflection of the over-borrowing of business firms just noted. The continuing dependence of banks on borrowing from the Bank of Japan is commonly referred to as the 'over-loaned condition' and is one of the most distinctive features of Japan's financial structure. Since November 1962, however, the Bank has followed the new formula of monetary regulation and has engaged actively in buying and selling bonds and debentures; this has tended to diminish the banks' dependence on borrowings from the Bank.

A fifth characteristic consists of the relationship between the monetary system and public finance. Following the Dodge Line of 1949, balanced budgets were for long the rule. Moreover, particularly during the high growth period, there was a tendency for revenue to exceed expenditure, and this encouraged resort to the 'over-loan' facility. From 1965 the large-scale flotation of government bonds helped to ease financial conditions for business firms, although this has not been as effective in relieving financial pressure as it might have been, since bonds have been issued by sales to the market.

Sixth, interest rates are largely ineffective. The fundamental reason for this is that interest rates have been subject to artificial regulations and have not been determined by the free play of demand and supply of funds. Regulation has been necessary because of the strong demand for funds by business firms. Contributory reasons can be found in 'over-loans' and in the consequent insufficient development of long-term and short-term markets.

These features derive essentially from Japan's rapid development since the Meiji period despite inadequate accumulation of capital. It must also be recognised that they have been strengthened by the high growth since 1955 under the stimulus of private investment. It may also be remarked that this financial structure has been conducive to the overheating of the economy, and that monetary policy has been subject to certain constraints.

Thus, the financial structure of Japan differs significantly from that of other nations; the impact upon it of the adoption of a more open economic system and of large-scale issues of government bonds deserves attention. Changes are no doubt desirable to diminish the extent of 'indirect financing', to encourage the development of security markets, and to permit the efficient operation of interest rates. Given, however, the deep roots of the features outlined above, an overnight change is scarcely to be expected. Nevertheless, an understanding of Japan's financial structure, whatever its susceptibility to change, is indispensable to the understanding of the country's financial system and financial policy.

CHAPTER 5

INVESTMENT, SAVINGS AND FINANCE

IT has been pointed out that the strongest driving force of the Japanese economy's high growth rate has been the vigorous fixed investment in plant and equipment of business firms. The high rate of investment has, needless to say, been supported by a high rate of savings. As a first step it is necessary to identify which sectors of the economy and in what ways savings have been formed and investment has been undertaken.

About 53 per cent of gross domestic investment (average of 1960–9) has been made by the corporate business sector. On the other hand, about 42 per cent of gross domestic savings (average of 1960–9) have been formed in the personal sector. Of net savings – that is, after deduction of provisions for capital consumption – 51 per cent (average of 1960–9) is represented by personal net savings. Thus, the corporate business sector and the personal sector have played important parts in economic development, the former as the principal investor and the latter as the principal saver. Investment activity in the corporate business sector was particularly marked during 1955–64 when growth was especially pronounced; at the peak, in 1959–61, it accounted for as much as 60 per cent of gross domestic investment. After 1965, however, its relative weight declined, chiefly because of expansion in public-sector investment, and in housing investment by the personal sector. Even so, it accounts for 50 per cent of gross domestic investment (average of 1965–9).

From the financial point of view the problem here is how the corporate business sector has raised the funds necessary for investment, and in what form the personal sector has employed its savings.

I. SOURCES OF FUNDS OF CORPORATE BUSINESSES

1. INVESTMENT AND SAVINGS OF CORPORATE BUSINESSES

(1) *Investment of Corporate Businesses*

The investment activity of corporate businesses can roughly be divided into fixed investment in plant and equipment (including housing investment) and investment in stocks. Fixed investment in plant and equipment plays a particularly prominent part in Japan. In the early post-war years, from 1946 to 1950–1, it was almost equal to investment in stocks. After 1956, when there was heavy fixed investment in plant and equipment for modernisation and innovation, the average scale of this type of investment became substantially larger than in the past, because plant and equipment have increased in average size. Moreover, inter-firm competition has intensified and has forced firms to make fixed investment for the sole purpose of enlarging their shares in their respective branches of trade. As a result, fixed investment in plant and equipment has come to surpass investment in stocks, until almost half of gross domestic investment has come to be represented by fixed investment of corporate businesses. It has thus become the crucial influence on the Japanese economy. As investment projects cannot be easily altered in response to changes in cyclical and financial conditions, the trend has been broadly upwards, although there have been some ups and downs.

From 1965 the burden of excess capacity in certain branches, as a result of a continuously high rate of investment for a number of years, temporarily dampened business firms' willingness to invest in plant and equipment. It revived, however, in 1967–8; not only did the liberalisation of capital transactions, etc., necessitate investment for strengthening international competitiveness, but the labour shortage also stimulated labour-saving investment. Thus, it is probable that fixed investment by corporate business in plant and equipment will continue to be the dominant influence upon the Japanese economy.

In contrast the relative significance of investment in stocks fell continuously during 1955–64. This is due to the fall in raw material prices caused by international surpluses, and to the improvement in the inventory management techniques of business firms. Despite this, investment in stocks still has a strong influence on business cycles, because it exhibits fairly wide fluctuations during a cycle, thus amplifying those caused mainly by variations in fixed investment in plant and equipment.

(2) *Savings of Corporate Businesses*

Gross savings of corporate businesses (provisions for capital consumptions and retained profits) have been about 37 per cent of total gross domestic savings. If we take retained profits (net savings) only, these account for about 21 per cent of total net domestic savings (average of 1960–9). Retained profits have a secular tendency to grow, which reflects the expansion in the scale of the economy, but they show fairly conspicuous ups and downs in a course of a business cycle. On the other hand, provisions for capital consumption (allowances for depreciation) have steadily increased year by year, reflecting the past high growth of fixed investment in plant and equipment. Their proportion to the total gross savings of corporate businesses has come to surpass that of retained profits.

As such gross savings are funds raised within corporate business itself, their proportion to gross investment may be termed the 'self-financing ratio'. The ratio in recent years has been as follows: it was in excess of 70 per cent in 1958, 1965 and 1966 when investment activity was at a low ebb, while in 1957 and 1961, years of high investment activity, the ratio was below 50 per cent. There is also a secular upward trend in the ratio, which results mainly from the increase in provisions for capital consumption, to which reference has already been made. Thus, in 1969, in spite of vigorous investment activity, the ratio was as high as 73 per cent. The figure, however, is still lower than in some other industrial countries. The deficiency had to be made good by borrowings from financial institutions and by issues of shares and debentures.

TABLE 5.1

Investment and Fund-Raising of Corporate Businesses

(hundred million yen)

	1959	1960	1961	1962	1963	1964	1965	1966	1967	1968	1969	1970
Plant and Equipment of Businesses	16,969	24,809	35,942	36,628	38,120	46,109	41,595	47,479	62,837	78,937	99,152	121,475
Houses	660	1,107	1,460	1,694	1,749	2,163	2,046	1,965	2,708	3,236	4,197	4,615
Inventory	3,314	4,190	13,698	4,018	8,080	9,383	5,675	7,823	18,623	19,882	22,938	25,808
Gross Investment Total (A)	20,943	30,106	51,100	42,340	47,949	57,655	49,316	57,267	84,168	102,055	126,287	151,898
Net Saving	4,783	9,564	10,497	9,660	9,162	11,626	9,546	14,490	22,925	32,747	38,950	41,381
Provisions for Depreciation	7,976	10,217	13,763	16,495	19,821	24,951	27,653	31,643	36,790	42,654	53,429	63,900
Gross Savings Total (B)	12,759	19,781	24,260	26,155	28,983	36,577	37,199	46,133	59,715	75,401	92,379	105,281
Borrowing	14,341	19,306	24,955	27,769	42,201	34,262	41,643	39,154	51,350	56,119	78,640	97,177
Industrial Debentures and Shares	4,286	7,028	13,502	9,053	7,509	8,923	4,902	5,843	5,932	5,644	7,800	12,677
(of which Industrial Debentures)	(1,447)	(1,528)	(3,858)	(1,330)	(1,638)	(1,525)	(2,195)	(2,251)	(2,781)	(1,546)	(2,907)	(3,460)
(of which Shares)	(2,839)	(5,500)	(9,644)	(7,723)	(5,871)	(7,398)	(2,707)	(3,592)	(3,151)	(4,098)	(4,893)	(9,217)
Foreign Liabilities	1,174	1,423	2,937	1,422	5,056	3,280	227	−1,588	3,447	3,658	5,443	5,424
External Funds Total	19,801	27,757	41,394	38,244	54,766	46,465	46,772	43,409	60,729	65,421	91,883	112,278
Fund-Raising Total (C)	32,560	47,538	65,654	64,399	83,749	83,042	83,971	89,542	120,444	140,822	184,262	217,558
Internal Fund-Raising Ratio (B/C)%	39·2	41·6	37·0	40·6	34·6	44·1	44·3	51·5	49·6	53·5	50·1	48·4
Self-Financing Ratio (B/A)%	60·9	65·7	47·5	61·8	60·4	63·4	75·4	80·6	71·0	73·9	73·2	69·3
Currency	2,059	3,132	2,659	4,385	14,010	4,636	9,690	6,483	6,475	7,198	15,200	15,818
Savings Deposits	3,503	3,797	5,274	9,767	11,805	8,124	10,459	11,317	10,759	12,717	15,470	20,883
Liquidity Total	5,562	6,929	7,933	14,152	25,815	12,760	20,149	17,800	17,234	19,915	30,670	36,701

2. METHODS OF FUND-RAISING

Corporate business needs funds for purposes other than investment, such as for the extension of trade credit (book credits, bills receivable and other trade receivables) and for the replenishment of liquidity on hand (cash and deposits). There are two sources of funds for these purposes: internal, by self-financing from savings; and external, by issues of shares and debentures, by borrowings from financial institutions or by taking trade credit (book debts, bills payable and other trade payables).

The total amount of funds raised by corporate business[1] displays a long-term tendency to increase in step with the expansion of the economy, although there has been a cyclical pattern, rising in phases of prosperity and of over-heating phases, and falling in recessions (see Table 5.1). In 1961, 1963 and 1967 the increases were particularly great.

Next, let us turn to the 'internal fund-raising ratio' – that is, the relative proportion of internal to total fund-raising. Although it has displayed certain cyclical fluctuations, it has an upward trend which reflects the rising tendency of the 'self-financing ratio'. In recent years the proportions of internal and external fund raisings to the total have been roughly 45–50 per cent and 50–55 per cent respectively.

Most of the funds raised externally (80 per cent) have consisted of borrowings from financial institutions; the relative importance of issues of shares and debentures (15 per cent) and borrowings from abroad (5 per cent) have been small (average of 1960–9). It is noteworthy that these relative proportions show considerable variations with changes in cyclical and financial conditions. In 1956–8 the proportion of borrowings was about 75 per cent and that of issues of shares and debentures was about 21 per cent, but in 1959–61 the former fell to 66 per cent, while the latter rose to 28 per cent. Capital and debenture issues multiplied during the latter period,

[1] Here, external fund-raising of corporate businesses is defined as those funds raised from the financial market in the wider sense of the term, such as borrowings, issues of shares and debentures, and borrowings from abroad, while trade credit is left out of account.

when conditions were favourable for them: there was a boom in the securities market, accompanied by rises in share prices, and investment trusts were rapidly gaining in popularity. When recession struck the market, however, the proportion fell uninterruptedly after 1962 until it reached 11 per cent in 1965–7, while the ratio of borrowings rose to 88 per cent.

If we examine the sources of funds of major and relatively large firms, it can be seen that the composition of their capital has, contrary to expectations, deteriorated over the years. This is because their investment activities have depended largely upon borrowings from banks (Table 5.2). The proportion of

TABLE 5.2

Financial Structure of Main Industrial Corporations

(percentages)

	1957	*1960*	*1963*	*1966*	*1969*
ASSETS					
Liquid Assets	49·4	47·7	50·5	53·1	56·6
Current Assets	20·9	26·2	29·3	36·3	39·1
(of which Cash and Deposits)	(6·7)	(8·9)	(9·8)	(10·1)	(9·4)
Trade Receivables	(14·2)	(17·3)	(19·5)	(24·9)	(28·4)
Inventories	20·0	15·0	12·5	12·1	13·1
(of which Finished Goods)	(6·2)	(5·2)	(4·9)	(5·2)	(6·0)
(„ „ Raw Materials)	(5·6)	(3·3)	(2·2)	(2·0)	(1·8)
Fixed Assets	52·3	51·9	49·0	46·5	43·2
Tangible Fixed Assets	46·2	43·6	38·6	35·0	32·6
Investments	5·7	7·8	9·8	10·9	10·1
Deferred Account	0·3	0·5	0·5	0·4	0·3
Total Assets (Liabilities, Net Worth)	100·0	100·0	100·0	100·0	100·0
LIABILITIES, NET WORTH					
Liquid Liabilities	45·4	45·2	47·7	50·0	51·9
(of which Trade Payables)	(13·8)	(15·5)	(17·8)	(20·2)	(23·1)
(„ „ Short-Term Borrowing)	(17·2)	(16·5)	(17·2)	(18·1)	(16·2)
Fixed Liabilities	21·5	25·8	26·2	26·8	28·6
(of which Long-Term Borrowing)	(14·7)	(16·4)	(17·3)	(17·4)	(18·7)
(„ „ Debentures)	(4·1)	(6·9)	(6·1)	(5·4)	(5·3)
Net Worth	33·1	28·9	26·1	23·3	19·6
(of which Capital)	(12·7)	(14·1)	(15·4)	(13·8)	(10·2)
No. of Companies	521	512	504	512	484

SOURCE: Bank of Japan, *Financial Statements of Main Industrial Corporations*. This is based upon balance sheets of companies of all industries at the end of fiscal years.

their external to their total liabilities rose from 62 per cent at the end of 1955 to 80 per cent at the end of 1969, while the ratio of the net worth fell from 38 per cent to 20 per cent. Moreover, of the net worth the proportion of paid-up capital has shown a slight decline from 11 per cent to 10 per cent in the meantime. Thus, the proportion of reserve funds fell markedly from 27 per cent to 9 per cent.

The causes of this deterioration in the capital structure can be summarised as follows: investment by corporate business has been too intense for finance by internal funds, as has been pointed out, so that they have had to depend upon external funds; big businesses have close connections with financial institutions, so that they have been able to raise funds more easily by borrowing from them than by issuing new securities, the cost of the former being less than that of the latter. It may be noted incidentally, that the ratios of net worth to total liabilities of firms in other major countries far exceed those in Japan: it was 58 per cent (end of 1967) in the United States, 56 per cent (end of 1966) in the United Kingdom and 39 per cent (end of 1966) in West Germany.

3. LIQUIDITY OF BUSINESS FIRMS AND TRADE CREDIT

The level of liquidity of a corporate business is usually represented by its holdings of currency (cash and deposit currencies). The level of currency holdings of corporate businesses has gradually risen with the growth in their transactions. As already noted, however, corporate business is heavily dependent upon bank finance, so that their liquidity, especially their holdings of deposit currency (current and short-term deposits), is determined largely by the lending attitudes of banks – and hence by the tightness or ease of credit. The ratio of the currency holdings of corporate business to sales has shown cyclical movements during these 10 years: it rose substantially in the easy money periods of 1958, 1963 and 1965, while it fell in the tight-money periods of 1961, 1964 and 1967. The memory of the credit squeeze of 1967–8 is, however, still fresh: corporate business liquidity was less pressed than in previous periods of monetary restraint, one cause being its high level during the preceding slack period of 1965.

Parallel with the development of corporate business liquidity, the behaviour of trade credit (trade receivables and payables) invites attention. Trade credit is the creditor-debtor relationship between buying and selling firms. Firms receiving the credit are thereby enabled to invest in inventories or in fixed capital, but firms giving credit have to raise funds to finance themselves: it is therefore a cause of increased borrowing.

During these 10 years the outstanding amount of trade credit has increased annually. In 1961–2, in particular, growth was conspicuous. At the end of 1969 the outstanding amount of book credits was 44,000 billion yen (equivalent to 3·3 months' sales proceeds). The marked increase in 1961–2 was primarily due to the worsening conditions of payment during a period of monetary restraint; this deterioration had a particularly severe impact, because fixed investment in plant and equipment continued at a high level despite the credit squeeze. A deterioration in payments tends, however, to occur in any period of credit squeeze and is usually reversed in easy-money periods. Nevertheless, in 1962–3, when monetary restraint was lifted, it was difficult to discern much improvement in payments. One cause of this was that firms were anxious to maintain their liquidity. Moreover, at about this time business firms were easing their selling terms, in order to maintain or even to raise the level of output. The impetus to this derived from the swelling of their overhead costs from the huge amount of past fixed investment in plant and equipment, and also from increased labour costs. If trade credit expands because of a marked worsening in settlement terms, business undertakings will naturally be endangered, because difficulties will arise in financing and in profitability. Since 1963 the outstanding amount of trade credit has continued to increase, but the ratio of trade receivables and payables to total turnover has remained relatively stable, so that the increase can be attributed principally to the growth in sales themselves.

II. FORMS AND VARIATIONS OF PERSONAL SAVINGS

1. VARIATIONS OF PERSONAL INCOME AND PERSONAL SAVINGS

(1) *Trends in Personal Income*

Personal income in Japan[1] is equivalent to about 90 per cent of the national income (average of 1960–9), and is steadily increasing with the growth of the economy (average growth per year was 17·3 per cent for 1960–9). Its movement is not particularly sensitive to business cycles[2] and its rate of increase is more stable than that of any other component of the national income. The reason is that the development of trade unions largely prevents a reduction in earned income during recessions: the same phenomenon is observable in Europe and America. Further, agricultural income is stabilised by the government's control of the price of rice.

(2) *Personal Expenditures and Personal Savings*

When taxes, contributions to social insurance and so on are deducted from personal income, the balance is called 'personal disposable income'. Personal disposable income is divided into consumption expenditure and savings, according to individuals' preferences. Personal-consumption expenditure grew at a fairly rapid pace from the immediate post-war years to about 1952–3, i.e. during the period when the level of consumption was recovering. From about 1953–4, when households of wage- and salary-earners in cities regained their pre-war (1934–6) levels of consumption, the growth rate of consumption expenditure

[1] The personal sector here includes personal households, unincorporated business firms, farmers, foresters, fishermen, non-profit-making organisations, etc. Personal income, therefore, includes individual proprietors' income, etc., besides compensation of employees.

[2] The proportion of personal income to the national income exhibits fairly wide fluctuations in the course of a business cycle: it goes down in the upward phase of the business cycle and goes up in the downward phase. This is not because personal income itself is susceptible to change, but rather because corporate income – that is, corporate profits, fluctuates widely in the course of a business cycle.

has somewhat slackened. Total personal income, however, continued to rise, so that the average ratio of consumption to income fell from a peak of 92 per cent in 1952–4, until it reached 80 per cent in 1961. This fall in the rate of personal consumption reflects, in fact, the rise in the rate of personal savings. Thus, the proportion of income which went into savings rose from 1953 to 1954, when the level of consumption re-attained its pre-war level. Since 1962, however, the rate of savings has ceased to rise; indeed, it has begun to fall. This is probably because it has already reached a considerably high level; a contributory factor may be the rise in consumers' prices which has continued for several years.

As personal income has shown a secular tendency to grow and the average rate of savings has continually been on a high level, the amount of personal savings has kept on increasing at a fairly rapid pace: in 1969 they were 4·2 times the level of 1960, while personal income was 3·7 times that level.

2. WHY IS THE RATE OF PERSONAL SAVINGS HIGH?

A characteristic feature of the Japanese economy, then, is the exceedingly high rate of personal savings. Rates of personal savings in Europe and America – 7 per cent for the United States (1967), 7 per cent for the United Kingdom (1967), 12 per cent for West Germany (1967) – are far lower than in Japan, which was 20 per cent in 1967. The causes of so high a rate may be summarised as follows.

First, as a result of the high growth rate of the economy personal income has increased rapidly, so that the increase in personal consumption has lagged behind and the rate of savings has increased. It tends to rise in booms and to decline in recessions. This is probably because the level of consumption tends to adjust itself to the highest level of income in the nearest past, irrespective of the level of current income. The rate of savings goes up when income is increasing rapidly, because the growth of consumption lags behind that of income.

Second, the proportion of extraordinary allowances, such as summer and year-end bonuses, to total wages or salaries is comparatively large in Japan. The proportion saved from such remuneration is substantial. It is estimated that about 50 per cent of the bonuses are saved: the custom generally is that routine expenditure is met from monthly wages and salaries.

Third, the system of social security is not so well developed in Japan as in Europe and America, although it has been expanded considerably in recent years. People must therefore provide against contingencies such as sickness and old age. It is not clear what proportion of personal savings is attributed to such motives, but they can be considered as strong incentives to saving.

Fourth, the absolute level of total personal assets is still relatively low in Japan, although the volume both of monetary savings and of tangible assets such as houses has rapidly recovered from the unusually low levels of the immediate post-war years. The willingness to accumulate such assets remains, therefore, quite strong, and accumulation continues at a fairly rapid pace. (This will be discussed later in Chapter 8.) The ratio of personal financial assets to disposable income, however, is only about 160 per cent, and is much lower than the 290 per cent of the United States. The accumulation of tangible assets, such as housing, also continues to be inadequate.

Fifth, because consumer credit is not fully developed, savings are necessary for acquiring houses and other consumers' durables.

Sixth, in the national income statistics of Japan, unincorporated businesses are included in the personal sector, along with individual households, farmers, foresters and fishermen. It must be stressed that the rate of savings in these unincorporated businesses is extremely high, so that their inclusion gives an upward bias to the savings rate of the personal sector as a whole. Such a high rate of savings may be explained by a variety of circumstances. First, their credit standing is lower than that of big business, so that they are compelled to depend more on self-financing. Next, the savings of unincorporate businesses are subject to special consideration. In corporate businesses more than half of corporate income (i.e. corporate profits) leaves firms in the form of corporate tax and of dividends, so that corporate net savings – that is, retained profits – are only a fraction of their income. In contrast, unincorporated businesses can retain that part of income which corresponds with dividends in corporate businesses. Moreover, unincorporated businesses cannot borrow so easily as big business from financial institutions. They must therefore maintain their liquidity at fairly high levels.

Finally, and fundamentally, the high rate of savings reflects traditional habits, based on such national characteristics as diligence, widespread education, a strong desire to raise the standard of living, and so on.

3. FORMS OF PERSONAL SAVINGS

Personal savings fall into two parts: one is devoted to increments in tangible assets, such as housing and investment in inventories and in plant and equipment by unincorporated businesses; the other is employed in acquiring financial assets, such as cash, deposits and securities.

Let us first turn to the real investment. House-building has risen markedly in recent years (the average yearly growth rate of 1963–7 was 18 per cent). Furthermore, investment by unincorporated businesses is less susceptible to cyclical changes than that by corporate businesses, and grows at a steady pace. The relative share of personal investment in total domestic investment has been steady at 20–25 per cent, although this percentage shows cyclical fluctuations and has recently tended to rise. In the personal sector the ratio of total investment to total savings has remained at about 40 per cent, so that there has been a marked excess of savings over investment; this means that personal savings are employed mainly in the acquisition of financial assets.

In what forms of financial assets are personal savings invested? Table 5.3 shows the increases in the financial assets of the personal sector, such as currency, deposits and securities. From the table it can be seen that the financial assets of individuals showed particularly large increases in the boom years of 1959, 1960, 1961 and 1966. Currency accounts for about 20 per cent of the increase, and its growth reflects that of personal income and of the transactions of unincorporated businesses. Holdings of savings deposits, trust and insurance funds, etc., represent, however, the larger part of the increase in personal financial assets. Claims on financial institutions,

TABLE 5·3

Increases in Personal Financial Assets

(hundred million yen)

	1959	*1960*	*1961*	*1962*	*1963*	*1964*	*1965*	*1966*	*1967*	*1968*	*1969*	*1970*
Currency	3,141	4,413	5,613	5,007	6,648	7,208	6,941	10,250	11,904	13,179	20,492	16,686
Cash	1,062	1,524	1,983	1,342	1,636	2,335	2,645	3,509	4,627	4,208	6,327	6,793
Demand Deposits	2,079	2,889	3,630	3,665	5,012	4,873	4,296	6,741	7,277	8,971	14,165	9,893
(Component Ratio, %)	(18·1)	(19·9)	(19·3)	(19·2)	(20·8)	(19·4)	(17·2)	(19·6)	(19·6)	(18·8)	(21·9)	(16·2)
Savings Deposits, etc.	11,036	12,329	13,528	15,133	20,020	23,960	30,669	37,347	44,155	50,652	62,872	72,201
Savings Deposits	8,255	9,054	9,601	10,460	14,782	18,074	21,894	25,863	31,430	35,508	44,738	50,462
Trusts	755	857	1,077	1,438	2,000	2,663	3,339	4,145	4,398	4,768	5,411	6,172
Insurance	2,026	2,418	2,850	3,235	3,238	3,223	5,436	7,339	8,327	10,376	12,723	15,567
(Component Ratio, %)	(63·8)	(55·8)	(46·4)	(58·2)	(62·6)	(64·4)	(76·0)	(71·4)	(72·6)	(72·3)	(67·0)	(70·0)
Securities	3,133	5,368	9,989	5,877	5,300	6,051	2,721	4,716	4,771	6,210	10,450	14,197
Bank Debentures	700	501	274	735	1,028	1,442	1,950	2,907	2,949	2,621	4,231	3,522
Other Bonds and Debentures	130	396	356	507	261	474	1,284	1,969	2,052	1,951	2,302	3,327
Shares	1,288	1,901	4,231	3,688	3,442	3,899	1,183	1,107	556	2,110	2,298	4,933
Investment Trusts	1,015	2,570	5,128	947	569	236	−1,696	−1,267	−786	−472	1,619	2,415
(Component Ratio, %)	(18·1)	(24·3)	(34·3)	(22·6)	(16·6)	(16·2)	(6·8)	(9·0)	(7·8)	(8·9)	(11·1)	(13·8)
Total	17,310	22,110	29,130	26,017	31,968	37,219	40,331	52,313	60,830	70,041	93,814	103,084
(Component Ratio, %)	(100·0)	(100·0)	(100·0)	(100·0)	(100·0)	(100·0)	(100·0)	(100·0)	(100·0)	(100·0)	(100·0)	(100·0)
(For Reference) Rate of Personal Savings %	16·7	17·4	19·2	18·6	18·0	19·7	17·8	17·9	19·4	19·7	20·2	—

SOURCE: Bank of Japan, *Flow of Funds Accounts*.

including demand deposits (which are included in currency) account for 85 per cent of the total increase (average of 1965–9). The relative share of investment in securities is only 9 per cent. In 1961, however, when the stock market was experiencing a boom and investment trusts were gaining in popularity, its relative weight rose to 34 per cent of the total increase. After 1962 the stock market experienced a severe slump, so that the volume of resources put into investment trusts and shares declined substantially; indeed investment trust funds recorded net decreases in the three years 1965–7. Investment in bank debentures, however, steadily grew, because they are akin to savings deposits and trusts.

Experience elsewhere has shown that, as personal financial assets accumulate, a wider range of assets other than deposits comes to be held, and that a preference emerges for direct investment in securities which promise capital gains. In Japan too, such a tendency may appear in the long run, but, as the securities market is still not well-developed, deposits will remain for some time the principal form of financial asset.

The accumulated total of outstanding personal financial assets amounted to 57,300 billion yen at the end of 1969 (Table 5.4) and was 1·5 times personal disposable income. Compared with the amount 10 years ago (end of 1961, 9,900 billion yen) there has been a sixfold growth in the accumulated total. By type of assets, the increases in trusts and insurance funds, and in bank debentures, are outstanding.

Thus, personal financial assets are increasing at a considerable pace, but their absolute level is still low in comparison with that of the United States. For instance, financial assets per head in the United States ($8013 at the end of 1967) are 6·7 times those of Japan ($1205).[1] This gap is greater than that in personal disposable income per head in the two countries ($2744 versus $761). The ratio of outstanding financial assets to personal disposable income is 2·9 in the United States and 1·6 in Japan.

The foregoing has outlined the trend of personal savings, which is reflected in additions to personal financial assets. All in all, the bulk of personal financial savings is absorbed

[1] It is customary to evaluate the amount of shares at their face values, but here they are valued at current prices for the sake of international comparison.

by financial institutions in the form of deposits, etc. In this we see clearly one of the characteristic features of the financial structure of Japan – that is, indirect financing.

FIG. 5.1 *Break-down of outstanding personal financial assets and variations in their ratio to personal disposable income*

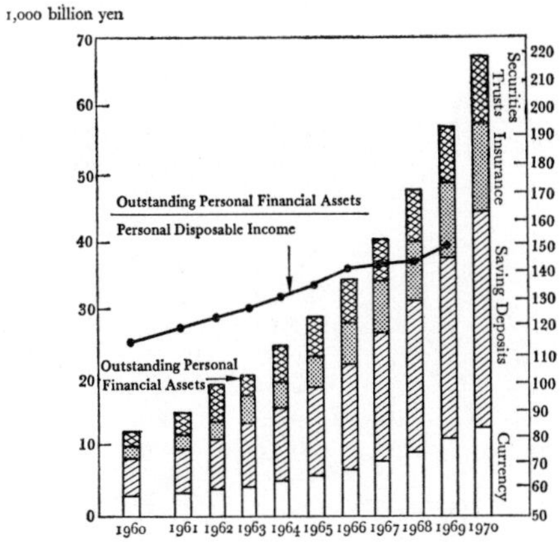

SOURCE: Bank of Japan, *Flow of Funds Accounts.*

TABLE 5.4

Expansion in the Outstanding Amount of Personal Financial Assets

(hundred million yen)

	End of 1960 (A)	*End of 1965* (B)	*End of 1970* (C)	(C)/(A)	(C)/(B)
Currency	26,378	57,683	130,194	4·94	2·26
Cash	9,300	19,241	44,705	4·81	2·32
Demand Deposits	17,078	38,442	85,489	5·01	2·22
(Component Ratio, %)	(21·6)	(19·6)	(22·6)		
Savings Deposits, etc.	72,554	180,860	448,087	4·80	1·92
Savings Deposits	56,217	130,345	318,346	5·66	2·44
Trusts	3,842	14,359	39,253	10·22	2·73
Insurance	12,495	36,156	90,488	7·24	2·50
(Component Ratio, %)	(59·5)	(61·5)	(60·5)		
Securities	23,078	55,582	97,419	4·22	1·75
Bank Debentures	2,023	7,245	23,475	11·60	3·24
Shares	14,039	33,033	44,273	3·15	1·34
Investment Trusts	5,501	10,685	12,194	2·22	1·14
Others	1,515	4,619	17,477	11·54	3·05
(Component Ratio, %)	(18·9)	(18·9)	(16·9)		
Total (D)	122,010	294,125	675,700	5·54	2·30
(For Reference)					
Personal Disposable Income (E)	106,864	218,261	—	—	—
(D)/(E) %	114·2	134·8	—		

SOURCE: Bank of Japan, *Flow of Funds Accounts.*

CHAPTER 6

PUBLIC FINANCE, BALANCE OF PAYMENTS AND BANKING

I. THE RELATIONSHIP BETWEEN PUBLIC FINANCE AND BANKING

In the contemporary world public finance exerts important influences on banking and economy through various channels. First, both the absolute size and the individual items of the government revenue and expenditure greatly affect the level of domestic effective demand. Second, the government as a borrower of money has a strong impact on financial markets. In Japan, however, the government did not figure prominently as a borrower until recent years, because the principle of balanced budgets was observed from the time of the Dodge Line in 1949. Indeed, during the high-growth period of the economy treasury receipts generally exceeded expenditures, because revenues from taxes rapidly increased. Since January 1966, however, there have been large-scale issues of government bonds, and the flows of funds have substantially been diverted from their previous channels, because of the emergence of the government as an important borrower. Third, the government itself is engaged in financial activities: if the government undertook only purely fiscal operations, it would go into financial markets only as a borrower, but it also makes investments and loans, so that it becomes a lender in markets as well. Fourth, the Treasury's account with the public will be reflected in the Bank of Japan's credit position with the government, which will directly influence markets.

The above four are the major points of contact between public finance and banking. These must now be examined in more detail in order to explore the recent behaviour of

TABLE 6.1

Ratio of the Outstanding National Debt to Gross National Product

(hundred million yen)

End of Fiscal Year	*1930*	*1935*	*1944*	*1950*	*1960*	*1964*	*1965*	*1966*	*1967*	*1968*	*1969*
Outstanding National Debt (A)	62	103	1,095	4,596	12,005	11,496	14,645	22,997	34,192	43,174	49,610
Long-term Domestic Bonds (B)	45	85	1,067	2,408	4,468	4,332	6,883	14,218	21,550	26,748	30,775
(of which Delivery Bonds)	(—)	(—)	(—)	(262)	(1,791)	(1,913)	(2,471)	(3,073)	(3,204)	(2,116)	(2,185)
Short-term Bills (C)	2	5	19	1,181	6,796	6,556	7,186	8,235	12,056	15,846	18,255
Foreign Bonds (D)	15	13	9	1,007	741	608	576	544	586	580	580
Gross National Product (E)	139	167	745	39,467	162,070	295,305	326,504	381,179	448,015	527,882	624,333
Ratios (A)/(E) (%)	44·6	61·7	147·0	11·6	7·4	3·9	4·5	6·0	7·6	8·2	7·9
(B)/(E) (%)	32·4	50·9	143·2	6·1	2·8	1·5	2·1	3·7	4·8	5·1	4·9
(For Reference)											
Government-Guaranteed Bonds (F)	—	—	—	6	2,552	6,334	8,931	12,543	15,708	17,763	19,249
Ratio [(A)+(F)]/(E) (%)	44·6	61·7	147·0	11·7	9·0	6·0	7·2	9·3	11·1	11·6	11·0

SOURCE: Bank of Japan.

TABLE 6.2

Balance of Payments

(million dollars)

	1961	*1962*	*1963*	*1964*	*1965*	*1966*	*1967*	*1968*	*1969*	*1970*
1. *Balance of Current Transactions*	−982	−48	−780	−480	932	1,254	−190	1,048	2,119	2,014
Balance of Trade	−558	401	−166	377	1,901	2,275	1,160	2,529	3,699	4,019
(of which Exports)	(4,149)	(4,861)	(5,391)	(6,704)	(8,332)	(9,641)	(10,231)	(12,751)	(15,679)	(19,021)
(of which Imports)	(4,707)	(4,460)	(5,557)	(6,327)	(6,431)	(7,366)	(9,071)	(10,222)	(11,980)	(15,002)
Balance of Service Transactions	−383	−420	−569	−784	−884	−886	−1,172	−1,306	−1,399	−1,798
Unilateral Transfers	−41	−29	−45	−73	−85	−135	−178	−175	−181	−207
2. *Balance of Long-term Capital*	−11	172	467	107	−415	−808	−812	−239	−155	−1,597
(of which Japanese Capital)	(−312)	(−309)	(−298)	(−451)	(−446)	(−706)	(−875)	(−1,096)	(−1,508)	(−2,037)
(of which Foreign Capital)	(−301)	(481)	(765)	(558)	(31)	(−102)	(63)	(857)	(1,353)	(440)
3. *Balance of Short-term Capital*	21	107	107	234	−61	−64	506	209	178	757
4. *Errors and Omissions*	20	6	45	10	−51	−45	−75	84	141	200
5. *Overall Balance*	−952	237	−161	−129	405	337	−571	1,102	2,283	1,374
6. *Monetary Movements*	−952	237	−161	−129	405	337	−571	1,102	2,283	1,374
Foreign Currency Reserves	−338	355	37	121[a]	108	−33	−69	886	605	903[b]
Others	−614	−118	−198	−70	297	370	−502	216	1,678	593
7. *Foreign Currency Reserves*	1,486	1,841	1,878	1,999	2,107	2,074	2,005	2,891	3,496	4,399

[a] At the end of March 1964 gold transfers with the I.M.F. to the amount of $180 million were included in foreign currency reserves.

[b] At the end of 1970 the allocation of SDR $122 million was included in foreign currency reserves.

SOURCE: Bank of Japan, *Monthly Report of Balance of Payments Statistics*.

the Japanese economy and, for that matter, of Japanese banking.

To begin with the scale of fiscal operations, the magnitude of the government's expenditure in the fiscal year 1969 can be gauged from the fact that its purchases of goods and services[1] were about 17 per cent (including local authorities) of the gross national product, which is not a particularly high percentage compared with other nations.

If we distinguish between investment expenditure and consumption expenditure, the former is 51 per cent and the latter is 49 per cent of the total. Investment expenditure (including that of local authorities) is equivalent to 21 per cent of gross domestic investment.

The most important branch of Treasury operations consists of the General Account. Taxes, including individual income tax, corporation tax and various indirect taxes, account for 81 per cent of the total revenue of the Account (average of fiscal years 1967–8). The incidence of taxation may be expressed as the ratio of tax revenue to the national income distributed, which is about 12 per cent. In expenditure, increases for public works, social security and tax distributed to local governments are conspicuous in recent years (the sum of these three items represent on average 52 per cent of total expenditure in the General Account in the fiscal years 1967–9). Expenditure for public works is the most important item both quantitatively and qualitatively.

Treasury investments and loans made through special accounts and public corporations are another form of the government's fiscal operations. Their scale has shown a remarkable growth since 1961 and is equivalent to 36 per cent of the General Account (average of fiscal years 1967–9).

Turning next to the operation of the Government as a borrower, the initial consideration is that the galloping inflation after the war drastically reduced the real burden of the huge national debt which Japan had accumulated during the war. Furthermore, the super-balanced budgets of the fiscal years 1949–50 made possible large-scale redemption of debt. More-

[1] Sum of 'general government consumption expenditure', 'gross fixed capital formation of the government', and 'increase in stocks of the government enterprises' in the national income statistics.

over, the Public Finance Law of 1947 aimed to establish the principle of 'sound finance'. Thus, the new law prohibited the issue of long-term government bonds, except for the purpose of raising funds for public works and investments and loans.[1] At this stage, however, the issue of new government bonds was not a practical problem: during the period of rapid economic growth the automatic expansion of tax revenue, though fluctuating somewhat from year to year, provided persistent budget surpluses. Further, the national railways and other government enterprises, which had been operated under special accounts, were reorganised into public corporations after the war, so that their bonds (public corporation debentures) were no longer included in the national debt.

Due to these post-war circumstances, the government became insignificant as a borrower. The proportion of the outstanding long-term government bonds to the gross national product was only 1·5 per cent at the end of 1964. Even if government-guaranteed debentures – public corporation debentures, of which the government guarantees the payment of principal and interest – and government short-term bills be included, the proportion would only be 6·2 per cent.

After the fiscal year 1962, however, the lower growth rate of the economy brought about slower increases in tax revenue, which in turn led to financial difficulties, so that it eventually became necessary to issue government bonds from the fiscal year 1965. Under the Law in regard to Extraordinary Fiscal Measures in the Fiscal Year 1965 government bonds to the amount of 20 billion yen were issued to make good the budget deficit. Since 1966 large amounts of Public Works Bonds under Article 4 of the Public Finance Law have been floated: 675

[1] After the enforcement of the Public Finance Law the following long-term bonds, excluding the delivery bonds, had been issued up to 1964 (fiscal year): 4% and 5% Reconstruction Treasury Bonds (72·6 billion yen during 1947–51), which were issued to raise funds for the national railways and the electrical communication system; Special Tax Reduction Bonds (14·1 billion yen during 1953–4), which were issued to raise funds for industrial investments; American Dollar Bonds ($57 million during 1959–63), which were issued to raise funds for loans to the Electric Power Development Joint-Stock Company; Swiss Franc Bonds (50 million francs in 1964), which were issued to raise funds for loans to the Development Bank of Japan and to the Japan Highway Public Corporation; Deutschmark Bonds (200 million marks in 1964) issued for the same purpose as the Swiss Franc Bonds.

billion yen in 1966, 720 billion yen in 1967, 471 billion yen in 1968 and 420·6 billion yen in 1969 (years are fiscal years). As percentages of the total revenues of the General Account, they are as follows: 5·2 per cent in 1965, 14·8 per cent in 1966, 13·6 per cent in 1967, 7·8 per cent in 1968 and 5·9 per cent in 1969. Thus, the peak was reached in 1966, after which the ratio declined. In the 1970 budget the ratio was expected to fall still further (to 5·4 per cent).

Meanwhile, the ratio of outstanding long-term government bonds to the gross national product rose rapidly from the trough of 1·5 per cent at the end of fiscal year 1964 to 4·9 per cent at the end of fiscal year 1969, or to 11·0 per cent if government-guaranteed bonds and government short-term bills are included. Even this ratio is much lower than the corresponding ratios in Europe and America.

Government short-term bills are issued to finance temporary deficits of the Treasury: at present Treasury bills are issued for the General Account, while Food bills and Foreign Exchange Fund bills are issued for the Foodstuff Control Special Account and the Foreign Exchange Fund Special Account respectively. (The maximum limits of their issues in the fiscal year 1969 were 500 billion yen for Treasury bills – including temporary borrowings – 1900 billion yen for Food bills, and 500 billion yen for Foreign Exchange Fund bills.) Beside these, some of the other special accounts also have the legal right to issue short-term bills, but no bills of this category have been issued since the fiscal year 1950.[1]

The current principle is that these government short-term bills should be issued by public tender, but banks and other private financial institutions purchase only a negligible part of the bills issued, because their yield is lower than other market rates of interest, and because banks are in over-lent positions,

[1] Temporary deficits of special accounts within a fiscal year are usually financed by transfer of temporary surpluses of other accounts and not by the issue of short-term bills or by borrowings. The transferred funds must be repaid *in toto* at the end of the fiscal year. (In the fiscal year 1967 such transfers were made to seven special accounts – Foodstuff Control, Foreign Exchange Fund, Industrial Investments, Welfare Insurance, Funds Accruing from Purchase of U.S. Agricultural Commodities, Measures for Coal Mining and Taxes Shared or Transferred to Local Governments – and to the Japan Monopoly Corporation. The peak in the outstanding amounts at the end of the months was 442·3 billion yen, in February 1968.)

as will be discussed later (see below, pp. 132–5). Most of the bills are therefore issued through purchase by the Bank of Japan, and are held by the Bank, the Trust Fund Bureau and other government agencies. Thus, the market for government short-term bills is not well-developed, and this greatly affects the financial markets (this will be discussed below, pp. 82–4).

The third point of contact between public finance and banking reflects the operations of the government as a lender. The government absorbs savings through the national network of post offices by postal savings deposits, post office life insurance, post annuities and so on. These savings are then employed in investments in and loans to the public sector, such as public corporations and local authorities, and to specific branches of the private sector, such as export industries, small businesses, agriculture and fisheries through government financial institutions, including the Trust Fund Bureau, Export–Import Bank, Development Bank of Japan and various other finance corporations.

The bulk of these funds consists of individual savings, such as postal savings deposits, post office life insurance and postal annuities, but the Trust Fund Bureau also receives 'social savings' in the form of deposits from the Welfare Insurance and the National Pensions Schemes. In recent years these have gradually gained in importance, as the social security system is developed. Further, the Local Public Enterprise Finance Corporation, the Housing Loan Corporation and others are issuing a greater volume of corporation bonds, and there is a growing amount of investment by the General Account, the Industrial Investment Special Account, etc., in the Export-Import Bank and other undertakings.

The plans for Treasury investments and loans are drawn up at the same time as the annual budgets. Their scale and contents are related to national policy and to prevailing economic conditions. Since the fiscal year 1961 there has been vigorous public investment in the modernisation of agriculture and of small businesses, house-building and road construction; while since the fiscal year 1964, with a rapid increase in export credits and in foreign lending, investments and loans for these purposes have greatly expanded. The total amount of investments and loans by various government financial institutions is equivalent to about 20 per cent of those of private financial institutions. These official lenders form an important component of the Japanese financial system both as suppliers of funds to the public sector, such as public corporations and local authorities, and as sources of funds to close gaps in the private sector which private financial institutions are unable to fill. (More detailed explanation of this point will be given in the chapter on government financial institutions (Part Three, Chapter 22).)

Finally, we come to the significance of Treasury Accounts with the public and of their impact on financial markets. The balance of accounts of the General Treasury Fund with the public (i.e. excluding those of the Foreign Exchange Fund Special Account and of long-term government bonds) shows wide cyclical fluctuations (Fig. 6.1), e.g., an excess of expenditure in 1958–9 and 1962–3, and of a large excess of receipts in 1960–1. Since the resumption of long-term bond-issues, however, the pattern of such fluctuations has changed: a large excess of expenditures of the General Treasury Fund has appeared, but, if we allow for receipts through bond-issues, the final balance is a small excess of receipts.

In the shorter term, a marked cyclical pattern is observable in the General Treasury Fund's accounts with the public: an excess of expenditure in the first quarter of the fiscal year (April–June) and the third quarter (October–December), with an excess of receipts in the second (July–September) and the fourth (January–March) quarters. In the third quarter the excess of expenditures is particularly large, because payments are made for foodstuffs purchased and for the year-end settlements. In the fourth quarter a large excess of receipts appears, because taxes are paid in, while large out-payments fall.

Thus, the accounts of the General Treasury Fund with the public experience substantial cyclical and seasonal variations. Such movements produce powerful effects on the demand and supply of money in financial markets for the following reasons. The government does not hold deposit accounts with commercial banks, so that the Bank of Japan is the sole depository for government funds. Moverover, government short-term bills are mostly issued via purchase by the Bank, as already explained. Private institutions therefore hold few such bills. The consequence is that, when the government is temporarily short of

FIG. 6.1 *Treasury accounts with the public and credit given by the Bank of Japan*

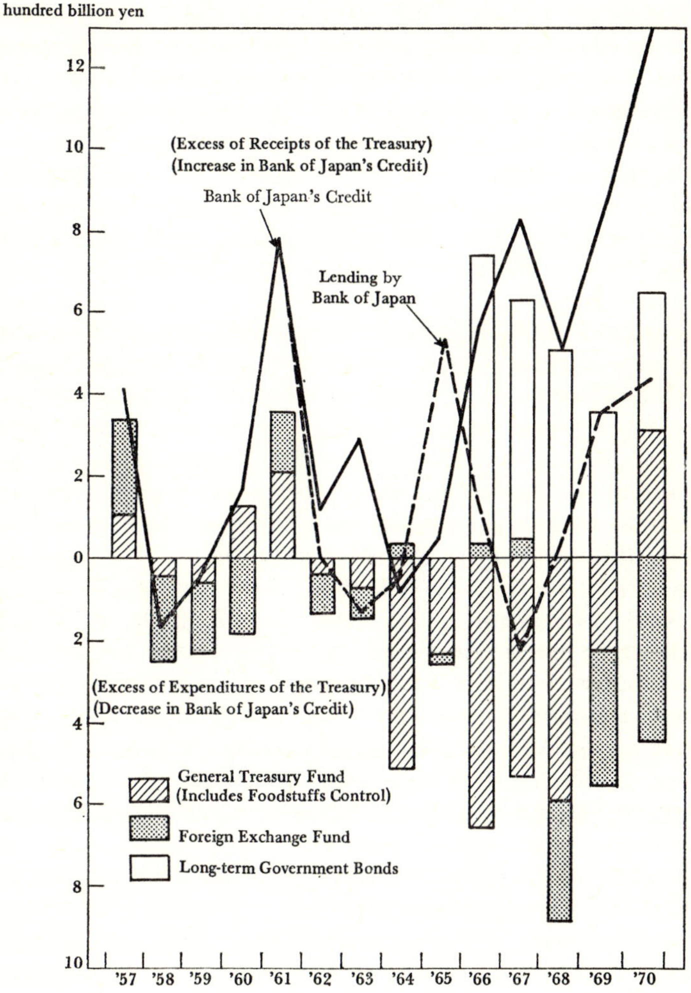

SOURCE: Bank of Japan.

money, the necessary funds are raised outside financial markets. Thus, money is unilaterally pumped into the market. Contrariwise, when there is an excess of public revenue over expenditure, government short-term bills will be redeemed; these are mostly held by the Bank – that is, outside the market – so that money is absorbed unilaterally by the government from the market. Such variations in public revenue and expenditure, especially cyclical variations, continue to exist despite the flotation of government bonds.

APPENDIX: LOCAL GOVERNMENT FINANCE

The scale of local government finance almost equals that of the central government: the purchase of goods and services by local authorities is about 9 per cent of the gross national product, approximately the same percentage as that of the central government. The composition, however, is different: consumption expenditure is 58 per cent, while investment expenditure is 42 per cent of the total in the fiscal year 1968. Thus, the relative weights of investment and consumption expenditure are the reverse of those of the central government.

Local government finance suffered from cumulative deficits in the early years of the decade 1955–64 as a result of increased expenditure. The budgets of 80 per cent of prefectures and of half of the cities, towns and villages were in the red. Subsequently, however, measures for financial reconstruction were adopted which cut down expenditure and increased tax revenue. The situation has thus been gradually improved until about only 10 per cent of local authorities remain in the red. Financial needs are, however, rapidly growing due to increased official salaries and to a rapid expansion in public investment; this is particularly true of local public enterprises such as waterworks, sewerage and transport. Borrowing by local authorities from the Trust Fund Bureau, the Post Office Life Insurance and Postal Annuity Funds and by the issue of local government bonds has increased substantially. The relationship to financial markets of local government finance differs from that of central government finance. As has been remarked, national finance is outside the market, but local governments place their deposits (public deposits) with banks. In addition their deficits are financed not only by investment and loans from government institutions, such as Trust Fund Bureau, but also by private financial institutions which, for example, hold local government bonds. In this sense, for private financial institutions local governments are akin to ordinary customers.

2. BALANCE OF PAYMENTS AND THE FINANCIAL SYSTEM

The balance of international payments greatly affects the domestic economy. Not only do the variations of exports and imports have great repercussions on Japan, the dependence of which on foreign trade is high, but also movements of long-term and short-term capital are beginning to have a direct influence on domestic monetary and financial conditions, as the liberalisation of capital transactions progresses.

(1) *Balance of Payments and Business Cycles*

The balance of payments (following the I.M.F. formula) is divided into the balance of current transactions (current account) and the balance of capital transactions (capital account and monetary movements). The former mainly records the receipts and expenditures on transactions of goods and services between Japan and foreign countries, while the latter principally registers the movements of long-term and short-term capital.

Current transactions are divided into three categories: trade transactions – that is, exports and imports; service transactions, which arise as a result of trade and capital transactions, as, for example, freights, insurance and investment income; transfers, such as reparations and donations. The balance of trade is closely related to domestic activity. With improvements in trade imports of raw materials and manufactured goods increase, while in the 'over-heating' phase of the cycle the rate of expansion of exports declines and the balance of trade goes into the red, because prices rise and shortages of supply in relation to demand for export goods develop. Contrariwise, in recessions imports decrease, while pressure accumulates to produce forced exports, so that the balance of trade improves, and thereby contributes to domestic recovery. During the past ten years or so, the Japanese economy has experienced four business cycles, and in each such a process was clearly discernible, although there were differences of degree from cycle to cycle. In 1957, 1961, 1964 and 1967, among others, the over-heating of the economy engendered such adverse balances of trade that foreign exchange reserves sank to crisis levels, necessitating monetary restraints.

Thus, the balance of trade has a cyclical pattern, but since 1965 it has displayed a trend towards bigger and bigger surpluses. This has chiefly been due to increased exports of products of heavy and chemical industries, which, following the large-scale fixed investment in plant and equipment between 1955 and 1964, have acquired a greater capacity to meet international competition. During roughly the same period there have been increased deficits in the balances of service and long-term capital transactions (above, Table 6.2, p. 77). Thus, surpluses in the balance of trade are financing deficits in the balances of service and long-term capital transactions. This is a general pattern observable in advanced countries.

Deficits in the balance of service transactions have grown rapidly since about 1961–2. This is mainly due to sharp increases in freight rates, time charters of ships and other expenses accompanying foreign trade, the expansion in which far outpaced that of the Japanese merchant fleet's tonnage. It has also been due to increased interest payments as foreign capital has flowed in.

Capital transactions are divided into four categories: transactions in Japanese capital (external investments of Japan); foreign capital (investments in Japan of foreign countries); short-term capital; and monetary movements (short-term assets and liabilities of the authorities, such as the government and the Bank of Japan, and of exchange banks). Between 1955 and 1964 there was a large-scale inflow of foreign capital in the form of untied loans, bond-issues and so on, which greatly contributed to the high growth rate of the Japanese economy. From 1965, however, there was a notable slowing down in the rate of inflow: changes in international interest-rate differentials, other nations' tighter controls on external transactions for balance of payments purposes, and slackness in domestic demand for money have been factors in the change. In 1968, however, the inflow began to increase again, and regained the level of 1962–4. On the other hand, the net outflow of Japanese capital increased from about 1964, and the tendency is expected to continue. This is because there has been a change in the composition of export goods: the relative weight of exports of ships and heavy machinery has risen, and these are exported on a credit basis. Another reason is that economic aid to developing nations in South-East Asia is growing.

The overall balance brings together the current balance, the long-term capital balance (Japanese capital-assets, and foreign capital-liabilities), short-term capital balance (includes B/C usance,[1] shippers' usance and so on, which are not recorded in monetary movements), and errors and omissions.

The overall balance tallies with the balance of monetary movements. Of the latter, the column entitled 'commercial banks' shows movements in the short-term external assets and liabilities of the exchange banks. These are largely dominated by the financing of exports and imports: in particular borrowing from foreign banks (to finance imports) reflects fluctuations in imports, which in turn affects domestic business conditions.

The final balance of these manifold transactions is focused in the fluctuations in foreign exchange reserves recorded in monetary movements. These amount to only about 25 per cent of Japan's imports, a relatively low percentage, which allows little margin for their decrease. An adverse balance of trade as a result of a domestic boom, therefore, makes it necessary to take immediate anticyclical measures.

(2) *Relationship between the Balance of Payments and the Monetary System – the Operations of the 'Foreign Exchange Fund Special Account'*

The Japanese government, through the Foreign Exchange Fund Special Account, holds the bulk of the country's foreign

[1] 'Usance bills for collection.'

exchange reserves (see Part Four, Chapter 24). The Special Account is the sole agent of the authorities in foreign currency dealings with the private sector (exchange banks). Although the Bank of Japan holds some foreign exchange through purchase from the Special Account, it does not deal directly with private institutions. Thus, fluctuations in foreign exchange reserves resulting from transactions with the private sector are directly related to yen receipts of and yen payments by the Special Account – a factor in Treasury receipts and payments. Increases in foreign exchange reserves (sales of foreign exchange by the public to the government) produce an excess of payments over receipts for the Special Account, while decreases (sales of foreign exchange by the government to the public) lead to an excess of receipts.

When foreign exchange reserves are increasing, the Foreign Exchange Fund Special Account finds itself short of yen funds. If other accounts of the Treasury are in surplus, the deficiency could be met by transfer to the Special Account. Hitherto, however, most of the deficits have been financed by the Bank of Japan. One method is by the outright sale of the Special Account's foreign exchange to the Bank; an alternative method is to issue Foreign Exchange Fund Bills, the maximum permissible issue in the fiscal year 1969 being 500 billion yen. (In principle, these bills should be issued by public tender, but in practice they have mostly been taken up by the Bank.)

When foreign exchange reserves are decreasing, surplus yen funds accumulate in the Special Account. They will be used for the repayment of funds transferred from other accounts and/or for the redemption of Foreign Exchange Fund Bills held by the Bank. Thus, a favourable balance of payments which leads to the accumulation of foreign exchange reserves (excess of payments of the Special Account) causes currency to be supplied from the Bank to the public; an adverse balance of payments, leading to decreases in foreign exchange reserves (excess of receipts of the Special Account) causes currency to be absorbed by the Bank. The balance of payments, therefore, directly affects financial markets.

FIG. 6.2 *The Balance of Payments, 1960–70*

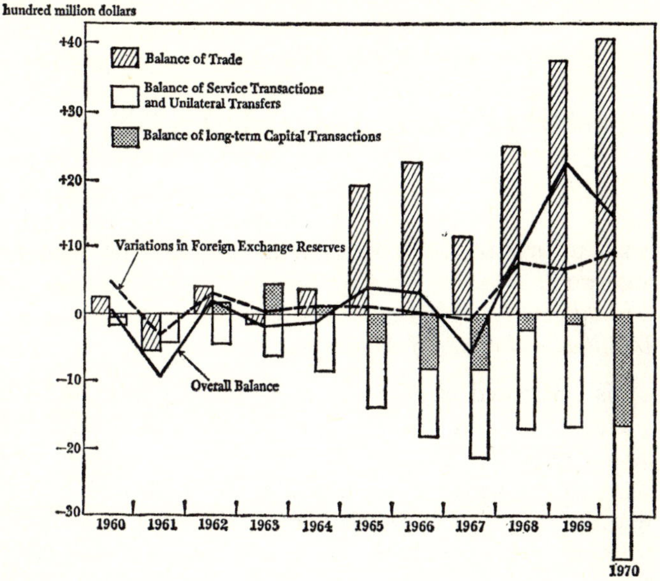

SOURCE: Bank of Japan, *Monthly Report of Balance of Payments Statistics.*

CHAPTER 7

SUPPLY OF MONEY

I. VARIOUS KINDS OF MONEY AND TRENDS IN THEIR AMOUNTS

(1) *Definition and Kinds of Money*

Money is composed of cash currency, such as bank-notes and coins, and of deposit money – that is, demand deposits, such as current deposits. Usually the term 'money supply' relates to money in the wider sense, and includes both cash currency and deposit money; the reason is that, although they are used for different purposes, both share two essential functions of money, i.e. they are a means of settlement and a store of purchasing power. Deposit money usually includes current deposits, ordinary deposits, deposits at notice and special deposits at banks and other major financial institutions. Current deposits are the most liquid, being subject to withdrawal by cheques and bills. This is deposit money in the narrowest sense of the word. Ordinary, notice and special deposits differ from current deposits, in that they are not subject to withdrawal by cheques, but they are demand or short-term deposits. We may distinguish them from current deposits by applying the general description of 'short-term deposits'. On the whole, these short-term deposits have a strong monetary character, although the degree of moneyness differs, according to whether the holders are business firms or general consumers. Business firms keep only minimum balances in current deposits for settlements in the immediate future. Their temporary surpluses are employed as short-term deposits – that is, as ordinary, notice and special deposits. Short-term deposits of business firms, therefore, are 'latent money', waiting to be transferred to current deposit and to be used for payments.

In practice there is constant transfer between current and short-term deposits, so that the turnover of business firms' short-term deposits seems to be fairly high. Thus, it seems to fit the facts if we include in 'money' not only current deposits but also short-term deposits.

A considerable proportion of time deposits of corporate businesses, on the other hand, is immobilised as compensating balances for their borrowing, and the remainder has fixed maturities. Thus, for corporate businesses, the liquidity of time deposits is much lower than that of short-term deposits. Nevertheless, an examination of the behaviour of business firms' deposits in recent years reveals that time deposits perform functions similar to those of money (cash currency and deposit money), so that they have increasingly come to be regarded as near-money.[1]

Part of the ordinary deposits of individuals resembles savings deposits, although subject to withdrawal on demand, but total balances in ordinary deposits are treated as deposit money, because the precise composition cannot be determined. In addition, postal transfer savings can be included in deposit money (demand deposits), because they are used to settle small transactions by unincorporated businesses and by non-profit-making associations.

(2) *Variations in the Supply of Money*

The survey of money supply in Japan during 1959–69 (Table 7.1) shows that the outstanding amount of money has grown with the expansion of the economy, although there have been some cyclical fluctuations. Its ratio to gross national product – that is, the 'Marshallian *k*', has had a secular upward trend. It has reached a level as high as 30–32 per cent since 1963. If we break it down into cash currency and deposit money the proportion of cash currency to gross national product has been stable at about 7 per cent during these ten years, while that of deposit money has risen from 19 per cent to 23–25 per cent. One

[1] It should be noted that, in the statistics of money supply composed by the Bank of Japan, the treatment of savings deposits has altered since December 1967. Formerly, they were treated as negative elements in the money supply, but now they are treated as near-money, and the overall movements of money and near-money can now be grasped.

TABLE 7.1

Money Supply

(hundred million yen)

End of the Year	*Cash Currency* (M_1)	*Deposit Money* (M_2)	*Money Supply* (M)	*Gross National Product* (Y)	*Ratios* (M_1)/Y	(M_2)/Y	(M)/Y
1959	9,312	25,551	34,863	129,263	7·2	19·8	27·0
1960	11,062	31,359	42,421	154,992	7·1	20·2	27·4
1961	13,312	38,267	51,580	191,255	7·0	20·0	27·0
1962	15,110	45,794	60,904	211,992	7·1	21·6	28·7
1963	17,305	59,724	77,029	244,640	7·1	24·4	31·5
1964	19,872	67,172	87,044	288,379	6·9	23·3	30·2
1965	22,642	80,232	102,874	317,869	7·1	25·2	32·4
1966	25,890	91,272	117,162	365,445	7·1	25·0	32·1
1967	31,136	102,552	133,688	431,070	7·2	23·8	31·0
1968	35,947	115,603	151,550	511,481	7·0	22·6	29·6
1969	43,191	139,634	182,825	597,047	7·2	23·4	30·6
1970	50,978	162,617	213,595	706,177	7·2	23·0	30·2

SOURCE: Bank of Japan, *Money Supply and Related Data.*

important cause of this was that corporate businesses rushed to borrow in 1963, when the credit squeeze was lifted, in order to provide for future needs for funds, and the money borrowed went to swell their deposits. Another important reason is that part of the ordinary deposits of individuals, which are in effect income or savings deposits, have shown a secular tendency to increase, and these are included in deposit money.

The annual figures for the supply of money (Fig. 7.1) display fairly marked cyclical fluctuations. They reflect the vicissitudes of financial and business conditions. For instance, in 1960, 1963, 1965 and 1969 – that is, in the upswings of the business cycle – the rate of increase was substantial, whereas it was much lower in 1961, 1962 and 1964, when measures of monetary restraint were introduced. The two components of money display contrasting behaviour in this respect: the amount of cash currency has a relatively stable growth rate, while that of deposit money fluctuates widely in response to business conditions. This is especially true of current deposits.

In order to understand the bearing of these monetary movements on general economic trends, it is necessary to consider both the demand for and the supply of money. The demand side

TABLE 7.2

Indices of Money Supply

(hundred million yen)

	End of 1963		End of 1965		End of 1967		End of 1968		End of 1969		End of 1970	
	Amount	*Ratio to GNP*	*Amount*	*Ratio to GNP*	*Amount*	*Ratio to GNP*	*Amount*	*Ratio to GNP*	*Amount*	*Ratio to GNP*	*Amount*	*Ratio to GNP*
1. *Monetary Survey*												
Cash Currency	17,305	7·1	22,642	7·1	31,136	7·2	35,947	7·0	43,191	7·2	50,978	7·2
Deposit Money	59,724	24·4	80,232	25·2	102,552	23·8	115,603	22·6	139,634	23·4	162,617	23·0
Total	77,029	31·5	102,874	32·4	133,688	31·0	151,550	29·6	182,825	30·6	213,595	30·2
2. *Flow of Funds Accounts*												
Cash Currency	16,925	6·9	21,995	6·9	30,424	7·1	35,099	6·9	42,129	7·1	49,677	7·0
Current Deposit	10,451	4·3	13,434	4·2	16,313	3·8	15,843	3·1	17,932	3·0	19,020	2·7
Short-term Deposits	57,847	23·6	78,753	24·8	103,746	24·1	120,357	23·5	147,705	24·7	172,313	24·4
Total	85,223	34·8	114,182	35·9	150,483	34·9	171,299	33·5	207,766	34·8	241,010	34·1
Gross National Product	244,640		317,869		431,070		511,481		597,047		706,177	

SOURCE: Bank of Japan, *Money Supply and Related Data* and *Flow of Funds Accounts*.

FIG. 7.1 *Factors in changes in the money supply*

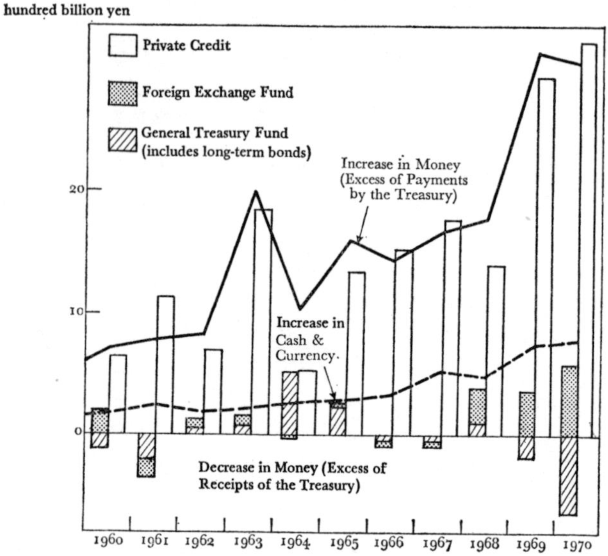

SOURCE: Bank of Japan, *Money Supply and Related Data.*

has already been discussed in connection with the demand of corporate business for investment funds and with trends in personal consumption and in personal savings. Here, therefore, attention will be focused on the supply side, i.e. the mechanism of the money supply and the factors affecting it.[1]

[1] There are three kinds of statistics which relate to the analysis of monetary movements: 'Money Supply and Related Data' and 'Monetary Survey' are compiled by the Statistical Department of the Bank of Japan, while the 'Flow of Funds Accounts' are compiled by the Research Department of the Bank. 'Money Supply' and 'Monetary Survey' differ in that the former lays stress on the flow analysis of money supply, while the latter concentrates upon the stock analysis, taking account of outstanding amounts by sectors, but they derive data from the same financial institutions and the items investigated coincide. 'Flow of Funds Accounts' show financial assets and liabilities, including money, of various sectors. They differ from the former two, in obtaining data from all financial institutions.

2. THE MECHANISM OF MONEY SUPPLY AND INFLUENCES UPON THE MONEY SUPPLY

(1) *The Mechanism of Money Supply*

The factors causing increases in the supply of money (cash currency and deposit money) are (1) payments of the General Treasury Fund; (2) increases in foreign exchange reserves (excess of payments of the Foreign Exchange Fund Special Account); (3) increases in lending by private financial institutions; (4) increases in private financial institutions' holding of securities; and (5) other factors. These, however, are not only factors in the increase of the money supply; they are also factors in the increase of time deposits – hereafter referred to as 'near-money' – in the banking system (banks and other financial institutions which handle current deposits). As has been pointed out, the Bank of Japan is the sole custodian of Treasury funds, and lends to the government. Thus, changes in the supply of money through (1) excess of payments by the General Treasury Fund, and (2) excess of payments by the Foreign Exchange Fund Special Account can arise only through the Bank's lending to the government or by the sale of foreign exchange to the Bank. On the other hand, increases in (3) private financial institutions' lending, and (4) in private financial institutions' holdings of securities, represent credit-giving activities by the banking system. It goes without saying that they correspond with changes in the supply of deposit money and increases in time deposits.

These determinants of the supply of money and near-money can be expressed in the following equations:

(Increase in money) + (Increase in near-money) = (Increase in cash currency) + (Increase in deposit money) + (Increase in time deposits) = (Excess of payments of the General Treasury Fund) + (Excess of payments of the Foreign Exchange Fund Special Account) ≠ (Increases in private financial institutions' lending) + (Increases in private financial institutions' holdings of securities) (Equation 1).

Equation 1 has been derived by consolidating and adjusting

accounts of the Bank of Japan and other banks for the sake of convenience and by offsetting the overlapping items. Equation 1 is, in fact, composed of Equations 2 and 3 below. Equation 2 shows movements in the accounts of the Bank (determinants of changes in cash currency); Equation 3 shows movements in the accounts of banks (determinants of changes in deposit money and time deposits.)

(Increase in cash currency) = (Increase in foreign exchange reserves) + (Increase in the Bank's credit to the government ≠ [(Increase in the Bank's credit to private financial institutions) − (Increase in private financial institutions' deposits with the Bank)]

(Equation 2).

'Increase in foreign exchange reserves' means an excess of payments by the Foreign Exchange Fund Special Account, which leads to an increase in foreign exchange holdings by the Bank and/or to purchase by the Bank of Foreign Exchange Fund Bills. 'Increase in the Bank's credit to the government' means an excess of payments by the General Treasury Fund. It must be noted that the Bank's credit position *vis-à-vis* the government may be affected by increases or decreases of government deposits at the Bank.

(Increase in deposit money) + (Increase in time deposit) = (Increase in lending) + (Increase in securities investment) − [(Increase in the Bank's credit to private financial institutions) − (Increase in private financial institutions' deposits with the Bank) − (Increase in cash in hand)]

(Equation 3).

In Equations 2 and 3 items in square brackets are transactions between the Bank of Japan and private financial institutions and can be offset.

Cash currency on the left-hand side of the Equation 2 includes bank-notes and coins. As coins are issued by the government, they are, properly speaking, to be regarded as its liabilities, but the Bank receives all new coins from the government *en bloc* and puts them into circulation together with its bank-notes, so that increases in the outstanding amount of coins may be deemed to represent increases in the

Bank's credit to the government. Then, part of the supply of cash currency goes to swell cash on hand in the banking system and does not go into the general circulation. As the increase in cash currency in Equation 1 refers to additions to the general circulation outside the banking system, it is equal to the balance by subtraction of the increase in cash on hand in banks from the total supply of cash from the Bank of Japan, which is shown on the left-hand side of the Equation 2. It must also be noted that in Equation 2 the increase in the Bank's credit to private financial institutions includes both the increase in lending and purchases and sales of bonds and debentures by the Bank (market operations). The same applies to increases in the Bank's credit to private financial institutions in Equation 3, which records the transactions at the level of private financial institutions.

In the next place, if we transpose time deposits from the left-hand side to the right-hand side of the Equation 3, which shows determinants of the increase and decrease of both deposit money and near-money, Equation 3* is derived; this shows the determinants of the variations in the amount of deposit money:

(Increase in deposit money) = (Increase in lending + Increase in Securities Investment − Increase in time deposits) − [(Increase in the Bank's credit) − (Increase in deposits with the Bank) − (Increase in Cash on hand)] (Equation 3*).

(Increase in lending + Increase in Securities investment − Increase in time deposits) may be thought of as representing the credit-creating activities of the banks.

(2) *Factors in the Money Supply*

From the statistics of 'Money Supply' we shall now examine the factors in the supply of money (cash currency and deposit money – see Table 7.3).

If we look at the trend which emerges after the elimination of cyclical fluctuations the General Treasury Fund continued to have an excess of receipts until about 1961 and was a restrictive factor in the money supply; thereafter it came to have an excess of payments, becoming in 1964 as

TABLE 7·3

Factors affecting the Money Supply

(hundred million yen)

Years	*Increase and Decrease in Money*			*by Factor*					(For Reference)
	Total	*Cash Currency*	*Deposit Money*	*Time Deposits* (A)	*General Treasury Fund*	*Foreign Exchange Fund Special Account*	*Lending and Others* (B)	*of which lendings*	*Credit-Creation* (B)–(A)
1961	9,159	2,251	6,908	11,871	– 2,087	– 1,458	24,576	(21,999)	12,705
1962	9,324	1,797	7,527	16,032	400	918	24,038	(24,396)	8,006
1963	19,777	2,195	17,582	19,964	765	731	38,245	(39,404)	18,281
1964	10,015	2,567	7,448	18,531	5,163	– 318	23,701	(28,790)	5,170
1965	15,830	2,770	13,060	22,889	2,366	231	36,122	(32,900)	13,233
1966	14,288	3,248	11,040	26,995	– 487	– 367	42,137	(40,111)	15,142
1967	16,526	5,246	11,280	29,224	– 518	– 421	46,689	(46,172)	17,465
1968	17,862	4,811	13,051	32,699	928	3,008	46,625	(45,198)	13,926
1969	31,275	7,244	24,031	41,185	– 1,724	3,494	70,690	(68,378)	29,505
1970	30,770	7,787	22,983	47,605	– 6,367	4,466	80,276	(80,224)	32,671
Total 1961–1970	174,826	39,916	134,910	266,995	– 1,561	10,284	433,099	427,572	166,504

NOTES:

1. This table has been drawn up by consolidating (offsetting the overlapping accounts) and by adjusting (by aggregating or breaking down various items of accounts) the accounts of principal financial institutions, which supply cash currency or deposit money, i.e. the Bank of Japan, the Foreign Exchange Fund, all banks (excluding trust accounts), mutual loans and savings banks, credit associations, the Central Co-operative Bank of Agriculture and Forestry, and the Central Bank for Commercial and Industrial Co-operatives.
2. Bank-notes and coins held by the above financial institutions are excluded from 'cash currency'.
3. The 'General Treasury Fund' is the sum of the Treasury Accounts with the Public, and coins issued.

SOURCE: Bank of Japan, *Money Supply and Related Data*.

important a factor in money supply as credit-creation by the banks (i.e. the difference between banks' lending and other assets on the one hand, and their time deposits on the other). After 1965, however, the excess of payments dwindled and an excess of receipts reappeared in 1966 and 1967, when government bonds were issued. The Foreign Exchange Fund Special Account did not figure greatly as the supplier of money until 1968, because foreign exchange reserves did not show wide fluctuations. Since 1968 it has become one of the biggest sources of money supply, as foreign exchange reserves have kept on increasing. Throughout the period, however, much of the increased money supply has come from increases in bank lending, i.e. through credit-creation by banks. This reflects the fact that economic growth during the period has been based mainly on increases in private investment.

Cyclically the supply of money has experienced considerable fluctuations from year to year in response to changes in business and financial conditions, as has been pointed out. Also, the factors affecting the money supply have varied in importance over time.

The General Treasury Fund usually has an excess of receipts in the upswings and in the over-heating phases of the business cycle, while an excess of payments appears in downswings. Since the fiscal year 1963, however, this pattern has been less apparent. One reason is that the scale of supplementary budgets became larger after that fiscal year. Another reason may lie in the obstacles to the realisation of large surpluses in boom periods with the development of bond-issues after the fiscal year 1965.

In contrast, the Foreign Exchange Fund Special Account becomes a supplier of money in the recovery phases of the cycle, because a favourable balance of trade brings gains in foreign exchange reserves; but in the over-heating phases an adverse balance of trade develops, and causes losses, so that the Special Account emerges as an absorber of money. It must be pointed out, however, that this pattern has also recently become less pronounced; because foreign exchange reserves have recently been on the increase, even during the period of business expansion.

Bank lending increases rapidly in upswings, while during

over-heating and recessions the tight-money policy causes it to slow down. Thus, credit creation by banks registered large increases in 1961, 1963, 1967 and 1969, while in 1962 and 1964 there were markedly slower rates of growth.

3. SUPPLY OF CASH CURRENCY

The above seeks to explain changes in the total supply of money, including deposit money. The supply of cash currency will now be considered. As already pointed out, the outstanding amount of cash currency bears a relatively stable ratio to the scale of the economy (i.e. to gross national product). The Bank of Japan is the supplier of cash currency, mostly through financial institutions, although a very small portion may pass directly to business firms and individuals from the Bank; in order to dispense cash in this way financial institutions must have liquid resources, in the form of cash on hand and deposits with the Bank; these two items constitute their cash reserves.

A part of the cash currency supplied by the Bank is therefore retained by financial institutions as their cash on hand (at the end of 1969, 885·5 billion yen, or 17 per cent of the total outstanding amount), but most of it circulates in the private sector (at the end of 1969, 4213 billion yen, or 83 per cent). We may distinguish cash circulating in the private sector from cash on hand in financial institutions; the former may be termed 'cash in circulation', most of which is used for wages and for personal expenditure, although some is employed for payments by small business. Thus, the increase in cash in circulation predominantly reflects growth in personal incomes, which is a result of past investment by business firms. It is therefore very difficult to control the demand for cash, once it has materialised in the withdrawal of deposits from financial institutions.

In the foregoing section the determinants of the supply of cash currency have been expressed in Equation 2. By transposing Equation 2 we obtain Equation 4.

(Increase in cash currency) = (Increase in cash on hand at financial institutions) + (Increase in cash in circulation) = (Increase in foreign exchange reserves) + (Increase in the Bank's credit to the government) + (Increase in the Bank's credit to private financial institutions) − (Increase in private financial institutions' deposits with the Bank) (Equation 2).

(Increase in cash reserves of financial institutions) = [(Increase in cash on hand at financial institutions) + (Increase in private financial institutions' deposits with the Bank)] = [(Increase in foreign currency reserves) + (Increase in the Bank's credit to the government) + (Increase in the Bank's credit to private financial institutions)] − (Increase in cash in circulation) (Equation 4).

When the cash in circulation increases with the expansion of the economy the cash reserves of private financial institutions generally decrease. The decrease is, however, counteracted by (1) an excess of payments by the Foreign Exchange Fund Special Account, when the balance of payments is favourable and foreign currency reserves are increasing; or by (2) an excess of payments by the General Treasury Fund, which is financed by an increase in the Bank's credit to the government.

In major European countries, such as West Germany and Italy, purchase by the central banks of gold and foreign exchange replenishes the cash reserves of financial institutions. In Japan, however, both the rate of increase of foreign exchange reserves and the excess of payments of the General Treasury Fund have been comparatively modest. Indeed they have been too small to offset decreases in the cash reserves of financial institutions, which has resulted from the rapid growth of the amount of cash in circulation. The gap has mostly been filled by credit from the Bank of Japan. However, the situation is now changing owing to a considerable increase in foreign exchange reserves.

In general, a central bank has three instruments of credit control: (1) lending policy; (2) open-market operations; and (3) reserve requirements. As the open market is well-developed in the U.S.A. and in the U.K., open-market operations are carried out daily to regulate cash reserves. In Japan, with its less-developed open market, such operations were little used before 1962 (see pp. 156–7 below). As for reserve requirements under the Reserve Deposit System the legal reserve ratio has been very low, so that there has been little scope for its reduction. Thus, the cash reserves of financial institutions have been replenished mainly through lending by the Bank of Japan. Since November 1962, however, following the introduction of the 'New Measure for Monetary Regulation', the Bank has come to supply the desired volume of currency largely through purchases and sales of bonds and debentures.

4. SUPPLY OF MONEY AND MONETARY POLICY

The central bank is in a position to control the total amount of money. It cannot, however, directly influence the amount of cash in circulation in the short run. By using the weapons of monetary policy it regulates the credit-creating activities of banks and can eventually control the tempo of economic activity; in other words, the central bank can regulate the cash reserves of banks or alter the terms on which they can be replenished. As lending by banks is conditioned largely by the level of their cash reserves the central bank can significantly affect banks' lending attitudes and thereby business investment. Thus, the cash reserves of banks, along with interest rates, are the most important objective of monetary policy. In this way the monetary policy of the central bank can, in the last analysis, control the amount of cash in circulation by regulating bank lending, thus influencing the pace of economic activity.

The total amount of money is thus regulated by monetary policy, but *ex-ante* calculation of the correct amount of money is scarcely possible. Money is supplied through daily financial transactions, such as depositing, lending, purchases and sales of securities, between the central bank and the banks. The verdict on whether or not the money supply is at an appropriate level depends on success in maintaining stability in the value of money, which is one objective of monetary policy, and also on the achievement of balanced growth in the economy. Thus prospective future movements in prices and in the balance of payments are important yardsticks. Amongst other indices bearing directly or indirectly upon these movements are those relating to the state of domestic demand and the demand for and supply of labour, as well as the attitudes of management in business firms. All these provide data for the formation of an overall judgement.

(hundred million yen)

Years	Bank-notes	Treasury Fund				Credit of the Bank of Japan				Others (C)
		Total	*General Treasury Fund (A)*	*Foreign Exchange Fund*	*New Issues of Long-term Bonds*	*Total*	*Lending*	*Purchase and sale of Securities*	*Others (B)*	
1960	2,046	624	−1,264	1,888	—	1,638	1,622	1	15	− 216
1961	2,460	−3,546	−2,089	−1,457	—	7,845	7,844	—	1	−1,839
1962	2,658	1,318	400	918	—	1,001	6	995	—	339
1963	3,115	1,496	765	731	—	2,872	−1,295	4,167	—	−1,253
1964	2,415	4,845	5,163	−318	—	−959	−453	−506	—	−1,471
1965	2,649	2,597	2,366	231	—	535	5,173	−2,985	−1,653	−483
1966	3,496	−854	6,514	−367	−7,001	5,590	1,133	2,809	1,648	−1,240
1967	4,981	−939	5,349	−421	−5,867	8,008	−2,261	9,792	477	−2,088
1968	6,304	3,936	5,932	3,008	−5,004	5,127	481	5,517	−871	−2,759
1969	7,694	1,770	2,063	3,494	−3,787	8,854	3,785	4,893	−659	−2,930
1970	7,447	−1,901	−3,143	4,466	−3,224	13,352	4,116	7,866	2,205	−4,004
Total 1960–70	45,265	9,346	22,056	12,173	−24,883	53,863	20,151	32,549	1,163	−17,944

NOTES:

1. Minus signs indicate:
   (*a*) Bank-notes, net withdrawals;
   (*b*) Treasury Fund, net receipts;
   (*c*) Lending, net repayments;
   (*d*) Securities, excess of sales.
2. (A) Includes Foodstuffs Control Special Account.
   (B) Includes purchase and sale of foreign currency bills, bills sold under repurchase agreements and purchase and sale of short-term bills of the government.
   (C) Includes reserve deposits, deposits with agencies, coins and redemption of bonds and debentures held by the Bank.

SOURCE: *Factors for Changes in Bank-notes Issued.*

CHAPTER 8

FLOW OF FUNDS

I. SURVEY OF THE FLOW OF FUNDS

The financial market in the widest sense of the term embraces the flow of funds as a whole in the national economy. The financial market is where borrowers and lenders or investors of funds, i.e. lending and borrowing, are regulated, and where the price of funds – that is, the interest rate – is determined.

As the sum total of financial transactions in the national economy constitutes the financial market in the widest sense, all sorts of economic units, such as business firms, households, the government, banks and other financial institutions, are participants in the market. In the Japanese financial market households' savings figure as the principal source of funds, while the principal takers of funds are business firms which undertake investment. Financial institutions act as intermediaries between these two; adjusting the demand or the supply of funds, they play an important role in the working of the financial market. The government, which is the principal in fiscal activity, is at the same time a supplier and a taker of funds. The Bank of Japan is the pivot of the financial system, being the issuing bank, bankers' bank and the government's bank. Figure 8.1 shows the pattern by sector of saving and investment activities, and of borrowing and lending and other financial transactions by subdividing them into five processes (figures are averages of 1968–70).

The figure shows that: (1) the bigger saver is the personal sector, the savings of which amount to 42 per cent of gross national savings, while savings by the corporate business sector are 38 per cent and those by the public sector are 20 per cent of the total; (2) the personal sector is also the biggest provider of funds in the market, supplying 67 per cent of the total, while the relative share of the corporate business sector is only 27

FIG. 8.1 *Flow of funds from saving to investment (average of 1968–70)*

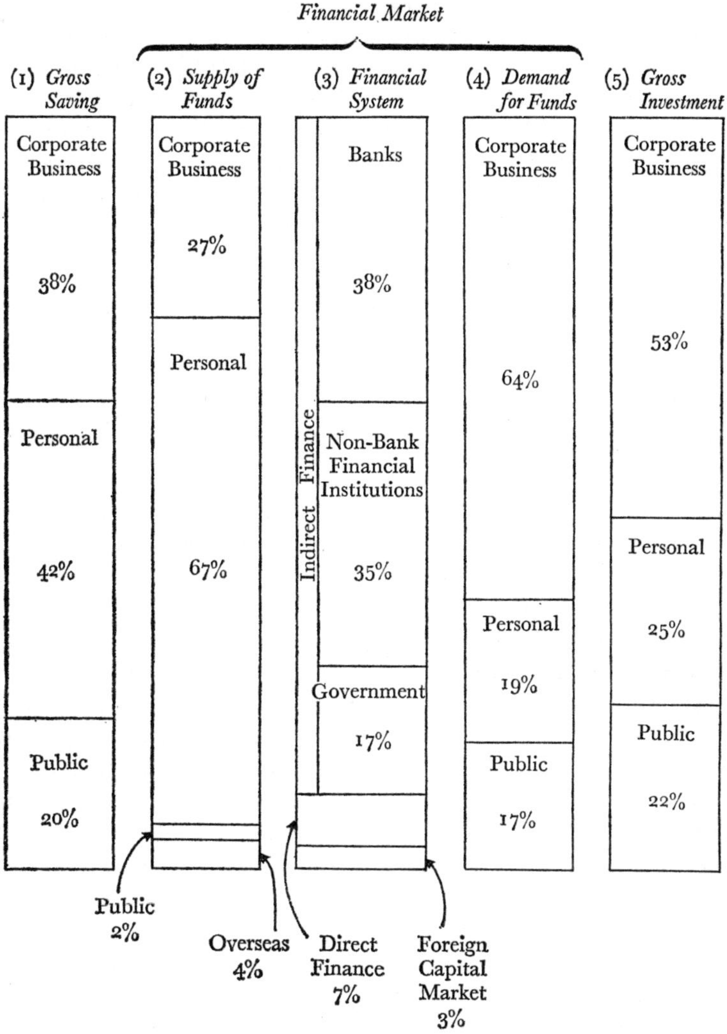

per cent; (3) in the flow of funds, so-called 'indirect financing' – that is, the flow via financial institutions – predominates, accounting for 90 per cent of the total flow; 'direct financing', namely, investment in securities by individuals and corporate businesses, is equal to only 7 per cent. Moreover, indirect financing through banks accounts for 38 per cent of the total;

(4) the biggest borrower of funds is the corporate business sector, which absorbs 64 per cent of the total funds raised, while the public sector takes 17 per cent and the personal sector takes 19 per cent of the total; (5) of the funds ultimately used for investment, the relative share of the corporate business sector is 53 per cent, while that of the public sector is 22 per cent and that of the personal sector is 25 per cent. The distinctive feature of Japan's financial structure is that 'indirect financing' through financial institutions, particularly banks, predominates in the flow of funds from the personal sector (savers) to the corporate business sector (investors). This situation is, however, changing, as will be explained in the next section.

2. RECENT TRENDS

(1) *Investment and Fund-raising*

The investment activities of the private sector, including the corporate business sector, have been discussed in Chapter 5. Here, trends in investment and in the raising of funds (borrowing from financial institutions, issue of securities, and inflow of foreign capital) by sector (i.e. trends in (4) and (5) in Fig. 8.1) will be discussed from the national point of view (Fig. 8.2).

Gross domestic investment shows a steep upward trend, although there were periods of temporary stagnation in 1962 and 1965. Net investment (gross investment less depreciation) has also tended to increase rapidly, but there is a growing gap between net and gross investment. This reflects larger provisions for depreciation, and shows that much investment in plant and equipment has been financed from depreciation allowances.

The volume of funds raised has increased at about the same pace as net investment, although there have been fluctuations from year to year. The increase was particularly large in the boom years of 1961, 1963, 1967 and 1969.

The breakdown of the procurement of funds shows that the growth in the demand of the corporate business sector has dominated the behaviour of the demand for funds in the economy as a whole. It has already been remarked that the corporate business sector has been the biggest borrower of funds; in boom

FIG. 8.2 *Investment and funds raised*

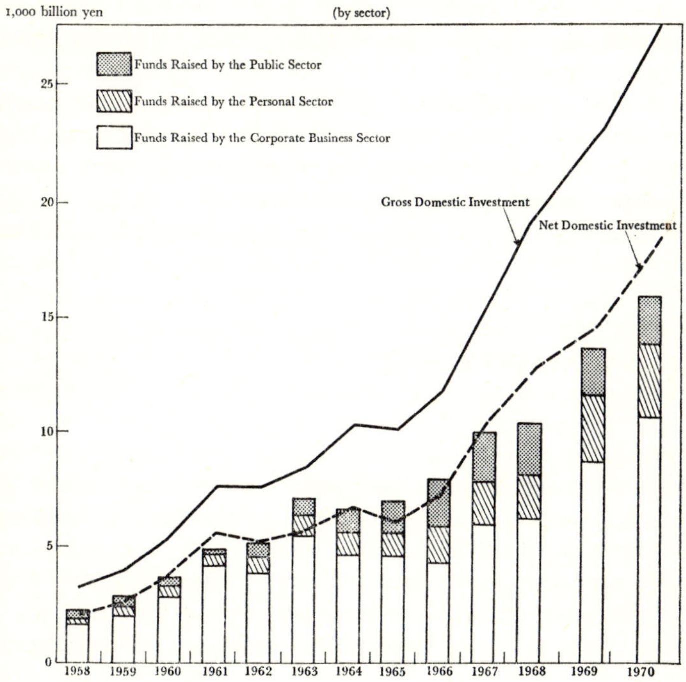

SOURCE: Bank of Japan, *Flow of Funds Accounts.*

years, such as 1960–1 and 1963, the preponderance of this trend has been particularly marked. A prominent feature of recent years, however, has been the greatly increased demand for funds by the public sector since about 1965, due to increased public investment and to government bond-issues. The demand for funds by the personal sector is also rising rapidly because of vigorous housing investment. Thus, the relative share of the corporate business sector in the total funds raised reached a peak in 1961 and has since declined; the rise in the self-financing ratio of the sector has further contributed to the decline.

(2) *Composition of the Financial Market*

Changes in the relative importance of the financial, security and the foreign capital markets and of various financial institutions (i.e. trend in (3) of Fig. 8.1) will now be examined (Fig. 8.3).

The relative importance of direct financing increased briefly in 1960–1, when security markets were booming and investment trusts were soaring in popularity; but the subsequent depression of the market caused it to fall back again. The inflow of foreign capital scarcely increased after 1963–4, when there was such activity in the issue of securities in foreign markets and in the taking up of untied loans that foreign borrowing supplied almost as large a proportion of the total funds raised as direct financing.

Lending and security investment by financial institutions therefore constitute the bulk of the funds supplied in the financial market in the widest sense.

There have been some changes in the relative shares of various kinds of financial institutions in the total of indirect financing; that of all banks has remained at about the same level of 40 per cent during these 10 years, while that of non-bank private financial institutions has risen at a rapid pace since approximately 1955–64, and is now almost as big as that of banks.

(3) *Savings and Supply of Funds*

Next, trends in the supply of funds (deposits, trust, insurance, security investment and inflow of foreign capital) in the financial market in the widest sense will be examined (i.e. trends of (1) and (2) in Fig. 8.1).

The relative shares of the various sectors in gross domestic savings, which are the source of funds, are as follows: averages of 1960–9, personal sector, 42 per cent; corporate business sector, 37 per cent; public sector, 21 per cent. These relative shares have on the whole remained static. In the supply of funds, too, the personal sector has been dominant, providing 60–65 per cent of the total, although there have been some cyclical fluctuations in this ratio.

By use of funds financial institutions have been absorbing increasing amounts. By form of employment the relative importance of deposits, particularly of savings deposits, is rising. They now absorb as much as 71 per cent of the funds supplied (average of 1965–9). The relative share of trusts and insurance is 16 per cent of the total (6 per cent for trusts and 10 per cent for insurance (averages of 1965–9)). This is not a high percentage, but it is growing significantly.

3. ACCUMULATION OF FINANCIAL ASSETS

The expansion of the financial market in the widest sense brings an increase in the outstanding volume of financial assets. Table 8.1 makes comparisons of the amounts outstanding of principal financial assets at the end of 1969 with those of five and ten years before. The sum of outstanding financial assets (Table 8.1, D) has increased about sixfold during these ten years.[1]

Thus, the rate of accumulation of financial assets is far in excess of the growth rate of gross domestic product during the same period (G.D.P. was 4·6 times as great as previously). The outstanding amount of these assets, like the willingness to accumulate them, had been depressed to extremely low levels by the post-war inflation, so that the subsequent stability in the value of money and the high growth of the economy prompted their rapid recovery and expansion.

Among the various kinds of financial assets, insurance has shown the biggest increase (8·8 times as large in 1969 as in 1959), followed by trusts (7·4 times), savings deposits (5·9 times) and lending (5·7 times). The smallest increase is that of cash currency (4·7 times). Among securities (5·4 times), corporation debentures, local bonds and bank debentures have registered great increases, whereas there has been a striking stagnation in the growth of shares and investment trusts. A remarkable

[1] Lending is an asset of the financial sector and is to be set off against money and savings deposits, so that duplication ensues if we include it in the outstanding financial assets. Even if we exclude, however, financial assets have multiplied by about six times during these ten years – that is, roughly the same result is obtained whether we include or exclude them.

TABLE 8.1

Outstanding Amounts of Financial Assets

(hundred million yen)

	End of 1960 (A)	*End of 1965* (B)	*End of 1970* (C)	(C)/(A)	(C)/(B)
Cash Currency	12,968	26,976	58,974	4·55	2·19
Deposit Money	35,630	92,475	191,978	5·39	2·08
Savings Deposits	80,148	200,810	466,178	5·82	2·32
Trusts	6,429	20,983	52,240	8·12	2·49
Insurance	12,495	36,156	90,488	7·24	2·50
Securities	71,367	170,388	342,063	4·79	2·01
(of which Government Bonds)	(9,792)	(14,417)	(55,114)	(5·63)	(3·82)
(,, ,, Local Bonds/Corporation Debentures)	(5,293)	(25,416)	(74,434)	(8·96)	(2·93)
(,, ,, Bank Debentures)	(10,540)	(28,847)	(61,753)	(5·86)	(2·14)
(,, ,, Industrial Debentures)	(6,925)	(17,486)	(30,431)	(4·39)	(1·74)
(,, ,, Shares)	(32,747)	(72,481)	(107,266)	(3·28)	(1·48)
(,, ,, Investment Trusts)	(6,070)	(11,741)	(13,065)	(2·15)	(1·11)
Loans and Discounts	148,018	375,304	836,879	5·65	2·23
(of which Loans and Discounts to the Private Sector)	(120,807)	(314,518)	(701,300)	(5·81)	(2·23)
(of which Loans and Discounts to the Government)	(27,211)	(60,786)	(135,579)	(4·98)	(2·23)
Total (D)	367,055	923,092	2,038,800	5·55	2·21
(Excluding Loans and Discounts) (E)	219,037	547,788	1,201,921	5·49	2·19
Gross National Product (GNP)	154,992	317,869	706,177	4·56	2·22
(D)/(GNP)	2·37	2·90	2·89		
(E)/(GNP)	1·41	1·72	1·70		

tendency during the last five years has been the increase in government bonds, and the net decrease in investment trusts.

4. RELATIVE SHARES OF VARIOUS FINANCIAL INSTITUTIONS AND CHANGES IN THEM

As Fig. 8.3 shows, the relative importance of various financial institutions in giving credit has undergone some change. The same is true of their relative shares in the absorption of funds.

Table 8.2 shows variations in the relative shares of (and in outstanding amounts held by) various financial institutions in the use (lending and security investment) and in the raising (deposits and bank debenture issues) of funds. Both in lending and in deposits banks overwhelm others with shares of about 50 per cent (end of 1969), but their relative position has had a marked tendency to decline during the last ten years. City banks especially have lost ground, while country banks, long-term credit banks and trust banks (banking accounts) have held their own. In contrast to city banks, the relative importance of financial institutions for small businesses, such as credit associations, those for agriculture and fisheries, insurance companies and trust banks (trust accounts), has risen greatly. During the same period the relative weight of government financial institutions has declined.

Thus, the relative positions of various financial institutions have changed considerably, but the decline in the relative share of banks and the rise in that of financial institutions for small businesses have accelerated, particularly since 1961. The causes may be summarised as follows: (1) the fall in the relative share of banks has been particularly pronounced during periods of monetary restraint, because banks have been most strongly affected by the Bank of Japan's moral suasion or by restrictions on lending; (2) financial institutions for small businesses have been treated favourably in the setting up of new branches and by other administrative regulations; (3) the high growth of the economy accelerated the accumulation of financial assets by individuals, so that credit associations, trust accounts and so on, the major business of which is the

FIG. 8.3 *Funds extended through various channels*

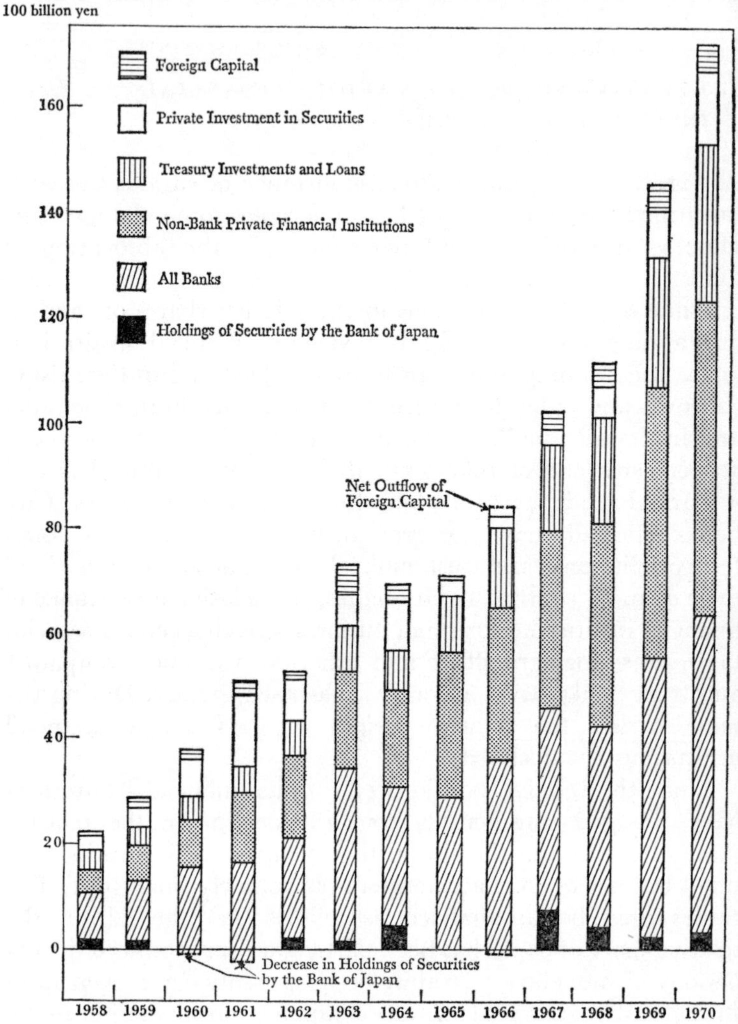

SOURCE: Bank of Japan, *Flow of Funds Accounts.*

absorption of personal savings deposits, grew at a relatively rapid pace.

The relative decline in the role of commercial banks and the consequent improvement in the relative position of non-bank financial institutions are phenomena observable also in European and American countries. Japanese banks, however, are differently situated from European and American banks in that they have carried on 'mixed banking' from the Meiji period: besides commercial banking, they engage in savings deposits business and take time deposits from the general public, while on the other hand they finance fixed investment by corporate business in plant and equipment. Thus, the reason for the fall in their relative share is not necessarily the same as that applying to overseas banks. None the less, the growth of non-bank financial institutions during the last decade has been striking.

TABLE 8.2

Loanable Funds of all Financial Institutions (Outstanding Balances)

(hundred million yen)

	Loans and Discounts, Investment in Securities (Employment of Funds)					
	End of 1960		*End of 1965*		*End of 1970*	
	Total	%	*Total*	%	*Total*	%
All Banks	95,586	54·9	225,863	51·3	459,047	45·9
(of which City Banks)	(54,771)	(31·5)	(126,935)	(28·9)	(251,145)	(25·1)
(,, ,, Country Banks)	(27,911)	(16·0)	(65,500)	(14·9)	(136,842)	(13·7)
(,, ,, Long-term Credit Banks)	(10,036)	(5·8)	(25,071)	(5·7)	(53,938)	(5·4)
(,, ,, Trust Banks)	(2,868)	(1·7)	(8,357)	(1·9)	(17,122)	(1·7)
Financial Institutions for Small Businesses	21,564	12·4	69,373	15·8	165,485	16·6
(of which Mutual Loans and Savings Banks)	(10,143)	(5·8)	(28,959)	(6·6)	(57,558)	(5·8)
(,, ,, Credit Associations)	(8,327)	(4·8)	(26,437)	(6·0)	(71,577)	(7·2)
(,, ,, Credit Co-operatives)	(1,541)	(0·9)	(6,315)	(1·4)	(17,388)	(1·7)
Financial Institutions for Agriculture and Fisheries	9,074	5·2	29,415	6·7	83,861	8·3
Insurance[b]	7,204	4·1	20,587	4·7	56,863	5·7
Trusts[c]	7,383	4·3	22,535	5·1	54,666	5·5
Government[d]	33,222	19·1	72,149	16·4	179,790	18·0
Total	174,033	100·0	439,922	100·0	999,712	100·0

Deposits (Source of Funds[a])

	End of 1960		End of 1965		End of 1970	
	Total	%	Total	%	Total	%
All Banks	81,202	56·0	193,599	51·1	404,204	47·0
(of which City Banks)	(42,793)	(29·5)	(99,316)	(26·2)	(205,012)	(23·8)
(,, ,, Country Banks)	(26,472)	(18·3)	(62,726)	(16·6)	(130,639)	(15·2)
(,, ,, Long-term Credit Banks)	(9,582)	(6·6)	(24,587)	(6·5)	(53,032)	(6·2)
(,, ,, Trust Banks)	(2,355)	(1·6)	(6,970)	(1·8)	(15,521)	(1·8)
Financial Institutions for Small Businesses	23,743	16·4	72,980	19·3	166,632	19·3
(of which Mutual Loans and Savings Banks)	(10,365)	(7·1)	(29,278)	(7·7)	(57,295)	(6·6)
(,, ,, Credit Associations)	(9,449)	(6·5)	(30,297)	(8·0)	(75,039)	(8·7)
(,, ,, Credit Co-operatives)	(1,881)	(1·3)	(7,650)	(2·0)	(19,361)	(2·3)
Financial Institutions for Agriculture and Fisheries	9,962	6·8	31,875	8·4	84,578	9·8
Insurance[b]	5,477	3·8	20,944	5·5	55,227	6·4
Trusts[c]	6,429	4·4	20,983	5·6	52,240	6·1
Government[d]	18,282	12·6	38,230	10·1	98,538	11·4
Total	145,095	100·0	378,611	100·0	861,419	100·0

NOTES:

[a] The source of funds is the sum of current deposits, short-term deposits, savings deposits, trusts, insurance and the issue of bank debentures.

[b] Employment of insurance funds includes both life and non-life insurance, but the source of insurance funds is for life insurance only.

[c] Trusts do not include securities investment trusts.

[d] The source of funds of the government includes Postal Savings Deposits, Post Office Life Insurance and Postal Annuity.

SOURCE: Bank of Japan, *Flow of Funds Accounts*.

CHAPTER 9

RATES OF INTEREST

I. THE PRINCIPAL RATES OF INTEREST AND THEIR REGULATION

Rates of interest are the prices of funds lent and borrowed in the financial market in the wider sense of the term. The financial market consists of various specialised markets, including the securities market and the financial market in the narrower sense, in each of which various interest rates are formed. At present, the Temporary Money Rates Adjustment Law places ceilings on the main interest rates. Since before the Second World War interest rates for bank deposits and lending had been fixed by agreement between banks, but the law of 1947 concerning the prohibition of private monopolies and the maintenance of fair trade raised doubts about the legality of these agreements. The banks therefore abolished the agreements before the Fair Trade Commission gave any verdict on them. Some regulation was still thought to be necessary, however, because of the prevailing inflation; in the same year, therefore, the Temporary Money Rates Adjustment Law provided for the imposition of limits on interest rates.

This law regulates in principle all interest rates of private financial institutions, but it does not cover those of the Bank of Japan and of government financial institutions, nor those regulated under other laws. The Minister of Finance has the initiative in proposing appropriate ceilings for interest rates to the Policy Board of the Bank, which, after consultation with the Money Rates Adjustment Council, fixes maximum rates. The Council is an advisory body of the Policy Board and has fifteen members: the Chief of the Banking Bureau of the Ministry of Finance, the Chief of the Adjustment Bureau of the Economic Planning Agency, the Vice-Governor of the Bank, seven representatives of financial institutions, three representatives of industry, and two men 'of learning and experience.' The maximum rates as fixed in this way are published in 'Notifications' of the Ministry of Finance. The procedures by which various rates of interest are determined in Japan will be explained below (see Table 9.1 for principal rates of interest).

(1) *The Bank Rates*

The Bank rates are the standard rates of interest applied to borrowing from the Bank of Japan. At present, there are five such rates, the choice of which depends on the nature of the bills discounted or of the securities and bills which serve as collateral. (For details, see p. 151.) The discount rate for commercial bills is, in practice, regarded as the basic rate, and when reference is made to the current Bank rate it is this rate which is meant.

The Policy Board of the Bank of Japan is the sole body with authority to determine the Bank rates. As they are the rates for lending by the Bank, alterations in them directly affect the cost to other banks of borrowing from it. In addition, the banks' lending rates are geared to the Bank rate. Furthermore, call money rates are influenced by changes in the Bank rate. Thus, the Bank rate exerts great influence on the overall levels and the structure of interest rates, and is the key rate in the structure of interest rates. The Bank alters the rate whenever this appears to be necessary and tries thereby to adjust demand for and supply of funds.

It should be added that if exceptional circumstances lead a bank to borrow in excess of its credit line, the Bank can charge a higher penal rate (4·0 per cent per annum above the Bank rate).

(2) *Lending Rates*

Bank lending includes bill-discounting, loans on promissory notes, loans on deeds, overdrafts, and so on. Interest rates on such lending vary according to the credit standing of borrowers, to the intended uses of the borrowing, etc. They also vary with changes in financial conditions.

TABLE 9.1

Principal Interest Rates (end of May 1971)

(percentage)

	Interest Rates	*Remarks*
BANK RATE		
Discount rate on commercial bills and interest rate on loans secured by government bonds and specially designated securities	5·50	Special Higher Rate 9·5%
Discount rate on export usance bills in yen	5·00	Exempted from application of Special Higher Rate
Discount rate on export advance bills	5·25	
Interest rate on loans secured by export advance bills	5·50	Special Higher Rate 9·75%
Interest rate on loans secured by bills and securities other than above	5·75	
INTEREST RATES ON DEPOSITS, ETC.		
Banks		
Ordinary Deposits	2·25	Represents the ceiling of deposits interest rate set forth by the guideline of the Bank of Japan
Time Deposits (3 months)	4·00	
Time Deposits (6 months)	5·00	
Time Deposits (1 year)	5·75	
Time Deposits (1 year and 6 months)	6·00	
Post Offices		
Ordinary Savings	3·60	Government Ordinance under Postal Savings Law
Time Savings (Less than 1 year)	4·25	
Provisional Dividend (Rate on Money in Trust, 5 years)	7·23	
Provisional Dividend (Rate on Loan Trust, 5 years)	7·47	

LENDING RATES OF BANKS, ETC.				
Discount rate of, and interest rate on, loans secured by bills of high creditworthiness, such as commercial bills eligible for Bank of Japan rediscount (Standard Rate)	5·75			9·5
Discount rate of, and interest rate on, loans secured by export usance bills eligible for Bank of Japan rediscount	5·75	Voluntary Regulations of the National Federation of Bankers' Associations (Maximum)	Maximum Rates under Temporary Money Rates Adjustment Law	9·5
Discount rate of, and interest rate on, loans secured by export advance bills eligible for Bank of Japan rediscount	6·00			9·5
Discount rate of, and interest rate on, loans secured by export advance bills other than those eligible for Bank of Japan rediscount	6·25			9·5
Discount rate of, and interest rate on loans secured by other bills	7·50			9·5
Overdrafts	8·50			10·25
Average Agreed Rates of Interest on Loans, Advances and Discounts of All Banks	7·663	March 1971		
CALL LOAN RATE (Unconditional Money)	6·50	8 May 1971		
AVERAGE YIELDS TO SUBSCRIBERS OF SECURITIES				
Short-term Government Bills	5·423	Term 60 days (May 1971)		
Long-term Government Bonds	7·011	,, 7 years		
Government-guaranteed Debentures	7·434	,, 7 years		
Local Bonds	7·831	,, 7 years		
Bank Debentures (Interest-bearing)	7·638	,, 5 years		
Bank Debentures (Discount)	6·213	,, 1 year		
Industrial Debentures (Grade A)	8·046	,, 7 years		
Industrial Debentures (Grade D)	8·483	,, 7 years		
AVERAGE YIELD OF SHARES	4·17	Average Yield of All Shares Listed in the First Section of the Tokyo Stock Exchange end of December 1970		

At present, a ceiling is placed upon the rate for short-term lending by banks (of maturities of less than one year and of amounts in excess of one million yen) by the 'Notification' of the Ministry of Finance under the Temporary Money Rate Adjustment Law, which has been in force since January 1948. In this legal control of interest rates there is, however, an inherent risk that the pegging of rates may inhibit their function of adjusting the demand and supply of money, and of impairing the autonomy of financial institutions. Maximum lending rates have therefore come to be fixed by voluntary agreements among members of the Federation of Bankers' Associations of Japan since June 1958, following a reduction in Bank rate. These voluntary maxima do not exceed the ceilings set under the Temporary Money Rates Adjustment Law.

Later, when Bank rate was cut in February 1959, the system of a 'standard rate' was instituted, on the model of the prime rate in the United States. From March of that year the standard rate was linked to Bank rate, moving by the same amount. Thus, it became the leading index of the banks' lending rates. It is applied to the discount of and loans secured by bills of high creditworthiness, such as commercial bills eligible for the Bank rediscount. By the adoption of this system the lending rates of banks became more closely linked to Bank rate.

By a 'Notification' under the Temporary Money Rates Adjustment Law, the maximum lending rates of trust banks (designated 'money in trust'), of insurance companies (excluding loans to policy-holders) and of the Central Co-operative Bank for Agriculture and Forestry (lendings to non-affiliated organisations) are fixed as follows: those of trust banks and of insurance companies are to be 0·5 per cent higher than the maximum lending rates of banks,[1] while those of the Central

[1] By an agreement of December 1954 among members of the Trust Bank Association the lending rate of designated money in trust of trust banks was reduced from April 1956 to 0·365 per cent above the ceiling on banks' lending rates under the Temporary Money Rates Adjustment Law. Then, by an agreement of August 1968 among the Association's members, the maximum rate was fixed at 0·365 per cent higher than the banks' maximum lending rate by their voluntary regulation. After September 1969 the maximum rate was fixed at 0·25 per cent higher than the banks' maximum rate remarked above.

By agreements among members of Marine and Fire Insurance Association and of Life Insurance Association the maximum rate on short-term lending by insurance companies was 0·73 per cent higher than the banks' maximum rate (of

Co-operative Bank for Agriculture and Forestry are to be 0·25 per cent higher.

The maximum lending rates of mutual loans and savings banks, credit associations and credit co-operatives are not regulated by 'Notifications' under the Temporary Money Rates Adjustment Law, but by the respective laws governing these institutions. For instance, the lending rates of mutual loans and savings banks are subject to approval by the Minister of Finance under the Mutual Loans and Savings Banks Law. The maximum lending rates in this case are stipulated in their Conditions of Operations. Their actual lending rates are higher than those of banks, because both the cost of funds and the risks attendant on their lending are higher. The lending rates of government financial institutions are subject to approval by the Minister of Finance. The maxima are stipulated in the respective laws governing them or in their Conditions of Operations. For policy reasons these rates are fixed at relatively low levels.

(3) *Interest Rates on Deposits*

There are numerous kinds of deposits of banks and other financial institutions, each of which has its own rate of interest. By 'Notifications' under the Temporary Money Rates Adjustment Law maximum limits are imposed upon interest rates on deposits of banks and other private financial institutions, upon those on mutual deposits among financial institutions and upon provisional dividend rates on designated money in trust. The maximum interest rates on deposits of non-bank financial institutions are the same as those on bank deposits. For instance, ceilings on rates for deposits of mutual loans and savings banks are the same as those for bank deposits. For the time being, however, deposits with credit associations, credit co-operatives, agricultural co-operatives and other co-operatives are permitted to carry maximum rates 0·1 per cent higher than those on corresponding deposits in banks. These maximum rates are

discount on bills nor eligible for rediscount at the Bank) by their voluntary regulation. In September 1969 the maximum rate was 0·75 per cent higher than the banks' maximum rate mentioned above and in November 1970 the maximum rate was 0·5 per cent higher.

those actually paid by banks and others on their deposits. The maxima under the Temporary Money Rates Adjustment Law were altered in April 1970 for the first time in nine years. The inelasticity and the relatively high levels of rates on deposits are outstanding features of Japan's financial system.

Interest rates on postal savings deposits are fixed by government ordinance under the Postal Savings Law; they were changed in April 1970 for the first time since April 1961. (In October 1961 postal time savings deposits were introduced.) The interest rate on ordinary postal savings deposits is fixed at a higher level than that on ordinary deposits in banks; the purpose is to give favourable treatment to small savings.

(4) *Call Loan Rates*

Call loan rates are the rates of interest on money lent for very short periods, mostly through brokers, between financial institutions and/or securities companies. Its fluctuations, therefore, are a sensitive indicator of the situation of financial institutions. In Japan, where the market for government short-term bills and for commercial bills is not well-developed, the call loan rate is the leading short-term rate of interest and is the best indicator of market conditions.

No regulation, legal or otherwise, is at present imposed upon changes in call loan rates. They are determined by negotiations between call loan dealers and financial institutions in a comparatively competitive atmosphere, and they therefore fluctuate in response to ease or tightness in the money market. Their movements are, however, usually linked to changes in the Bank rate, one reason being that the Bank thereby adjusts the demand and supply of the money in the market.

Call loans are a form of reserve asset for those who lend in this way. Liquidity rather than profitability should therefore be their prime concern. Thus, under normal conditions, call loan rates should be lower than lending rates or Bank rate. City banks, the major takers of call loans, are, however, in chronic over-lent positions and are permanently indebted to the Bank for substantial amounts, and are always under pressure from it to repay. Hence, there is a tendency for Bank rate to provide a floor for variations in the call loan rate.

(5) *Interest Yields on Securities*

Fixed-interest securities include government bonds, local bonds, government-guaranteed debentures, and bank and industrial debentures. For those securities it is necessary to distinguish between their terms of issue and their yields to subscribers when newly issued, and market yields on existing securities. The terms of new issues vary according to the degree of certainty of repayment and liquidity (i.e. maturity and negotiability). In principle the terms for new issues should be related to the yields on existing securities, but this relationship does not necessarily prevail. One reason is that the market for public bonds and debentures has only recently (February 1966) been reopened; occasionally, notably in periods of monetary restraint, there has been a considerable divergence between these rates.

(6) *Interest Rates on Government Securities*

Government short-term bills are now issued at rates fixed initially by the Minister of Finance under the Regulation in Regard to Procedures of Raising Funds for the Government. These rates had rarely been altered until April 1968, when they were raised for the first time in five years. At that time short rates were rising because of the credit squeeze; since then, they have varied with Bank rate.

The issue terms of long-term government bonds are in principle fixed by the Minister of Finance under the Law Concerning Government Securities, but in practice they are the result of negotiations with the underwriting syndicate and others.

(7) *Interest Rates on Other Bonds and Debentures*

The issue terms of bonds and debentures other than government bonds are arranged by the interested parties, but they do not necessarily reflect the market's valuation. For instance, the rates of interest on industrial debentures are classified into five groups according to the credit standing of the issuers, but the differentials between these five groups are too small. The terms of issue of other kinds of bonds and debentures are uniform.

2. VARIATIONS OF INTEREST RATES

As already noted, Bank rate is the key interest rate, and it has been changed fairly freely in accordance with changes in business conditions. We now turn to examine the fluctuations of interest rates, including Bank rate, during post-war business cycles (see Fig. 9.1).

FIG. 9.1 *Variations in interest rates*

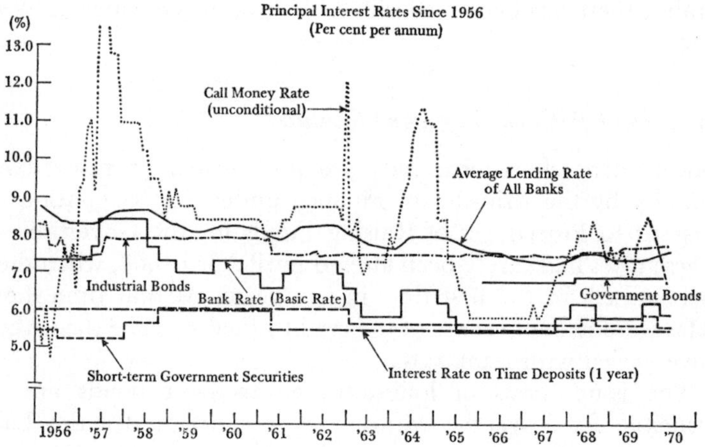

With the restoration of monetary policy in various countries around 1950, when many economic controls had been lifted and the market economy had been revived, there was also a new understanding of the function of interest rates and of the importance of Bank-rate policy. It was after the foreign exchange crisis of autumn 1953 that the Bank of Japan began to employ interest-rate policy in earnest as a countercyclical measure. It must be noted, however, that the interest-rate policy in this case was not Bank-rate policy as such, but 'the Higher Interest Rates Application System'. Coupled with the abolition of priority for import finance, the tightening of this system succeeded in adjusting the economy. This is regarded as the 'restoration of monetary policy' in Japan, because since then the importance of interest-rate policy has again been recognised, although the 'restoration' came a little later than in other countries and the policy was applied in a somewhat distinctive fashion.

Interest-rate policy based upon the higher rates application system was apparently abnormal in the sense of divorcing Bank rate from market rates. Thus, in August 1955, the Bank of Japan raised Bank rate sharply from 5·84 per cent to 7·30 per cent, which was roughly equal to its average effective lending rate. This was a preliminary to a policy of controlling finance by a flexible Bank rate. By this step the higher interest-rates application system ceased to be the principal instrument of interest-rate policy, and reverted to its original function of supplementing Bank rate in special cases.

Since then Bank rate has been changed frequently. In 1957, when the economy was over-heated, it was raised by 1·095 per cent in two instalments. Then, in 1958 (recession) and in 1959 (stability), it was lowered by 1·46 per cent in three steps. Towards the end of 1959 it was feared that the pace of the boom was excessive, so the rate was raised by 0·365 per cent as a precaution; but as these fears subsided it was reduced in August 1960 and again in January 1961, by 0·365 per cent on each occasion. In the latter half of 1961, however, the economy began to be over-heated again, so that the rate was twice increased, by 0·365 in July and in September respectively. The effects of anti-cyclical measures became apparent in 1962 and the rate was lowered twice by 0·365 per cent in October and again by 0·365 per cent in November. Two further reductions of 0·365 per cent on each occasion followed in March and April 1963. The aim was to promote the normalisation of financial conditions by a flexible interest-rate policy, and by establishing a normal structure of rates.

The rate was raised by 0·73 per cent in March 1964, to help prepare for the transition of the Japanese economy to an open system. By this it was intended to adjust the economy and to ensure a favourable trend of the balance of payments. In 1965, when business was fully adjusted and the domestic economy was entering a mature stage of development, the rate was lowered by 1·095 per cent in three instalments, in January, April and June, reaching its lowest level in post-war years (5·475 per cent for the discount of commercial bills). After January 1966, when the issue of government bonds began, business activity again picked up. In 1967, however, the balance of payments showed a large deficit so that the rate was increased by 0·365 per cent in September 1967 and by the same amount the following January. Subsequently, the balance of payments improved markedly, and the rate was cut by 0·365 per cent in August 1968, to 5·84 per cent.

As economic activity showed a fairly rapid expansion in 1969 Bank rate was raised by 0·41 per cent in spite of the favourable balance of payments. After about one year's tight-money policy the economic activity tendedto calm down. In this situation the Bank of Japan, in October 1970, reduced Bank rate by 0·25 per cent to 6·0 per cent.

When Bank rate was raised in May 1957 the maximum lending rate of banks under the Temporary Money Rates Adjustment Law was increased by 0·365 per cent. This was the first occasion since the war that changes in the banks' lending rates had been linked with that of the Bank rate. That link continues. Further, although the ceiling on the banks' lending rates under the law has been maintained at the same level, the system of the standard rate was introduced in March 1959. This standard rate is changed by mutual agreement among banks in the light of changes in Bank rate, but it never exceeds the maximum imposed under the Temporary Money Rates Adjustment Law. As the standard rate provides the norm for variations in other lending rates the latter are also linked to Bank rate. In practice, however, only short-term lending rates of banks have conformed relatively well to this rule. Thus, there has been reasonable flexibility in the lending rates of city banks since the introduction of the standard-rate system, because much of their lending is of the type to which the standard rate is applicable; on the other hand, the rates of country banks and of long-term credit banks have not varied very much, because the former engages in relatively little of that type of lending, while the latter are concerned chiefly with long-term loans. In the long run, however, the banks' lending rates have tended to decline. Thus, during the last decade the average agreed rate of interest on loans and discounts has fallen from 8·395 per cent to 6·8 per cent.

Lending rates have thus experienced flexible, though narrow, fluctuations. Interest rates on deposits, in contrast, have been fairly rigid. Recently there have been only three changes, upward in 1957, downward in 1961 and upward in 1970.

Call loan rates were in principle linked to alterations of the Bank rate from July 1957, when the banks decided to fix maximum rates on call loans by mutual agreements among themselves. Subsequently, however, actual market rates far exceeded such maximum rates in times of monetary restraint. Such abnormally high rates on call loans were the result of the credit squeeze by the Bank of Japan, which it enforced despite the banks' over-lent positions. These abnormally high levels of call loan rates therefore reflected distortions in Japan's financial structure. In 1965, however, call loan rates declined rapidly due to successive reductions in Bank rate and to the general slackness of the money market. Throughout 1966 the rate on unconditional call money remained unchanged at 5·84 per cent. During the monetary restraint of 1967–8, however, it rose again until it reached the peak of 8·395 per cent (June 1968). Since the reduction of Bank rate in August 1968 it has fallen again. It should be noted that the agreements among banks on call loan rates were abandoned in September 1967. During the monetary restraint of 1969–70 it rose again (8·5 per cent at the peak).

As already noted, it was decided in May 1965 that government short-term bills should henceforward be issued in the market for public subscription. The method of issue was not, however, the ideal system of issue through public tender, but by offerings of bills to the public at a fixed discount rate of 5·292 per cent. The rate was raised by 0·365 per cent in December 1957, and by the same amount in September 1958; it was eventually reduced by 0·365 per cent in June 1963. Thereafter, the rate remained unchanged for five years, but it was raised by 0·1825 per cent in April 1968 and was lowered by the same margin the following August. Except for conversion bonds, with a yield to subscribers of 6·432 per cent since September 1960, long-term government bonds had not been issued for a long time until January 1966, when new bonds (6½% Treasury bonds) were issued for the first time in many years. The yield to subscribers was 6·795 per cent at first, but was revised to 6·902 per cent in February 1968, and again to 7·011 per cent in April 1970. The terms of issue of government-guaranteed debentures, local bonds, industrial and bank debentures, which had remained almost stationary from July 1957 to April 1961, were raised in April 1968, in March 1969 (only industrial debentures) and in March 1970.

The market for public bonds and debentures was reopened in February 1966. From then until the spring of 1967, when relative ease prevailed in financial markets, the market yield on existing securities was fairly close to the subscribers' yield on newly issued securities. From the middle of the year, particularly after September, when a credit squeeze was applied, the market yield began to climb, so that a substantial gap developed between market yields and subscribers' yields. Accordingly, the terms of issue of government bonds and other debentures were revised in February and April of 1968. As a result the subscribers' yield on these securities was raised by about 0·1 per cent; the market yield, however, continued to rise, so that the gap between the subscribers' and market yields again widened. Therefore the above-mentioned terms of issue of government bonds and other debentures were revised again in 1970.

3. THE STRUCTURE AND LEVEL OF INTEREST RATES

One of the characteristics of the Japanese financial system is the existence of constraints on the free movements of interest rates, so that they cannot fully perform their function of regulating the demand for and supply of funds.

For interest rates to be able to perform their proper functions, the development of free money and capital markets would be an important prerequisite. It is in the open market that interest rates are most freely determined, and in such markets even slight variations in rates can adjust the demand for and supply of funds; moreover, the development of such markets would facilitate transference of funds between markets, thereby creating structural relationships between rates. An orderly structure of rates would thus emerge; only with such a structure would an optimum distribution of funds be possible.

In Japan, however, the formation and development of free markets have been impeded by such factors as the chronic excess demand for call money caused by the over-lent positions of city banks, by the retarded development of the capital market owing to excessive dependence on indirect financing, and by artificial regulation of interest rates. Consequently, the interrelationships between various interest rates have been relatively weak, so that distortions have developed in the structure. For instance, call loan rates, which should not normally exceed Bank rate, have hitherto usually been above it. Moreover, in tight-money periods, call loan rates have very often exceeded even long-term rates, although one reason for this has been the rigidity of long rates. Furthermore, in spite of variations in lending rates, deposit rates have remained at the same level for a relatively long period. Such distortions in the structure of rates are partly due to the absence of free markets, but it must be noted that a vicious circle has been engendered, in that the distortion itself has hampered the normal development of the markets by deflecting the flow of funds.

A like distortion has arisen from the constant effort to lower the level of rates in Japan, which allegedly has been high by international standards. It cannot be declared unequivocally that the level in Japan is higher than that of other countries, because the structure of rates differs from one country to another; further, the level itself is subject to cyclical fluctuations. For instance, high levels of interest rates have prevailed all over the world during recent years, so that the level in Japan has not necessarily been higher than in other countries. On a long-run view, however, the level may well have been higher in Japan. For instance, it can readily be seen that the average lending rate of banks has been relatively high, although this has fallen recently; a straightforward comparison with other countries is scarcely possible because detailed statistics on rates in foreign countries are not available, and because differences in requirements for compensating balances must also be taken into account.

The root cause of high rates of interest is, needless to say, the persistently strong demand for funds. In a sense, it is natural for such a phenomenon to occur in an economy with a high rate of private investment and with an annual growth rate as high as 10 per cent. Lags in the development of various financial markets, together with the over-lent positions of banks have contributed to the distortion in the structure of interest rates, most notably in the unduly high levels of short-term rates.

It follows that fundamental changes, such as a cooling-off in the demand for funds and improvements of the financial structure, are essential to moderate the dearness of money. Moreover, although it is frequently contended that Japanese business firms suffer from an excessive burden of interest payments, the possibility must be considered that the burden arises less from the existence of high interest rates than from the greater dependence of business firms in Japan on external borrowings than is the case in other countries. It is, of course, desirable that a fall in interest rates should be in prospect, but a hasty reduction in disregard of the prevailing demand for funds must be avoided, because this would impair their function of adjusting the demand for and supply of funds. In this connection a noteworthy suggestion has been made (July 1970) by the Committee on Financial System Research; a report of its Special Committee on Private Financial Institutions, entitled On the Desirable Conditions of Ordinary Private Financial Institutions, has suggested that the functions of interest rates may be utilised to good purpose.

It goes without saying that in an open economy free movements in interest rates would become more important than hitherto in regulating of the demand and supply of funds. At the same time international movements of funds in response to interest-rate differentials between nations would create more complex problems for the economy. Fairly flexible interest-rate policies are now adopted by advanced countries, so that on occasions some rates may become lower in Japan than in other countries. In future, therefore, interest-rate policies will need to be more adaptable and more flexible.

Finally it was traditional to express Bank rate, commercial banks short-term lending rates, the interest rate on ordinary deposits, and so on, in terms of one day's interest per 100 yen before September 1969, when the annual rate basis was adopted.

FIG. 9.2 *Structure of interest rates*

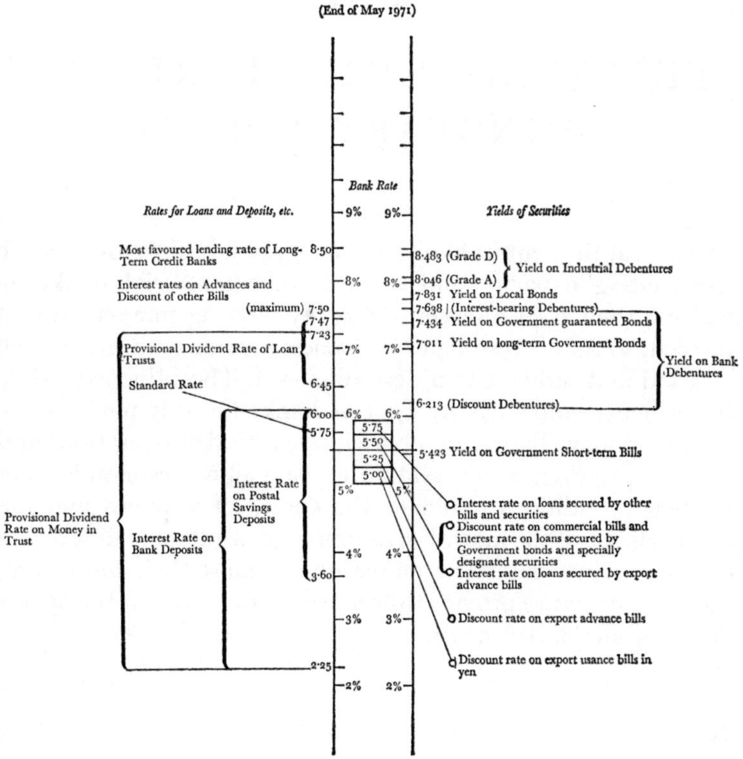

CHAPTER 10

FINANCIAL STRUCTURE AND MONETARY POLICY

IN general the central bank's monetary policy aims to influence the lending capacity and attitude of commercial banks by varying their cash reserves and/or by altering market rates of interest, so that investment by business firms may eventually be affected and brought to a desirable level. The principal policy instruments employed by central banks for this purpose are lending policy (Bank-rate policy), open-market operations and reserve requirements.[1] Naturally prevailing economic and financial conditions influence the choice of weapons and the achievement of the aims. Furthermore, considerable differences on these points exist between nations, because their contrasting financial structure provide differing environments for the operation of policy instruments.

1. MONETARY POLICY UNDER OVER-LOANS

The characteristic features of the financial structure of Japan have already been discussed. Among them, over-loans of commercial banks, especially of city banks, affect monetary policy most of all. Over-loans can be defined as a condition in which commercial banks are in over-lent positions, and are habitually dependent to a significant extent upon borrowing from the Bank of Japan or from the call money market.

Over-loans of commercial banks are fundamentally a result of the high growth rate of the Japanese economy. In post-war Japan business firms have invested at a rapid rate, so that their demand for funds has been extremely strong. In spite of this the development of the capital market has lagged, so that

[1] See, for particulars, Part Three, Chapter 12, 'The Bank of Japan'.

business firms have had to procure funds by borrowing from commercial banks. Under these circumstances close relationships have tended to develop between commercial banks and business firms. Thus banks have been willing to meet this demand for funds, and in consequence they have been chronically short of cash and liquid reserves. The cash deficiency has been made good by borrowing from the Bank of Japan or from the call money market. This is particularly true of city banks, because big firms, which have provided the driving force in the high growth of the economy, are their major customers.

The over-lent positions of banks temporarily disappeared in 1955–6, when there was a large-scale disbursement of Treasury money due to export growth and to a bumper crop of rice. However, the over-loan situation reappeared and was intensified during the high growth period of 1955–64 (see Table 10.1). When the growth rate was too high the demand for cash currency rapidly increased and Treasury accounts with the public showed a large excess of receipts over payments, because the balance of payments became adverse and large natural increments developed in tax revenue. On such occasions the Bank of Japan replenished the cash reserves of commercial banks, mainly by lending to them, so that over-loans tended to be aggravated whenever the growth of the economy accelerated too rapidly.

Provided that the high growth of the economy is pushed forward by active private investment in plant and equipment, and provided that the currency necessary for the growth is supplied through lending by the Bank of Japan, such over-loans are virtually inevitable. It is undeniable, however, that over-loans have restricted the employment of orthodox instruments of monetary policy, so that excesses in economic activity have tended to proceed unchecked.

In other words, if substantial borrowing from the Bank becomes normal, commercial banks become accustomed to such facilities, and eventually come to regard their lines of credit with the Bank as being tantamount to cash reserves. In such circumstances they will lose sight of the criteria by which they should regulate their lending; they will come to be neither willing nor able to regulate it in response to changes in their cash reserves. Thus, they will tend more readily to accede to

TABLE 10.1

Indices of Over-loans

(percentages)

End of the Year	*Lending Ratio* (A) *All Banks*	*Lending Ratio* (A) *City Banks*	*Ratio of External Liabilities* (B) *All Banks*	*Ratio of External Liabilities* (B) *City Banks*	*Ratio of Borrowing from the Bank of Japan* (C) *All Banks*	*Ratio of Borrowing from the Bank of Japan* (C) *City Banks*
1953	103	111	12	18	10	14
1954	99	106	9	15	7	11
1955	89	91	3	7	1	1
1956	92	94	6	10	3	4
1957	100	107	12	19	10	15
1958	96	101	9	14	5	9
1959	93	98	8	14	4	7
1960	93	98	8	14	5	8
1961	96	103	13	22	11	18
1962	96	105	12	22	9	16
1963	96	102	10	19	7	12
1964	96	104	12	21	5	9
1965	93	99	10	19	5	9
1966	92	97	9	17	6	10
1967	93	99	8	16	4	8
1968	91	96	7	15	4	8
1969	91	97	8	16	5	8
1970	92	99	9	18	5	8

NOTES:

$$(A) = \frac{\text{Lending}}{\text{Real Deposits} + \text{Debentures Issued}} \times 100$$

$$(B) = \frac{\text{Borrowing from Financial Institutions} + \text{Borrowing from Call Loan Market} - \text{Lending to Call Loan Market}}{\text{Real Deposits} + \text{Debentures Issued} + \text{Borrowing from Financial Institutions} + \text{Borrowing from Call Loan Market} - \text{Lending to Call Loan Market}} \times 100$$

$$(C) = \frac{\text{Borrowing from the Bank of Japan}}{\text{Real Deposits} + \text{Debentures Issued} + \text{Borrowing from the Bank of Japan}} \times 100$$

SOURCE: Bank of Japan, *Economic Statistics Annual*.

business firms' vigorous demand for funds. Such a state of affairs is not only undesirable from the point of view of the sound management of banks: it will also impair the efficacy of monetary policy, which presupposes that banks operate rationally. Furthermore, with commercial banks permanently dependent upon borrowing from the Bank, call loan rates never go below the Bank rate, even in easy money periods. Such high rates of call money have impeded the development of the market for public bonds and debentures.

Thus, over-loans have limited the usefulness of the three instruments of monetary policy. For instance, the lag in the development of the market for public bonds and debentures has made it difficult for interest rates to perform their functions properly: in particular, systematic relationships between variations of short-term and long-term interest rates could hardly be expected, so that it has been difficult to undertake open-market operations in a flexible fashion. As banks have been short of cash reserves the effects of reserve requirements have been circumscribed. For these reasons only limited results could be expected from orthodox policies, which aim at affecting the lending capacity and attitudes of commercial banks by varying their cash reserves or by causing changes in market rates of interest. Until the autumn of 1962, therefore, the Bank of Japan relied mainly on lending policy, especially Bank-rate policy, to regulate credit. In addition, particularly in periods of monetary restraint, the Bank has used 'window guidance' as a supplementary weapon, by which direct controls have been imposed upon lending by individual banks.

2. MONETARY POLICY AFTER THE ADOPTION OF NEW MEASURES FOR MONETARY REGULATION

Until the autumn of 1962 the Bank of Japan relied largely on lending policy and window guidance. In over-loan conditions commercial banks were heavily dependent upon borrowing from the Bank, so that a higher Bank rate imposed heavy burdens in the extra cost of funds; moreover, at any time pressure could be applied for repayment. As cash currency was supplied through Bank lending, the volume of this could thus be effectively controlled by the Bank.

There were difficulties in using open-market operations and reserve requirements, so the Bank had to rely upon lending policy; if, however, the Bank were to depend permanently upon lending policy as the principal monetary control, its lending would continue to grow with the economy, as more cash currency was needed. In the circumstances, over-loans by banks would scarcely be put right. In November 1962, therefore, the Bank decided to adopt the New Measure of Monetary Regulation, by which currency necessary for growth was to be supplied through purchases and sales of bonds and debentures by the Bank, while maximum lines of credit with the Bank were set for those city banks which were the most heavily indebted to it. Lending in excess of the limits was in principle prohibited, to avoid a cumulative increase in the Bank's lending.

As the market for public bonds and debentures was closed at the time, resale conditions were attached to the purchases and both purchase and sale were effected at nominal, theoretical prices back-calculated from the subscribers' yields. The transactions were made after negotiations with individual financial institutions. When circumstances changed subsequently, various alterations were made in the system. In particular since February 1966, when the long-closed market for public bonds and debentures was reopened on the occasion of the issue of government bonds, purchases and sales have come to be made at market prices and without resale conditions. This was an advance towards true open-market operations. Shortly before this, in January 1966, the Bank started to buy and sell government short-term bills with call loan dealers. These changes are doubly important; they furthered the original aim of the new measure for monetary regulation, to limit the continued increases in the Bank's lending and to put right the banks' overloans; and they also increased the efficacy of monetary policy.

3. FUTURE PROBLEMS

Since the adoption of the new measures for monetary regulation the Bank of Japan has followed a flexible policy in buying and selling bonds and debentures, thereby checking the steady rise in the Bank's net lending hitherto. Even so, some undesirable features of over-loans persisted. Thus, even since the adoption of the new measure the Bank has had to resort to window guidance to support increases in Bank rate during credit squeezes. Efforts must therefore be made to eradicate the bad effects of over-loans and to create conditions conducive to an efficient monetary policy. For this three things are indispensable: (1) to establish the principle that commercial banks should maintain a fixed ratio of cash reserves and that they should voluntarily regulate the volume of credit given by reference to their cash reserves; (2) to foster the growth of the market for public bonds and debentures, to secure a balanced development of short-term and long-term markets; (3) to make efficient use of interest rates and to achieve a realistic rate structure.

The precise future shape of Japan's financial structure cannot be foreseen, but in the formulation of monetary policy the following two points at least must probably be taken into account.

First, the Japanese economy has become 'an economy with a national debt'. As the relative importance of the public finance in the economy rises, and as the outstanding amount of the national debt increases, it will become more important to harmonise credit policy with fiscal and debt-management policies. Monetary policy, moreover, will have to adjust itself fully to the change in the flows of funds resulting from the issue of government bonds.

The second point is that Japan opted for an open economy, appropriate to her status as an advanced industrial country, when she adopted Article 8 of the I.M.F. Agreement in April 1964, and when she became a regular member of the O.E.C.D. Consequently, credit policy must have close regard for the international monetary situation, such as interest-rate differentials, if external and internal equilibrium are to be achieved.

In short, if monetary policy is to be effective it is necessary to create appropriate conditions as well as to develop, to improve and to diversify policy instruments in response to the continuing structural changes in Japan's financial system.

PART THREE

Existing Financial Institutions

CHAPTER II

GENERAL SURVEY

THE financial system in Japan has undergone various historical changes (see Part One). It was radically reorganised after the war, and now consists of the following financial institutions. The Bank of Japan, the central bank, is the pivot of the financial system; surrounding it are various well-developed private financial institutions, such as commercial banks, long-term credit banks, trust banks, financial institutions for small businesses, financial institutions for agriculture and fisheries and insurance companies. Besides these, there are call loan dealers, securities finance companies and securities companies, which may be counted as financial institutions in the wider sense, although they differ somewhat in character. Further, there are a few government financial institutions, with functions supplementing those of private institutions.

These institutions operate either on a national scale or locally. Nowadays every town has offices of commercial banks, mutual loans and savings banks, credit associations or credit co-operatives. Every village has a post-office and an agricultural or fishery co-operative. The total number of offices of financial institutions taking deposits from the public is about 50,000, or roughly one office for each 2000 of population, or one for every 500 households.

Financial institutions can be classified in various ways, but the classification adopted here is that commonly used, which does not necessarily agree with the legal one. For instance, the term 'commercial banks' cannot be found in the legal code, but they can be distinguished from others in that they are primarily engaged in short-term finance. They include city banks, country banks, foreign exchange banks and foreign banks domiciled in Japan. Legally, city banks, country banks and foreign-domiciled banks are banks established under the

Banking Law, of which the first two have traditionally been described as 'ordinary banks'. The specialised foreign exchange bank[1] is a bank established under the Foreign Exchange Banks Law. Trust banks are also governed by the Banking Law and engage in commercial banking through their banking accounts, but trust business is their chief concern, so they are not included with commercial banks.

This classification is not always ideal from the functional viewpoint. In the U.S.A. and the U.K. financial institutions other than the central bank are divided into two categories, that is, those with credit-creating capacities and those which are primarily financial middlemen. The former comprise commercial banks, while the latter includes savings banks, life insurance companies and other non-bank financial intermediaries. In Japan, however, as has been pointed out in Part One, the various kinds of financial institutions reflect their respective and unique historical development, so that it is often impossible to classify them exactly. For instance, nearly half of ordinary banks' deposits are time deposits of one year's maturity, while their medium- and long-term loans are substantial. They cannot therefore be regarded as pure commercial banks. Moreover, a few ordinary banks operate trust accounts. Thus, ordinary banks in Japan are 'mixed banks', which combine credit-creating with credit-intermediating functions. On the other hand, financial institutions for small businesses, such as mutual loans and savings banks, credit associations and credit co-operatives, and agricultural financial institutions, such as agricultural co-operatives, provide current account facilities; in that respect they can create credit in the same way as banks. Thus, it is rather difficult to make a clear-cut division of Japanese financial institutions into those with credit-creating abilities and those with credit-intermediating functions only. Instead we shall distinguish them by the fields in which they mainly operate, and review them accordingly.

First, city banks play a leading role in the short-term finance of large-scale business. Although country banks also have such

[1] Legally, banks established under the Foreign Exchange Banks Law are referred to as 'foreign exchange banks', but the term is used in common parlance to denote 'authorised foreign exchange banks' under the Foreign Exchange and Foreign Trade Control Law. In common usage the former are termed 'specialised foreign exchange banks'. Here, the conventional terminology is adhered to.

connections with big firms, their main borrowing customers are local and small.

Second, in foreign exchange and in the finance of foreign trade the specialised foreign exchange bank and city banks are dominant, although long-term credit banks, foreign domiciled banks, country banks and trust banks are also active.

Third, in medium- and long-term finance, long-term credit banks, trust banks and life insurance companies predominate, but, as already noted, city banks, country banks, financial institutions for small businesses and financial institutions for agriculture, forestry and fisheries include a considerable volume of medium- and long-term financing in their respective activities.

Fourth, in the finance of small business, country banks and financial institutions traditionally specialised in this field, such as mutual loans and savings banks, credit associations and credit co-operatives, predominate. City banks engage in this field to a limited extent.

Fifth, agriculture and fisheries are financed mainly by a hierarchy of co-operative organisations, with the Central Co-operative Bank for Agriculture and Forestry on the top, the Credit Federation of Agricultural Co-operatives in the middle and member co-operatives at the base. It goes without saying that commercial banks, particularly country banks, are involved in this field also.

Sixth, finance of securities markets is the concern of specialised securities finance companies, although commercial banks and others also participate in this activity.

The above is a broad survey of the fields covered by private financial institutions. To supplement them, government financial institutions and special accounts of the Treasury have been established. They perform important functions in the finance of industrial development, foreign trade, housing, small businesses, agriculture and fisheries and so on. The biggest source for such Treasury loans and investments is funds mobilised through the network of post-offices, such as postal savings and premiums for post-office life insurance.

There are three open markets in long-term and short-term finance: the call money market, the foreign exchange market and the securities market. The foreign exchange market, though developing, does not yet play a very important role. The call money market is fairly well-developed, and the principal operators are the call loan dealers. Although the market for public bonds and debentures is not yet fully evolved, the market for transactions in existing shares is comparatively well-developed; the securities companies play the major role in this market.

As has been stressed previously, business investment has up to now been the main driving force of Japan's economic development. As lenders to business, banks have figured much more largely than the securities market; big banks, such as city banks and long-term credit banks, have therefore been able to exert great influence on the economy, both quantitatively and qualitatively. This must not obscure the importance of other financial institutions, such as mutual loans and savings banks and credit associations which have developed rapidly along with the development of small businesses, in the finance of which they have specialised. There are likely to be shifts in the relative importance and roles of the different financial institutions, because the background against which they operate has been changing rapidly in recent years; one may cite, for example, the flotation of government bonds and the internationalisation of the economy.

In this context, following the report of the Committee on Financial System Research on 'the Ideal System of Finance of Small Businesses' in October 1967, the government enacted in June 1968, two 'Financial Laws'. One amended the Mutual Loans and Savings Banks Law and the Credit Associations Law, etc.; the object was to reorganise and improve the system of finance of small businesses. The other was a law concerning amalgamations and conversions of financial institutions. By these new laws it is hoped to improve the scope and efficiency of finance for small businesses, by encouraging the financial institutions concerned to meet contemporary needs through amalgamations or by conversion from one type of institution into another. The Committee on Financial System Research reported on 'the Desirable Conditions of Ordinary Private Financial Institutions' in July 1970, and investigated problems of financial efficiency in general and the business conditions of various kinds of financial institutions.

Recently, therefore, there have been serious efforts to re-organise the financial system; this concern has been focused in the debates of the Committee on Financial System Research. The success of these efforts will be watched closely in the light of future changes in both internal and external economic conditions.

FIG. II.1 *Organisation map of existing financial institutions (end of December 1970)*

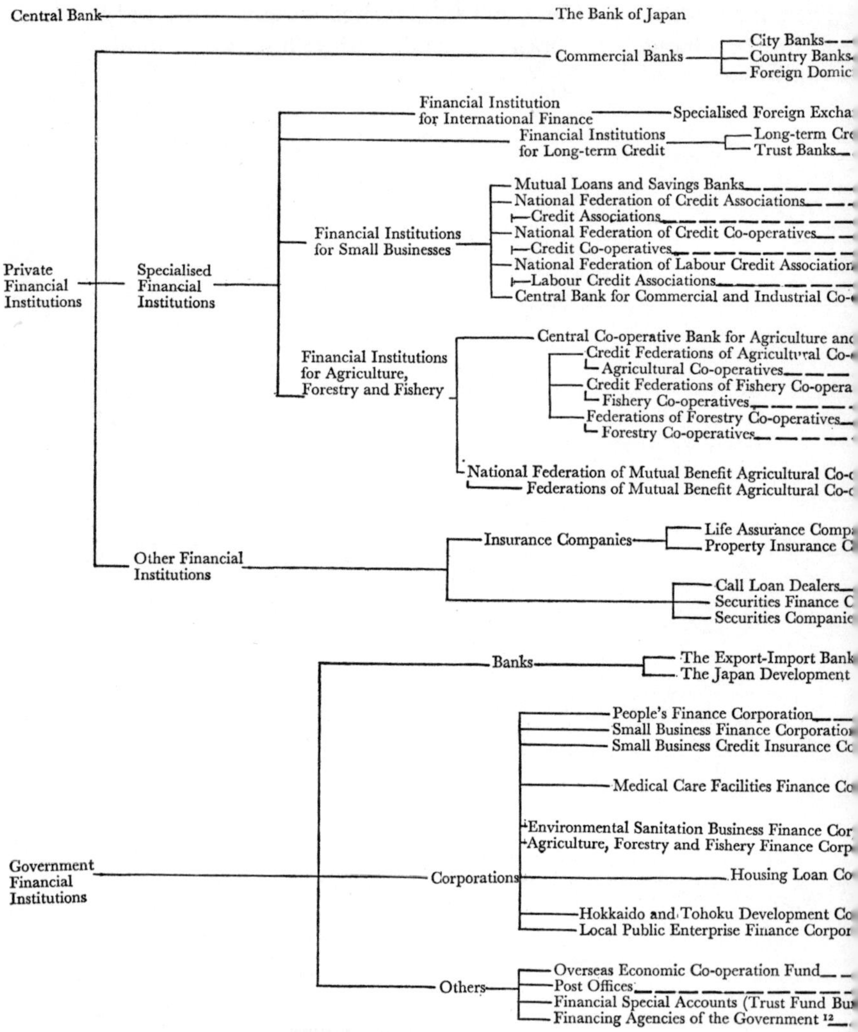

1 Does not include overseas offices.
2 Total of banking accounts (deposits) and trust accounts (loan trusts, money in trust and pension trusts) of seven specialised trust banks.
3 Includes instalments.
4 Includes special lending to depositors.
5 Assets employed.
6 Reserves for outstanding insurance contracts.
7 Borrowing from the call loan market.
8 Call loans.
9 The number of reporting companies was 254.
10 Foreign Currency Debentures.
11 Total of Trust Fund Bureau, Post Office insurance, postal annuity, Industrial Development Special Account, *City Development Fund Special Account* and *Finance of Settlers Special Account*. For particulars, see Chap. 12.
12 See Chap. 12.

Number of Institutions	*Number of Offices*[1]	*Capital*	*Deposits and Debentures Issued*	*Lending*	*Securities*
14	2,377	3,890	236,295	209,432	38,757
61	4,335	1,566	145,001	117,649	20,050
18	38		3,378	5,918	
1	32	200	6,687	8,016	706
3	34	740	54,493	47,293	7,133
7	262	741	16,867[2] **	11,639 **	4,629 **
72	2,869	604	63,665[4]	52,422[4]	5,440
1	20	50	5,514	5,027	1,389
502	3,871	1,222	77,395	66,142	6,375
1	10 **	22	913	1,060	378
532	2,098	540	19,778	17,245	603
1	1	2	563	119	369
46	363	90	3,575	3,009	209
1	72	327	11,737	12,040	224
1	33	100	22,975	14,045	5,382
46	405	372	34,792	12,182	7,753
6,077	15,392 **	1,969	61,867	31,123	2,234
34	132	35	1,891	1,659	33
1,696	n.a.	268	2,274	2,364	115
46	46	9		18	
3,199	n.a.	74		786	
1	1	9 *	1,123[5]	418	635
46	46	71 *	10,028[5]	4,538	2,534
20	17,552 **	2 *	46,732[6] **	37,051	12,595
21	2,555 **	621 *	7,417[6] **	3,367	4,376
6	10	4	18,169[7]	19,173[8]	25
3	9	34		2,665	
270	1,851	948 *		4,280 **	2,009 **
1	2	4,453		15,220	46
1	10	2,340	287[10]	17,051	25
1	113	200		7,089	
1	45	252	2,058	8,952	26
1	1	687		635	
1	2	115		1,433	3
1	1	10		1,229	
1	16	1,703		9,554	97
1	14	972	34	10,697	25
1	3	75	1,481	1,846	40
1	1	37	4,194	4,162	63
1	1	793		1,344	39
20,700			72,844		
				119,646[11]	41,208***
11		2,803	223	9,335	—

* End-March 1970
** End-September 1970
*** End-March 1971
n.a. not available

CHAPTER 12

THE BANK OF JAPAN

I. FUNCTIONS OF THE BANK OF JAPAN

The Bank of Japan is the central bank: it acts as the bank of issue, as the bankers' bank and as the government's bank; through its operations in the above three capacities it manages the monetary system.

The purpose of the Bank's operations is to stabilise the value of money and thereby to contribute to the stable development of the Japanese economy. Stability of the value of money is an intrinsic objective of the central bank as the issuer of currency. It is at the same time extremely important for stable economic growth. With this aim in mind the Bank exercises the functions listed above, regulates money and credit and supports and supervises the financial system.

2. THE BANK OF JAPAN AS THE BANK OF ISSUE

The Bank of Japan is the sole issuing bank in Japan: its notes are legal tender to unlimited amounts. Notes are issued through purchase of gold and foreign currency by the Bank, through credit granted to the government or to the private sector, and by other routes. The present system of note-issue is termed 'the flexible maximum limit system', the salient features of which are as follows:

(1) The Bank of Japan Law (Article 29) simply stipulates that 'The Bank of Japan issues bank-notes' and there is no clause imposing upon it the duty of convertibility of notes.

(2) The maximum limit for note-issue is fixed by the Minister of Finance after consultation with the Cabinet. In November 1970 the maximum was set at 4900 billion yen.

(3) The Bank can issue notes in excess of the limit, if necessary, but if the excess remains in circulation for more than fifteen days the Bank must seek the approval of the Minister of Finance. Moreover, the Bank must pay an excess issue tax from the sixteenth day, which at present is 3 per cent per annum.

(4) The Bank of Japan must hold reserves to the same amount as the notes issued. Commercial and other bills, loans, government and other bonds and debentures, foreign exchanges, gold and silver bullion and others may be included in these reserves. The Minister of Finance sets a maximum limit on each item in the reserve, except for gold and silver bullion and foreign exchange, which can be held in unlimited amounts.

Notes may be issued in nine different denominations, from 10,000 yen down to 1 yen, although notes for 50 yen or less are at present not issued. There are five kinds of subsidiary coins,[1] of 100 yen, 50 yen, 10 yen, 5 yen and 1 yen; the amount outstanding is only 6 per cent of the total cash currency in circulation, including bank-notes.

3. THE BANK OF JAPAN AS THE BANKERS' BANK

The Bank of Japan is the bankers' bank and deals exclusively with private financial institutions, if we exclude its transactions with the government, of which explanations will be given later. Deposit and lending transactions with business firms and individuals are the sphere of the commercial banks and other financial institutions. At present the Bank deals with the following financial institutions: commercial banks, long-term credit banks, trust banks, mutual loans and savings banks, credit associations, National Federation of Credit Associations, Central Bank for Commercial and Industrial Co-operatives, Central Co-operative Bank for Agriculture and Forestry, securities finance companies, securities companies, call loan dealers and so on. Thus, the Bank does business with practically all the principal financial institutions. The main business it conducts with them as the bankers' bank is as follows:

[1] Olympics commemorative silver coins of 1000 yen and 100 yen were issued in 1964, and in 1970, for the Japan World Exposition commemorative coins of 100 yen were issued.

(1) *Current Deposits*

The Bank holds current accounts for its financial customers; they are utilised for clearing, in making remittances between districts, and in settling other transactions between financial institutions, such as dealings in call loans. They are used also to settle the Bank's transactions with financial institutions, such as lending and the purchase and sale of securities. Reserve deposits under the reserve deposit requirement system, which will be explained later, are paid into these accounts. As an adjunct to its current deposit business, the Bank handles clearing business for clearing houses in places where it has offices. The Bank also undertakes remittance business between the offices of financial institutions which are its customers or between such financial institutions.

(2) *Lending*

The Bank of Japan discounts bills held by commercial banks and others and also makes advances on such bills.

Bill-discounting is a form of credit-giving, by which the Bank rediscounts eligible bills discounted by financial institutions which are its customers. At present, commercial bills, export advance bills and export usance bills are rediscountable at the Bank. Commercial bills are bills of exchange or promissory notes drawn for the finance of purchases of goods for resale, of which the payers are the buyers. Rediscount of such bills had traditionally been considered to be the standard form of lending by the Bank of Japan. Export advance bills are bills drawn to raise funds necessary for the manufacture, purchase, processing, etc., of export goods, on which irrevocable letters of credit have already been opened. Finally, export usance bills are bills in yen drawn by Japanese exporters to obtain advance payments for exported goods, the ultimate settlement of which appears secure, and which are made through non-residents' free yen accounts. Export advance bills and export usance bills are rediscounted at more favourable rates than commercial bills. Not all commercial, export advance and export usance bills are eligible for rediscount at the Bank. For eligibility they should have maturities of less than three months (five months on usance bills) from the day of acceptance or of rediscount, and in principle they must carry, besides the endorsement of the discounter, those of one or more solvent persons.

Advances on bills are a form of credit-giving, by which the borrowers issue their promissory notes to the Bank on the security of eligible bills, bonds and debentures and the Bank discounts the notes. At present, the Bank recognises the following bills, bonds and debentures as eligible security for advances on bills: long-term government bonds, government short-term bills, government-guaranteed debentures, bank debentures, designated local bonds, industrial debentures, commercial bills and export advance bills eligible for rediscount at the Bank, ineligible export advance bills, import trade bills and other bills (ordinary bills), which the Bank recognises as adequate security.

There are five[1] different rates of interest for discounts and loan by the Bank (i.e. the official rates); which rate is actually applied depends upon the quality of the discounted bills or of the security. The Bank rate, when this is quoted, is the rate of discount for commercial bills.

Official Rates of the Bank of Japan
(May 1971)

Discount rate on commercial bills and interest rate on loans secured by government bonds and specially designated securities	5·50%
Discount rate on export usance bills	5·00%
Discount rate on export advance bills	5·25%
Interest rate on loans secured by export advance bills	5·50%
Interest rate on loans secured by bills and securities other than the above	5·75%

In addition to these discounts and loans the Bank has instituted the system of Loans Against Foreign Exchange Assets with the approval of the Minister of Finance. This is a special kind of loan on bills to authorised foreign exchange banks on the security of foreign assets held by them. The interest rate on these loans is determined separately from other official

[1] Since October 1972 there have been only two Bank rates, the first four listed being merged into a single rate.

rates (5·00 per cent from May 1970). To supplement this system the Bank initiated, from December 1965, the purchase of foreign currency bills drawn by authorised foreign exchange banks on the security of foreign currency usance bills originating from export trade.

(3) *Purchase and Sale of Bills, Bonds and Debentures*

The Bank of Japan buys from or sells to customers financial institutions various bills, bonds and debentures. At present the principal items bought and sold are long-term government bonds, government-guaranteed debentures and government short-term bills. Transactions in long-term government bonds and government-guaranteed debentures (those within one year from their issue are not bought) are at market prices with commercial banks, long-term credit banks, trust banks, mutual loans and savings banks, National Federation of Credit Associations, Central Co-operative Bank for Agriculture and Forestry and securities companies having current deposit accounts with the Bank. Transactions in government short-term bills have usually been with call loan dealers since 1966.

(4) *Other Transactions*

The buying and selling of gold and silver bullion is naturally one of the Bank's functions. The Bank can also buy and sell foreign exchange if it deems that to be necessary. In post-war years, however, the Bank has undertaken such transactions only with the government; when it deals with private organisations it does so on the government's account (the Precious Metals Special Account or Foreign Exchange Fund Special Account).

The Bank is also the clearing house for domestic exchange transactions. The system operates as follows: private financial institutions make daily clearings (in the same way as for the clearing of cheques and bills) at various places in order to settle mutual debts and claims arising from remittances, collection of bills and so on; the unsettled balances are converted into claims and debts of private financial institutions with the Bank, and then they are settled through an Exchange Settlement Account at the Bank.

4. THE BANK OF JAPAN AS THE GOVERNMENT'S BANK

The Bank of Japan receives deposits from and lends to the government. It is also entrusted under various laws with certain governmental functions, such as the receipts and disbursements of Treasury funds, management of the national debt and of the foreign exchanges.

(1) *Government Deposits*

As will be explained later (see (3) A, this chapter) the Bank manages the receipts and payments of the Treasury Fund. Apart from transfers between various Treasury accounts, these are all made by payments to or from the government balance at the Bank. Taxes and other government revenues are all deposited with the Bank, while government disbursements are effected by drawing government cheques on it.

(2) *Advances to the Government*

The Bank of Japan Law places no restriction on the Bank's grant of accommodation to the government; the law expressly states that the Bank may make advances to the government without taking any collateral and subscribe to or take up government loan issues. This reflects the origin of the law as a piece of war-emergency legislation. The Finance Law of 1947, however, forbids in principle the issue of long-term government bonds through absorption by the Bank and also long-term lending by the Bank to the government (Article 5, the Finance Law). In practice, too, the Bank at present neither purchases newly issued long-term government bonds nor lends to the government on long-term. In recent years, even short-term lending to the government is rare, except on a temporary basis at the end of a fiscal year. Almost all government short-term bills, however, are issued through purchase by the Bank, although the principle is to issue them by public subscription: private financial institutions take up few of them, partly because the interest rate is low and partly because they are short of liquidity.

(3) *Business delegated to the Bank*

The Bank manages the following business for the government under various laws.

A. Treasury Funds

The Bank of Japan Law stipulates that the Bank shall undertake the management of Treasury Funds. This extends beyond routine receipts and payments; it includes a variety of accounting responsibilities, and includes the receipt, delivery and custody of securities owned by or deposited with the government. Thus, the Bank's Treasury business is extremely large. Some of it is undertaken by banks all over the country, which are appointed by the Bank as Treasury agents or national revenue agents (which handle business relating to Treasury revenue only), because the Bank's head office and branches cannot handle all the business themselves.

B. Management of the National Debt

The Bank acts as manager of the national debt. This involves the flotation and servicing of bonds and bills, issue and registration of bond certificates, the payment of its principal and interest and associated matters. In this field also further agents are appointed: the Treasury agents referred to previously handle many matters relating to the national debt, and national debt agents are appointed throughout the country for the limited purpose of making payments of the principal of and interest on the debt.

C. Foreign Exchange Business

Japan's foreign currency reserves are at present concentrated in the hand of the Foreign Exchange Funds Special Account. The management of the account which involves receipts and payments of yen exchange and foreign exchange, is entrusted to the Bank by the Minister of Finance. In this capacity as the Minister's agent the Bank operates in foreign currencies with authorised foreign exchange banks. Acting under the Foreign Exchange and Foreign Trade Control Law and the Law concerning Foreign Investment, it also undertakes certain government transactions in foreign exchange, foreign trade and foreign capital.

5. MONETARY REGULATION

The three functions of the central bank, i.e. those of note-issuer, of the bankers' bank and the government's bank, are the basis of the Bank's regulation of the monetary system. It employs the following policy instruments:

(1) *Lending Policy*

Lending policy (alterations in Bank rate) occupies a central position among the Bank's policy weapons. Changes in the terms of lending, such as in eligibility and in the type of security required and alterations of credit ceilings for city banks are important features of this policy.

A. Bank-Rate Policy

Bank rate has been altered fairly flexibly in response to changes in business conditions. Short-term lending rates of commercial banks have progressively become geared to the Bank rate since 1957. This is a result of a mutual agreement among the banks. Particularly since 1959, when the 'standard' rate was instituted, changes in it have been strictly linked to those of Bank rate, which is the rate of discount on commercial bills eligible for rediscount at the Bank, and also the rate for advances on such bills and on other bills of similar credit standing.[1]

Changes in Bank rate have had a considerable influence because they have a marked effect upon the cost and availability of funds for banks and business firms; one reason for this is that business firms are highly dependent upon banks, which, in turn, rely upon the Bank of Japan for funds. Moreover, Bank rate policy is the classical weapon of a central bank, so that a change of the rate is regarded as a signal of economic change. It is therefore closely watched not only by financial and securities circles, but also by industrialists, big and small alike.

[1] See, for details, Part Three, Chapter 13, 'Commercial Banks'.

B. Credit Ceiling Application System

The Bank of Japan sets limits to its lending to each city bank, in view of their dependence upon such borrowings. Thus, the ease of borrowing from the Bank by financial institutions is restricted. Lending in excess of limits is in principle refused, but, if banks wish to borrow in excess of the limits in exceptional circumstances, a penal rate is charged; this exceeds Bank rate by 4·00 per cent.

This system was introduced in November 1962, when the so-called New Measures for Monetary Regulation were introduced. In order to correct the abnormal situation in which financial institutions in general were excessively dependent on the Bank, these included a flexible policy of purchases and sales of securities; credit ceilings were applied in order to end the excessive reliance of certain financial institutions on borrowing from the Bank. Before the adoption of this system the Higher Interest Rates Application System had been in operation, by which penal rates in excess of Bank rate were applied to lending to those financial institutions which borrowed beyond their respective limits. That system was an important adjunct of Bank-rate policy.

(2) *Open-Market Operations*

Properly speaking, the central bank's purchases and sales of securities in the open-market aim to regulate credit directly, by changing the cash reserves of private financial institutions, and indirectly by causing variations in interest rates.

In Japan, however, the open market was undeveloped, so that, up to 1962, the Bank bought and sold bonds, debentures and bills by direct negotiation with individual financial institutions. Moreover, this was done only a few times each year. After the war the Bank of Japan undertook the following operations: it bought government bonds and Reconversion Finance Bank Bonds during the Dodge Line phase; it sold bills to absorb seasonal surpluses of the Central Co-operative Bank for Agriculture and Forestry and of country banks; and it purchased government-guaranteed debentures from commercial banks to alleviate monetary stringency due to seasonal movements in the Treasury Fund. These, however, were a far cry from true open-market operations.

In November 1962 the Bank decided to adopt a flexible policy in purchases and sales of bonds and debentures in addition to the above-mentioned system of credit ceilings. The purpose was to add a new weapon to the Bank's armoury and to normalise the monetary system. Cash currency necessary for economic growth had been supplied through Bank lending, but it now came to be provided through its buying operations. These transactions in bonds and debentures differed from open-market operations in Europe and America in that they involved direct negotiations with financial institutions and were done at fixed rates of interest and with repurchase agreements. Since then, there have been frequent purchases and sales of securities.

A further development, in January 1966, was the issue of long-term government bonds and the reopening of the markets in public bonds and debentures. In February that year the Bank decided to make purchases and sales of bonds and debentures at market prices without repurchase agreements. This was a step towards real market operations. Dealings in long-term government bonds and government-guaranteed debentures are at present done in this way. Furthermore, from January 1966, transactions in government short-term bills have been undertaken with call loan dealers; this provides an additional weapon of short-term monetary control.

(3) *Reserve Deposit Requirement System*

The Reserve Deposit Requirement System is an instrument of monetary policy, by which private financial institutions are compelled to redeposit with the central bank a certain proportion of their deposits; these cash reserves may be varied, and thereby the credit-creating capacity of the financial institutions is affected. As changes in the reserve ratio are uniform and compulsory, the effect may be powerful and lasting.

In Japan the system was introduced under a law of 1957. The reserve ratio was first fixed in September 1959, and subsequently it has been altered several times. At present the following financial institutions are subject to these reserve requirements: commercial banks (including foreign-domiciled banks and the specialised foreign exchange bank), trust banks, long-term credit banks, mutual loans and savings banks and credit associations respectively with more than 20 billion yen of deposits, Central Co-operative Bank for Agriculture and Forestry. These financial institutions must lodge a certain proportion of their deposits – the proportion is different for time deposits and for other deposits – in cash with the Bank. The legal maximum reserve ratio is 10 per cent, but, as private financial institutions in Japan are generally short of cash, and as city banks in particular are permanently dependent upon borrowings from the Bank, reserve ratios are much lower than those of other countries, as will be seen from the following table.

Reserve Ratios in Force (16 September 1969)

	Time Deposits %	*Other Deposits* %
1. Commercial Banks, Long-term Credit Banks and Trust Banks		
(1) Banks with more than 100 billion yen of deposits	0·5	1·5
(2) Banks with deposits of more than 20 billion, but less than 100 billion yen	0·25	0·75
(3) Banks with deposits of less than 20 billion yen	0·25	0·75
2. Mutual Loans and Savings Banks and Credit Associations		
(1) Those with deposits of more than 100 billion yen	0·25	0·75
(2) Those with deposits of more than 20 billion, but less than 100 billion yen	0·25	0·75
3. Central Co-operative Bank for Agriculture and Forestry	0·25	0·75

(4) *Window Guidance*

In its daily contacts with financial institutions, the Bank of Japan gives guidance on various matters, including their lending activity. Particularly in times of monetary stringency, the Bank on occasion indicates the amount of lending it deems proper under prevailing circumstances; this supervision is known as 'window guidance', the content of which differs from time to time. Before 1964, for instance, the Bank fixed monthly for each city bank a guideline for lending. From 1964 a specific rate of increase in lending was determined for each quarter and was applied uniformly to all city banks, etc. More recently, from the third quarter of 1967 to the third quarter of 1968, increases were regulated more by reference to the individual bank's financial position. This system has been suspended since September 1968.

Window guidance is, in its nature, a supplementary tool of orthodox instruments of monetary policy – that is, Bank rate, open-market operations and reserve deposit requirements. It is used more as a weapon of monetary restraint than otherwise; it is employed to regulate the total amount of commercial bank credit and is not a tool for the qualitative control of lending. It must be stressed that it is a form of moral suasion, so that it presupposes co-operation on the part of financial institutions.

6. ORGANISATION

The Bank of Japan is legally a special corporation under the Bank of Japan Law enacted in 1942, in the middle of the war. Since the war several attempts have been made to revise it, but only one important amendment has been made; this involved the setting up of the Policy Board by the amendment of 1949.

(1) *Capital*

The capital of the Bank of Japan is 100 million yen, of which 55 million was subscribed by the government and 45 million by the public. The subscribers are entitled to receive dividends at a maximum rate of 5 per cent per annum, but otherwise they have no rights; there is no general meeting of subscribers, nor are they granted any rights to participate in the management of the Bank; the balance of profits, after deducting dividends to subscribers and additions to reserves must be paid to the Treasury.

(2) *Policy Board of the Bank of Japan*

The supreme decision-making body of the Bank is the Policy Board. The duty of the Board is to direct the administration of the Bank's business to regulate money and credit and to carry out other financial policies in accordance with the needs of the national economy. More specifically, the Board is responsible for all the principal policy instruments, including lending policy, open-market operations and reserve deposit requirements, and it also exercises control over the maximum interest rates of private financial institutions. Changes in reserve ratios under the reserve deposit requirement system, however, are subject to the approval of the Minister of Finance; changes in ceilings on the interest rates of private financial institutions may be made only after consultation with the Interest Adjustment Council, to which the Minister of Finance refers proposals for such changes.

The Policy Board has seven members: the Governor of the Bank, two representatives of the government (one from the Ministry of Finance and the Economic Planning Agency respectively), four appointed members (having considerable experience and knowledge of city banking, of country banking, of commerce and industry, and of agriculture respectively). The government representatives do not have voting rights. Appointed members are nominated by the Cabinet with the consent of both houses of the Diet. Their tenure of office is four years, and is renewable. The Chairman of the Board is elected by and from the five voting members, but traditionally the governor of the Bank is elected to the post.

(3) *The Management*

The officers of the Bank are the governor, vice-governor, three or more directors, two or more auditors and a few advisers. The governor represents the Bank and executes the general business in accordance with the policies formulated by the Policy Board. The vice-governor and the directors assist the governor in the execution of the business, while the auditors audit its management. The governor and the vice-governor are appointed by the Cabinet, while the directors are nominated by the Minister of Finance from among the candidates recommended by the governor. Auditors are appointed by the Minister of Finance. The terms of office are five years for the governor and vice-governor, four years for the directors, three years for the auditors and two years for the advisers, and are renewable. The Head Office of the Bank is in Tokyo, while branches (31 at present) and sub-branches (13) are established at important cities all over the country. In addition, the Bank maintains representatives in various overseas countries.

(4) *Relationship with the Government*

Under the current laws the Bank is subject to fairly extensive supervision by the government. The Minister of Finance is empowered to issue general directives and may give supervisory orders to the Bank. The Minister also appoints the Comptroller of the Bank of Japan, who superintends its business. The Minister can also dismiss the officers of the Bank. In addition to this general supervision, the government has power to permit, approve and decide various individual matters of the Bank's business, so that almost all aspects of its activities, including policies, organisation, note-issue and accounting, are under the government's control. In practice, however, the government and the Bank are constantly in close touch and mutual co-operation is always maintained, so that the supervisory powers of the government have never been exercised.

Incidentally, when in 1958–60 the Committee on Financial System Research (an advisory body of the Minister of Finance) discussed the revision of the Bank of Japan Law, the central issue was the extent to which the Bank should be independent of the government, but a unanimous conclusion was not achieved. Thus, the Committee's Report offered two alternative proposals: when the Minister of Finance considers that the policy of the Bank is at variance with the policy of the government, and when an agreement cannot be reached to adjust policies after consultation with the governor, the Minister can (*a*) issue directives to the Bank; or (*b*) he can demand that the decision of the Policy Board be postponed for a certain period (after which the Policy Board may reconfirm the original decision). It was up to the government to adopt one of these proposals, but so far it has adopted neither.

TABLE 12.1

Principal Accounts of the Bank of Japan

(hundred million yen)

End of the Year	*1958*	*1963*	*1968*	*1969*	*1970*
ASSETS					
Gold Bullion	4	255	309	309	309
	(—)	(1·1)	(0·6)	(0·6)	(0·5)
Bills Discounted	503	1,438	3,399	3,645	4,086
	(4·6)	(6·0)	(7·3)	(6·6)	(6·4)
Advances	3,290	10,118	12,234	15,773	19,448
	(30·2)	(42·2)	(26·2)	(28·4)	(30·2)
Government Securities	5,360	3,460	14,341	18,215	23,813
	(49·1)	(14·5)	(30·7)	(32·9)	(37·0)
Other Securities	—	5,062	9,375	7,904	4,432
	(—)	(21·1)	(20·1)	(14·3)	(6·9)
External Assets	1,209	3,314	6,108	8,563	11,232
	(11·1)	(13·8)	(13·1)	(15·4)	(17·5)
Other Assets	546	316	924	1,031	971
	(5·0)	(1·3)	(2·0)	(1·8)	(1·5)
Total	10,912	23,963	46,690	55,440	64,291
LIABILITIES					
Bank-notes in Circulation	8,910	20,574	40,419	48,114	55,560
	(81·7)	(85·9)	(86·6)	(86·8)	(86·4)
Deposits of Financial Institutions	26	1,087	1,598	2,172	2,983
	(0·2)	(4·5)	(3·4)	(3·9)	(4·6)
Government Deposits	626	331	741	617	428
	(5·7)	(1·4)	(1·6)	(1·1)	(0·7)
Reserves	643	1,466	3,006	3,440	4,099
	(5·9)	(6·1)	(6·4)	(6·2)	(6·4)
Other Liabilities	707	505	926	1,096	1,221
	(6·5)	(2·1)	(2·0)	(2·0)	(1·9)

NOTE: Figures in parentheses are percentages of the total.

SOURCE: The Bank of Japan, *Economic Statistics of Japan.*

CHAPTER 13

COMMERCIAL BANKS

I. GENERAL SURVEY

Commercial banks, or deposit banks, are short-term financial institutions, deposits being their principal source of funds. One of their principal functions is to receive on deposit the savings of individuals and of business firms and to employ them in lending and investment. This intermediary function of connecting the supply of and the demand for money is shared by other financial institutions, but commercial banks differ from them in the following ways.

First, they handle current accounts, which are payable on demand, and on which depositors can draw cheques to be used as means of payment in the same way as cash. Moreover, commercial banks can exchange and settle cheques, bills and other means of payment and remittances among different localities either through the network of branches of the same bank or through joint arrangements. Furthermore, they can create deposits through their lending and investments, such deposits being a multiple of their cash reserves, because they can economise upon reserves by the mechanism of inter-bank transfers and of bill-clearings (see Part Two, Chapter 7). In Japan, virtually all types of financial institutions, in addition to commercial banks, operate current-account facilities, although the amounts outstanding are much smaller. Deposit-creation by commercial banks is therefore the main target of the central bank's monetary policy.

In Japan it is mainly the so-called ordinary banks which provide commercial banking. They are established under the Banking Law of 1927. At that time there were more than one thousand ordinary banks; but liquidations and amalgamations among smaller banks followed the financial crisis and the enforcement of the Banking Law, and there were also mergers under the 'one prefecture one bank' principle during wartime, so that their numbers had fallen to 61 (8 city banks and 53 country banks) by the end of 1945. After the war, some special banks (the Nippon Kangyo Bank, the Hokkaido Takushoku Bank and the Yokohama Specie Bank) and a savings bank (Savings Bank of Japan) were converted into ordinary banks. Moreover, some banks, which had been amalgamated with others during the war, broke away. Since 1949 a few new country banks have been established. More recently a mutual loans and savings bank has converted itself into an ordinary bank. On the other hand, there have been a few, though not many, amalgamations between city banks and country banks, and amongst country banks. As the result of these changes the number of commercial banks at the end of December 1970 was 76, consisting of 14 city banks,[1] 61 country banks and 1 specialised exchange bank. In addition, some foreign banks have opened branches in Japan since the war. At present, 18 of them are accorded the same treatment as commercial banks.

Commercial banks have contributed significantly to the development of the Japanese economy from the Meiji era, and it is largely due to them that, despite her meagre accumulation of capital, Japan has been able to industrialise rapidly. The deposits of commercial banks have represented nearly one-half of those of all financial institutions. These funds have been supplied to business firms for working capital and for their new investment, which has been the driving force of economic development. Even in recent years about one-third of the funds raised by business have been supplied by commercial banks.

[1] The number includes, beside the 12 already in existence, the Taiyo Bank (formerly Mutual Loans and Savings Bank of Japan) and the Saitama Bank. The former was converted into a (city) bank under a law in December 1968, while the latter seceded from the Local Bankers' Association in March 1969 and became a city bank in the following month. 'City banks' in common usage often includes the specialised foreign exchange bank, in which case the number of city banks would be 15.

2. CHARACTERISTICS

The characteristics of commercial banks in Japan are as follows:

(1) *Mixed Banking*

First, commercial banks in Japan have traditionally been engaged in long-term finance in addition to commercial banking proper (mixed banking). Since the pre-war years, however, the ideal has always been that they should be engaged chiefly in short-term finance on the model of British banks. Attempts have thus been made to separate the long- and short-term lending by establishing long-term credit banks (special banks before the war). In spite of these efforts about 10 per cent of the total lending of commercial banks is even now for terms of one year or more. Moreover, some apparently short-term lending is repeatedly renewed and is in practice employed for long-term purposes. If we include this form of long-term lending, its proportion will be considerably higher than 10 per cent. Furthermore, commercial banks hold about one-quarter of outstanding bank debentures, the issue of which is the chief source of funds for long-term credit banks, while commercial banks' portfolios include about 50 per cent of outstanding industrial debentures. Thus, as large-scale subscribers, they exert great influence on the issue market. Moreover, they lend money for subscription to newly issued shares of corporate business, while they themselves take up about 10 per cent of such shares.

Thus, commercial banks in Japan directly or indirectly are closely involved in the field of long-term finance and are a strong influence in this market. As has been pointed out, this is chiefly due to the fact that the capital market in Japan is not fully developed, so that personal savings are deposited largely with commercial banks. Thus, more than half of their total deposits consists of time deposits with maturities of more than three months (more than 80 per cent of time deposits are for one year).

(2) *Over-loans*

City banks are in a state of more or less permanent over-loan (see Part Two, Chapter 10). Since the war, city banks have stretched their credit-creating capacities to the extreme in order to meet the demands of their business customers. The resultant shortage of cash reserves has been made good by large and continuous borrowing from the Bank of Japan and/or by borrowing from the call loan market. Consequently, their cash and liquidity ratios have become much lower than those of banks abroad. Thus, they have had to ensure their liquidity by holding bonds and debentures which may be bought or sold by the Bank of Japan, and they also hold bills and debentures eligible for rediscount or as collateral security for borrowing from the Bank. Country banks, however, are differently situated. Although they are commercial banks, they have more liquidity, borrow little from the Bank and are substantial lenders in the call loan market.

(3) *Branch Banking*

The third characteristic is that Japanese banking has always included branch banking. This contrasts with American banking, in which unit banks predominate. City banks have nationwide networks of branches, while country banks have branches in the prefectures in which they are situated. This is a legacy of the war-time principle of one bank in one prefecture. Recently, however, country banks have begun to open offices in big cities. Thus, the average number of offices per bank is fairly large: about 170 for a city bank and about 70 for a country bank. Moreover, commercial banks agree among themselves to act as mutual correspondents, and they all have accounts with the Bank. Thus, they are integrated into a unified commercial banking system with the Bank of Japan at its pivot. As the offices of commercial banks are found everywhere, and as they are knit together in a unified system, they are well placed to provide an adequate public service, to contribute to the spread of the banking habit and to increase the efficiency of the utilisation of funds.

(4) *Close Ties with Business Firms*

Fourth, commercial banks in Japan, particularly city banks, have had very close relationships with their business customers. A big firm rarely banks with one bank exclusively, but usually has accounts with a number of banks, although in many cases one is the chief banker and has a particularly close connection with the firm. In post-war years, moreover, with the dissolution of Zaibatsu holding companies, banks have become the nuclei of various groups of big firms. Further, the Anti-Trust Law forbids banks to hold more than 10 per cent of the total stock issued by a joint-stock company, but there is no legal restriction on bank lending; it is not uncommon, therefore, for more than 30 per cent of a big firm's borrowing to come from its principal banker.

A bank too closely linked with a particular business firm may easily be involved in the latter's competition with other groups, so that banks are liable to extend credit too freely; it has to be recognised that this has been a factor making for overheating of the economy.

3. PRINCIPAL BUSINESS

The Banking Law restricts the business of banks to receiving deposits, loans and advances, bill-discounting, exchange transactions and other ancillary business of banking (safe custody, underwriting, purchase, sale and lending of securities, receipt and payment of public money, receipt of subscriptions for new shares, payment of dividends, money-changing, collection of debts, guarantee of debts, acceptance of bills, letters of credit and so on). Banks are prohibited from engaging in other business. They are, however, permitted under another law of 1943 to engage in savings-bank business and trust business. At present, however, banks do little savings-bank business, except for instalment savings; and only one commercial bank now engages in trust business, because in response to the government's policy of separating trust and banking business, most commercial banks have gradually discontinued such business or have established separate specialised affiliates.

We turn now to the principal business of commercial banks.

(1) *Deposits*

Deposits are the most important source of commercial banks' funds. Beside cash, cheques, bills and other paper can be paid into deposit accounts, provided they can be immediately encashed through bill-clearings.

Interest is given on all types of deposits except current accounts; in accord with a notification under the Temporary Money Rates Adjustment Law; ceilings have been imposed upon interest rates, and these ceilings correspond with the rates paid by the banks. The government, however, accords favourable treatment to deposits in order to encourage savings, for example by tax exemption on small savings (interest income from deposits less than one million yen is not subject to tax).[1]

A. Current Deposits

Current deposits are normally subject to withdrawal on demand only by cheque. There is, however, an exception to the rule: if a bill drawn by a depositor is made payable at the bank office at which he holds his current account, the balance in it can be used to settle the bill without a cheque, provided that it is passed through the clearing house, or that the person presenting it is also a depositor of the bank.

As the risk and trouble of holding, receiving and delivering of cash can be avoided by the use of cheques, business firms settle their accounts almost wholly in this way, so that most have current accounts. In recent years individuals have also come to open current accounts and to make payments by cheques, although the practice is not yet universal. Banks take care, however, to choose only credit-worthy firms and individuals as current account customers. For this there are several reasons: management of current deposit accounts requires considerable trouble; as it is unpredictable when and for what amounts cheques may be drawn, banks must hold considerable cash reserves against deposits; and there is a danger that customers may overdraw. It should be noted that no interest has been allowed on current accounts since 1944.

[1] Such favourable treatment in regard to tax is also applied to income from interest, dividends on deposits of financial institutions other than banks and debentures, and from dividends on trusts (money in trust, loan trusts and securities investment trusts).

B. Ordinary Deposits

Ordinary deposits are payable on demand like current deposits, but cheques cannot be drawn on them. Withdrawal can be made only upon presentation of a passbook and of a seal registered with the bank. Interest is allowed on such deposits (at present below 2·25 per cent per annum). Anybody can open an ordinary deposit account and as small a sum as one yen can be paid into the account, so that ordinary deposits are a popular outlet for the small savings and temporarily idle money of individuals. At the end of September 1968 there were 54 million ordinary deposit accounts with commercial banks, of which close to 51 million were held by individuals. Business firms which have no current accounts also utilise these facilities, many big firms keeping such accounts for their cash on hand because they carry interest. In fact, almost one-half of the outstanding amount of ordinary deposits is held by corporate business.

C. Deposits at Notice

Deposits at notice are not withdrawable for seven days after depositing. Thereafter, they can be withdrawn on two days' notice. As they are a relatively stable type of deposit, a higher rate than on ordinary deposits attaches to them (at present, below 2·5 per cent). By mutual agreement among banks, sums of less than 50,000 yen cannot be deposited. Most of the outstanding amount consists of business firms' temporarily redundant money, so that they resemble interest-bearing current deposits rather than ordinary deposits.

D. Time Deposits

Time deposits have fixed maturities, such as three months, until the expiry of which they are not withdrawable. They are, therefore, the most stable source of funds for banks and carry the highest rate of interest. The bulk of savings deposits in Japan is held in this form. Not only individuals but also corporate businesses hold time deposits; the latter hold almost one-half of the outstanding amount of time deposits at commercial banks. Sums of 100 yen or more can be paid into the account. A certificate or a passbook is issued for each account.

There are several kinds of time deposit: the most popular is the ordinary time deposits, for which there are three kinds of maturities, of three months (at an interest rate of below 4 per cent), six months (below 5 per cent) and one year (below 5·75 per cent).

Other varieties include anonymous time deposits (special time deposits); neither the name nor the address of the depositor is disclosed to the bank, the only identification being his seal registered with it; and instalment time deposits, in which money is paid in regularly for a definite period or until it reaches a predetermined sum.

E. Instalment Savings

In return for a promise to pay a pre-determined sum to the depositor at an agreed date, money is paid in at regular intervals over a certain period of time. Instalment savings are commonly referred to as 'monthly instalment savings', the peculiar feature of which is that money is collected by clerks on outside duty. This kind of deposit is akin to instalment time deposits in that money is paid in at definite intervals, for a definite number of times and in a definite amount. The difference is that the interest is represented by the difference between the sum of instalments and the money paid by the bank at the expiry of the contract term (at present, below 3·9 per cent). Instalment savings are popular with mutual loans and savings banks and with credit associations, but only a few commercial banks are engaged in this kind of business.

F. Deposits for Tax Payments

Deposits for tax payments were newly instituted in May 1949. The purpose was to alleviate the burden on the taxpayers. They are, in principle, withdrawable only when the depositor makes payments of the tax with the money. The interest rate is 0·75 per cent higher than on ordinary deposits (at present, below 3·0 per cent), and is free from the tax on interest income and there is an exemption from stamp duty on the passbook.

G. Special Deposits

Special deposits are also known as 'miscellaneous deposits', and take a variety of forms. In fact, they are not so much deposits as money for temporary custody. The principal items include: government revenue paid in to banks, which are the Bank of Japan Agents or National Revenue Agents (such money must be paid over to the Bank two days after the receipt of money); public money of local authorities, which is paid into banks acting as their revenue agents; dividends on shares, which the banks have been entrusted to pay to the shareholders; money for the payment of the principal or the interest of public bonds and debentures; subscriptions for new shares; and money for the payment of cashiers' cheques issued by the bank. In fact, money in temporary custody is treated as deposits solely for book-keeping convenience. There are therefore no fixed maturities for these deposits, except in special cases, and they carry no interest in most instances (the legal rate is below 2·25 per cent).

(2) *Lending*

While deposits are the most important credit-receiving business of commercial banks, lending plays the crucial role on the credit-giving side. The importance of lending is not simply that it is the biggest source of profits for banks: variations in the amount of lending greatly affects the productive and investment activities of business firms.

A. Types of Lending

Lending takes the following four forms: bill-discounting, loans on bills, loans on deeds and overdrafts.

(*a*) *Bill-discounting*. Bill-discounting is the purchase of bills after deduction of interest for the period to maturity. Commercial bills form the more important class of bills discounted. They are drawn for the settlement of commodity transactions (a maturity of three months is customary). Their quick and final payment is ensured by the sale of goods in the hands of the drawees. More than one person is interested in a bill, so that, in case of the payee's default, the right of recourse can be exercised against endorsers, including the discounter. For this reason the discounting of commercial bills is considered to be the ideal form of lending by commercial banks. Moreover, fine commercial bills are rediscountable at the Bank of

Japan[1] or can be used as collateral for borrowings from the Bank.

In addition to commercial bills, banks discount bank acceptances – that is, bills the payment of which are guaranteed by banks, and documentary bills, to which bills of lading or warehouse receipts are attached. The former are deemed to be particularly safe, but they are seldom seen in Japan, except in connection with foreign trade.

(*b*) *Loans on Bills*. Loans on bills are lending in the form of discount of self-addressed (single-name) promissory notes issued by the borrower in favour of the Bank; the bulk of lending in Japan is now done in this form. Promissory notes in this case are not created for the finance of commodity transactions, as is the case with commercial bills, but are made out for the sole purpose of serving as instruments for borrowing money from the bank. Loans on bills are mainly for the finance of working capital of the manufacturers, so that the terms of notes usually range from two to three months. They are, however, often renewed and used for the finance of long-term working capital and of fixed investment in plant and equipment.

(*c*) *Loans on Deeds*. In this case the debtor gives the bank, not his promissory note, but a bond of debt. This form is principally used in long-term lending, such as the loan of funds for fixed investment, which are secured by real estate, or in loans to local authorities. Banks, however, prefer loans on bills even for long-term loans, because this is a more flexible form: the terms of loans can be more easily altered, and repayments can be secured more easily under the law on bills, and the bills are transferable by endorsement.

(*d*) *Overdrafts*. Under an overdraft agreement a customer is allowed to overdraw his current account within a given limit during a given period. This is most convenient for borrowers

[1] Commercial bills eligible for rediscount at the Bank are restricted to bills drawn for the settlement of goods bought for the purpose of resale. Thus, they are only a portion of commercial bills in general banking terminology. For instance, bills drawn by merchant firms or factors on manufacturers for raw materials bought by the latter are generally treated as commercial bills, but are not eligible for rediscount at the Bank. It may be noted that promissory notes of the Export Joint Sales Company of Agricultural and Fishery Products drawn in favour of financial institutions for money borrowed to finance the consignment of goods for export (single-name notes) are not commercial bills in any sense, but, from June 1964, they have been accorded the privilege of being eligible for rediscount at the Bank.

with frequent receipts and payments, and is the standard method of accommodating bank customers in the United Kingdom and other countries. Overdrafts, however, are more difficult to administer than bill-discounting and loans on bills, and are not eligible for refinancing by the Bank of Japan. Consequently, Japanese banks are reluctant to grant customers this facility, although the rate of interest is higher than that on loans on bills.

B. Discount of and Loans on Foreign Trade Bills

Commercial banks' discount of and loans on foreign trade bills are accorded the following preferential treatment.

(*a*) *Export Trade Bills*. Banks discount or make loans on export advance bills, against which payments are assured from the foreign currency proceeds of exports. Such accommodation is granted before or upon shipment, at lower rates than against other bills, because the Bank of Japan accords them favourable treatment. Export advance bills are drawn by exporters or manufacturers on commercial banks for finance of manufacture, and the collection and processing of goods under export contracts, or they are bills drawn on exporters for the same purposes. Export advance bills become 'export advance bills' eligible for rediscount at the Bank, if irrevocable letters of credit are opened for the export transactions in respect of which bills are drawn, and if the bills have three months or less to run to maturity. Bills for which the existence of export contracts can be confirmed, but for which irrevocable letters of credit have not been opened, or which have more than three months to run to maturity (in principle, there should be not more than six months to maturity) are treated as export advance bills eligible as collateral for loans on bills by the Bank. Documentary usance bills in yen, drawn by Japanese exporters for the settlement of exports, the payment of which is assured from balances in free yen accounts, and which mature within five months of acceptance by authorised foreign exchange banks having discount or borrowing accounts with the Bank, are also export usance bills eligible for rediscount at the Bank (yen export usance bills).

In addition to discounts of and loans on export advance bills and export usance bills, commercial banks finance export trade by granting overdraft facilities to merchant firms; such facilities are usually termed 'export accounts' (export advance finance). Joint loans are also made with the Export–Import Bank of Japan on long- and medium-term for the finance of exports (at present, the Export–Import Bank provides 70–80 per cent of such loans, while commercial banks lend the remaining 20–30 per cent). These joint loans are principally to finance exports of ships and plants sold on credit; the period of repayment is usually about 5–7 years (in exceptional cases, 15 years).

(*b*) *Import Trade Bills.* If domestic importers import goods, for which bills are drawn upon them in foreign currency payable at sight, they must have yen funds ready for purchase of foreign currency when the bills fall due. Time is, however, needed until the imported goods are sold and payment is received. Importers have therefore to borrow the necessary yen from banks. Promissory notes issued by importers in favour of banks in order to borrow from them are called 'import settlement bills'. Commercial banks distinguish advances on these bills from other loans and discounts and record the total separately as 'loans for settlement of import bills'. Import settlement bills with maturities of less than two months (three months for imports from distant areas) were formerly given preferential treatment by the Bank as 'import trade bills' eligible as collateral for loans. Bills drawn to finance payments of freight and insurance on imported goods (import freight bills), with maturities of less than two months (three months for imports from distant areas), were also treated as 'import trade bills'. Documentary usance bills in yen drawn by overseas exporters on Japanese importers, on which payments were made through non-residents' free yen accounts and which had a tenor of less than two months (three months for imports from distant areas) were also included in this category (import usance bills in Japanese currency) if accepted by authorised foreign exchange banks with discount and borrowing accounts at the Bank.

From about 1965, however, interest rates in overseas countries rose, while they fell in Japan, so that interest-rate differentials have narrowed. Thus, the reason for giving preferential treatment to import finance has disappeared, and such treatment of import trade bills was discontinued by the Bank from January 1966. Accordingly, commercial banks have also ceased to accord preference to such bills.

C. Lending Rates

By a notification under the Temporary Money Rate Adjustment Law and by a guideline of the Bank, ceilings may be imposed upon the lending rates of commercial banks (see Table 13.1). Interest rates on lending for more than one year or of less than one million yen, are not, however, subject to such regulations (but loans on and discounts of export and import trade bills are subject to them). In practice, however, maximum lending rates lower than the legal ceilings are fixed by mutual agreement among banks (see Table 13.1). Within these limits,

TABLE 13.1

Ceilings on Interest Rates of Commercial Banks' Lending (May 1971)

(percentages)

	Maximum Rates by Notification under the Temporary Money Rates Adjustment Law	*Maximum Rates by Voluntary Regulations*
1. Standard Rate. Discount rate of, and interest rate on, loans secured by bills of high credit-worthiness, such as commercial bills eligible for Bank of Japan rediscount	9·5	5·75
2. Discount rate of, and interest rate on, loans secured by export usance bills eligible for Bank of Japan rediscount	9·5	5·75
3. Discount rate of, and interest rate on, loans secured by export advance bills eligible for Bank of Japan rediscount	9·5	6·0
4. Discount rate of, and interest rate on, loans secured by export advance bills other than those eligible for Bank of Japan rediscount	9·5	6·25
5. Discount rate of, and interest rate on, loans secured by other bills	9·5	7·50
6. Overdrafts	10·25	8·50

NOTES:

1. These rates are also applied to lending by long-term credit banks and trust banks.

2. These rates are not applied to loans with maturities exceeding one year nor to bills of face value under one million yen, which are not export or import trade bills.

3. The above structure of commercial banks' interest rates was replaced in October 1972, on the simplification of the Bank of Japan's official rates (see p. 151), by a threefold classification of rates for : (1) discounts of, or loans on, bills of especially high credit standing; (2) discounts and loans in respect of other bills; (3) overdrafts.

SOURCE: Bank of Japan.

commercial banks decide the interest rate for each lending transaction, taking into account the customer's credit standing and other circumstances.

D. Collateral Security

For lending other than bill-discounting it is customary to require borrowers to provide personal or real security, including deposits with the lending bank (time deposit or deposit at notice) or real estate, such as land, buildings, ships and factories under construction. When the borrower's credit standing is low the personal guarantee of company officials or the guarantee of the associated companies or of credit-guarantee associations is required. Loans on the security of merchandise, debentures or shares have been relatively rare in the post-war years. It should be added that it has hitherto been customary for banks to require borrowers to deposit a certain proportion of the borrowed money in the form of time deposit or deposit at notice; these are the so-called 'compensating balances'. This practice can, however, easily degenerate into a means of expanding deposits for window-dressing purposes or it may lead to a *de facto* raising of interest rates. The extravagant use of this device is, therefore, now restrained by mutual agreement among banks. Lending on the security of such deposits, or lending that involves compensating balances, should be made at rates of interest lower than on ordinary lending.

(3) *Investment in Securities*

Investment in securities is next in importance to lending among bank assets.

There are two reasons for banks to hold securities: first, they are earning assets, the profitability of which is inferior only to lending; and, second, they are easily negotiable in securities markets, so that they are a species of liquid assets for banks. In post-war Japan, however, there has been little inducement for banks to hold securities. Banks have been in over-lent positions; indirect finance has predominated; and the yield on fixed-interest securities has been kept low, so that they have been unattractive investments. Further, the securities market has been underdeveloped, so that realisation of securities has been difficult. Thus, commercial banks acquired securities only if they had special relations with the companies issuing them, or when the securities involved were the objects of buying operations by the Bank or were eligible as collateral for borrowing from it; such, for example, were national bonds, government-guaranteed debentures or bank debentures.

It should be said that Japanese banks are permitted to underwrite the issues of national bonds, but the underwriting of issues of shares and industrial debentures is the sole prerogative of securities companies under Article 65 of the Securities and Exchange Law.

(4) *Domestic Remittance Facilities*

Domestic remittance facilities are a service by which banks act as intermediaries for payments between people in different localities. Remittances through banks may be made in four different ways. First, by ordinary remittance, the remitting bank draws a remittance cheque on a correspondent bank, and this is given to the remitter; he mails the cheque to the payee, who presents it to the paying bank for payment. Second, telegraphic remittance is used when a quicker method than mailing remittance cheques is required; in this case, the paying bank is instructed by telegraph to pay to the payee, who is advised by telegraph. Third and fourth respectively, the crediting of current accounts and the telegraphic crediting of current accounts may be used when payees have current or ordinary deposit accounts with the paying banks, which are credited upon instruction by the remitting banks. As these last two methods are safe and reliable, they are more widely utilised than the other two.

Conversely, the creditor may collect money from the debtor through a bank. In this case, it is usual to draw bills of exchange. The drawer entrusts a bank to collect from the debtor; the bank sends the bill to its own office or to a correspondent bank in the place where it is payable, and the bill is presented for payment either through the clearing house or directly to the debtor.

When such transactions take place between offices of the

same bank they are settled within it by debiting or crediting inter-office accounts. When they involve transactions with other banks the debts and credits are settled through the domestic clearing system. The paying bank acquires a claim on the remitting bank when it pays the money to the payee on behalf of the latter, and the claim is paid by an office of the Bank of Japan on behalf of the remitting bank, from which it collects the money. Before this stage is reached, however, commercial banks in the same locality exchange their claims on each other in the same way as in clearing bills and cheques; only the net balances are settled by debiting or crediting the respective banks' balances at the Bank of Japan. The system greatly helps the rational operation of banking and the effective employment of money. One point to note is that commercial banks are required to keep their exchange clearing accounts at the Bank in funds, so that the Bank does not become their creditor by making payments on their behalf.

(5) *Foreign Exchange Business*

Commercial banks cannot engage in foreign exchange business unless they are licensed to do so by the Minister of Finance under the Foreign Exchange Bank Law (only the Bank of Tokyo is so licensed at present) or unless they are permitted to do so by the Minister under the Foreign Exchange and Foreign Trade Control Law. Banks with such authorisation are called 'authorised foreign exchange banks'. A distinction can be made between Japanese foreign exchange banks and foreign-domiciled banks. There are at present 90 Japanese foreign exchange banks; of these the Bank of Tokyo is the specialised foreign exchange bank, 13 are city banks and one is a long-term credit bank. These 15 banks have overseas offices. There are 18 foreign-domiciled banks. Others (57 banks) comprise country banks, trust banks and the Central Bank for Commercial and Industrial Co-operatives.

Foreign exchange banks conduct ordinary foreign exchange business, including the purchase and sale of foreign currency, opening and receiving of letters of credit, purchase of export bills, payment of import bills, collection of bills of exchange, payment of money orders for remittance, purchase and sale of foreign exchange with customers and with other banks. They maintain overseas branches in order to perform such business. They can also conclude correspondent contracts with overseas banks or foreign-domiciled banks, with which they open their own accounts, in which they are allowed to deposit foreign currency funds necessary for their foreign exchange dealings.

With the vast expansion in the volume of foreign trade of Japan, and with the liberalisation of foreign exchange transactions, the amount of foreign money employed by thc foreign exchange banks has greatly increased. Part of the foreign currency assets is held in liquid form,[1] such as cash, deposits with correspondent overseas banks, call loans and securities, but the bulk is employed in the financing of foreign trade, such as purchase of export bills, granting of import usance credit and loans in foreign currency to overseas agents of Japanese merchant firms. In some cases the foreign currency assets they have acquired are converted into and employed in yen. There are three ways for banks to raise the necessary foreign currency: (1) to purchase it with their own yen; (2) to accept deposits in foreign currency; and (3) to borrow from foreign banks. In general the liquidity position of Japanese banks has been low and interest rates in Japan have been relatively higher than in foreign countries, so that banks have been reluctant to purchase foreign currency with their own yen funds. Such purchases have been made only to the extent that they have been able to borrow at low-interest rates from the Bank of Japan on the security of previously bought export usance bills (System of Loans against Foreign Exchange Assets) or to sell export usance bills to the Bank (System of Purchase of Foreign Bills). Thus, foreign currency deposits and borrowings from overseas banks have been the main sources of foreign money for the banks. Foreign currency deposits include both deposits in foreign currency, such as Euro-dollar deposits, and non-residents' free yen deposits, to which foreign currency is paid in.

[1] From June 1962 old Japanese Class A foreign exchange banks have been required to hold a certain percentage of their short-term liabilities in foreign currencies in a liquid form as minimum reserves. This is called the 'Foreign Currency Reserves System'.

Borrowing from foreign banks arises from their acceptance of usance bills; refinance credit received from foreign banks on the security of claims on importers, to whom Japanese banks have lent money to settle sight import bills; clean loans; and overdrafts. In addition, the government deposits part of its foreign currency holding with the foreign exchange banks, which may employ some of it as ordinary working capital.

4. ASSETS AND LIABILITIES: PROFIT AND LOSS

We shall now turn to recent trends in commercial banks' assets and liabilities and in their profit and loss accounts, which reflect the results of their operation (see Tables 13.2 and 13.3).

(1) *Liabilities*

More than 70 per cent of commercial banks' liabilities consist of deposits, their main source of funds.[1] More than half are time deposits, of which over 80 per cent have maturities of one year. A prominent feature of commercial banking in Japan is that time deposits, especially those of one year, form such a large part of total deposits. This enables banks to employ their money for relatively long periods. Time deposits in commercial banks have increased at a comparatively steady pace in the post-war years. One reason is that individuals' preference for them has consistently been strong. Another reason is that it has been advantageous for companies to hold their liquid assets in this form: as the market for bonds and debentures is not well-developed, companies have been heavily dependent upon borrowing from banks, and it has therefore been prudent for them to hold time deposits with banks. Next to time deposits, current and ordinary deposits are important,

[1] The sum of various kinds of deposits is termed 'gross deposits', but this includes cheques and bills paid into deposit accounts, which cannot be employed as money until they have been settled through clearing. In most instances, therefore, cheques and bills on hand (which are included in cash on hand) are deducted from gross deposits and the resulting 'real deposits' (i.e. net deposits) are used as indices of the actual resources of banks. Further, when necessary, foreign currency deposits of the government with commercial banks are deducted from real deposits to obtain 'deposits on net basis'.

TABLE 13.2

Principal Accounts of Commercial Banks
(end of 1970)

(hundred million yen)

	City Banks	*Country Banks*	*Total*
ASSETS			
Cash	27,127	9,168	36,295
(of which Bills and Cheques on hand)	(23,638)	(6,421)	(30,059)
Deposits with Financial Institutions	5,954	3,615	9,569
Call Loans	123	5,635	5,758
Securities	39,463	20,050	59,513
Bills Discounted	74,109	38,411	112,520
Loans and Advances	143,339	79,237	222,576
(of which Loans on Notes)	(126,109)	(63,429)	(189,538)
Foreign Exchange	25,828	183	26,011
Domestic Exchanges Paid	1,334	973	2,307
Customers' Liability for Acceptances and Guarantees	39,589	8,886	48,475
Bank Premises and Real Estate	6,143	3,143	9,286
Other	5,880	2,849	8,729
Total	368,889	172,150	541,039
LIABILITIES			
Deposits	242,983	145,001	387,984
(of which Real Deposits)	(219,344)	(138,580)	(357,924)
Borrowing	26,754	597	27,351
(of which borrowing from the Bank of Japan)	(21,237)	(431)	(21,668)
Call Money	20,437	109	20,546
Foreign Exchange	10,425	51	10,476
Domestic Exchanges Unsettled	1,144	1,792	2,936
Acceptances and Guarantees	39,589	8,886	48,475
Reserves	6,903	3,170	10,073
Capital	4,090	1,566	5,656
Legal Reserves	900	995	1,895
Surpluses	9,460	8,467	17,927
Other	6,204	1,516	7,720

SOURCE: Bank of Japan, *Economic Statistics Annual.*

which account respectively for 12 and 16 per cent of total deposits. As already noted, current deposits serve mainly as a means of settling inter-firm transactions, so that they exhibit wide seasonal and cyclical fluctuations. Deposits at notice and instalment savings are not very popular, their respective shares in the total being respectively 9 and 2 per cent.

The net worth of commercial banks consists of capital, legal

TABLE 13.3

Composition of Assets and Liabilities of Commercial Banks

(percentages)

End of the Year	*1930*	*1948*	*1953*	*1958*	*1963*	*1968*	*1969*	*1970*
ASSETS								
Cash and Deposits with Financial Institutions	7·4	14·4	10·1	12·5	11·6	9·4	9·1	8·5
Call Loans	1·5	0·6	0·6	1·1	0·8	1·0	0·9	1·1
Securities	23·5	18·4	8·6	11·2	10·1	12·6	11·7	11·0
Loans, Advances and Discounts	51·2	55·7	64·5	62·3	60·5	62·0	56·6	55·8
(of which Bills Discounted)	(4·7)	(9·1)	(24·7)	(20·3)	(21·3)	(21·5)	(20·9)	(20·8)
(„ „ Loans on Notes)	(31·2)	(44·6)	(35·2)	(40·0)	(37·8)	(36·5)	(35·7)	(35·0)
Foreign Exchange	1·1	—	3·4	1·9	3·8	4·1	4·3	4·8
Bank Premises and Real Estate	3·2	0·4	1·4	1·4	1·1	1·7	1·7	1·7
Other	12·1	10·5	11·4	9·6	12·1	9·2	15·7	17·1
Total	100·0	100·0	100·0	100·0	100·0	100·0	100·0	100·0
LIABILITIES								
Deposits	65·6	77·6	70·3	77·1	71·9	74·0	73·0	71·7
Borrowing	5·4	7·4	8·0	5·0	6·5	4·7	5·0	5·1
Call Money	0·8	0·5	1·2	2·4	2·8	2·6	3·3	3·8
Foreign Exchange	0·5	—	2·5	0·6	2·6	2·3	2·1	1·9
Capital	15·3	2·1	1·1	1·0	1·0	1·2	1·1	1·0
Reserves and Surpluses	5·3	0·9	2·6	3·2	2·9	3·4	3·5	3·7
Other	7·1	11·5	14·3	10·7	12·3	11·8	12·0	12·8

SOURCE: Bank of Japan, *Economic Statistics Annual.*

reserves (capital reserves, revaluation reserves and revenue surplus), surpluses (voluntary reserves and profits) and reserves (reserves for possible loan losses, reserves for price fluctuations and reserves for retirement allowances). Sometimes reserves are not included in net worth in the narrower sense. The net worth is important for covering the risks that commercial banks incur in the employment of money, and as the final reserve against external liabilities, including deposits. For this reason commercial banks are required by the Banking Law to retain a higher proportion of profits (revenue surplus) than ordinary joint-stock companies.[1] Moreover, a part of reserves is treated as

[1] Ordinary joint-stock companies have to retain a tenth of their profits until the accumulated total reaches one-fourth of the capital (Article 288, Commercial Law), but banks have to 'retain more than one-fifth of profits as reserves whenever dividends are paid out of profits, until the accumulated total becomes equal to the capital' (Article 8, Banking Law).

TABLE 13.4

Composition of Deposits with Commercial Banks

(percentages)

End of the Year	*1930*	*End of September 1952*			*End of September 1963*			*End of September 1970*		
			City Banks	*Country Banks*		*City Banks*	*Country Banks*		*City Banks*	*Country Banks*
Current Deposits	12·7	19·9	24·2	10·7	17·5	20·1	12·6	11·2	12·3	9·3
(of which Deposits by Corporate Businesses)		(95·8)	(96·7)	(91·1)	(96·4)	(97·2)	(94·1)	(82·6)	(96·1)	(91·8)
Ordinary Deposits	20·8	16·4	15·0	19·6	16·0	15·2	17·6	16·5	15·4	18·5
(of which Deposits by Corporate Businesses)		(38·5)	(40·1)	(35·9)	(44·3)	(47·3)	(39·6)	(45·3)	(47·6)	(42·0)
Deposits at Notice	5·8	6·5	7·3	4·7	8·1	9·3	6·0	8·8	10·0	6·9
(of which Deposits by Corporate Businesses)		(91·7)	(92·1)	(90·4)	(93·6)	(94·0)	(92·6)	(95·3)	(95·5)	(94·7)
Other Short-term Deposits	3·3	5·7	7·0	2·9	5·9	7·4	3·3	6·1	6·4	3·6
Time Deposits	57·3	48·7	45·4	55·8	50·5	47·7	55·7	56·8	55·9	58·3
(of which Deposits by Corporate Businesses)		(37·4)	(42·4)	(28·5)	(48·4)	(54·2)	(39·3)	(47·9)	(51·8)	(39·0)
(of which Deposits of One Year's Maturity)		(75·5)	(74·2)	(77·6)	(79·7)	(76·6)	(84·3)	(84·1)	(82·3)	(87·0)
Instalment Savings	0·1	2·8	1·1	6·3	1·9	0·3	4·8	0·6	0·2	3·4
Total	100·0	100·0	100·0	100·0	100·0	100·0	100·0	100·0	100·0	100·0
(of which Deposits by Corporate Businesses)		(56·0)	(62·5)	(42·1)	(62·7)	(68·7)	(51·5)	(58·8)	(63·7)	(50·2)

SOURCE: Bank of Japan, *Economic Statistics Monthly*.

losses in the calculation of income liable to corporation tax under the Special Taxation Measures Law. Formerly, additions to reserves were left to the discretion of banks, but from the latter half of the fiscal year 1967 a unified accounting standard in this respect has been in operation, under an administrative regulation of the Ministry of Finance. In pre-war years the net worth of commercial banks was equivalent to nearly 20 per cent (of which capital represented 15 per cent) of their total liabilities, but in recent years it has been only about 6 per cent (of which capital accounts for 1 per cent), even if reserves are included. Such a small percentage of net worth is chiefly due to the extremely rapid growth of deposits and lending; but a contributory reason can be found in the difficulties that banks experience in increasing their capital, because the capital market is underdeveloped and because administrative regulation imposes limitations upon the dividend rates on bank shares.

In contrast to the fall in the relative weight of net worth, borrowing from the Bank of Japan, from other financial institutions and from the call money market has markedly increased. This is particularly true of city banks. In pre-war years they borrowed practically no money from the Bank or from the call money market, but since the war their borrowing from these sources has greatly expanded. This is a reflection of the brisk demand for money from business firms during the periods of reconstruction and of high growth. In tight-money periods in particular, borrowing from financial institutions and from the call money market sometimes exceed 15 per cent of their total liabilities.

(2) *Assets*

Both before and since the war, lending (discounts, loans and advances) has represented the greater part of commercial banks' assets. In post-war years it has been equal to about 60 per cent of total assets and to almost 100 per cent of 'real deposits'. The relative weight of commercial bills discounted greatly increased and is now equivalent to more than 30 per cent of total lending (they were less than 10 per cent in pre-war years). One cause of this is that the self-financing capacity of factors and manufacturers has weakened since the war, so that they have had to rely more upon settlements by bills. Another reason is that the Bank of Japan has accorded favourable treatment to commercial bills in its provision of rediscount facilities. In contrast, loans on deeds and overdrafts, which represented more than 10 per cent of the total in pre-war years, have markedly declined in relative importance; in recent years the former have accounted for about 7 per cent, while the latter have been equivalent to about 1 per cent of the total. Such contrasting tendencies may be explained by the circumstances that settlement of commercial bills can confidently be expected in relatively short periods; whereas bills are eligible for rediscount at the Bank or as security for loans from it, loans on deeds and overdrafts lack such attractions, so that banks short of funds have preferred to discount bills with high liquidity. Loans on bills have, however, been the dominant form of lending since the war as they were before, and they represent more than half of the total.

Most commercial banks' lending is to business firms. Loans to individuals are insignificant, although they are increasing with the notable growth of consumer credit, such as housing loans and the finance of consumer durables. By industry, lending to manufacturing industry predominates (see Table 13·5). It absorbs about half of total lending. Next comes wholesale trade, lending to which is equal to a little under 30 per cent of the total. Then follow, in order of importance, retail trade, construction, services, transport and communication and other public utilities, real estate, agriculture and forestry and fishery, and mining. In lending to manufacturing industry, that to light industries, such as textiles and foodstuffs, was formerly the most important, but, with the growth of the heavy and chemical industries, lending to chemical, steel, machinery and metal industries, etc., has in recent years come to account for about 60 per cent of the total.

Lending to business firms can roughly be divided into the finance of working capital and the finance of fixed investment in plant and equipment. The latter is about 10 per cent of total lending, but it is probable that, if we include renewals of nominally short-term lending, the ratio is higher than this.

Business firms require working capital for various purposes. In Japan a considerable proportion of inter-firm transactions

TABLE 13.5

Outstanding Amounts of Lending by Commercial Banks, by Industry (end of 1970)

(hundred million yen)

	City Banks			*Country Banks*		
		of which loans for fixed invest-ment	*of which lending to small businesses*		*of which loans for fixed invest-ment*	*of which lending to small businesses*
Manufacturing Industries	98,152	9,791	21,687	46,562	3,800	23,449
(of which Foodstuffs)	(5,257)	(576)	(1,344)	(4,388)	(465)	(3,149)
(,, ,, Textiles)	(10,713)	(463)	(3,374)	(7,387)	(573)	(5,070)
(,, ,, Chemical and Allied)	(11,840)	(2,095)	(1,460)	(4,452)	(404)	(746)
(,, ,, Iron and Steel)	(10,214)	(1,520)	(913)	(2,422)	(179)	(578)
(,, ,, Machinery)	(8,683)	(446)	(2,931)	(4,587)	(300)	(2,351)
(,, ,, Electrical Machinery, Equipment and Supplies)	(10,741)	(341)	(1,632)	(3,272)	(170)	(947)
(of which Transportation Equipment)	(13,030)	(695)	(1,068)	(3,904)	(272)	(968)
Agriculture, Forestry and Fishery	973	150	341	2,510	631	2,149
Mining	1,339	102	157	815	83	366
Construction	10,597	390	3,033	6,363	484	4,336
Wholesale Trade	61,028	1,272	10,766	24,572	944	10,499
Retail Trade	7,525	2,585	3,474	10,330	2,240	6,918
Real Estate	5,922	1,534	2,915	4,953	1,265	3,151
Transport, Communication, Electricity, Gas and Water	9,003	3,403	1,230	4,034	1,352	1,577
Services	7,482	2,500	3,132	7,236	3,306	5,353
Individuals	8,385	2,726	8,385	6,793	3,260	6,793
Others	4,864	544	414	2,694	660	280
Total	215,270	24,997	55,536	116,862	18,025	64,871

NOTES:

1 Do not include overdrafts.

2 Lending to small business is lending to business firms with capital of less than 59 million yen (for wholesale and retail trades and

in raw materials and commodities is settled by bills, most of which are brought to banks for discount. Then, money needed in anticipation of production and for the payment of corporate taxes and dividends is often borrowed from the banks. Thus commercial bank lending for working capital increases seasonally in the months in which business transactions are customarily settled (March, September and December), and in those in which the accounts of business firms are closed (June and December). Moreover, bank lending is strongly influenced by the business cycle, for Japanese firms are generally short of liquidity.

By size of borrower, about two-thirds of bank lending is for large enterprises with capital of more than 50 million yen. Particularly in the case of city banks, more than 70 per cent of their loans, advances and discounts are for large firms. In comparison, more than half the lending of country banks is for small businesses with capital of less than 50 million yen, so that country banks are important lenders to this sector.

Investment in securities is the next important item in the employment of funds. In pre-war years investments accounted for more than 20 per cent of total assets, but in post-war years commercial banks have been reluctant to hold securities for reasons which have already been enumerated. Thus, the proportion of investments in total assets has declined to about 10 per cent. The type of security held is as follows (see Table 13.6): bank and industrial debentures and shares were the most important at the end of 1969 and they were followed by public corporation debentures, local and government bonds. The amount of government bonds held by commercial banks increased rapidly after January 1966, when the government began to issue long-term bonds. In more recent years, however, the increase has slowed down, because banks sell them to the Bank of Japan when the Bank undertakes buying operations and because the issue of long-term bonds has decreased.

Among the assets of commercial banks, cash on hand and deposits with other financial institutions are, so to speak, their first-line reserves. As has already been pointed out, the cash reserves of Japanese banks are extremely small. Deposits with other financial institutions include compulsory deposits

TABLE 13.6

Composition of Securities Held by Commercial Banks

(percentages)

End of the Year	*1930*	*1958*	*1963*	*1968*	*1969*	*1970*
Government Bonds	42·0	4·8	2·0	11·4	10·5	7·8
Local Bonds	9·9	9·0	10·0	11·4	12·1	12·9
Public Corporation Debentures		12·4	12·5	12·1	11·6	14·2
Bank Debentures	36·4	31·5	26·0	24·7	23·0	24·6
Industrial Debentures		28·2	29·7	19·3	25·4	21·8
Shares	10·6	13·6	19·2	20·5	16·9	18·0
Other	1·1	0·5	0·6	0·6	0·5	0·7
Total	100·0	100·0	100·0	100·0	100·0	100·0

SOURCE: Bank of Japan, *Economic Statistics Annual.*

with the Bank under the reserve requirements system. Even when these are included, net cash reserves (i.e. excluding cheques and bills on hand) are equivalent to only about 4 per cent of real deposits. For this reason they have to borrow from the Bank whenever their customers withdraw large sums, for instance, for payments of wages and salaries or when the Treasury accounts with the public show a large excess of receipts. Call loans form a second line of reserve, but city banks tend to be borrowers of such funds, although country banks are lenders (call loans are equal to a little over 3 per cent of their 'real deposits'). Thus, the liquidity of commercial banks, particularly of city banks, is extremely low. This is both the most striking characteristic and the weakness of commercial banks in Japan.

(3) *Profit and Loss*

The composition of the assets and liabilities of commercial banks is reflected in their profit and loss.

The bulk of their current income comes from earnings on lending (discount on bills and interest on loans and advances). Other income, including interest on securities held, is less than 30 per cent of the total.

On the other hand, interest payments on deposits constitute more than half of current expenses. As a large part of commercial bank deposits consists of time deposits, which carry high rates of interest, the average interest cost on total deposits is relatively high at 4·1 per cent (in the first half of fiscal year 1969). If other expenses, such as expenditure on personnel and materials and taxes, are added to this, deposit costs amount to 6·2 per cent. These costs are, however, being reduced year by year, as deposits per head of bank employee increase and as costs of personnel and materials fall with more rational management and the increasing mechanisation of clerical work. In recent years, however, the reduction has slowed down. The cost of borrowing from other financial institutions and from the call money market rose substantially during the period of high growth in 1955–64; this was a reflection of over-loans by commercial banks and of the rise in call loan rates. Especially during credit squeezes, when these external liabilities rapidly increase, these costs have far exceeded the average interest rates on loans and discounts, so that at such times bank managements have been hard hit.

5. TYPES OF BANKS AND BANKING ORGANISATIONS

All commercial banks in Japan are private financial institutions on joint-stock principles. They are subdivided into several groups (city banks, country banks, specialised foreign exchange bank, foreign-domiciled banks) with slightly different functions. In what follows, not only the banks but also the bankers' associations will be discussed in broad outline; the majority of their members are commercial banks, although membership is not confined to them.

(1) *City Banks*

City banks base their operations on big cities, but they also have nationwide networks of branches. From April 1969 there were fourteen such banks: the Fuji Bank, the Sumitomo Bank, the Mitsubishi Bank, the Sanwa Bank, the Tokai Bank, the Dai-ichi Bank, the Mitsui Bank, the Nippon Kangyo Bank, the Kyowa Bank, the Daiwa Bank, the Bank of Kobe, the Hokkaido Takushoku Bank, the Taiyo Bank and the Saitama Bank.

The city banks have been the most important private

TABLE 13·7

Profit Rates and Costs of Commercial Banks

(percentages)

First Half of the Fiscal Year	*1930*	*1948*	*1953*	*1958*	*1963*	*1966*	*1967*	*1968*	*1969*	*1970*
Costs on Deposits and Debentures (A)	5·31	6·63	7·08	6·86	6·32	6·69	6·60	6·27	6·22	6·23
Interest Rates on Deposits and Debentures	3·88	1·61	3·30	4·21	4·04	4·11	4·11	4·12	4·14	4·17
Rates of General Expenses (Personnel and Supplies)	1·22	4·89	3·42	2·35	1·94	1·89	1·80	2·20	1·96	1·95
Tax Rate	0·20	0·13	0·37	0·30	0·34	0·69	0·69	0·13	0·12	0·11
Interest Rates on Lending, Call Loans and Securities Held (B)	5·80	7·05	8·79	8·32	7·67	7·32	7·20	7·47	7·37	7·67
Interest Rates on Lending and Call Loans	5·73	8·35	8·89	8·48	7·70	7·36	7·22	7·54	7·41	7·74
Interest Rates on Securities Held	5·94	3·91	8·02	7·40	7·54	7·09	7·15	7·14	7·20	7·34
Profit Rates (A) – (B)	0·49	0·42	1·71	1·46	1·35	0·63	0·60	1·20	1·15	1·45

NOTES:

1. Tax rates since the first half of 1966 are calculated by the new formula under an amendment to the Commercial Law.
2. Figures for 1968 were calculated from revised profit-and-loss statements.

SOURCE: Bank of Japan, *Economic Statistics Annual.*

financial institutions since Meiji times. At present their deposits represent about one-fourth of those of all financial institutions, and 60 per cent of those of all commercial banks. They provide about 30 per cent of the funds required by private businesses, and they therefore exert considerable influence on the national economy.

Large firms figure prominently as borrowers from city banks, about half of whose outstanding advances are for sums exceeding 500 million yen; more than 60 per cent of their outstanding deposits are deposits by corporate businesses, most of which are in sums of more than a million yen. Time deposits by individuals are about one-fourth of the total. City banks are therefore characterised by having large firms as their principal customers, the expansion of which provided the main driving force of the high growth of the economy in post-war years; city banks have therefore played an important part in that development. They have, however, engaged in severe competition among themselves, so that they have been only too glad to lend to big firms to meet their almost insatiable demand for money. Indeed, they have sometimes lent more than their credit-creating capacity warranted in order to maintain their ties with such firms; this has unquestionably been a factor in the aggravation of the over-loans situation of city banks.

(2) *Country Banks*

Country banks have their head offices in provincial cities and operate mainly in their local prefectures. After April 1969 there were 61 country banks. Some are as large as city banks, but most are medium or small banks; the customers they finance are chiefly small local businesses. More than half of their total advances are for firms with capital of less than 50 million yen. Nearly half of their deposits are personal accounts, of which about three-fifths are time deposits (mostly of one year's maturity). Thus, they resemble savings banks. Their liquidity position is better than that of city banks, because of the low turnover of their largely personal deposits and also because their lending is mostly to local small businesses. Investments form a higher proportion of their assets than in the case of city banks, and they are also important lenders in the call loan market. Very few country banks are permanently in debt to the Bank of Japan.

Their main function is the finance of local industries, but they naturally lend substantial sums to large firms too. In periods of monetary restraint large firms and their affiliates tend to turn to country banks for money which they cannot borrow from city banks.

(3) *Specialised Foreign Exchange Bank*

A specialised foreign exchange bank is a bank established under the Foreign Exchange Banks Law of 1954. Its principal business is dealings in foreign exchange and the finance of foreign trade. At present there is only one such bank (the Bank of Tokyo). As already pointed out, the difference between its foreign exchange business and that of authorised foreign exchange banks (old class A) is slight, and is one of degree. It receives favourable treatment from the government in opening overseas branches and in foreign currency deposits. However, it cannot open domestic offices, except in places closely concerned with foreign trade and foreign exchanges nor can it lend money for other purposes. To compensate for such obstacles to the acquisition of deposits, a specialised foreign exchange bank is permitted, by an amendment to the law in 1962, to issue debentures up to five times its capital and reserves, to provide a further means of raising yen funds.

(4) *Foreign-domiciled Banks*

Foreign-domiciled banks are branches, sub-branches or agencies in Japan of foreign banks. There are at present 18 of them, each of which requires a licence under the Banking Law; they can therefore accept deposits in yen and make advances in the same way as Japanese banks, but their principal business is in foreign exchange, all of them being authorised foreign exchange banks (old Class A). Foreign-domiciled banks played an important role immediately after the war, when the credit standing of Japanese banks was low. In recent years, however, their relative importance has been declining, as the foreign exchange business of Japanese banks has become better organised. Lately they have been actively engaged in providing untied (impact) loans to first-class firms in Japan, in lending to financial institutions and to the call loan market; this is in addition to their usual business, such as the rediscount of export bills purchased by Japanese banks, the confirmation of letters of credit issued by them, and the collection and acceptance of import bills.

(5) *Bankers' Associations and the Clearing Houses*

Commercial banks maintain clearing houses and have bankers' associations in Tokyo and other major cities. The associations are members of the Federation of Bankers' Associations of Japan. In addition, country banks organise the Local Bankers' Association. Trust banks and long-term credit banks are also members of the clearing houses and of the bankers' associations.

A. Clearing Houses

A clearing house is an organisation at which financial institutions in the same locality exchange and settle cheques and bills payable at other banks, interest coupons on public bonds and debentures, dividend warrants and so on at a fixed time every day. Clearing houses are either auxiliaries of the bankers' associations in various places or are independent organisations. At the end of 1970 there were in all 121 clearing houses, which are authorised by the Minister of Justice. Not only commercial, trust and long-term credit banks, but also mutual loans and savings banks, credit associations, and credit co-operatives participate in the clearings either directly or through their correspondent banks. In addition, offices of the Bank of Japan and principal post-offices are associate members of clearing houses and participate in clearings to collect government revenue paid into commercial banks, to claim payment of bills rediscounted and to exchange and settle government cheques, post-office cheques and postal money orders. The clearing balances of individual financial institutions are usually settled by transfers of current deposits with the Bank of Japan, but in places where there is no office of the Bank, settlements are effected through transfers of inter-bank deposits with a particular bank in the locality. Cheques and bills brought to the clearing houses are regarded as having been legally presented for payment. If such bills and cheques are dishonoured for reasons such as insufficiency of deposits, the drawers become liable to the closure of their banking accounts. It should be added that, since 1958, domestic exchange clearing departments have been opened in clearing houses at places where the bank has offices; these are therefore designated 'settlement offices'. Drafts on other banks are exchanged and settled there in the same way as bill-clearings.

B. The Federation of Bankers' Associations of Japan

The Federation of Bankers' Associations of Japan (hereafter referred to as 'the Federation') was established in September 1945 as the joint organisation of the bankers' associations. It represents all the banks. It undertakes research into financial and economic problems. It promotes liaison and co-operation among bankers' associations, and between banks and other economic organisations, while it makes contacts with, and makes representations and proposals to, governmental authorities. In addition, it undertakes various projects conducive to improvement and progress in banking in general. The Federation has been especially active in securing the voluntary regulation of various aspects of banking, for instance, by setting up the Committee on Bank Fund Adjustment. The more important aspects of such voluntary regulations will now be described.

(*a*) *Voluntary Regulation of Lending Rates.* Under the Temporary Money Rates Adjustment Law ceilings are placed upon interest rates on loans, advances and discounts of commercial, trust and long-term credit banks by the Policy Board of the Bank of Japan, after the Minister of Finance has consulted with the Interest Rates Adjustment Council (interest rates on lending for more than one year or in amounts below one million yen are not subject to the legal control, but there is a legal maximum for interest rates on discounts of or advances on export or import bills, whatever their maturity or face value). Since June 1955, however, the Federation by voluntary agreement among the members, has fixed a maximum rate lower than the legal ceiling, on discounts of or advances on ordinary bills — that is, bills other than those eligible for rediscount at the Bank or foreign trade bills. Further, in June 1958, when Bank rate was lowered, the Federation reduced its voluntary maximum rate by the same margin as Bank rate, although the legal ceilings under the Temporary Money Rates Adjustment Law were not altered. At the same time the Federation set voluntary maximum rates on discounts of, or on advances on, commercial bills eligible for rediscount at the Bank, and on foreign trade bills, for which such voluntary controls had not existed. In March 1959 the Federation introduced the system of the standard rate on the model of the prime rate in the United States: thereafter this became the leading rate for commercial banks' lending. As movements in the standard rate are geared to those of Bank rate the banks' lending rates as a whole have come in principle to move with Bank rate. The standard rate is applied to the discounts of and loans secured by bills of high creditworthiness, such as are eligible for rediscount at the Bank. Such discounts and advances account for about 10 per cent of total lending by banks.

Call rates had been subject to guidance by the Bank of Japan until August 1955, when it was discontinued. Then, in May 1957, the ceiling on day-to-day money rates under the Temporary Money Rates Adjustment Law was lifted. Accordingly, the Federation imposed voluntary ceilings on rates offered in the call loan market, but in September 1967 these, too, were abolished.

(*b*) *Voluntary Regulation on Deposits.* Interest rates on deposits with commercial and other banks are limited by ceilings under the Temporary Money Rates Adjustment Law and guidelines of the Bank of Japan, but keen competition for deposits has existed among banks, so that some of them at times offered special rates above the legal maximum. It has also been common for banks to require borrowers to maintain compensating balances. The administrative guidance of the Ministry of Finance, together with the self-discipline applied by the Federation, did, however, put an end to the practice of special deposit rates, which had been a problem since about 1951. As for compensating balances, the Federation decided in 1952 to eradicate the practice, and from time to time it has tried to enforce voluntary regulation. In particular, in June 1964, when the Diet and the Ministry of Finance requested the Federation to take effective steps in this matter, it adopted new measures of self-discipline, by which such deposits were to be reduced by half within six months and to zero after a year. Moreover, each bank office had to submit a report on the outstanding amount of such deposits. Thanks to these measures the practice is fast disappearing. Self-discipline was further strengthened in November 1966, when the members of the Federation agreed to reduce the ratio of compensating balances to lending as well as interest rates on them.

(*c*) *Restraint of Non-essential Accommodation and of Loans for the Finance of Fixed Investment.* The Federation set up the Voluntary Credit Restraint Committee in 1951, when the Bank of Japan and the Ministry of Finance asked it to secure the voluntary restriction of non-essential lending. The Committee established criteria for such lending and for long-term loans for fixed investment in plant and equipment, which banks were asked to observe. In December 1957 the Committee and the Committee on Lending and Investment were merged into the Committee on Bank Funds Adjustment, which checks non-essential lending and controls long-term loans for fixed investment. The Committee also co-ordinates bank investments and loans with Treasury investments and loans.

(*d*) *Joint Rules of Bank Lending.* From about 1963 it has been increasingly agreed that the past over-heating of the economy was aggravated by the absence of sound rules for the operations of business firms and of financial institutions, so that monetary policy lacked effectiveness. The Banking Credit Adjustment Council therefore requested the Federation to consider the establishment of sound rules of finance, which would contribute to stable growth in the future. Accordingly the Federation resolved in July 1965 to adopt the Joint Rules of Bank Lending. With the aim of normalising finance and of establishing sound principles of finance the Rules laid down a code for banks: it involved the improvement of the ratio of advances plus discounts to deposits; due regard to the financial ratios and financing programmes of business firms; rationalisation of conditions for advances; and steps to ensure the soundness of loans for fixed investment in plant and equipment and of loans to merchant firms.

(*e*) *Voluntary Restraint of Advertisement.* In order to prevent excessive advertising competition among banks the Federation established Measures for the Rationalisation of Advertisement in 1953; these imposed limits on the extent of advertisement and propaganda by banks. If banks seek to go beyond the restrictions they must first consult the Federation.

C. Local Bankers' Association

This association was organised in 1936, so that it is older than the Federation. While the Federation is a federal body of nationwide bankers' associations, the members of the Local Bankers' Association are individual banks. As country banks do not on the whole compete among themselves, this is a tight-knit body. It is active in organising the joint training of bank employees, handles collective receipts and payments of public money, organises co-operation in regard to various facilities, such as a common cheque system, underwrites the issue of government bonds and of government-guaranteed debentures and makes representations and proposals to the authorities concerned.

6. RELATIONS WITH THE BANK OF JAPAN

It goes without saying that with their crucial role in the financial system, particularly in credit-creation, commercial banks maintain a most intimate relationship with the Bank of Japan as the bankers' bank. First, the Bank receives money on deposit from, discounts bills for, makes advances to, and makes purchases and sales of securities with, commercial banks. The clearing of bills, cheques and domestic exchanges is another aspect of relationships between the Bank and the commercial banks (see p. 193). Second, the Bank operates its monetary policy through these transactions, the major target of which is therefore the commercial banks. Moreover, the officials of commercial banks are in close touch with the Bank, and the Presidents of some commercial banks are appointed as advisers of the Bank (consultants of the Governor). It is traditional for the governor to attend and to make a speech at the National Convention of Bankers. In various other ways the chief executives maintain close contacts and exchange opinion and information.

A further consideration is that by the letter of agreements with the Bank commercial banks are subject to inspection by it. This goes beyond mere examination of their operating conditions: it includes guidance by the central bank on the improvement and rationalisation of their management. The resultant insight into the state of banks' business is useful in enforcing monetary policy. Long-term credit and trust banks have comparable close relationships with the Bank.

7. SUPERVISION AND GUIDANCE BY THE GOVERNMENT

The Banking Law provides the legal foundation for supervision of banks by the government (Treasury). The current law contains detailed provisions relating to the establishment and organisation of banks, but it treats their actual running as the banks' own concern. The government, however, through the Treasury, regulates their managements in various ways, the principal objects of attention being as follows:

(1) *Approvals and Orders under the Banking Law*

The Banking Law provides that banking business cannot be undertaken without a licence from the Minister of Finance. Equally, the Minister's approval is required for amalgamations, closures, liquidations, increases in capital and the holding of more than one post by bank officials. The Minister may also ask banks at any time to submit reports on their business and accounts, and can inspect them. He can order a bank to close or impound its assets in a deposit office, or issue any other orders deemed necessary, should a bank commit illegal acts or the Minister considers that a deterioration in its financial condition necessitates such measures to protect depositors.

(2) *Regulation of establishment of Offices*

Under Article 6 of the Banking Law the opening of new banking offices is subject to approval by the Minister of Finance. Banks' business activities, including the taking of deposits, are closely affected by the number and distribution of offices, so that this ministerial power is a basis for government supervision and guidance of banks. The main purposes of this regulation are the promotion of savings, better banking services, the improvement and rationalisation of bank management and prevention of excessive competition among banks.

(3) *Administrative Guidance of Accounts of Banks*

The observance of sound banking is the main purpose of administrative guidance and is concerned with the protection of depositors. The Ministry of Finance advises banks by circulars from the Director of the Banking Bureau and by other means; on the ratio of advances plus discounts to deposits. It also gives advice on the remedying of the over-loans situation and the chronic dependence on borrowing from the Bank. To encourage banks to adhere to sound banking principles the Ministry directs them to lower this ratio to less than 80 per cent.

Liquidity Ratios. Here, the aim of the guidance is to raise the ratio to deposits of liquid assets (cash, deposits with other financial institutions, money in trust, call loans, loans to other financial institutions, securities and bank acceptances) to more than 30 per cent on average, in order to improve the composition of assets and to improve banking liquidity.

Ratio of Real Property for Business Use. In order to prevent locking up of funds and to normalise the composition of assets, the Ministry requests banks to keep the ratio of real assets for business use to owned capital in the narrower sense to less than 50 per cent, and to reduce it to 40 per cent in the near future.

Ratio of Net Worth. In order to protect depositors the ratio of net worth to outstanding deposits when balance sheets are made up must be more than 10 per cent.

Dividend Rates. The Ministry maintained the strict rule on the dividend rates until September 1970. The purpose was to limit as far as possible the outflow of profits through dividends and to increase banks' net worth. This rule was liberalised to some extent in September 1970, and banks can now pay out dividends up to 10 per cent. For those banks with excellent profit records dividend rates can go up to 15 per cent.

In addition to guidance on these points the Ministry instructs banks to observe reality, clarity and continuity in their accounts. Accurate accounts should be kept of profits and costs on the basis of the accrual principle. Further, all banks are expected to adopt the same accounting methods in providing for depreciation and other reserves. Since the half-year ending September 1967 a unified standard of accounting has been adopted by all the banks. Accordingly, a year later the Ministry discontinued its guidance on the ratio of banks' current expenses to their current income (since the fiscal year 1952, the guidance had been that the ratio should be less than 78 per cent); the purpose of this was to ensure sound management and to reinforce banks' internal reserves.

CHAPTER 14

LONG-TERM CREDIT BANKS

I. SURVEY OF LONG-TERM FINANCE

If we leave internal reserves out of account, business firms raise long-term funds by the three methods of the issue of new shares, the issue of debentures and by long-term borrowing. As Table 14.1 indicates, the ratio of long-term borrowing to total fund sraised externally is very high in Japan. Long-term funds can be borrowed from various financial institutions since most of them engage in both short-term and long-term finance. Private financial institutions, particularly long-term credit banks established to facilitate long-term finance, play a dominant role in this field. Recently, however, trust banks, mutual loans and savings banks and credit associations have increased in importance as suppliers of long-term funds. The rise in the relative weight of life insurance companies also commands attention. As for financial institutions outside the private sector, long-term finance by Treasury funds contributed substantially to the reconstruction of the Japanese economy, but, as will be explained later (Chapter 22), its relative importance has gradually declined with the completion of reconstruction. In recent years Treasury funds have come in principle to play a role complementary to that of private finance, although an element of competition between them remains. The acquisition of funds through share and debenture issues acquired temporary importance between 1955 and 1964, but in recent years with stagnation in securities markets their relative significance has considerably declined.

The relative shares of various sources of funds for fixed investment in plant and equipment fluctuate cyclically. Tables 14.1 and 14.2 show that in easy-money periods there is an increase in the relative proportions of long-term funds borrowed from long-term credit banks together with those raised by the issue of industrial debentures, while the relative weight of funds borrowed from city banks falls. The reverse movement is observable in tight-money periods. The reason for

TABLE 14.1

Composition of Supply (Net Increase) of Industrial Equipment Funds

(percentages)

Years	*1960*	*1962*	*1964*	*1966*	*1968*	*1969*	*1970*
WINGS							
Private Financial Institutions							
Banking Accounts of All Banks	21·2	16·0	19·9	19·5	20·6	25·2	24·7
(of which Long-term Credit Banks)	(12·8)	(9·5)	(12·1)	(11·0)	(10·4)	(10·4)	(13·7)
Trust Accounts of All Banks	9·8	10·9	11·8	8·2	14·6	12·1	11·4
Mutual Loans and Savings Banks	4·3	3·9	1·0	4·3	2·4	2·8	2·2
Credit Associations	1·8	2·0	2·6	7·5	3·9	5·0	3·6
Others	11·9	12·5	15·4	16·2	24·9	22·6	25·7
Total (A)	49·0	45·3	50·7	55·7	66·4	67·7	67·6
Government Funds							
Government Financial Institutions	8·7	9·2	10·2	15·0	14·4	11·3	10·5
Special Accounts for Financial Purposes	4·3	3·3	3·1	4·6	3·3	2·4	1·8
Total (B)	13·0	12·5	13·3	19·6	17·7	13·7	12·3
Total Borrowings (A+B)	62·0	57·8	64·0	75·3	84·1	81·4	79·9
STOCKS AND SHARES	26·9	34·6	28·7	12·6	11·5	12·2	13·8
INDUSTRIAL DEBENTURES	11·1	7·6	7·3	12·1	4·4	6·4	6·3
Grand Total	100·0	100·0	100·0	100·0	100·0	100·0	100·0

NOTE: The item 'Trust Banks' is the sum of banking accounts and trust accounts of trust banks.

SOURCE: Bank of Japan, *Economic Statistics Annual.*

the cyclical behaviour is that financial institutions, particularly city banks, take up a substantial proportion of new debenture issues. In tight-money periods financial institutions, particularly city banks, are less able to purchase new debentures. The new issue market rapidly shrinks and the demand for funds for fixed investment converges on city banks; the principal borrowers from these are big firms, which under other

TABLE 14.2

Composition of Net Increase in Loans of All Banks for the Finance of Fixed Investment in Plant and Equipment

(percentages)

Years	*1958*	*1959*	*1960*	*1961*	*1962*	*1963*	*1964*	*1965*	*1966*	*1967*	*1968*	*1969*	*1970*
City Banks	17·9	7·4	17·9	19·7	18·0	13·9	12·7	10·9	9·1	15·0	21·7	28·5	24·9
Country Banks	4·5	8·9	8·9	10·6	7·8	12·4	11·2	10·7	28·1	20·5	16·5	15·6	16·2
Long-term Credit Banks	50·6	47·8	41·3	36·1	34·6	32·3	37·3	37·9	35·3	30·3	24·5	24·8	26·3
Trust Banks	27·0	35·9	31·9	33·6	39·6	41·4	38·8	40·5	27·5	34·2	37·3	31·1	32·7
Total	100·0	100·0	100·0	100·0	100·0	100·0	100·0	100·0	100·0	100·0	100·0	100·0	100·0

NOTE: The item 'Trust Banks' is the sum of banking accounts and trust accounts of trust banks.

SOURCE: Bank of Japan, *Economic Statistics Annual*.

circumstances might issue industrial debentures. The loans of long-term credit banks acquire importance in easy-money periods, because their issues of bank debentures are more easily saleable then, while in tight-money periods they suffer from shortage of resources, so that their relative importance declines. This structure in the supply of funds for fixed investment in plant and equipment is responsible for cyclical variations in their composition.

2. CHARACTERISTICS AND SUMMARY

Three special banks which had played important parts in long-term finance in pre-war years, namely, the Industrial Bank of Japan, the Hypothec Bank of Japan, and the Hokkaido Colonial Bank, were exempted from closure by the General Headquarters of the Allied Forces after the war. The post-war inflation, however, coupled with the discontinuance by the Deposit Bureau of the Ministry of Finance in January 1946 of purchases of their debentures, was a severe blow to their ability to raise funds. They were also hard hit by the discontinuance of war-time compensation. Thus, their operations were greatly circumscribed in the immediate post-war years. At that time, General Headquarters were of opinion that long-term funds should be raised in the capital market; their policy was therefore to abolish these special banks, the resources of which chiefly depended upon debenture issues and the main function of which was long-term finance. Thus, the Hypothec Bank of Japan and the Hokkaido Colonial Bank were converted into commercial banks.[1] In 1949 the Reconstruction Finance Bank, which had been virtually the sole supplier of long-term funds, ceased making new loans. Nevertheless, the capital market could hardly be expected to provide the entire volume of long-term funds required. In 1950, therefore, when the system of special banks was abolished (so that the Industrial Bank of Japan was also converted into a commercial bank), the Law Concerning Debenture Issues of Banks was promulgated, in order to facilitate the supply of long-term funds; under this law all banks were authorised to issue debentures under certain conditions.

[1] As the Nippon Kangyo Bank and Hokkaido Takushoku Bank respectively.

Bank debentures were issued by the Nippon Kangyo Bank, the Industrial Bank of Japan, the Hokkaido Takushoku Bank, the Central Co-operative Bank of Agriculture and Forestry, the Central Bank for Commercial and Industrial Co-operatives and the Bank of Tokyo (once only). There was, however, a strong feeling that such a state of affairs would reduce the distinction between long-term and short-term financial markets. A thorough examination of the system of long-term finance thus became desirable, and the government decided to foster specialised long-term financial institutions in order to establish a more orderly system of long-term finance. After consultation with the Temporary Financial System Council set up at the end of 1951, the Debenture Issues Law, mentioned above, was repealed and replaced by the Long-term Credit Banks Law.

Long-term credit banks differ from the pre-war special banks in that they are purely private financial institutions under a comprehensive law, so that their legal status is similar to that of banks under the Banking Law, whereas the old banks had been established under special laws. The main function of long-term credit banks is, needless to say, to make long-term loans. They were established primarily to separate long-term from short-term lending and thus to ease the demands on commercial banks. They can issue debentures to raise the long-term funds required for such lending, but they are prohibited from receiving deposits except from specific customers. Thus, the sources of their funds differ markedly from those of commercial banks.

There are at present three long-term credit banks: the Industrial Bank of Japan, the Long-term Credit Bank of Japan and the Nippon Fudosan Bank; the first two were established in December 1952 and the third in April 1957. These banks have far fewer offices than commercial banks because of the nature of their business, but they operate on a nationwide scale. The first two bank mainly for big firms, while the last-mentioned deals chiefly with small enterprises.

Both the resources and the outstanding amount of loans of these banks have greatly increased thanks to the high growth rate of the Japanese economy (see Table 14.3). In particular the vigorous demand for funds for fixed investment in plant and equipment, in spite of the retarded development of the capital market, was favourable to their growth. In recent years, however, great changes have developed in the conditions under which they obtain and employ their funds: for instance, the self-financing potential of business firms has been reinforced, bond issues by the government have brought about easier trends in industrial finance and city banks have reduced their subscriptions for bank debentures. Thus, a focal point in recent discussions about reorganisation of the financial system has been the proper place of long-term credit banks in the system.

TABLE 14.3

Resources and (Outstanding) Lending of Long-term Credit Banks

(hundred million yen)

End of Year	*Deposits and Outstanding Debentures*			*Loans, Advances and Discounts*		
	Long-term Credit Banks (A)	*All Banks* (B)	(A)/(B)	*Long-term Credit Banks* (A)	*All Banks* (B)	(A)/(B)
			%			%
1955	3,326	40,104	8·3	3,240	31,958	10·1
1956	3,847	50,976	7·5	3,799	40,662	9·3
1957	4,585	59,023	7·8	4,673	50,244	9·3
1958	6,036	70,146	8·6	6,027	58,129	10·4
1959	7,668	80,991	9·5	7,488	68,028	11·0
1960	9,663	97,522	9·9	9,343	81,826	11·4
1961	11,625	113,871	10·2	11,090	97,701	11·4
1962	13,786	133,759	10·3	12,916	114,946	11·2
1963	16,990	171,930	9·9	15,720	145,626	10·8
1964	20,272	196,931	10·3	18,849	168,297	11·2
1965	25,038	229,600	10·9	22,483	192,179	11·7
1966	30,136	265,455	11·4	26,039	220,460	11·8
1967	35,733	299,241	11·9	30,696	253,230	12·1
1968	40,894	347,235	11·8	34,858	290,328	12·0
1969	47,149	402,749	11·7	40,504	337,844	12·0
1970	55,358	461,169	12·0	47,293	394,793	12·0

NOTE: The item 'All Banks' comprises only the banking accounts of all banks.

SOURCE: Bank of Japan, *Economic Statistics Annual*.

3. BUSINESS

(1) *Issue of Debentures*

The principal source of funds of long-term credit banks, it has been noted, is the issue of bank debentures. They are authorised to issue them up to twenty times the sum of their capital and reserves.[1] Commercial law provides that the outstanding amount of debentures of a joint-stock company cannot exceed the sum of its capital and reserves, but, as long-term credit banks rely on debenture issues as their chief source of funds, the maximum limit of their issues is far greater than that for ordinary companies.

Long-term credit banks issue interest-bearing debentures (maturity of five years) and discount debentures (one year). In principle, they are bearer debentures, but they may be registered at the request of subscribers or holders. Before the issue of new debentures the banks must submit a report to the Minister of Finance stating the amount and the terms of issue. At the end of 1969 the amount of debentures outstanding was 4063·6 billion yen; 3026·3 billion of these were interest-bearing and 1037·3 billion were discount debentures. They are equivalent to 11 per cent of the total amount of deposits outstanding at all banks.

Banks other than long-term credit banks also issue debentures: Agriculture and Forestry Debentures are issued by the Central Co-operative Bank of Agriculture and Forestry, Commerce and Industry Debentures are issued by the Central Bank for Commercial and Industrial Co-operatives, and the Bank of Tokyo has issued debentures. Newly issued interest-bearing debentures are purchased largely by commercial banks, particularly city banks. Discount debentures are issued directly by the banks concerned and the bulk is sold to individual investors through securities companies (see Table 14.4). The volume of bank debentures to be issued is decided by mutual agreement among the parties concerned. The issuing terms are identical for all

[1] For newly established long-term credit banks (i.e. banks other than those which were in existence when the Long-term Credit Banks Law was promulgated and which were converted into long-term credit banks at the time), the limit is thirty times the sum of capital and reserves for five years after their establishment.

TABLE 14.4

Subscriptions for Bank Debentures (during 1970)

(hundred million yen)

	Interest-bearing Debentures		*Discount Debentures*		*Total*	
	Amounts	*Composition* %	*Amounts*	*Composition* %	*Amounts*	*Composition* %
City Banks	3,481	34·1			3,481	12·5
Country Banks	1,074	10·5			1,074	3·9
Trust Banks	30	0·3			30	0·1
Insurance Companies	488	4·8	1	0	489	1·8
Central Co-operative Bank of Agriculture and Forestry, Agricultural Co-operatives	34	0·3	5	0	39	0·1
Credit Associations	754	7·4			754	2·7
Mutual Loans and Savings Banks	1,012	9·9			1,012	3·6
Individuals and Others	3,330	32·7	17,627	100·0	20,957	75·3
Total	10,203	100·0	17,633	100·0	27,836	100·0
Trust Fund Bureau	338		1,401		1,739	
Post Office Life Insurance and Postal Annuity	74		28		102	
Grand Total	10,615		19,062		29,677	
(of which Debentures of Long-term Credit Banks)	(8,285)		(12,368)		(20,653)	

SOURCE: The Industrial Bank of Japan, *Monthly Statistics of Bonds and Debentures.*

kinds of bank debentures, and are infrequently altered, although they are liable to change with material changes in financial conditions. The current terms of issue are shown in Table 14.5 (these have been current since March 1970 for interest-bearing debentures and since May 1970 for discount debentures).

(2) *Deposits*

Certain restrictions are imposed upon the taking of deposits by long-term credit banks. They can accept deposits only from the government, local authorities, borrowers, companies which have entrusted the business of debenture issue to them, those for whom the banks provide safe custody of property, and exchange

TABLE 14.5

Terms of Issue of Bank Debentures

	Interest-bearing Debentures[a]	*Discount Debentures*
Nominal Yield	7·5%	5·83%
Issue Price	99·50 yen	94·15 yen
Maturities	5 years	1 year
Subscribers' Yield	7·638%	6·213%

[a] Other than Bank of Tokyo Debentures.

SOURCE: Bank of Japan.

correspondents. Thus, they cannot take deposits from the general public. This limitation is justified on several grounds: short-term money, such as deposits, is by nature an inappropriate source of funds for long-term credit business; the traditional principles of protection for depositors require that the general public, ignorant of the business of such banks, should be prevented from making deposits with them lest they be involved thereby in unexpected losses; and competition for deposits with commercial banks should be avoided, so that the two types of banks may operate on a complementary basis. The outstanding amount of deposits with long-term credit banks is therefore not large, but they are indispensable for their business activities, for instance, in the administration of credits.

(3) *Lending*

On the asset side the principal business of long-term credit banks is the provision of funds for fixed investment in plant and equipment, and for long-term working funds, the discount of bills, and the guarantee of debts and the acceptance of bills. Thus, they can engage in the supply of short-term working funds (with maturities of less than six months) as a subsidiary activity, although their main function is the provision of long-term funds for fixed investment and of long-term working funds. There is, however, a condition that short-term lending should not exceed the amount of deposits. They are also permitted to lend long-term funds (of longer maturities than six months) for non-business purposes, such as housing loans and consumer loans on the security of real estate.

By their nature long-term credit banks have to pay particular attention to the management of securities. The Long-term Credit Banks Law specifically provides that 'A long-term credit bank shall give particular consideration to ensuring the repayment of debts arising from long-term loans by such means as demanding sound security and/or allowing the debtors to pay in instalments'. (Article 7.)

The outstanding loans of long-term credit banks, it has been noted, increased annually at a steady pace from their foundation, so that their existence has been amply justified (Table 14.3). Since 1964, however, there have been signs of a slowing down of the rate of increase. This is largely due to three circumstances. From 1962 to 1965 the rate of increase in fixed investment in plant and equipment stagnated; since 1966 the issue of government bonds has eased business finance, and has tended to reinforce the self-financing capacity of business firms; and commercial banks have reduced their take-up of newly issued bank debentures.

By use of funds loans for fixed investment in plant and equipment grew rapidly until 1964, but subsequently their rate of increase has dropped. In contrast it is notable that lending to provide working funds has expanded considerably since then. (Table 14.6.)

By industry manufacturing absorbs the bulk of long-term credit banks' loans for both fixed investment and for working capital. (Table 14.7.) The relative weight of loans to basic industries, such as iron and steel and electricity, has remained substantial, but that of loans to new industries, such as petrochemicals and automobiles, has grown in step with their development. Thus, long-term credit banks play an important role in supplying funds for fixed investment in plant and equipment, as is evident from the proportion that their loans bear to the total of such loans by all banks.

In most cases the lending rates of long-term credit banks are not subject to regulation under the Temporary Money Rates Adjustment Law, by which interest rates on lending for periods of more than one year are exempted from its provisions.

(hundred million yen)

Year-Ends	Loans, Advances and Discounts of Long-term Credit Banks: Loans for Fixed Investment in Plant and Equipment	Rate of Increase	Loans for Working Capital	Rate of Increase	Total	Rate of Increase	Proportions to and Total of Loans, Advances and Discounts of All Banks: Loans for Fixed Investment in Plant and Equipment	Loans for Working Capital	Total
		%		%		%	%	%	%
1953	1,354	—	781	—	2,135	—	45·2	3·3	8·0
1954	1,901	40·4	833	6·7	2,735	28·1	52·2	3·3	9·4
1955	2,327	22·4	913	9·6	3,240	18·5	60·3	3·3	10·2
1956	2,896	24·5	902	−1·2	3,798	17·2	57·2	2·5	9·4
1957	3,759	29·8	914	1·3	4,673	23·0	53·3	2·1	9·4
1958	4,949	31·7	1,077	17·8	6,027	29·0	56·4	2·2	10·5
1959	6,287	27·0	1,200	11·4	7,488	24·2	59·5	2·1	11·1
1960	8,020	27·6	1,322	10·2	9,342	24·8	59·6	2·0	11·5
1961	9,671	20·6	1,418	7·3	11,090	18·7	58·6	1·8	11·4
1962	11,347	17·3	1,567	10·5	12,915	16·5	58·4	1·7	11·3
1963	13,819	21·8	1,900	21·3	15,720	21·7	57·5	1·6	10·9
1964	16,397	18·7	2,450	28·9	18,847	19·9	57·7	1·8	11·3
1965	19,231	17·3	3,251	32·7	22,482	19·3	58·4	2·1	11·8
1966	21,311	10·8	4,727	45·4	26,038	15·8	57·3	2·6	11·9
1967	24,576	15·3	6,118	29·4	30,694	17·9	55·4	3·0	12·2
1968	28,101	14·3	6,750	10·3	34,851	13·5	52·5	2·9	12·1
1969	32,975	17·3	7,526	11·5	40,501	16·2	49·1	2·8	12·1
1970	39,078	18·5	8,210	9·1	47,288	16·8	46·9	2·7	12·1

NOTES:

1. Do not include overdrafts.
2. Loans, Advances and Discounts of All Banks are those on the banking accounts only.

SOURCE: Bank of Japan, *Economic Statistics Annual*.

TABLE 14·7

Outstanding Loans, Advances and Discounts of Long-term Credit Banks (end of 1970)

(hundred million yen)

	Loans and Advances for Fixed Investment in Plant and Equipment			*Loans for Working Capital*		*Total*		
	Outstanding Amounts	*Com-position*	*Proportion to Totals of All Banks*	*Outstanding Amounts*	*Com-position*	*Outstanding Amounts*	*Com-position*	*Proportion to Totals of All Banks*
Manufacturing	22,792	58·4	62·2	3,238	39·5	26,030	55·1	14·9
(of which Textiles)	(1,556)	(4·0)	(59·9)	(316)	(3·8)	(1,872)	(4·0)	(9·2)
(„ „ Chemical and Allied)	(4,409)	(11·3)	(63·6)	(279)	(3·4)	(4,688)	(9·9)	(21·7)
(„ „ Iron and Steel)	(4,436)	(11·4)	(72·2)	(386)	(4·7)	(4,822)	(10·2)	(27·0)
(„ „ Machinery)	(960)	(2·5)	(56·1)	(332)	(4·0)	(1,292)	(2·7)	(8·7)
(„ „ Electrical Machinery, Equipment and Supplies)	(1,449)	(3·7)	(73·7)	(372)	(4·5)	(1,821)	(3·9)	(11·1)
(of which Transportation Equipment)	(2,640)	(6·8)	(70·7)	(774)	(9·4)	(3,414)	(7·2)	(16·3)
Agriculture, Forestry and Fisheries	360	0·9	31·5	55	0·7	415	0·9	10·5
Mining	390	1·0	67·8	48	0·6	438	0·9	16·1
(of which Metals)	(70)	(0·1)	(73·7)	(5)	(0)	(75)	(0·2)	(8·7)
(„ „ Coal)	(117)	(0·3)	(81·8)	(26)	(0·3)	(143)	(0·3)	(15·9)
Construction	641	1·6	41·1	421	5·1	1,062	2·2	5·7
Wholesale and Retail Trade	3,018	7·7	30·0	1,597	19·4	4,615	9·8	4·1
Transport and Communications	4,353	11·2	55·1	186	2·3	4,539	9·6	29·3
(of which Shipping)	(1,464)	(3·7)	(58·9)	(66)	(0·8)	(1,530)	(3·2)	(42·1)
Electricity, Gas and Water	3,067	7·8	70·5	11	0·1	3,078	6·5	55·7
(of which Electricity)	(2,859)	(7·3)	(72·3)	(9)	(0·1)	(2,868)	(6·1)	(60·8)
Others	4,458	11·4	61·6	2,655	32·3	7,112	15·0	12·3
Total	39,079	100·0	46·9	8,211	100·0	47,289	100·0	12·1

However, interest rates on loans to the electrical industry and to the shipping industry to finance planned shipbuilding have been set voluntarily by these long-term credit banks at 8·5 per cent. These are *de facto* standard rates for long-term loans of ordinary banks.

(4) *Securities Business*

Long-term credit banks are authorised to engage in the following business, on condition that they do not interfere with the business of securities dealers under the Securities Transaction Law:

(*a*) Acting as trustee for the issue of government and local bonds, industrial debentures, etc.
(*b*) Acting as trustee for mortgages of secured debentures.
(*c*) Registration of debentures under the Debentures Registration Law.
(*d*) Servicing of debentures, receiving deposits of subscription money for new shares, acting as agents for payment of dividends on shares and other agency business.
(*e*) Subscription for, purchase of, and taking up of securities (the taking up of newly issued debentures and shares for the purpose of resale is prohibited).

The amount of such securities business handled by long-term credit banks varies from bank to bank, but they figure prominently as trustees and registration agents of debentures. This business can be outlined briefly.

Table 14.8 shows the number of trusteeships (number of issuers) of bonds and debentures. Long-term credit banks hold the second biggest share after that of city banks, but as the former are far fewer than the latter their voice in the issue market is relatively strong. Further, in Japan most bonds and debentures are registered and the actual documents are rarely made out; registration is usually made at the trustee bank (a single or representative bank), and in this way, too, long-term credit banks play a significant role.

TABLE 14.8

Number of Bond and Debenture Issues by Trustee (Single or Representative)

	Government-guaranteed Debentures	*Local Bonds*	*Industrial Debentures*	*Total*
Long-term Credit Banks	9	1	66	76
City Banks	—	7	234	241
Country Banks	—	1	—	1
Trust Banks	—	—	12	12
Total	9	9	312	330

NOTE: Only issues for public subscription are listed. (End of September 1970.)

SOURCE: Bond Underwriters' Association, *Directory of Bonds and Debentures.*

(5) *Other Business*

Long-term credit banks can also engage in ancillary business, such as exchange transactions and safe deposit, just like commercial banks. Exchange business includes both domestic and foreign transactions.

4. COMPOSITION OF ASSETS AND LIABILITIES: PROFIT AND LOSS

The nature of the business of long-term credit banks reflects itself in the composition of their assets and liabilities. Table 14.9 shows their principal accounting items at the end of 1958 and 1966–9. Some prominent features of their assets and liabilities will now be discussed.

(1) *Composition of Liabilities*

The outstanding amount of debentures, the issues of which are the principal source of funds for long-term credit banks, account for more than 70 per cent of their total liabilities. This corresponds roughly with the proportion of deposits to total liabilities of commercial banks; in contrast, deposits in long-term credit banks are less than 10 per cent of the total.

TABLE 14.9

Principal Accounts of Long-term Credit Banks

(hundred million yen)

Year-ends	*1958*		*1966*		*1967*		*1968*		*1969*		*1970*	
		Composition %		*Composition* %		*Composition* %		*Composition* %		*Composition* %		*Composition* %
ASSETS												
Loans, Advances and Discounts	6,028	81·0	26,039	74·1	30,696	74·4	34,858	73·5	40,504	73·6	47,293	72·2
Securities	457	6·1	4,487	12·8	5,152	12·5	5,753	12·1	6,418	11·7	7,133	10·9
Cash and Deposits with Other Financial Institutions	226	3·0	1,302	3·7	1,542	3·7	2,703	5·7	2,104	3·8	2,478	3·8
Call Loans	48	0·6	321	0·9	607	1·5	506	1·1	523	1·0	427	0·7
Other	684	9·3	3,010	8·5	3,271	7·9	3,622	7·6	5,463	9·9	8,149	12·4
Total	7,443	100·0	35,159	100·0	41,268	100·0	47,442	100·0	55,012	100·0	65,480	100·0
LIABILITIES												
Deposits	735	9·9	3,167	9·0	3,900	9·4	4,676	9·9	6,090	11·1	8,092	12·4
Outstanding Debentures	5,302	71·2	26,969	76·7	31,833	77·1	36,218	76·3	41,059	74·6	47,266	72·2
Borrowings from the Bank of Japan	58	0·8	313	0·9	308	0·8	309	0·7	313	0·6	486	0·7
Borrowings from other Sources	87	1·2	51	0·2	151	0·4	185	0·4	210	0·4	168	0·3
Call Money	264	3·5	73	0·2	—	—	—	—	80	0·2	—	—
Capital	111	1·5	470	1·3	520	1·3	520	1·1	700	1·3	740	1·1
Reserves and Surpluses	216	2·9	1,019	2·9	1,173	2·8	1,313	2·8	1,490	2·7	1,673	2·6
Other	670	9·0	3,097	8·8	3,383	8·2	4,221	8·8	5,070	9·1	7,055	10·7

SOURCE: Bank of Japan, *Economic Statistics Annual.*

(2) *Composition of Assets*

In the second half of the 1950s loans, advances and discounts of long-term credit banks accounted for more than 80 per cent of their total assets, but recently the ratio has fallen slightly to 74 per cent. The ratio of cash, deposits with other financial institutions and call loans to the total of assets is exceedingly low. This is due partly to the fact that they do not need so much reserve for payment because deposits are a small fraction of their liabilities, and partly to the fact that they do not have large amounts of bills and cheques on hand. The ratio of securities investments is also lower than in the case of commercial banks, but is increasing; this reflects the expansion of the issue market.

(3) *Profit and Loss*

The biggest source of income for long-term credit banks is interest on loans, while the bulk of their expenses consists of interest on their debentures. This is only to be expected from the nature of their business (Table 14.10).

As they raise money chiefly by the issue of debentures the cost of their funds is high, but the yield from the employment of funds is also high, because most of their loans are long-term. Another characteristic is that their expenses ratio is much lower than that of commercial banks (see Table 14.11); as they have fewer offices and employees in relation to their resources, the proportion of personnel expenses is lower.

TABLE 14.10

Income and Expenditure of Long-term Credit Banks (March 1970 to September 1970)

(hundred million yen)

	Current Income			Current Expenditure	
		Composition			Composition
		%			%
Income from Loans, Advances and Discounts	1,847	84·4	Interest on Deposits and Debentures	1,665	80·5
Interest on Call Loans	27	1·2	Interest on Borrowing and Call Money	18	0·9
Income from Investments in Securities	242	11·1	Expenses	259	12·5
Other	73	3·3	Other	127	6·1
Total	2,189	100·0	Total	2,069	100·0

SOURCE: Bank of Japan.

TABLE 14.11

Cost of Funds (March 1970 to September 1970)

(percentages, annual return)

	Interest Rate on Deposits[a]	Rate of Expenses			Cost of Deposits[a] (A)	Interest Rates on Loans, Advances, Discounts, Call Loans and Securities Investments (B)	Margin (A) – (B)
			Rate of Personnel Expenses	Rate of Supplies Expenses			
Long-term Credit Banks	6·81	1·06	0·26	0·72	7·87	8·26	0·39
Trust Banks	6·34	1·37	0·73	0·58	7·71	8·18	0·47
City Banks	4·19	2·08	1·16	0·80	6·27	7·55	1·28
Country Banks	4·13	2·03	1·30	0·65	6·16	7·91	1·75

[a] Deposits here include outstanding debentures and principal of trusts.

SOURCE: Bank of Japan.

CHAPTER 15

TRUST BANKS

I. DEVELOPMENT AND CHARACTERISTICS OF TRUSTS

Trust is defined in the Trust Law as the transfer or other acts of disposal of the title to property from the truster to the trustee, who is entrusted with administration of the property for certain specified objectives on behalf of a designated beneficiary (the truster himself or a third party). Trust companies in themselves, therefore, are essentially financial intermediaries and do not have the credit-creating capacity of commercial banks.

The significant development of modern trust business in Japan began with the promulgation of the Trust Law and of the Trust Business Law in 1922. By the 1930s trust companies under the Trust Business Law had become important financial institutions, the principal resources of which were money in trust. Thereafter, war-time financial control led to amalgamations and liquidations, until only seven specialised trust companies (of which one was an investment trust company) were left at the end of 1945. In addition, there were 11 commercial banks, which had absorbed trust companies at around the end of hostilities and which were thus engaged in trust business as a sideline.

The post-war runaway inflation dealt a particularly heavy blow to trust companies. Money in trust, which is a form of long-term savings, continued to decrease until 1948, so that specialised trust companies faced serious difficulties. To ease this situation the General Headquarters of the Allied Forces suggested that they might engage in banking as well. Accordingly, six companies were converted into banks under the Banking Law to operate both trust and banking business. Their name was changed to 'trust banks'[1] and they commenced

[1] In the legal code there is no such term as 'trust banks'. In theory the present trust banks are ordinary banks under the Banking Law, which engage in trust

operation under the new system from the summer of 1948. (The one remaining trust company was converted into a securities company.) Since then their resources, which had been decreasing, began to recover. The increase was principally due to their attraction of deposits. Within two years of the conversion the amount of deposits exceeded that of money in trust. Thus, they made a fresh start under favourable conditions.

Thereafter, with the stabilisation of the value of money, their trust departments also resumed activity. Moreover, new kinds of trust business were developed; they became trustees of the securities investment trusts, which were restarted in 1951, while loans trusts were commenced in 1952. Loan trusts marked an epoch in their development. In 1957, five years after the inception of business, the outstanding amount of loan trusts exceeded that of money in trust. Thereafter, between 1955 and 1964, they grew annually by 30 to 40 per cent. From 1965 the pace slackened, but the amount outstanding at the end of 1969 was 4·1 times that of money in trust, and represented 60 per cent of the total resources of all trust banks on both banking and trust accounts (i.e. the sum of deposits, principal of funds in trust, principal of loan trusts and principal of pension trusts). Thus, thanks mainly to the growth of loan trusts, trust banks were enabled to regain their former position as long-term financial institutions.

In the meantime the government has adopted the policy of separating banking from trust business in order to promote specialisation in the various fields of finance. Since December 1954 it has pursued this objective through administrative supervision. The six trust banks have been divided into two groups: four were to become specialised trust banks with trust business as their main activity, while the remaining two were eventually to become ordinary banks with banking as their principal business. Two groups were accorded different treatment by the government in its supervision of their trust business and in its regulation of their offices.

Furthermore, from 1959, city banks engaged in trust business

---

business under the Law in regard to Ordinary Banks, etc. Engaging in Saving Banks Business and/or Trust Business. Trust business is regulated by the Trust Law and by the Trust Business Law, but there is at present no trust company under the latter law.

began to hive off their trust departments, which amalgamated either among themselves or with the trust departments of trust banks. By this process two new specialised trust banks have been created. Thus, at present, there is only one city bank with a trust department, the Daiwa Bank. There are, at present, seven specialised trust banks (Mitsubishi, Mitsui, Sumitomo, Yasuda, Toyo, Chuo and Nippon). Seven country banks used to engage in trust business, but all closed their trust accounts between 1956 and 1966. Thus, only eight banks are now engaged in trust business.[1]

Thus, with the stabilisation of the economy and the growth of personal incomes, the foundations of trust banks have been consolidated, while new fields have been opened to them. As a result, the amount of funds in trust[2] has come in recent years to represent a considerable proportion of the total resources of all financial institutions. At the end of 1969, the ratio of the resources of trust banks to those of all banks was 13 per cent, and exceeded that of long-term credit banks, which was 10 per cent. The ratio is roughly the same as in pre-war years, when trust development was at its peak.

The characteristics of trust business in Japan are as follows:

First, trusts are a form of long-term financial institution. Particularly since the expansion of 1955–64, they have played an important role in long-term finance. For instance, the relative share of trust accounts in the new supply (net increase) of funds for fixed investment in industrial plant and equipment is quite close to that of long-term credit banks (see Table 14.1, p. 202). As institutional investors in bonds, debentures and shares, however, they do not stand out, if we exclude the securities investment trusts.[3]

Second, in modern Japan trusts function as institutions

[1] Trust of mortgage debentures under the Mortgage Debenture Trust Law is an exception to this. As will be explained later (pp. 229–30), ordinary city banks handle this business.

[2] The sum of the trust accounts of the eight trust banks, whether specialised or otherwise, is usually termed 'Trust Accounts of All Banks', but this includes trusts, which have nothing to do with the flow of funds. Therefore, only the outstanding amounts of money in trust, loan trusts and pension trusts are used as indices of the resources of trusts.

[3] Securities investment trusts are managed by securities dealers, who are trusters. All the initiative and responsibility rest with them. Trust banks, who are trustees, handle only the receipts and disbursements.

for the public's savings. Pre-war trust companies resembled agencies for managing the assets of the well-to-do, but the war brought about profound changes: inflation wiped out the pre-war propertied class. Nowadays, their important customers are non-profit-making organisations, such as mutual benefit associations, and the general public. Needless to say, this reflects the redistribution of income and the rise in income levels. A contributory reason is that the backward state of the capital market caused the public to turn to trusts as an outlet for their savings. At the same time the trust banks adapted themselves to the realities of the post-war world by subdividing the minimum units of loan trusts and by making beneficiary certificates encashable before maturity. Such a profound transformation compared with the pre-war situation poses one of the most difficult problems in establishing a clear demarcation between various kinds of financial institutions.

2. BUSINESS

Trust banks are concurrently engaged in both trust and banking business. As these differ in nature, trust banks must segregate the two types of accounts, so that trust banks and city banks engaged in trust have accounts for banking and for trust respectively.

The banking business of trust banks is the same as that of ordinary commercial banks, but 'trust' includes extremely diverse types of business, a classified list of which is shown in the accompanying table (Table 15.1) 'Survey of Trust Business'. Some explanation of the principal kinds is desirable.

(1) *Money Trusts*

In money trusts the trusted property is money. This includes money in trusts, loan trusts, pension trusts, securities investment trusts and money trusts other than money in trust.

A. Money in Trust

Money is accepted as trusted property, and the beneficiary receives earnings from its employment during the trust period, while the principal is returned to him at the end of the period.

According to the method of operation, there are three categories: designated money in trust, specified money in trust, and money in trust without designation or specification.

(A) DESIGNATED MONEY IN TRUST. Most of the money in trust belongs to this category. When a trust contract is drawn up the trusters give general instructions on the employment of funds, but the details are left to the discretion of the trust banks. In practice, the banks themselves decide upon the plan of employment, with the agreement of the trusters, which involves two types of operation, joint and unit.

(*a*) *Joint Operation* (*Designated 'Joint'*). In this case trust banks employ jointly the money trusted by a number of trustors and the yields are distributed in proportion to the amounts entrusted. Trust banks are authorised to make contracts guaranteeing the principal or a minimum dividend rate. 'Money in trust with special clause' is a trust to which a special contract is attached at the truster's request: there are various kinds of special contracts, such as trusts for education funds, housing fund trusts, living expenses trusts, pension trusts and trusts for mutual aid associations funds, trusts for retirement allowances reserves and for pension funds and so on. This is considered to be a promising branch of the trust business. The bulk of money in trust is of the 'designated joint operation' variety: 66 per cent of the beneficiaries are individuals,[1] while 31 per cent are corporations and 3 per cent are anonymous (end of September 1970).

Provisional dividend rates on designated joint operation trusts with maturities of over one year are exempt from interest-rates control under the Temporary Money Rates Adjustment Law, and are fixed independently by trust banks.[2] The current provisional dividend rates are as follows:

Maturities	*Provisional Dividend Rates on 'Designated Joint Operations' Money in Trust*	*Notes*
1 year and less than 2 years	not more than 5·25%	valid from July 1972
2 years and less than 5 years	not more than 5·8%	valid from July 1972
5 years and over	not more than 6·63%	valid from July 1974

[1] The minimum unit for trust money is 5000 yen, as agreed by members of the Trust Association.

[2] Money in trust of shorter maturities than one year have been discontinued since January 1956.

(*b*) *Unit Operation* (*Designated 'Unit'*). Trust properties of large amounts may be employed independently. In contrast to designated joint operation trust money, there is no guarantee of the principal, and most of the beneficiaries are corporations. As dividend rates on designated unit operation on trusts are outside the regulations under the Temporary Money Rates Adjustment Law, high rates of dividends for short-term contracts were paid for a time after the war, so that this type of trust attracted much money. The Ministry of Finance, however, regarded such high dividends as disruptive of the structure of interest rates and took steps to restrain them. Subsequently, the outstanding amount fell and it is now very small. With this type of trust the principle is that dividend rates are determined by the actual results of operations, but trust banks have voluntarily agreed since April 1956 to keep rates below 6·205 per cent. The period of trust is over one year and the minimum unit is five million yen.

(B) SPECIFIED MONEY IN TRUST. The truster gives specific directions as to the methods of employment of the entrusted properties. Contracts guaranteeing the principal and minimum dividend rates are prohibited; on the other hand there is no limitation on the period of trust. Most of the beneficiaries are corporations.

(C) MONEY IN TRUST WITHOUT DESIGNATION OR SPECIFICATION. The truster gives no instruction as to the method of employment, so that in this the trust banks have complete freedom of decision. The employment of these unspecified trusts is, however, legally restricted to subscription for government bonds or for debentures of special companies established under special laws, loans on the security of these bonds and debentures, deposits with post offices and deposits with banks. Thus, this type of trust is unattractive and is not used at all.

B. Pension Trusts

Trust banks are entrusted with the management and employment of pension funds, of which there are two types: trusts for qualified retirement pension funds, and for welfare annuity funds.

(A) QUALIFIED RETIREMENT PENSION TRUST. This is a new type of trust started in April 1962, by which business firms (trustors) entrust to trust banks (trustees) their own contributions or those made jointly with their employees. The money is managed by the trust banks, which pay the employees (beneficiaries) their pensions in accordance with the regulations of the firms concerned.

For reasons of social policy special tax reductions are granted to pension funds if they meet the requirements of the Minister of Finance. On the other hand, there are quite severe restrictions on the employment of such resources because the scheme puts a premium on safety and reliability. Only ten channels for the employment of funds are open to this kind of trust, movable and real property in trust, pension investment fund trust[1] and so on. Moreover, more than 60 per cent of the entrusted property must be employed in forms which carry guarantees of the principal or in which there is specific provision for repayment of the principal. However, as the schemes extend over long periods, the real value of the property must be protected against inflation. For this reason more risky investments are permitted if they do not exceed 50 per cent of the total (of which shares should be less than 30 per cent and investments in the beneficiary rights of real property in trust and in real estate should be less than 20 per cent). Thus, there is scope for flexibility.

(B) WELFARE ANNUITY FUND TRUST. This system was initiated in October 1966. The government delegates to the welfare annuity funds established by business firms part of the management of old-age pensions (collection of contributions and payment of pensions) under the welfare annuity insurance scheme. Contracts are concluded between trust banks and welfare annuity funds, by which banks manage and employ the funds. Employment of the entrusted property is, in principle, subject to the same limitations as those applying to Qualified Retirement Pension Trusts.

As pension trusts have been started only recently, their resources are not yet substantial (at the end of 1969 the principal outstanding was 86·0 billion yen for Qualified Retirement

[1] Pension investment fund trusts were started in May 1963. The purpose was to aggregate a number of pension funds and to make joint investment in shares and real estate. The system was instituted because individual pension funds, which had just been started, had insufficient resources to employ independently.

Pension Trusts and 64·7 billion yen for Welfare Annuity Trusts), but, by judging by European and American experience, their future prospects seem bright.

C. Loan Trust

Loan trusts were newly introduced in June 1952 under the Loan Trust Law. This defines a loan trust as 'money in trust', by which the trustee jointly employs money received under a uniform trust contract from a number of trusters principally in loans and/or in discounting bills, and of which the beneficiary rights are evidenced by a beneficiary certificate (Article 2). Loans trusts are similar to 'joint operation designated money in trust' in that the money is jointly employed, but differs in that the employment of funds is restricted to loans and discounts, and also because beneficiary certificates, embodying beneficiary rights, are sold openly to the public. A trust bank fixes a period of a month or two up to a stated date, during which it will receive money from the public; this is pooled and treated as a unit, and is employed in long-term loans to important industries. Only the seven specialised trust banks can handle loan trust business.

The period of trust is either two or five years. The beneficiary certificates may be registered or may be bearer certificates. Bearer certificates are issued in six denomimations of 10,000 yen, 100,000 yen, 500,000 yen, 1,000,000 yen, 5,000,000 yen and 10,000,000 yen. Registered certificates have face values of 10,000 yen or multiples of 10,000 yen. Bearer certificates are transferable before the expiry of the trust period; after the lapse of one year from the issue, holders can request the trustees to repurchase certificates. Although a uniform provision dividend rate is fixed by mutual agreement among trust banks, the principle is to make distributions according to the actual results of employing the funds. The dividend rate is therefore subject to variation if these returns change during the trust period. In this respect the certificates differ from fixed-interest-bearing bonds and debentures. At present the trust banks have a voluntary agreement that the dividend rate for five-year certificates should be 7·47 per cent (from March 1970), and that for two-year certificates should be 6·45 per cent (from March 1970). A further point is that trust banks build up 'special reserves' and make contracts to guarantee the principal of their funds.

Investment plans and changes in them are subject to approval by the Minister of Finance. At one time restrictions had been imposed upon loans to other than the four key industries (shipping, electricity, coal, iron and steel), but they have been relaxed. Moreover, the employment of trust property received before the closing date and of surplus money accrued from investment (interest on money lent and repayments before maturity) are not subject to such limitations.

At the end of September 1970, 65 per cent of the beneficiaries of loan trusts were individuals, while 23 per cent were corporations and 12 per cent were unregistered.

D. Securities Investment Trust

Securities investment trust is the trust of property collected from a number of customers by investment trust managing companies. The trustees are trust banks (or banks engaged in trust business as a subsidiary activity). The investors become beneficiaries, to whom beneficiary certificates are issued. The truster companies, which are specialists in securities investment, direct the trustees (trust banks) as to the forms of investment, such as shares, bonds or debentures, or call loans. The trust banks execute these instructions, administer the trust property, receive interest and dividends and keep accounts of the property; the resultant profits are distributed to the beneficiaries in proportion to their investments (the distribution is made according to the actual results and there is no guarantee of the principal). The truster companies and the trust banks receive remuneration from the trust property for managing the funds.

Securities investment trusts were started in 1941, but it was not until after 1951 that the wholesale development of stock investment trusts, which invest trust property mainly in shares, began. At present, nine security companies, including medium-scale ones,[1] have affiliated truster companies. The trustees are the six trust banks and the one bank engaged in trusts as

[1] There were 14 stock investment truster companies in 1961. In 1964 seven of them amalgamated to form two new companies; the purpose was to improve the constitution of investment trusts and to separate the trust business. There are thus nine truster companies at present.

subsidiary business. In addition, the 'bond investment trust' concerned mainly with investment in bonds and debentures was introduced in 1961.

Securities investment trusts achieved considerable growth between 1955 and 1964 when the stock markets were booming. Investors favoured them because despite the diversification of risks in comparison with direct investment in individual shares, there was still a possibility of similar capital gains. After 1961, however, when the market slumped they stagnated, and from 1964 the amount still held by investors began to decline.

Securities investment trusts fall broadly within the scope of securities investment companies, so that a more detailed description will be given in Chapter 20.

E. Money Trust other than Money in Trust

In this type of trust, money is received as the entrusted property, but on the expiry of the trust period the trust property is not converted into cash, but is delivered to the beneficiary as it stands. For instance, money may be entrusted to trust banks for purchase of real estate with instructions as to the location, area of land and price.

(2) *Trusts other than Money Trusts*

A. Securities in Trust

Securities may be accepted as trust property from the start and be retained or employed to profits. There are three varieties of this kind of trust.

(A) SECURITIES ADMINISTRATION TRUSTS. Trust banks receive securities from the trusters and, after marking them as trust assets, they collect dividends, coupons and redemption money for the trusters, and dispose of the assets as directed; or they may act as proxies in other ways, including subscription for new shares. Only public bonds, industrial and other debentures and (listed) shares may be entrusted in this way. This type of trust is operated as a form of service to clients, and the amount outstanding is small.

(B) SECURITIES EMPLOYMENT TRUSTS. Securities entrusted by the trusters are employed in lending to third parties, who pay 'rent' for them. Such lending is of two types:

(*a*) Lending to industrial companies, which use the securities as a guarantee against deferred payments of liquor tax, sugar-consumption tax and so on. They can also use them as a guarantee for tenders for government and local-authority construction works.

(*b*) Lending to securities companies, which use them as security for borrowed call money.

In the case of (*a*), however, cash or securities are not always required as a guarantee, but the surety of banks or trust banks suffices in most cases, so that the outstanding amount of such lending is decreasing. Thus, lending in category (*b*) predominates now. As shares cannot be used in these ways there is in practice little resort to share-employment trusts.

(C) SECURITIES DISPOSAL TRUST. Securities are entrusted for sale; the purpose may either be the sale in itself or may be the profit upon sale, but, in any case, there is little use of this type of trust.

B. Monetary Claims in Trust

The purpose of the trust is the collection of the principal and interest of monetary claims; the preservation and execution of mortgage rights; and the performance of other tasks necessary to safeguard and invest the monetary claims in trust. Examples of this type of trust are those of life insurance and the assets of closed institutions; life insurance predominates overwhelmingly.

In life insurance trusts the policy-holder becomes the truster, for whom the trust bank (trustee) receives money on the expiry of the policy, or in the event of an accident insured under it. The trustee then manages and employs the money for the beneficiary in accordance with the trust contract. Until the receipt of the insurance money the trust ranks as monetary claims in trust, but thereafter it becomes designated money in trust. There are two varieties: funded life insurance in trust, where the trust bank, to which the life insurance is entrusted, pays in the insurance premiums; and plain life insurance in trust, where the trust bank is entrusted with the right to receive the insurance money only, while the premiums are paid by the trustor himself.

C. Movable Property in Trust

The entrusted property in this case is commodities, the management and disposal of which are the purpose of the trust. Such business is usually the function of factors and warehouse companies, and it is not appropriate for financial institutions to undertake it. Originally, such trusts were not recognised by the authorities, but they have, however, permitted trust banks to become trustees of 'rolling-stock and other transportation equipment and machinery'; rolling-stock trusts are now the predominant type.

In this type of trust rolling-stock is delivered to trust banks as trust property by the manufacturer. In most instances the latter borrows the manufacturing costs from the former on the security of their beneficiary rights. The trust bank leases the vehicles to a railway company. The rental is paid to the beneficiary (rolling-stock company), which uses the money to repay the borrowing from the trust bank, so that in due course, the rolling-stock becomes the property of the railway company and the trust bank is fully paid. Recently, other kinds of movable property in trust have developed, such as the trust of ships, lorries and airplanes.

D. Real Property in Trust

Land, buildings and other real estate may be entrusted for the purpose of management or disposal. In trusts for management the trustee collects rents, administers and maintains the property; trusts for disposal are utilised when land is sold in lots after readjustment or when the landowner wants to sell the land to his tenant. Because of the expenses and troubles of such trusts, however, they are seldom used.

E. Mortgage Debenture Trust

A company issuing debentures becomes the truster, who entrusts to the trustee (ordinary or trust bank) mortgage rights to the property or the business. The mortgage consists of the estate (i.e. land, buildings, machinery, etc., are lumped together and treated as a single asset) such as real property, ships, railways, factories, mines and others. The trustee manages the mortgage rights in the interests of the debenture-holders.

As mortgage rights in general are a form of intangible asset, such rights may not be entrusted by themselves; but, in the case of mortgages connected with debenture issues, such trusts are recognised on the ground that the rights are an essential element. The trust was legalised by the Mortgage Debentures Trust Law of 1905, so that its history is older than that of ordinary trusts. Trusteeship of mortgage debentures requires a licence from the Minister of Finance. At present, 25 banks, including 7 trust banks, 14 city banks, 1 specialised foreign exchange bank and 3 long-term credit banks, have such licences. Most corporate debentures are issued with mortgage trusts. Usually banks or trust banks, which have close relations with the issuing company, are appointed as joint trustees.

3. EMPLOYMENT OF FUNDS

(1) *Lending*

The proportion of securities to the total assets of trust accounts appears fairly high, but, if we exclude those held by securities investment trusts, they are in fact a very small fraction of the total funds employed by the trust banks themselves. Loans, advances and discounts represent the biggest proportion of the assets. Needless to say, those on loan trust account are the most important component of the total.

Most lending on trust accounts consists of loans of funds for fixed investment in plant and equipment. This stems from the nature of trust banks as long-term financial institutions. At the end of 1969 loans for such purposes were 77 per cent of total lending on trust accounts. This is a very high percentage compared with that of commercial banks: about 12 per cent.

By industry, lending to manufacturing industries, public utilities, transport and communication amounts to as much as 74 per cent of the total on trust accounts. In the case of commercial banks the proportion is about 50 per cent. On the other hand, lending to the wholesale and retail trades, which accounts for about 30 per cent of the total lending of commercial banks, is less than 10 per cent of the total loans, advances and discounts on trust accounts. The relative weight of housing loans is rising gradually (1·6 per cent at the end of 1969).

By size of borrowers, 92 per cent of the total lending on trust accounts is for firms with more than 50 million yen of paid-up capital, while the ratio of such lending to the total for commercial banks is about 63 per cent. Thus, nearly the whole of trust banks' lending is for large firms with high credit standing.

To sum up, long-term loans with ample margins for safety are favoured outlets for funds of trust accounts.

(2) *Investment in Securities*

The bulk of securities held on trust accounts are the property of securities investment trusts; other types of trust hold only about a quarter as much. Close to half of the securities of investment trusts are corporate debentures; next come shares. Nearly half of the corporate debentures are held on the accounts of bond investment trusts, which started in January 1961. At present, government bonds are held, and there is little investment in local bonds.

4. ASSETS AND LIABILITIES: PROFIT AND LOSS

(1) *Assets and Liabilities of Trust Accounts*

A. Liabilities

About 97 per cent of the liabilities of trust accounts consist of those of money trusts. Of these, the outstanding amount of securities investment trusts has steadily increased since their inauguration in 1952; their liabilities accounted for as much as 55 per cent of the total in 1961. Thereafter, however, the stock market slumped, so that their growth slowed down and eventually became negative. In contrast, loan trusts have shown a marked increase, until, by the end of 1969, they had come to represent more than half the total liabilities. One factor in this development was the fall in share prices, which prompted individual investors to seek stable investments; another reason was that the dividend yield of loan trusts exceeded that of money in trust and that of interest on deposits. Thus, at the end of 1969, loan trusts represented 79 per cent of the total liabilities of money trusts other than securities investment trusts. Next came the liabilities of jointly operated designated money in trust, which accounted for 15 per cent of the total. Other kinds of money trusts represented mere fractions of the total: specified money in trust accounted for 0·9 per cent and pension trusts for 1·2 per cent of total liabilities. Trusts other than money trusts represent only about 4·5 per cent of the total liabilities of all kinds of trusts. The bulk of such non-monetary trusts consists of securities in trust.

B. Assets

Until about 1962 the composition of the assets of trust accounts reflected the growth of securities investment trusts. The relative proportion of securities held by them rose, while that of loans fell from 70 per cent in 1956 to 39 per cent in 1961. After 1962, however, when investment trusts ceased to grow rapidly the tendency was reversed: the relative importance of loans began to climb again. At the end of 1969 they accounted for 68 per cent of total assets. As trust funds are employed mainly in making long-term loans or loans for fixed investment in plant and equipment, the amount of bills discounted has remained low throughout the period.

Given the nature of trust business, cash reserves (cash on hand and deposits with other financial institutions) are very small. Call loans, however, represent a relatively high proportion of the total assets employed: 5 to 7 per cent. In fact, of this, some 90 per cent are the reserve assets of securities investment trusts, so that the ratio of call loans to the total assets of trusts proper is just as low as that of cash on hand and deposits.

(2) *Banking Accounts of Trust Banks*

As has already been explained, specialised trust banks now operate banking accounts, as distinct from their trust accounts, so that they function as commercial banks as well. The relative importance of these banking accounts differs from bank to bank, depending on whether they intend to become pure trust banks in future or to become banks proper; naturally trust accounts are more important for the former, and banking accounts count for the latter. In all, 20 to 30 per cent of total assets and liabilities of all trust banks consists of banking accounts.

The ratio of the banking accounts of specialised trust banks to the total of all banks is very small: their deposits represented 4·0 per cent of total deposits at the end of 1969, while their lending accounted for 3·1 per cent, and their securities 6·6 per cent of the total.

All of the specialised trust banks operate in big cities and large firms are their principal customers on banking accounts. In this respect they resemble city banks. Most of their deposits are the so-called business deposits. The proportion of current to total deposits was 12 per cent at the end of 1969, which was roughly the same percentage as that of commercial banks.

(3) *Profit and Loss of Trust Banks*

Table 15.6 (p. 238) shows the income of trust banks. Interest on banking accounts represent about 60 per cent of their current income, while trust remuneration[1] from loan trusts, money in trust and so on provides only about 30 per cent. This small percentage derives from the calculation of trust remuneration on a net basis: that is, dividends to beneficiaries are deducted from the income from employment of the trust assets. If we take this circumstance into consideration and calculate on a gross basis, it will appear that the relative weight of income from trust accounts is much larger. Income from the so-called property management business, such as movable and real property in trust and securities in trust, is very small. Most of their income comes from money trusts, such as loan trusts, and from long- and short-term financial operations on banking accounts.

On the other hand, more than 80 per cent of current expenditure consists of expenses and interest payment on deposits; dividend payments to trust beneficiaries are not included in the current expenditure.

[1] The truster and the trustee (trust bank) agree on the amount of trust remuneration at the time of the trust contract. Dividends are paid out of the earnings from the employment of the trust property and the rest accrues to the trustee as their remuneration. At present standards and/or ceilings of remuneration are provided for in the trust contracts. For instance, the standard rate for loan trusts is 2·19 per cent for trusts of 2 years' maturity, and 1·46 per cent for those of 5 years' maturity, with a permissible spread of 0·365 per cent either side of the standard rate.

TABLE 15.1

Survey of Trust Business (end of 1968)

(hundred million yen)

	Outstanding Amount of Principal[a]
MONEY TRUSTS	
Money in Trust	
Designated Money in Trust: Joint Operation	9,773
Designated Money in Trust: Unit Operation	59
Specified Money in Trust	717
Money in Trust without Designation or Specification	0
Pension Trusts	
Qualified Retirement Pension Trusts	1,225
Welfare Annuity Fund Trusts	1,251
Pension Investment Fund Trusts	1,624
Loan Trusts	41,992
Securities Investment Trusts	
Unit Trusts / Open-end Trusts / Open-end Bond Trusts	13,462
Money Trusts other than Money in Trust	27
NON-MONETARY TRUSTS	
Securities in Trust	
Securities Administration Trusts	532
Securities Employment Trusts (Used as Collateral Security / Used for Loans)	3,006
Securities Disposal Trusts	0
Monetary Claims in Trust	
Life Insurance in Trust / Closed Institutions' Trusts	1
Movable Property in Trust	864
Real Property in Trust	
Administration Trusts / Disposal Trusts	429
Surface Rights and Leasehold in Trust (Land and Fixtures in Trust)	
Mortgage Debenture Trusts	
Open-end Mortgage	
Closed-end Mortgage	
ANCILLARY BUSINESS	
Safe Custody	
Guarantee of Debts	
Intermediation of Purchase and Sale of Real Property and of Loans of Money or Leases of Real Property	
Flotation of Public Bonds, Corporate Debentures and Stocks; Receipt of Subscription Money for them; Servicing them	
Execution of Wills relative to Property	
Auditing of Accounts	
Agency Business (Acquisition, Custody, Disposal or Lease of Property; Readjustment or Liquidation of Property, Collection of Debts; Performance of Obligations)	

[a] Includes the Daiwa Bank (Trust accounts).

TABLE 15.2

Outstanding Amount of Lending on Trust Accounts of All Banks, by Industry (end of 1970)

(hundred million yen)

Industry	*Outstanding Amounts*			
	Total	*Per Cent of Total*	*Loans for Fixed Investment in Plant and Equipment*	*Lending to Firms with less than 50 million yen of Capital*
Manufacturing	29,414	57·1	24,840	827
Agriculture, Forestry and Fisheries	268	0·5	166	18
Mining	519	1·0	404	11
Construction	1,708	3·3	854	119
Wholesale and Retail Trade	3,282	6·4	1,588	275
Transport and Communication	5,372	10·4	4,838	195
Electricity, Gas and Water	2,484	4·8	2,469	—
Services	1,375	2·7	1,045	271
Other	7,128	13·8	3,945	2,886
Total	51,550	100·0	40,149	4,602

SOURCE: Bank of Japan, *Economic Statistics Annual.*

TABLE 15.3

Outstanding Amount of Securities Held on Trust Accounts of All Banks (end of 1970)

(hundred million yen)

	Securities Investment Trusts		*Other Trusts*		*Total*	
Government Bonds	0	(0)	0	(0)	0	(0)
Local Bonds	1,017	(9·5)	743	(23·9)	1,760	(12·6)
Corporate Debentures	5,383	(49·8)	1,666	(53·5)	7,049	(50·7)
Shares	4,002	(37·0)	581	(18·7)	4,583	(32·9)
Other Securities	400	(3·7)	122	(3·9)	522	(3·8)
Total	10,802	(100·0)	3,112	(100·0)	13,914	(100·0)

NOTE: Figures in parentheses are percentages of the total.

SOURCE: Bank of Japan.

TABLE 15.4

Principal Items of Assets and Liabilities of Trust Accounts of All Banks

(hundred million yen)

End of the Year	*1956*	% of the Total	*1961*	% of the Total	*1966*	% of the Total	*1968*	% of the Total	*1969*	% of the Total	*1970*	% of the Total
ASSETS												
Loans and Advances	2,777	70·0	8,881	39·2	24,548	61·4	35,841	69·5	42,926	67·9	51,351	66·5
Bills Discounted	197	5·0	148	0·7	244	0·6	238	0·5	196	0·3	199	0·3
Cash and Deposits with Others	17	0·4	63	0·3	24	0·1	89	0·2	40	0·1	53	0·1
Call Loans	195	4·9	1,470	6·5	2,643	6·6	1,817	3·5	2,694	4·3	2,995	3·9
Securities Held for Securities Investment Trusts	586	14·8	11,028	48·7	8,295	20·8	7,861	15·3	9,351	14·8	10,802	14·0
Other Securities	73	1·8	222	1·0	1,155	2·9	2,084	4·0	2,536	4·0	3,115	4·0
Other	122	3·1	851	3·6	3,058	7·6	3,614	7·0	5,515	8·6	8,670	11·2
Total	3,967	100·0	22,663	100·0	39,967	100·0	51,544	100·0	63,258	100·0	77,185	100·0
LIABILITIES												
Money Trusts												
Money in Trust	1,615	40·7	2,876	12·7	5,232	13·1	7,460	14·5	9,065	14·3	11,006	14·3
Loan Trusts	1,593	40·2	6,742	29·7	23,412	58·6	32,164	62·4	37,502	59·3	43,724	56·6
Pension Trusts	0	0	0	0	246	0·6	910	1·8	1,535	2·4	2,539	3·3
Securities Investment Trusts	742	18·7	12,434	54·9	9,912	24·8	9,113	17·7	11,220	17·7	13,325	17·3
Pension Investment Fund Trusts	0	0	0	0	16	—	89	0·2	1,075	1·7	1,717	2·2
Sub-Total	3,950	99·6	22,052	97·3	38,818	97·1	49,736	96·5	60,397	95·5	72,342	93·7
Securities in Trust	12	0·3	538	2·4	849	2·1	1,278	2·5	2,047	3·2	3,545	4·6
Other Trusts	5	0·1	73	0·3	300	0·8	530	1·0	813	1·3	1,298	1·7

TABLE 15.5

Principal Assets and Liabilities of Specialised Trust Banks

(hundred million yen)

	Trust Account				*Banking Account*				
End of the Year	*Cash, Deposits, Call Loans*	*Securities*	*Lending*	*Sub-Total*	*Cash, Deposits, Call Loans*	*Securities*	*Lending*	*Sub-Total*	*Total*
ASSETS									
1956	152	382	2,212	2,746	326	127	1,160	1,613	4,359
	(3)	(9)	(51)	(63)	(7)	(3)	(27)	(37)	(100)
1960	1,148	5,356	6,255	12,759	652	423	2,529	3,604	16,363
	(7)	(33)	(38)	(78)	(4)	(3)	(15)	(22)	(100)
1965	2,098	8,502	20,208	30,808	1,538	2,462	5,919	9,919	40,727
	(5)	(21)	(50)	(76)	(4)	(6)	(14)	(24)	(100)
1968	1,764	7,718	33,462	42,944	1,915	3,763	9,588	15,266	58,210
	(3)	(13)	(58)	(74)	(3)	(6)	(17)	(26)	(100)
1969	2,523	9,207	39,926	51,656	2,599	4,335	10,512	17,446	69,102
	(4)	(13)	(58)	(75)	(4)	(6)	(15)	(25)	(100)
1970	2,786	10,710	47,694	61,190	3,401	4,826	12,402	20,629	81,819
	(3)	(13)	(58)	(75)	(4)	(6)	(15)	(25)	(100)

	Trust Account				*Banking Account*				
End of the Year	*Money in Trust*	*Loan Trusts*	*Securities Investment Trusts*	*Sub-Total*	*Deposits*	*Borrowings*	*Call Money*	*Sub-Total*	*Total*
LIABILITIES									
1956	664	1,537	446	2,647	1,196	47	186	1,429	4,076
	(16)	(38)	(11)	(65)	(29)	(1)	(5)	(35)	(100)
1960	1,383	4.931	5,689	12,003	2,864	122	232	3,218	15,221
	(9)	(33)	(37)	(79)	(18)	(1)	(2)	(21)	(100)
1965	2,310	19,553	9,739	31,602	8,112	87	425	8,624	40,226
	(6)	(49)	(24)	(79)	(20)	(—)	(1)	(21)	(100)
1968	3,976	32,164	7,840	43,980	12,030	71	327	12,428	56,408
	(7)	(57)	(14)	(78)	(21)	(—)	(1)	(22)	(100)
1969	4,872	37,502	9,681	52,055	14,405	81	238	14,724	66,779
	(7)	(56)	(14)	(78)	(22)	(—)	(—)	(22)	(100)
1970	6,068	43,724	11,436	61,228	17,011	151	207	17,368	78,597
	(8)	(56)	(15)	(78)	(22)	(—)	(—)	(29)	(100)

NOTE: Figures in parentheses are percentages of the totals.

SOURCE: Bank of Japan.

TABLE 15.6

Profit and Loss of Trust Banks (March 1970 to September 1970)

(hundred million yen)

	Current Income			Current Expenditure	
		% of the Total			*% of the Total*
Income from Lending	423	39·0	Interest on Deposits	263	33·0
Income from Securities Held	158	14·5	Interest on Call Money Borrowed	10	1·3
Trust Remuneration	304	28·0	Other Interest Paid	87	10·9
Commission Received	116	10·7	Expenses	382	47·9
Other	85	7·8	Other	55	6·9
Total	1,086	100·0	Total	797	100·0

SOURCE: Bank of Japan.

CHAPTER 16

FINANCIAL INSTITUTIONS FOR SMALL BUSINESS

1. CHARACTERISTICS AND DEVELOPMENT OF SMALL BUSINESS FINANCE

(1) *Characteristics and Problems of Small Business Finance*

Small businesses have a substantial role in the Japanese economy. For instance, the number of small enterprises with fewer than 300 employees represented 99·5 per cent of the total number of firms in manufacturing industry in 1966; thus big enterprises with more than 300 employees accounted for only 0·5 per cent of the total. By number of employees in industry, 69·7 per cent were employed by small businesses. Despite the predominance of small businesses by numbers of firms and of employees, they were responsible for only 53·6 per cent of the value added in industry that year (Ministry of International Trade and Industry, *Census of Manufacturers*). This remarkable productivity gap is a characteristic distinction between small and large enterprises.

Most small concerns in Japan are organised on joint-stock principles, but in practice they resemble private or family businesses. They lag behind big firms in managerial techniques, such as accounting and market research, so that their management is not rationalised in the same degree as big business. Needless to say, their productive equipment and technique are, in most cases, behind the times. Thus, in 1966 their labour productivity, which may be represented by the amount of value added per employee, was a little over 60 per cent of that of big firms. In consequence, the level of wages in small businesses is only about three-quarters of that in big concerns, despite the substantial reduction of the gap because of labour shortage in recent years.

In spite of the unfavourable contrast with large firms, small businesses, like agriculture which is similarly backward and lagging in productivity, have remained significant in the national economy, because of Japan's excessive population, which these labour-intensive industries absorb. This co-existence of modern industries with backward agriculture and small businesses constitutes the 'dual structure' of the economy and is one of the country's conspicuous economic characteristics.

The 'dual structure' is naturally reflected in finance. The problems of financing small businesses arising from this structure are as follows:

A. Low Credit-worthiness and High Rates of Interest

It is undeniable that small businesses in general are more risky borrowers than big firms. Moreover, they borrow only small amounts, so that the cost of accommodating them is inevitably higher than for big enterprises. On the other hand, the cost of funds for specialised private financial institutions for small businesses, such as mutual loans and savings banks, and credit associations, is higher than that of all banks, so that their lending rates are comparatively high (at the end of 1969, the average agreed interest rate on loans, advances and discounts of all banks was 7·605 per cent, while that of mutual loans and savings banks was 8·365 per cent). If compensating balances on loans and discounts are taken into consideration, the effective interest burden on small businesses must be much higher than that on big firms.

B. Difficulty of Going into the Capital Market

As small businesses are hardly able to raise funds in the capital market they have a persistent demand for borrowing from financial institutions. Although they have encountered less difficulty recently in borrowing from specialised financial institutions for small businesses, the resources of which have much increased, they experience financial difficulties during credit squeezes when the demand of big firms for money suddenly expands and when the banks become more selective amongst borrowers.

C. Subordination to Big Firms

Many small businesses are dependent upon big firms or upon wholesale dealers, so that in recessions they are in a weak position and consequently are liable to experience unfavourable settlement terms.

(2) *Development of Small-Business Finance*

As the problems of small businesses are deeply rooted in Japan's economic structure, their solution is not easy. Precisely because they are so difficult, however, serious concern has been paid to them: there have long been measures to support and strengthen small firms. As part of these measures the system of small-business finance has been much expanded and strengthened since the war, and various improvements have been made.

'Mujin' and other co-operative type specialised financial institutions for small businesses have been in existence from early years. Since the war they have been legally reorganised as mutual loans and savings banks, credit associations and credit co-operatives. The latter two types of organisations have central institutions in the National Federation of Credit Associations and in the National Federation of Credit Co-operatives respectively. It was previously noted (p. 30) that the Central Bank for Commercial and Industrial Co-operatives was founded in pre-war years under a special law and has been concerned with the finance of small businesses co-operatives. In addition, the government has established the Small Business Finance Corporation and the People's Finance Corporation for the purpose of channelling public funds into small businesses. Further, facilities to supplement the credit standing of small firms have been organised; Credit Guarantee Associations and the Small Business Credit Insurance Corporation. Moreover, prefectures make special loans to small businesses (System of Lending Money for Modernisation of Equipment of Small Businesses and System of Lending Money for Development of Small Businesses). The government gives aid to these schemes. In 1963, with the enactment of the Fundamental Law for Small Businesses, small-business investment companies were established, which aimed to replenish the capital of small businesses by subscribing for their new shares.

In the high growth period 1955–64 these specialised institutions contributed materially to the promotion and development of small businesses. At the same time the financial institutions themselves (particularly mutual loans and savings banks, credit associations and credit co-operatives) were remarkably active. For instance, it will be seen from Table 16.1 that in small-business finance the relative share of private specialised financial institutions, such as mutual loans and savings banks, credit associations and credit co-operatives, has greatly risen, while that of commercial banks has declined.

Since 1965, however, great changes have taken place in the financial environment, so that improvement in the financial system has become a leading issue: reforms have become inevitable because of the new demands of the new era. Since June 1966, therefore, the Financial System Council has been concerned with the overall reassessment of the Japanese financial system. As a first step attention was concentrated on the problem of small-business finance. Discussions about private specialised financial institutions have noted the great gap between hope and achievement; their business has tended to resemble that of commercial banks, and they have increasingly polarised into extremely large and extremely small institutions. Following protracted consideration of these tendencies, in October 1967 the Special Committee on Small Business Finance of the Financial System Council submitted to the Ministry of Finance a report entitled On the Ideal System of Small Business Finance. The report resulted in the two financial laws of June 1968 (Law Amending a Part of the Mutual Loans and Savings Banks Law, Credit Associations Law, etc., for the Purpose of Consolidating and Improving the System of Small Business Finance and Law Concerning Amalgamations and Conversions of Financial Institutions). The two laws are epoch-making, for they represented the first steps towards a reorganisation of the financial system. The underlying purpose of the laws is to facilitate the 'efficient financing' of small businesses; their more immediate aim is to widen the scope of mutual loans and savings banks, credit associations and other private specialised financial institutions for small businesses, in order to enable them to meet modern needs more effectively.

(percentages)

End of the Year	All Banks			Specialised Financial Institutions for Small Businesses					Total Including Other Financial Institutions
	Banking Accounts			Private				Government	
		City Banks	Country Banks		Mutual Loans and Savings Banks	Credit Associations	Credit Co-operatives	Central Bank for Commercial and Industrial Co-operatives, Small Business Finance Corporations, People's Finance Corporations	
1960	52·8	25·4	25·4	36·5	19·1	14·1	3·3	9·3	100·0
1961	50·1	23·3	24·7	39·1	20·0	15·4	3·7	9·1	100·0
1962	45·9	20·7	23·7	43·4	22·0	17·3	4·1	9·2	100·0
1963	48·7	21·7	24·8	41·4	20·3	17·0	4·1	7·8	100·0
1964	47·0	20·8	23·8	42·5	20·1	17·8	4·6	8·5	100·0
1965	45·6	20·1	23·1	43·5	20·4	18·2	4·9	8·9	100·0
1966	45·9	20·1	23·1	43·0	19·6	18·4	5·0	8·9	100·0
1967	45·4	19·3	23·0	43·3	19·4	18·6	5·3	8·8	100·0
1968	46·1	19·7	23·3	42·0	17·1	19·3	5·6	9·4	100·0
1969	44·9	19·5	22·2	43·1	17·2	20·2	5·6	9·4	100·0
1970	43·9	18·8	21·9	43·9	17·4	21·0	5·6	9·5	100·0

NOTES:

(1) Lending of All Banks is that made to joint-stock companies or individuals with capital of less than 50 million yen (before 1962, capital of less than 10 million yen), but, in the case of wholesale and retail trades and of catering industries, only that to firms with a capital of less than 10 million yen is included. Overdrafts, however, are not included in lending.

(2) Loans to financial institutions or to local authorities are excluded from the amounts of lending by financial institutions.

(3) 'Other financial institutions' in the Total column include the trust accounts of All Banks, the Japan Development Bank (lending to the same category of firms as in the case of All Banks is taken) and the National Federation of Credit Associations (only agency loans are included).

SOURCE: Bank of Japan, *Economic Statistics Annual*.

Let us now turn to the details of small-business finance. At the end of 1969, country banks were the most important suppliers of money in this sphere, their relative share being 21·6 per cent; they were followed by credit associations (21 per cent), city banks (20 per cent) and mutual loans and savings banks (17 per cent). Private specialised financial institutions, including credit co-operatives, supply 44 per cent of the total, which is about the same percentage as that supplied by all banks (banking account) to small businesses. The relative share of public financial institutions, such as the Central Bank for Commercial and Industrial Co-operatives, the Small Business Finance Corporation, and the People's Finance Corporation, has remained steady at about the level of 9 per cent during the last ten years.

The various specialised financial institutions have differing characteristics depending upon their origins. They will be described in the following sections, in which brief accounts will also be given of the systems of credit guarantee and credit insurance, which seek to underpin the credit status of small businesses, and of business investment companies.

2. MUTUAL LOANS AND SAVINGS BANKS

(1) *General Survey*

'Mujin' companies, which had been the traditional financial institutions for the general public, became mutual loans and savings banks under the Mutual Loans and Savings Banks Law of 1951. This law was part of the post-war reorganisation of the financial system.

Mutual loans and savings banks are financial institutions on joint-stock principles, the aim of which is 'to facilitate finance for the general public and to contribute to the augmentation of their savings'. Their special feature is their 'mujin' business, inherited from the 'mujin' companies. 'Mujin' is a combination of savings and loans by which long-term loans of small sums are repaid in instalments, a method which meets the needs of small businesses. They can, at the same time, engage in business similar to that of commercial banks, such as taking deposits, and lending. As they are specialists in small-business finance, however, they are treated somewhat differently from banks operating under the Banking Law. For instance, restrictions are imposed upon their areas of operation; this is intended to restore the money to the locality from which it has been absorbed. As financial institutions for the general public, the amount of their lending to a single borrower is rigidly limited.

Since their inception mutual loans and savings banks have made spectacular progress. For example, their resources increased from 218·8 billion yen at the end of 1952 to 5398·4 billion yen at the end of 1969, or by 25 times. In this process, however, their business has changed considerably. At the same time, some problems emerged. First, they have tended to become assimilated with commercial banks. To take an example, the business of mutual instalment savings and loans ('mujin'), which originally was very important, has gradually diminished, while the credit-creating activities which their current deposit business made possible have also expanded. These banks have increasingly come to deal with large firms, so that their lending of large sums has increased, while their areas of operation have been enlarged. Thus, they have in many ways outgrown their function as specialised financial institutions for small businesses.

Second, their development has produced differentiation into big and small units; differences in regional development have accentuated this tendency. Thus, some have acquired resources comparable to those of city banks.

For these reasons the Mutual Loans and Savings Bank Law has been amended. First, they have been defined as financial institutions, which in principle accommodate small businesses with less than 300 employees or with a capital of less than 200 million yen. Second, the minimum capital has been raised, in order to strengthen them.[1] Third, restrictions on their areas of operation have been abolished.

[1] Article 5 of the Mutual Loans and Savings Banks Law provides: mutual loans and savings banks with head offices in Tokyo or in cities with more than half a million of population, which are designated by the Minister of Finance, should have more than 300 million yen of capital (formerly 30 million yen).

Other mutual loans and savings banks should have more than 200 million yen of capital (formerly 20 million yen).

Thus, mutual loans and savings banks have been reorganised to meet contemporary needs as specialised financial institutions for small business. On the other hand, it has been made possible for some to be converted into commercial banks, provided that this is conducive to financial efficiency and that small-business finance is not thereby impeded. This is stipulated in the Law Concerning Amalgamations and Conversions of Financial Institutions.[1] The Mutual Loans and Savings Bank of Japan (Nippon Sogo Bank) was the first to be converted in December 1968, when its title was changed to Taiyo Bank.

At the end of 1969 there were 71 mutual loans and savings banks with 2786 offices. As they have become important financial institutions those with more than 20 billion yen of deposits have been subject to the Reserve Deposit System since April 1963. From March 1966 all the mutual loans and savings banks have been subject to the Bank of Japan's buying and selling operations of bonds and debentures. Thus, in recent years they have become direct targets of monetary policy.

(2) *Business*

A. Mutual Instalment Loans and Savings ('Mujin')

Only mutual loans and savings banks can engage in this kind of business, which is called their 'proper business'. A specific term and specific sum are agreed in advance with the customer, who regularly pays a given sum into the bank. At the expiry of or in the middle of the period this agreed sum is repaid. If the customer requires the money in the middle of the period, contracts stipulate the method of determining precedence among customers, and hence the order of payment. Thus, the mutual instalment business ('mujin') resembles the instalment savings deposit business in that fixed amounts are regularly

[1] Article 6 of the Law Concerning Amalgamations and Conversions of Financial Institutions lays down the following four criteria for deciding whether a particular amalgamation or conversion is permissible: 1. To be conducive to financial efficiency; 2. Not to impede the finance of small businesses in the region in question; 3. Not to disturb financial discipline; 4. To be able properly to execute business after amalgamation or conversion.

paid into the bank. The difference is that the latter's purpose is just savings, while the former combines loans before maturity. When loans are made, interest is added to the amounts of instalments subsequently paid.

There are two types of 'mujin'. The first is 'mujin' in the narrower sense (the typical 'mujin'), where a number of accounts is organised into a group and precedence in loans is determined by lot, by tender or by other similar methods. The second is the mutual instalment contract (or pseudo-*mujin*), where no group is organised and loans are not dependent on chance factors such as lots and biddings. Account-holders who have paid instalments for a certain period can borrow the money, or may have the use of it whenever they want. Thus, the irrational elements incidental to the typical 'mujin' are missing from this type, which represents the mutual instalment business.

B. Deposits, Lending etc.

In the same way as ordinary banks, mutual loans and savings banks can receive deposits (including current deposits) or instalment savings; can make loans and advances; discount bills of exchange; engage in domestic exchange business; and keep securities, precious metals and other commodities in safe custody. These are called 'common business', which resembles that of commercial banks. There are restrictions, however, on the amount of lending to one person (10 per cent of the capital or 200 million yen, whichever is the lower). They are also prohibited from dealing in foreign exchange.

In respect of interest rates the mutual loans and savings banks are also differently placed from ordinary banks. Their deposit rates are subject to control under the Temporary Money Rates Adjustment Law, but their maximum lending rates are fixed by their 'conditions of operation', which are submitted when they apply for licences. They are 12·75 per cent for loans, 11·75 per cent for overdrafts on current deposit accounts and 11·00 per cent for bill-discounting. Further, lower maxima for loans are fixed by mutual agreement among members of the National Mutual Loans and Savings Bank Association, although the maxima differ according to the size of the loans.

(3) *Recent Trends*

During the last five years their resources (instalment and deposits) have roughly doubled: the outstanding amount at the end of 1969 was 5398·4 billion yen. Instalments had accounted for 50 per cent of the total in 1956, but at the end of 1969 they represented only 2·9 per cent. This is because instalments have scarcely increased in this period; indeed, since 1963 they have in fact tended to decrease while deposits have grown tremendously. The greater part of the deposits, accounting for 76 per cent of the total, consists of fixed deposits, such as time deposits and instalment savings.

The amount of their lending (ordinary and instalment loans) has also approximately doubled during the five years to the end of 1969, when it amounted to 4393·3 billion yen. Instalment loans accounted for only 0·9 per cent; they have continually declined since 1963, while other forms of lending have shown marked increases.

Thus, commercial bank business has grown remarkably. This reflects the increased resources of small business, their customers, and their enhanced demand for loans in an atmosphere of economic expansion. On the other hand, the banks have increased their lending to big businesses. In contrast, their original business has notably declined. This is because business firms have found borrowing costs high, because they entail compensating balances (lower interest rates are paid on accumulated instalments than on outstanding loans, from which the amount of instalments paid is not deducted, so that interest is charged on the whole loans until maturity). In April 1961, to simplify the calculation of interest and to lower its real burden on mutual instalment loans, the mutual loans and savings banks therefore agreed to adopt the remaining balance system (instalments are regarded as repayments, so that monthly interest payments are calculated on the balance of the loan after subtraction of instalments). This change resulted, however, in a reduction of bank income. Since April 1964, moreover, their financial statements have offset loans against instalments. Thus, the mutual loans and savings business has continued to decline.

In lending to industry, by mutual instalment loans and in

other forms, the largest share has gone to wholesale and retail trades, but the relative importance of lending to manufacturing industries steadily increased from 1956 to about 1964. This rise reflected the modernisation of manufacturing industries as the economy has grown rapidly, although recently the relative weight of such lending has tended to fall (it was 25 per cent at the end of 1956 and 27·4 per cent at the end of 1969).

Mutual loans and savings banks, along with country banks and financial institutions for agriculture and forestry, have been important lenders to the call loan market. Monetary ease and the resultant declining trend in call loan rates in recent years (the average rate for unconditional call loans was 8·5 per cent at the end of 1969), however, caused them to shift funds from the call market to securities offering better yields. Further, the mutual loans and savings banks agreed to increase their holdings of securities as a form of reserve asset. Thus, at the end of 1969 their investment in securities (bank debentures, industrial debentures, shares and beneficiary certificates of loan and other trusts) amounted to 465·2 billion yen, or 8·6 per cent of their total resources. The percentage, however, was still below that of commercial banks.

3. CREDIT ASSOCIATIONS AND FEDERATION OF CREDIT ASSOCIATIONS

(1) *Credit Associations*

A. General Survey

The origin of credit associations may be traced to the credit co-operatives of the Meiji era, but their immediate predecessors are the credit co-operatives governed by the Law for Co-operatives of Small Businesses, etc., of 1949, which sought to organise small businesses into co-operatives; its essential purpose was to promote their autonomy. Thus, they could be freely established and official supervision was kept to the minimum. As the law governed all co-operatives other than those of farmers, fishermen and consumers (for each of which respective co-operative laws have been enacted), a wide variety of institutions were encompassed by the description of 'credit co-operatives': some

TABLE 16.2

Principal Accounts of Mutual Loans and Savings Banks

(hundred million yen)

End of the Year	*1956*		*1960*		*1965*		*1968*		*1969*		*1970*	
		%		%		%		%		%		%
ASSETS												
Mutual Instalment Loans	1,806	33·4	2,084	17·2	1,247	3·4	494	0·9	388	0·6	352	0·5
Other Loans, Advances and Discounts	2,496	46·2	7,445	61·5	25,174	69·0	35,811	67·6	43,545	67·9	52,070	68·3
Securities	204	3·8	653	5·4	2,554	7·0	3,866	7·3	4,652	7·3	5,440	7·1
Call Loans	70	1·3	193	1·6	690	1·9	876	1·7	1,243	1·9	1,760	2·3
Others	829	15·3	1,744	14·3	6,815	18·7	11,925	22·5	14,351	22·3	16,650	21·8
Total	5,405	100·0	12,119	100·0	36,480	100·0	52,972	100·0	64,179	100·0	76,272	100·0
LIABILITIES												
Mutual Instalment Savings	2,404	44·5	3,016	24·9	2,653	7·3	1,877	3·5	1,556	2·4	1,244	1·6
Deposits	2,361	43·7	7,827	64·6	29,547	81·0	42,657	80·5	52,428	81·7	62,421	81·8
(of which Time Deposits)	(1,555)	(28·8)	(5,489)	(45·3)	(19,596)	(53·7)	(28,500)	(53·8)	(34,553)	(53·8)	(41,466)	(54·4)
Borrowings	52	1·0	37	0·3	21	—	153	0·3	251	0·4	289	0·4
Others	588	10·8	1,239	10·2	4,259	11·7	8,285	15·7	9,944	15·5	12,318	16·2

NOTE: As the Nippon Sogo Bank (Japan Mutual Loans and Savings Bank) became an ordinary bank (its title being changed to Taiyo Bank) in 1968, the figures for the end of 1968 are not comparable with those for former years.

SOURCE: Bank of Japan, *Economic Statistics Annual*.

TABLE 16.3

Outstanding Amounts of Lending by Mutual Loans and Savings Banks, by Industry

(hundred million yen)

End of Year	Manufacturing Industries		Wholesale and Retail Trades		Catering Industries		Others		Total		The Relative Proportion of Loans for Fixed Investment
		%		%		%		%		%	
1956	1,068	24·8	1,519	35·3	835	19·4	877	20·5	4,299	100·0	14·4
1960	2,809	29·5	3,206	33·7	1,315	13·8	2,189	23·0	9,519	100·0	20·7
1965	8,686	32·9	8,318	31·5	3,061	11·6	6,329	24·0	26,394	100·0	19·8
1968	9,883	27·2	11,520	31·8	4,262	11·8	10,607	29·2	36,272	100·0	21·2
1969	12,028	27·4	13,574	30·9	4,919	11·2	13,371	30·5	43,892	100·0	21·4
1970	14,875	28·4	15,943	30·5	5,482	10·5	16,050	30·6	52,350	100·0	21·0

SOURCE: Bank of Japan, *Economic Statistics Annual*.

were genuine co-operatives, while others took deposits from the general public and resembled ordinary financial institutions. The latter were comparatively large associations, which had formerly been urban credit co-operative associations. It was thus imperative to strengthen them and to enhance their credit-worthiness in order to protect depositors, because like banks they were public institutions. In 1951, therefore, the Credit Associations Law gave this group a fresh start as credit associations, which were to function as financial institutions for small businesses. Subsequently they have developed spectacularly. They now play important roles in the finance of small businesses, along with mutual loans and savings banks. For instance, between the end of 1952 and the end of 1969 their resources multiplied by forty-four times, from 145·7 billion yen to 6408·4 billion yen. Thus, their growth far outstripped that of mutual loans and savings banks.

As with mutual loans and savings banks, however, their growth has brought considerable changes in their business. First, membership of the associations has become nominal. On the credit-giving side, anybody wishing for accommodation can become a member, so that membership has become a formality. On the credit-receiving side, deposits by non-members have increased. Thus, the business of credit associations has more and more come to resemble that of commercial banks. Another problem is that members have displayed no interest in the running of associations, so that the election of delegates and the proceedings of the delegates' council have become matters of routine; the principle that they should be run by the general consent of members is not properly observed. Second, the expansion of their business and differences in regional development have led to their differentiation into big and small units. The large number of small-scale credit associations is a particularly serious problem, because they are insecurely based (there were 507 credit associations at the end of 1969).

For these reasons there has been a fairly drastic reform of the system of credit associations in accordance with the report of the Financial System Council. The principal features are as follows. First, the qualification for membership has been altered. Only enterprises with fewer than 300 employees or with less than 100 million yen of capital[1] can become members. At the same time the minimum contribution per member[2] has been substantially increased. Second, the system of delegates' councils has been improved: the election procedure has been altered and the powers of the councils have been enlarged. Third, the minimum capital has been raised to ten times its previous level, and restrictions have been imposed upon their purchase of members' shares.[3] The purpose is to replenish their net worth and to increase their underlying strength. Fourth, as it will be explained later, the scope of their business has been extended: for instance, lending to non-members can now be made more freely. Moreover, non-members have been permitted to utilise the ancillary services of credit associations, such as domestic exchanges and facilities concerning securities. Fifth, the maximum accommodation to one person has been raised from 50 million to 100 million yen.

Finally, it should be noted that credit associations and mutual loans and savings banks with more than 20 billion yen of deposits have been subject to reserve deposit requirements since April 1963. Since June 1964, moreover, credit associations, having accounts with the Bank of Japan have participated in the Bank's buying and selling operations in bonds and debentures.

[1] Previously, the condition was that only business firms with fewer than 300 employees could join.

[2] The amount is 10,000 yen for members of credit associations, which have head offices in special wards of the Tokyo Metropolis, or in cities with more than half a million population, which have been designated by the Minister of Finance. For members of other credit associations the minimum is 5000 yen. (Article 11 of the Credit Associations Law.)

[3] When members wish to leave credit associations, they can do so by transferring their own shares to other members. When other members do not want to purchase the shares, however, they can ask the credit associations to buy the shares. (Section 1, Article 16, Credit Associations Law.) This is a special system, which has been instituted to replenish the net worth of credit associations, which are financial institutions and which must have stable financial foundations. If the association cannot quickly dispose of the shares, however, they may accumulate in their hands, so that their effective capital may be reduced. This is contrary to the need to replenish their capital. Consequently, a restriction has been imposed upon the amount of shares the associations can purchase from members. (Section 2, Article 16, Credit Associations Law.)

B. Business

The business of credit associations does not differ very much from that of ordinary banks and consists principally of taking deposits and lending. Credit associations, however, are specialised financial institutions for small businesses, just like mutual loans and savings banks. They are 'to facilitate finance for the people and to serve to increase their savings' (Article 1, Credit Associations Law). Thus, they are local financial institutions, maintaining close relationships with small businesses. For this reason their areas of operation are confined to their own localities. Moreover, they are co-operative type financial institutions which, in principle, can lend only to members. In this respect, they differ markedly from banks, and are rather more akin to credit co-operatives, although they differ from them in accepting deposits from the public.

Credit associations can accept deposits (including current deposits) from both members and non-members. Interest rates are subject to control under the Temporary Money Rates Adjustment Law. At present, however, because of the special character of their business, their maximum deposit rates are fixed at 0·1 per cent or 0·365 per cent above the corresponding rates of banks. On the other hand, lending (loans, advances and discounts) are in principle made only to members. As an exception, however, they may lend to non-members on the security of deposits or instalment savings. They are also allowed to lend to local authorities, banks and other financial institutions, provided that such lending does not interfere with that to members. So-called 'lending to graduates' and 'small lending to non-members' are also permitted on the same conditions.[1]

[1] 'Lending to graduates' and 'small lending to non-members' have been instituted by a recent amendment to the law in 1968. 'Lending to graduates' is a system by which business firms which were formerly members for a certain period (at least three years) and which have lost their membership because they have outgrown the necessary qualifications, can continue to obtain accommodation for a specified period thereafter (five years). (Figures in parentheses are stipulated in Notification No. 71 of the Ministry of Finance of 1 June 1968.)

'Small lending to non-members' is a system by which non-members could qualify for membership by subscribing for a share, can borrow up to 300,000 yen without joining the association. The system has been introduced because it has been considered to be unnecessary for small or temporary borrowers to be forced to become members by subscribing for a share, the minimum amount of which has been raised. (Notification No. 71 of the Ministry of Finance.)

The total of such lending to non-members (excluding that to financial institutions) cannot exceed 20 per cent of the total (excluding that to financial institutions). Interest rates on loans and advances and the discount rate of bills are not subject to regulations under the Temporary Money Rates Adjustment Law, but their maximum levels are stipulated in their 'conditions of operation' (at present the maximum is 10·95 per cent).

Credit associations also engage in other business including domestic exchanges; receipt of subscription money for new shares, debentures and bonds and the payment of principal, interest or dividends; safe custody; agency business of the People's Finance Corporation; and other business. All these services are open to the public.

C. Recent Trends

On the liabilities side the total deposits in credit associations have more than doubled during the five years to the end of 1969, when the outstanding amount was 6408·4 billion yen. The proportion of fixed deposits, such as time and deferred deposits and instalment savings, is as high as 88 per cent.

Their lending has similarly increased, to reach 5430·1 billion yen at the end of 1969. This was a larger amount than the outstanding lending of mutual loans and savings banks. Thus, their importance in small-business finance has been rising in recent years. The breakdown by industry of their outstanding lending shows roughly the same pattern as that of mutual loans and savings banks. Lending to wholesale and retail trades has recently levelled out. It is also noticable that the rate of growth of lending to manufacturing industries, which steadily increased until recently, has slowed down of late.

Investments in securities amounted to 562·3 billion yen at the end of 1969, equal to 8·9 per cent of outstanding deposits. They have been increasing fairly rapidly. As in the case of mutual loans and savings banks this reflects the fall in call loan rates from the latter half of 1965, which prompted them to shift funds from call loans to securities investment.

TABLE 16.4

Principal Accounts of Credit Associations

(hundred million yen)

End of the Year	*1956*	%	*1960*	%	*1965*	%	*1966*	%	*1967*	%	*1968*	%	*1969*	%	*1970*	%
ASSETS																
Loans, Advances and Discounts	2,781	59·9	7,720	66·2	25,071	68·0	29,213	66·1	35,792	66·7	43,461	68·0	54,301	69·1	66,142	70·1
Securities	305	6·6	823	7·0	2,631	7·1	3,287	7·4	3,899	7·3	4,692	7·3	5,623	7·2	6,375	6·8
Deposits with Other Financial Institutions	833	18·0	1,411	11·9	5,571	15·1	6,496	14·7	7,056	13·1	7,314	11·4	8,107	10·3	9,500	10·1
Call Loans	90	1·9	321	1·8	665	1·8	444	1·0	623	1·2	919	1·4	1,004	1·3	1,092	1·2
Others	631	13·6	1,540	13·1	2,940	8·0	4,752	10·8	6,305	11·7	7,509	11·9	9,514	12·1	11,149	11·8
Total	4,640	100·0	11,815	100·0	36,878	100·0	44,192	100·0	53,675	100·0	63,895	100·0	78,549	100·0	94,294	100·0
LIABILITIES																
Deposits	3,813	82·2	9,580	81·1	31,138	84·4	36,884	83·5	44,572	83·0	52,212	81·7	64,084	81·6	77,395	82·1
Borrowings	78	1·7	217	1·8	264	0·7	412	0·9	420	0·8	841	1·3	1,021	1·3	940	1·0
Capital	154	3·3	275	2·3	696	1·9	787	2·1	886	1·7	994	1·6	1,108	1·3	1,222	1·3
Others	595	12·8	1,743	14·8	4,780	13·0	6,109	13·5	7,797	14·5	9,848	15·4	12,336	15·8	14,737	15·6

SOURCE: Bank of Japan, *Economic Statistics Annual*.

(2) *The Federation of Credit Associations*

By the Credit Associations Law of 1951 official recognition has been given to the establishment of the Federation of Credit Associations, to which the credit associations belong. In principle, credit associations are local institutions, but the efficient utilisation of funds requires that they assist each other by adjusting amongst themselves surpluses and deficiencies of funds. The Federation has been set up as their central agency for this purpose.

TABLE 16.5

Outstanding Amounts of Lending by Credit Associations, by Industry

(hundred million yen)

End of the Year	Manufacturing Industries		Wholesale and Retail Trades		Catering Industries		Others		Total		The Relative Proportion of Loans for Fixed Investment
		%		%		%		%		%	%
1956	875	32·0	1,031	37·7	364	13·3	465	17·0	2,735	100·0	10·6
1960	2,379	31·1	2,460	32·1	677	8·8	2,145	28·0	7,661	100·0	13·2
1965	8,044	33·5	7,455	31·1	2,279	9·5	6,209	25·9	23,987	100·0	19·0
1968	13,106	30·2	12,308	28·4	3,866	8·9	14,062	32·5	43,342	100·0	22·9
1969	16,133	29·8	14,844	27·4	4,700	8·7	18,496	34·1	54,173	100·0	24·2
1970	19,711	29·9	17,661	26·8	5,572	8·4	23,046	34·9	65,990	100·0	24·6

SOURCE: Bank of Japan, *Economic Statistics Annual.*

Only a credit association can become a member of the Federation, although membership is not compulsory. At present there is only one such federation, the National Federation of Credit Associations, which operates on a national scale; this was set up in November 1951 and is the successor to the National Federation of Credit Co-operatives.

Its principal business is the taking of deposits and lending. Deposits are accepted from members, the government, local authorities and other non-profit-making corporations. It also receives on deposit members' short-term surplus funds, which are treated as borrowings of the Federation under the name of 'Short-term Funds of Associations'. It can lend both to members and to non-members, but lending to non-members is subject to the approval of the Minister of Finance. Lending to a member is limited to 20 per cent of the sum of the members' capital and reserves.

In addition, the Federation can engage in domestic exchanges, safe custody of securities and other businesses. The Federation also handles the Credit Associations' Development Deposit System. This is a system of mutual aid among credit associations, by which financial assistance is given to associations short of funds due to natural disasters and other contingencies. It can also be used to strengthen their credit standing.

The total resources of the Federation (deposits and Short-term Funds of Associations) more than doubled in the five years to the end of 1969. This reflects the development of the credit associations. Short-term Funds of Associations used to be the largest constituent of its resources, accounting for 53·5 per cent of the total at the end of 1964. By the end of 1969, however, the proportion had been reduced to 37·1 per cent. This decrease reflects the fact that the interest rate on the Short-term Funds of Associations is linked to movements in the call loan rate; when the latter fell from late 1965, the deposit of short-term Funds with the Federation became unattractive to the member associations, which moved their funds into time deposits with more favourable yields.

Lending is the most important asset, representing 62·2 per sent of total assets at the end of 1969. Lending to members accounted for only about 20 per cent of total lending; the rest consisted of agency loans made through member associations, loans to banks and loans to local authorities. Loans to banks are in fact a means of employing idle money and are really long-term call loans.

Recently, lending has tended to stagnate, reflecting largely the cessation in the growth of loans to banks. Instead, holdings of securities have significantly increased, accounting at the end of 1969 for 18·6 per cent of total assets.

It should be added that the Federation has participated in

the Bank of Japan's buying and selling operations in bonds and debentures since February 1966.

4. CREDIT CO-OPERATIVES AND FEDERATION OF CREDIT CO-OPERATIVES

(1) *Credit Co-operatives*

A. General Survey

Credit co-operatives operate under the Law for Co-operatives of Small Business, etc., of 1949. As has been discussed in the section on credit associations, those credit co-operatives akin to ordinary financial institutions have been converted into credit associations. Thus, although credit associations and credit co-operatives are organised on the same co-operative principles, the latter adhere more closely to them than the former. For this reason, stress is placed on their autonomy, so that superintendence and other guidance are kept to the minimum. On the other hand, they can, in principle, do business only with their members, so that the principles of co-operative finance may be more fully observed.

Regulations are, however, necessary to ensure sound management and the protection of depositors. Thus, in 1949, the Law Concerning Finance Business Conducted by Co-operatives imposed restrictions upon their employment of surplus funds. Administrative guidance is also imposed upon their reserve ratios, ratios of lendings to deposits, ratios of large lendings to net worth, and so on.

As in the case of mutual loans and savings banks and of credit associations, the remarkable development of credit co-operatives has brought a gap between principles and their observance. Hence, the law was amended in 1968 to enlarge the scope of their business: they have been authorised to make loans to local authorities on the security of their deposits, loans to financial institutions and other loans, while, on the other hand, the minimum amount of their capital has been raised[1] in

[1] The minimum capital of credit co-operatives situated in special wards of the Tokyo Metropolis and in cities designated by the Minister of Finance has been fixed at 20 million yen (5 million yen previously) and that of other co-operatives at 10 million yen (2 million yen previously).

TABLE 16.6

Principal Accounts of Credit Co-operatives

(hundred million yen)

End of the Year	1956		1960		1965		1966		1967		1968		1969		1970	
		Percentages		Percentages		Percentages		Percentages		Percentages		Percentages		Percentages		Percentages
ASSETS																
Loans, Advances and Discounts	558	70·9	1,600	67·5	6,276	66·9	7,741	67·5	9,694	66·3	11,734	66·4	14,743	69·2	17,245	68·6
Securities	13	1·7	55	2·3	242	2·6	328	2·9	396	2·7	450	2·5	521	2·4	603	2·4
Deposits with Other Financial Institutions	120	15·2	423	17·8	1,695	18·1	1,965	17·1	2,413	16·5	2,817	16·0	2,489	11·7	2,847	11·3
Others	96	12·2	293	12·4	1,171	12·4	1,436	12·5	2,108	14·5	2,663	15·1	3,540	16·7	4,434	17·7
Total	787	100·0	2,371	100·0	9,384	100·0	11,470	100·0	14,611	100·0	17,664	100·0	21,293	100·0	25,129	100·0
LIABILITIES																
Deposits	612	77·8	1,897	80·0	7,721	82·3	9,467	82·5	11,756	80·5	14,173	80·2	16,931	79·5	19,778	78·7
Borrowings	66	8·4	114	4·8	203	2·2	257	2·2	351	2·4	362	2·0	382	1·8	460	1·8
Capital	41	5·2	88	3·7	290	3·1	334	2·9	383	2·6	435	2·5	491	2·3	540	2·1
Others	68	8·6	272	11·5	1,170	12·4	1,412	12·4	2,121	14·5	2,694	15·3	3,489	16·4	4,351	17·4

SOURCE: Bank of Japan, *Economic Statistics Annual*.

order to replenish their net worth. The maximum amount that may be lent to one person has also been increased.[1]

Only 72 credit co-operatives remained after the conversion of major co-operatives into credit associations. Since then, however, numerous credit co-operatives have been organised, because approval for their establishment is almost automatic unless there are special reasons to refuse it. They differ from credit associations in this respect also. In all, there were 539 credit co-operatives at the end of 1969.

B. Business

On the liabilities side, credit co-operatives accept deposits or instalment savings from their members. They can also accept deposits from the government, local authorities, non-profit-making corporations, and from those related to members and who live with them. Interest rates are subject to regulation under the Temporary Money Rates Adjustment Law. The ceilings on deposit rates are, in principle, the same as those for banks, but for co-operatives which have been paying rates higher than these maxima, rates can be 0·1 or 0·365 per cent above those of banks.

On the assets side, they make loans and advances to, or discount bills for, members. In addition, they can lend to members' relatives living with them on the security of their deposits or of instalment savings. Lending to a member should not exceed 20 per cent of the net worth. Their 'conditions of operations' provide for lending rates to be less than 18·25 per cent.

Amongst other business credit co-operatives undertake domestic exchange business for members; the receipt of subscription money for new securities, and the payment of principal, interest or dividends; safe custody; and so on.

C. Recent Trends.

Deposits, which account for some 80 per cent of the total liabilities of credit co-operatives, roughly trebled during the five years to the end of 1969. Such a conspicuous growth is due partly to the increase in their numbers and partly to the

[1] The maximum is determined by the prefectural authorities, but in practice it is 100 million yen.

remarkable growth of small businesses, which provides their membership. On the other hand, lending has rather more than trebled during this period, and represents nearly 70 per cent of total assets, while securities holdings are very small.

(2) *Federation of Credit Co-operatives*

When most of the credit co-operatives were converted into credit associations in 1951 the National Federation of Credit Co-operatives was also reorganised, becoming the National Federation of Credit Associations. In 1954, however, organisation of credit co-operatives into a federation was permitted under the Law for Co-operatives of Small Business, etc. The National Federation of Credit Co-operatives was thus formed, operating on a national scale.

Like the National Federation of Credit Associations, its principal business on the liabilities side is the acceptance of deposits from members, the government, local authorities or non-profit-making corporations. On the assets side its chief business is to make loans to, or to discount bills for, its members, the credit co-operatives.

The outstanding deposits and borrowed money of the National Federation of Credit Co-operatives multiplied about 2·7 times during the five years ending in 1969, when the outstanding amount was 144·9 billion yen. In part the growth reflects the growth of credit co-operatives themselves; but deposits by local authorities, as a part of measures for financial assistance to small businesses, have contributed not a little to the increase (at the end of 1969 they accounted for 8·8 per cent of total of deposits and borrowed money). On the other hand, lending also multiplied about 5·5 times during those five years. The larger part of this, however, is accounted for by increases in 'loans of deposited money', which are a counterpart of the deposits by local authorities. At the end of 1969 the outstanding amount of lending was 91·0 billion yen, about 40 per cent of which was 'lending of deposited money'. Such lending is made to small businesses via their credit co-operatives. The attendant risk, however, is shouldered by the Federation.

5. LABOUR CREDIT ASSOCIATIONS AND FEDERATION OF LABOUR CREDIT ASSOCIATIONS

(1) *Labour Credit Associations*

A. General Survey

Labour credit associations are financial institutions on co-operative principles which engage in financial activities to improve the standard of living of workers and to promote the welfare or mutual-aid projects of trade unions, consumers' co-operatives and other associations of workers. A financial institution of this type for workers was first established in 1921. This was the Credit Co-operative Labour Bank authorised by the City of Tokyo (dissolved in 1926). It was, however, during the post-war years when the trade union movement developed rapidly that formation of labour credit associations came to be seriously contemplated. At the national convention of the Federation of Trade Unions in November 1949 the policy was formally adopted of founding 'labour banks'. The first labour credit association was established in Okayama prefecture in August 1950 (the Workers' Credit Co-operative of Okayama Prefecture). This gave the signal for the formation of a series of labour credit associations in various places.

These associations were at first ordinary credit co-operatives under the Law for Co-operatives of Small Business, etc. They differ considerably, however, from other financial institutions in that they are co-operative organisations under the aegis of organised labour and in being non-profit-making bodies, which accept the small savings of workers. A separate law for them was therefore enacted in 1953 under the name of the Labour Credit Associations Law. The thirty-two labour credit co-operatives then existing in thirty-two prefectures were, under this law, immediately converted into labour credit associations. In April 1955 the Federation of Labour Credit Associations was formed as their central agency. With the founding of Shiga Prefecture Labour Credit Association in July of that year, the current system of one association in each prefecture was completed.

At the end of 1969 there were in all 46 labour credit associations with 350 offices all over the country. Membership is restricted to trade unions, consumers' co-operatives and their federations, civil servants' organisations under certain laws, and other workers' associations aiming to improve their economic conditions by welfare activities, mutual aid or in any other ways. If, however, there is a provision in the articles of association, workers can become individual members. At the end of 1969 the total number of members was about 212,000.

B. Business

The principal business of labour credit associations is the acceptance of deposits and instalment savings on the one hand, and lending on the other. They can receive deposits from their members, constituent members of corporate members, husbands or wives or other relatives of individual members living with them, the government, local authorities and non-profit-making corporations. Lending can, however, be made only to members or to constituent members of corporate members. They are prohibited from lending for political contributions or for election campaigns or for any other political activities. They are also forbidden to lend money for the expenses of labour disputes, such as postage, travel expenses or conference expenses. Even if the money is ostensibly used as living expenses for trade union members, the associations are not allowed to make such loans, if the real purpose is to use them for labour disputes. The outlets for their idle funds are restricted to deposits with other financial institutions, investments in securities, and so on, so that they are not permitted to lend on the call loan market. As with credit associations and credit co-operatives, they are authorised by a notification under the Temporary Money Rates Adjustment Law to pay interest on deposits at rates 0·1 or 0·365 per cent above the corresponding deposit rates of banks. On the other hand, their maximum lending rate is stipulated in their conditions of operations; at the end of 1969 this was 12·5 per cent.

In addition, labour credit associations are authorised to engage in the business of safe custody of securities for members and they are also permitted to act as agencies of the Housing Loan Corporation.

C. Recent Trends

Deposits in labour credit associations have steadily increased with the increased numbers of their members. They approximately trebled during the five years to the end of 1969, when the outstanding amount was 283·8 billion yen. Time deposits account for about three-quarters of total deposits. On the other hand, lending more than trebled to 232·3 billion yen. The most important single item in lending is living expenses, which represented 33·5 per cent of the total in the fiscal year 1969 (by number of cases, it accounted for more than 80 per cent of the total). The relative weight of such lending, however, has not increased of late. A noteworthy feature in recent years has been the gradual rise in the relative importance of housing loans. This reflects the shift from the original functions of labour credit associations, which were almost wholly concerned with supporting the mere subsistence of workers, to cover the whole gamut of activities for their well-being.

(2) *Federation of Labour Credit Associations*

The Federation of Labour Credit Associations, established in 1955 as the central agency of all the country's labour credit associations, undertakes roughly the same activities as those of individual associations, namely the receiving of deposits and lending. The difference consists in the Federation's emphasis on the strengthening of mutual bonds among member associations and on the efficient employment of funds. Its chief functions are, therefore, to operate the centralised clearing of current accounts, the mutual-aid fund and other arrangements for special loans.

The centralised clearing of current accounts is a system for the settlement of payments between labour credit associations by the crediting or debiting of their current account balances with the Federation. It operates this clearing at the request of associations having current accounts. Through the Mutual Aid Fund the Federation takes time deposits from member associations, and uses them to protect depositors or to reinforce their credit standing in cases of unexpected disasters and other emergencies. The Federation can also make loans to member

TABLE 16.7

Principal Accounts of Labour Credit Associations

(hundred million yen)

End of the Year	*1956*	%	*1960*	%	*1965*	%	*1966*	%	*1967*	%	*1968*	%	*1969*	%	*1970*	%
ASSETS																
Loans, Advances and Discounts	126	64·6	304	61·8	872	56·7	1,059	55·4	1,350	62·1	1,794	65·9	2,323	68·1	3,009	69·8
Securities	20	10·3	59	12·0	69	4·5	123	6·4	165	7·6	204	7·5	203	6·0	209	4·8
Deposits with Other Financial Institutions	32	16·4	115	23·4	408	26·5	490	25·6	498	22·9	526	19·3	621	18·2	724	16·8
Others	17	8·7	14	2·8	189	12·3	240	12·6	162	7·4	200	7·3	262	7·7	370	8·6
Total	195	100·0	492	100·0	1,538	100·0	1,912	100·0	2,175	100·0	2,724	100·0	3,409	100·0	4,312	100·0
LIABILITIES																
Deposits	169	86·7	410	83·3	1,182	76·9	1,462	76·5	1,813	83·4	2,266	83·2	2,838	83·3	3,575	82·9
(of which Time Deposits	(113)	(57·9)	(292)	(59·3)	(871)	(56·6)	(1,089)	(57·0)	(1,367)	(62·9)	(1,725)	(63·3)	(2,172)	(63·7)	(2,737)	(63·5)
Borrowings	8	4·1	32	6·5	63	4·1	89	4·7	53	2·4	71	2·6	74	2·1	78	1·8
Capital	9	4·6	18	3·7	44	2·9	50	2·6	57	2·6	66	2·4	77	2·3	90	2·1
Others	9	4·6	32	6·5	249	16·1	311	16·2	252	11·6	321	11·8	420	12·3	569	13·2

SOURCE: Bank of Japan, *Economic Statistics Annual.*

TABLE 16.8

Lending by Labour Credit Associations, by Use of Loan Proceeds

(hundred million yen)

In the Course o the Year	*Living Expenses*		*Housing Loans*		*Money needed to make good wages and salaries in arrears*		*Money for Mutual Welfare Projects*		*Money for Activities of Consumers' Co-operatives*		*Total*	
		Percent-ages		*Percent-ages*		*Percent-ages*		*Percent-ages*		*Percent-ages*		*Percent-ages*
1965	458	35·2	220	16·9	224	17·2	244	18·7	156	12·0	1,302	100·0
1966	486	36·0	311	23·1	141	10·5	215	15·9	195	14·5	1,348	100·0
1967	589	35·4	458	27·5	142	8·5	175	10·5	302	18·1	1,666	100·0
1968	680	34·8	518	26·5	163	8·4	163	8·3	429	22·0	1,955	100·0
1969	818	33·5	651	26·7	200	8·2	221	9·1	551	22·6	2,441	100·0

SOURCE: Ministry of Finance, *Annual Report of Banking Bureau.*

associations at specially reduced rates of interest, should they fall into difficulties or meet extraordinary disasters.

At the end of 1969 the outstanding deposits of the Federation were 49·3 billion yen, of which 76·8 per cent were time deposits. On the assets side investments in securities amounted to 35·5 billion yen and were the biggest item (68·8 per cent of the total), followed by lending (18·2 per cent) and call loans (9·9 per cent).

6. GOVERNMENT FINANCIAL INSTITUTIONS FOR SMALL BUSINESSES

(1) *The Central Bank for Commercial and Industrial Co-operatives*

The Central Bank for Commercial and Industrial Co-operatives was established in 1936 under the Central Bank for Commercial and Industrial Co-operatives Law, to facilitate finance for co-operatives of small businesses. The bank is a financial institution on co-operative principles, so that it can only receive deposits from or lend to affiliated organisations, which are its shareholders, and members of these organisations. The affiliated organisations have changed considerably over time: at present they include business co-operatives[1] under the Law for Co-operatives of Small Businesses, etc., joint-enterprise co-operatives,[2] credit co-operatives, commerce–industry trade associations,[3] environmental sanitation trade associations, liquor producers' associations, liquor dealers' associations, shopping district development co-operative associations, domestic maritime associations, mutual fire-insurance co-operatives,

[1] Business Co-operatives – ordinary co-operatives of small businesses.

[2] Joint-Enterprise Co-operatives – these differ from business co-operatives in that small businesses participating in them merge completely to form a joint enterprise, in which the owners of small businesses become shareholders, and at the same time work as its employees. More than two-thirds of the shareholders should work thus as employees, and more than one-half of the total employees of the enterprise should be shareholders.

[3] Commerce–Industry Trade Associations – these are prefectural organisations of trades, the purposes of which are (1) the discouragement of excessive competition among members; (2) contribution to rationalisation of members' undertakings; (3) guidance and instruction, collection of information and data, research and investigations necessary for members' business, (4) joint economic ventures of the same nature as those undertaken by business co-operatives.

petty business co-operatives,[1] consolidated co-operatives[2] and the federations of these co-operatives and associations as well as export or import associations. At the end of 1969 the total number of affiliated organisations was 18,770.

The bank is a special corporation under a special law. The affiliated organisations elect delegates by mutual vote of their own members. The delegates are organised in an assembly which is the decision-making body of the bank. At first the capital of the bank was 10 million yen subscribed equally by the government and the member associations. As the scale of operations has expanded the capital has frequently been increased. At the end of 1969 the paid-up capital was 31·2 billion yen, of which 18·4 billion, or more than half, was subscribed by the government.

The operation of the bank is under the superintendence of the Minister of Finance and of the Minister of International Trade and Industry. The competent ministers have power to appoint the bank's officers, to issue directives to the bank, to take punitive action against it and to restrict its activities. Moreover, a wide variety of individual businesses is subject to their approval. In addition, a supervisor of the Central Bank for Commercial and Industrial Co-operatives watches over the conduct of the bank's business. Thus, the government intervenes in the affairs of the bank more closely than in those of ordinary financial institutions: on the other hand, it gives financial assistance by subscribing for its capital and for its debentures nearly 20 per cent of bank's resources coming from the government. Besides its head office in Tokyo the bank has 71 branches and offices (at the end of 1969) in various parts of the country. A number of credit co-operatives act as its agencies. Thus, the bank operates on a national scale.

The bank is authorised to issue debentures, which are its

[1] Petty Business Co-operatives – these are miniature business co-operatives, the members of which should be extremely small enterprises with less than five employees (less than two employees for undertakings in commerce or catering industries). Special tax deductions are granted to such co-operatives.

[2] Consolidated Co-operatives – the members merge part or the whole of their operations to set up a joint enterprise. These differ from business co-operatives or joint-enterprise co-operatives in that voting rights may be conferred on members in proportion to their contributions. In principle, only small businesses can become members, but big firms may also join them if their number does not exceed one-quarter of the total number of members.

chief source of funds. At the end of 1969 the amount outstanding was 718·3 billion yen and accounted for about three-quarters of its total resources. There are two varieties: interest-bearing Commercial and Industrial Debentures (maturity of five years) and Discount Commercial and Industrial Debentures (maturity of one year). The nominal yields are 7·5 per cent and 5·83 per cent respectively. The maximum amount that may be issued is 20 times the sum of paid-up capital and reserves on the capital account.

Originally the bank was permitted to receive deposits only from the member associations, but the restriction was subsequently relaxed: the bank may now receive deposits from constituent members of the affiliated associations, from public bodies and non-profit-making corporations and, subject to the approval of the appropriate ministers, from banks and other financial institutions. The bank, however, is not authorised to accept deposits from the general public, so that deposits represent only about 20 to 30 per cent of total resources. Interest rates on deposits are not subject to regulations under the Temporary Money Rates Adjustment Law, but are fixed by the chairman of the board of directors.

Lending is made to affiliated associations and their constituent members. They take the forms of term loans with maturities of less than five years; loans repayable in annual, semi-annual or monthly instalments with maturities of less than 20 years; discounting of bills; and overdrafts. Lending to constituent members of affiliated associations is mostly indirect through these organisations. By an amendment to the law in 1962 the bank has been allowed, subject to the approval of the ministers concerned, to make short-term loans to non-members, whether individuals or corporate bodies, on the security of Commercial and Industrial Debentures held by them.

For each business year the delegates fix the maximum limit of lending to an individual borrower. For the 1970 business year the maximum was 500 million yen for an association and 50 million yen for a constituent member of an association. The lending rates are not regulated by the Temporary Money Rates Adjustment Law, but are fixed by the chairman of the board of directors for each business year. They are, however, subject to approval by the relevant ministers. In August 1970 the rate of discount of ordinary commercial bills with maturities of less than one year and the rate on advances on such bills was 8·30 per cent for associations (8·50 per cent for their constituent members), while for loans on deeds with maturities of more than one year the rate was 8·6 per cent for associations (8·8 per cent for their members).

Owing to the increased demand for funds from small businesses in recent years the bank's lending increased by about 150 per cent during the five years to the end of 1968, when the outstanding amount of lending was 1016·5 billion yen; of this, about 70 per cent was for the finance of working capital and 30 per cent for the finance of fixed investment in plant and equipment. By sector, lending to manufacturing industries represented nearly half of the total and held the biggest share, followed by lending to wholesale and retail trades, catering industries and transport and communication.

(2) *The Small Business Finance Corporation*

The Small Business Finance Corporation is a government financial institution. It provides long-term working capital and funds for the fixed investment necessary for the development of small businesses, which experience difficulties in obtaining such accommodation from ordinary financial institutions. Before the founding of the corporation, government funds had been made available to small businesses through the Reconstruction Finance Bank, the U.S. Aid Counterpart Fund Special Account and the Japan Development Bank. In 1953, however, the corporation was established as a financial institution with capital subscribed entirely by the government; it took over the outstanding claims of the Reconstruction Finance Bank and others.

The Small Business Finance Corporation is not the sole government financial institution for small businesses: there are also the People's Finance Corporation and the Central Bank for Commercial and Industrial Co-operatives. It differs from the other corporations in that it lends on long-term at low-interest rates to all sorts of small enterprises, while the People's Finance Corporation lends money mainly to extremely small businesses; and the Central Bank for Commercial and

Industrial Co-operatives exists to finance co-operatives and associations of small firms.

The capital of the corporation was 25·2 billion yen at the end of 1969. As it is not authorised to receive deposits, borrowing from the government was formerly the only source of funds, if we exclude the capital. Since 1964, however, it has been permitted to issue Small Business Debentures, which are guaranteed by the government. The maximum limit of issue is twenty times its capital and at the end of fiscal year 1969 the amount outstanding was 169·3 billion yen. At present, besides the head office, the corporation has 35 branches and 9 sub-branches. In addition, various banks and credit associations are appointed as agencies. It therefore operates on a national scale.

The principal business is loans to small businesses to finance fixed investment in plant and equipment or long-term working capital. Loans are classified into ordinary loans and special loans for specific policy objectives. The method of lending distinguishes between direct loans by the corporation itself and agency loans.

Restrictions are imposed upon the scale and type of business firms entitled to receive ordinary loans; they are also required to restrict the use of the loans to the rationalisation of their undertakings. In order to distribute the corporation's funds as widely as possible loans to a single borrower are in principle limited to 50 million yen in the case of direct loans, and to 10 million yen for agency loans; the basic rate of interest is 8·2 per cent. Loans may be term loans or may be repayable by instalments, and maturities range from one to five years.

Special loans are related to particular policy objectives of the government: loans to specific branches of the machine industry, to specific export industries and for the modernisation of small businesses are examples of such loans. The eligibility of borrowers is closely restricted, as are the uses of loan proceeds; on the other hand, there is favourable treatment in respect of the amount of loans and of interest rates.

The outstanding amount of the corporation's loans was 748·0 billion yen at the end of 1969, of which ordinary loans accounted for more than 90 per cent. Agency loans represented 58 per cent of the total, while direct loans were equal to 42 per cent. By use, loans to finance fixed investment in plant and equipment accounted for about 80 per cent. This reflects the nature of the corporation. It is also responsible for the fact that loans to manufacturing industries were more than 60 per cent of the total, while those to wholesale and retail trades and to catering industries are infinitesimal.

When the Small Business Investment Companies were established in 1963 the corporation subscribed for their shares and also made long-term loans to them.

(3) *The People's Finance Corporation*

The People's Finance Corporation was founded in 1949 as a government financial institution succeeding to the business of the pre-war People's Bank and of the Pension Bank. Its purpose is to lend money for business to private individuals, who experience difficulty in borrowing it from banks or other ordinary financial institutions. The provision of relief funds to destitute people is thus not the original aim of the corporation: it has been founded to lend small sums of money necessary for people's trades. It thus differs from the Small Business Finance Corporation in that it lends small amounts to petty borrowers.

It is a public corporation with capital subscribed entirely by the government. Its resources consist of its capital and borrowings from the government; its capital was originally 1·3 billion yen, but at the end of 1969 it amounted to as much as 20 billion yen. An important feature of the corporation is the People's Finance Council of the Ministry of Finance which exists to reflect public opinion on the corporation's operations. The council consists of eight representatives from the private sector and two representatives from the government; it makes decisions on affairs of specific importance to the corporation, and in addition expresses views on important aspects of the corporation's activities, if requested by the Minister of Finance. It has 112 branches and appoints other financial institutions as its agents, so that it operates nationally.

Its principal business is to make loans which include both ordinary loans to small businesses and loans on the security of pensions, War-Bereaved Family Treasury Bonds, Repatriates Bonds, Special Benefits Bonds and so on. Ordinary loans account for about 90 per cent of the total. The basic rate of interest on ordinary loans is 8·2 per cent, while the interest rate on other kinds of loans is 6 per cent. The amount of loans to one person may not exceed 5 million yen. The maturities are less than five years for loans to finance working capital, and less than seven years for loans to finance fixed investment. The loans are usually made on the joint surety of a third person, but if the borrower so desires, he can dispense with the surety by offering collateral security. For loans above 2 million yen, mortgages on real property (or in exceptional cases securities) are, in principle, required.

The outstanding amount of loans has increased steadily since its foundation. At the end of 1969 it was 593·1 billion yen, which represented an increase of 160 per cent during five years. By use, 65 per cent of loans was to finance working capital, while loans for fixed investment represented only 35 per cent. By industry, the relative weight of the wholesale and retail trades was the biggest with 50 per cent of the total, followed by manufacturing industries (29 per cent), and catering industries (6 per cent).

7. CREDIT GUARANTEE AND CREDIT INSURANCE

(1) *Credit Guarantee Associations*

The principal business of credit-guarantee associations is to indemnify the obligations of small businesses, which have borrowed from ordinary financial institutions. Their origin goes back to pre-war years, but it was in 1953 that the Credit Guarantee Associations Law was enacted, to provide legal status for these organisations, and thereby to facilitate their operations.

Under the law, credit-guarantee associations are special corporations. Their establishment is subject to approval by the relevant ministers. They are established under the aegis of local authorities with the participation of various financial institutions, such as commercial banks, mutual loans and savings banks, credit associations and credit co-operatives. At present there are 51 of them in the country.

Their principal business is: (1) guarantee of obligations of small businesses, which have borrowed from banks or other

TABLE 16.9

Principal Accounts of Three Government Financial Institutions for Small Businesses

(hundred million yen)

	Central Bank for Commercial and Industrial Co-operatives		*Small Business Finance Corporation*		*People's Finance Corporation*	
	End of 1963	*End of 1970*	*End of 1963*	*End of 1970*	*End of 1963*	*End of 1970*
ASSETS						
Loans, Advances and Discounts	3,350	12,039	2,406	8,952	1,841	7,089
Securities	76	224	—	26	—	—
Deposits with other Financial Institutions	123	455	23	19	11	29
Call Loans	14	0	0	0	0	0
LIABILITIES						
Debentures Outstanding	2,196	8,439	0	2,058	0	0
Deposits	998	3,298	0	0	0	0
Borrowings	78	88	1,964	6,129	1,528	6,681
Capital	130	327	248	252	200	200

SOURCE: Bank of Japan, *Economic Statistics Annual.*

financial institutions; (2) guarantee of contingent liabilities of banks and other financial institutions, which have been incurred by their guaranteeing of debts of small businesses; (3) guarantee of the contingent liabilities of banks and other financial institutions which have arisen when they have been commissioned by the People's Finance Corporation or by the Japan Development Bank to lend to small businesses as their agents, or when they have lent to them as an agency of the Small Business Finance Corporation. The funds needed for their operations come from contributions by local authorities and borrowings from the Small Business Credit Insurance Corporation. The maximum amount of the contingent liabilities of each association is fixed by reference to their operating conditions. The maxima are in the range of 20–50 times their basic assets.[1] These multiples have, however, tended to increase

[1] The basic assets provide the basis for their activities. The maximum amount of contingent liabilities of each guarantee association is fixed by its statute at some

recently, because their guarantee business has been on the increase, while the expansion of basic assets has lagged.

When a small business with debts guaranteed by one of the associations defaults, the association takes responsibility for repayment to the lending institution, and also takes over any claim. This guarantee business is supported by the credit insurance system of the Small Business Credit Insurance Corporation, which will be explained in the next section.

During 1969 the associations agreed to guarantee 979,000 obligations, amounting to 1045·1 billion yen. In the same year repayments taken over totalled 23·4 billion yen. Their average amount per case is smaller than that of credit guarantee arrangements as a whole, demonstrating that defaults occur mainly among small debtors. At the end of March 1970 the outstanding amount of credit guarantee was 1054 billion yen, which was 28 times their basic assets of 37·8 billion yen.

(2) *The Small Business Credit Insurance Corporation*

In order to support the credit-guarantee associations described above and further to reinforce the credit standing of small business a credit insurance system for small business has been established under the Small Business Credit Insurance Law and the Small Business Credit Insurance Special Account Law of 1950. At first it was operated by a special government account, but in 1958 the Small Business Credit Insurance Corporation was founded to take over the business of the special account.

Initially the corporation insured credit for banks and other financial institutions, but, by an amendment to the law in 1961, its only customers today are credit-guarantee associations; it insures contingent liabilities arising from their credit guarantees and also lends them the necessary money.

The corporation is a government financial institution with capital subscribed entirely by the government. Its sources of

---

multiple of its basic assets. They are composed of the endowment fund and of reserves. The endowment consists of contributions of local authorities and financial institutions, while reserves are accumulated from the balance of receipts and disbursements of each settlement term. From the fiscal year 1967 the endowments have been increased by allotments to financial institutions (700 million yen at the end of the fiscal year 1967).

funds, besides the fund taken over from the Small Business Credit Insurance Special Account, are contributions from the General Account and the Industrial Investment Special Account. At the end of 1969 its paid-up capital amounted to 60·7 billion yen, of which 4·4 billion yen was the insurance reserve fund and 56·3 billion yen was the loan fund.

Its primary business, the insurance of the contingent liabilities of credit-guarantee associations, is of a blanket type: it insures the associations automatically, when they make contracts to guarantee debts, provided the outstanding amount of such contracts does not exceed a stipulated sum. When an association makes repayment on behalf of a small business in default, it can receive 70 per cent of the paid sum as insurance money from the corporation. Its insurance business has steadily expanded with the growth of lending to small businesses; during 1969 the amount of insurance contracts entered into was 952·8 billion yen.

The second function of the corporation is to make loans to credit-guarantee associations, which include long-term loans for the finance of operating capital needed to cover increased guarantee liabilities, and short-term loans to facilitate the repayment of guarantee money. The maturities are two years for the former and six months for the latter. The outstanding amount of such loans has grown steadily with the increased activity of the associations. At the end of 1969 it amounted to 55·6 billion yen, the greater part of which was long-term loans.

8. SMALL BUSINESS INVESTMENT COMPANIES

It was stressed in the Fundamental Law for Small Business of 1963 that it was necessary for the sound development of small businesses to replenish their net worth, the relative proportion of which to their total liabilities was lower than that of big firms. As already noted, however, it is difficult for them to raise capital in the securities market. Thus, in 1963 the Small Business Investment Companies Law was passed, and under it three Small Business Investment Companies were formed in Tokyo, Nagoya and Osaka.

Capital is 2·5 billion yen for the Tokyo company, 1·6 billion yen for the Nagoya company and 2·0 billion yen for the Osaka company. The capital is provided by the government, local authorities and various private institutions. The biggest subscribers are private financial institutions, while the government has subscribed through the Small Business Finance Corporation to the amount of 350 million yen for each company (since October 1968). The shares taken up by the corporation do not carry voting rights, but have preferential rights in the division of profits and over residual assets; they can also be redeemed from profits.

The business of investment companies can roughly be divided into investment and consultation. Investment is made by subscribing for the new shares (or convertible debentures) of joint-stock companies with a capital of less than 50 million yen in industries designated by a government ordinance (twenty-four industries are so designated). If the capital of the company exceeds 100 million yen after the issue of new shares (in the case of convertible debentures, after their conversion into shares) the investment company cannot, in principle, take them up. The amount of shares (or debentures) for which an investment company subscribed should be more than 15 per cent and less than 50 per cent of the total paid-up capital of the company. In 1965, however, the stock exchanges decided that only companies with more then 300 million yen of capital could qualify for listing in Tokyo and Osaka, while in Nagoya the minimum amount of capital was fixed at 200 million yen. This meant that, if the investment companies continued to adhere to the previous limitations as to the capital of companies in which they could invest, they would be unable to perform their functions of bridging, i.e. of assisting small businesses by subscribing for their shares until they can raise capital in the stock market. In 1966, therefore, amendments were made to the relevant articles of the law governing the investment companies; subject to approval by the Minister of International Trade and Industry, they may be authorised to subscribe for new shares until the capital of the company concerned reaches the minimum amount for listing in the stock exchanges. Their subscriptions during 1969 amounted to 2·5 billion yen (120 cases).

The investment companies hold shares thus acquired until

the small enterprise can offer its shares for public subscription, when the investment companies sell them by public tender. The selling price should be equal to the market price, if such has already been formed for them. The investment companies also give guidance on management and techniques to the small businesses in which they invested. This is their second function – consultation.

CHAPTER 17

FINANCIAL INSTITUTIONS FOR AGRICULTURE, FORESTRY AND FISHERY

1. CHARACTERISTICS AND DEVELOPMENT OF FINANCE OF AGRICULTURE, FORESTRY AND FISHERY

(1) *Characteristics of Finance of Agriculture, Forestry and Fishery*

The consequence of the growth and modernisation of the industrial structure has been a marked tendency for the relative importance of primary industries, such as agriculture, forestry and fishery to decline. For instance, their contribution to national income was almost halved, falling from 23 per cent in 1955 to 12 per cent in 1967, while the proportion of the total working population employed in them was reduced from 36 per cent to 21 per cent. Compared with the corresponding proportions in the advanced countries of Europe and North America, however, the relative weight of agriculture, forestry and fishery remains quite large. In Japan, moreover, the majority of economic units in these industries are extremely small in scale, while their productive activities are inevitably exceedingly sensitive to natural hazards. For these reasons the levels both of productivity and income are much lower than in modern industries. The existence side by side of modern industries, and small businesses, agriculture, forestry and fishery is usually termed the 'dual structure' of the Japanese economy. Since there is an urgent need to modernise these industries the government has made great efforts to protect them and to foster their development. Far-reaching changes, however, are occurring in their economic environment, for instance in the structure of consumption as a result of economic growth, in the exodus of workers from these industries, and in the growing competition from imported goods as a consequence of further internationalisation of the economy. Modernisation and structural reform of these primary industries are now therefore urgently required.

The characteristics of agriculture, forestry and fishery enumerated above are reflected in the financial sphere. For instance, agriculture, which is much the most important primary industry, has the following financial features:

A. Low Mortgage Value and Low Profitability

As most farms are excessively small, and as the household is scarcely distinguishable from the business aspect, both their mortgage values and their profitability are therefore likely to be low, so that the risk factor deters ordinary financial institutions from lending to them.

B. Long-term Nature of Funds Demanded

Relatively short-term funds suffice to finance the working capital of farms, in order to purchase fertilisers and farm chemicals. Low-interest loans with maturities ranging from several years to 20–30 years are, however, required to finance their structural reform, or to finance rationalisation to raise their productivity, for instance by the purchase of livestock or by improving equipment or land. Since 1961, when the Fundamental Law of Agriculture was enacted, it has been a particular concern of agricultural policy to close the gap between agriculture and other industries, and to secure stability in the supply of agricultural products. More long-term finance is necessary, however, to achieve these aims.

C. Seasonality of Demand for Money

As rice is the principal crop the financial requirements of agriculture for working capital is strongly seasonal: demand is active from spring to summer, so that lending to agriculture increases while savings decrease; from autumn to winter payments are made for agricultural products, so that savings increase while lending is repaid. Thus, agricultural finance tightens from spring to summer, while it slackens from autumn to winter.

These conditions are shared more or less by forestry and

fishery, and make it difficult to provide for their smooth financing.

(2) *Development of the Finance of Agriculture, Forestry and Fishery*

Because of the peculiarities enumerated above, agriculture, forestry and fishery have difficulty in borrowing from commercial banks and other private financial institutions. For this reason the government has encouraged the development of co-operative financial institutions and specialised financial institutions; these have borne the main burden of meeting their financial needs. In the past these financial institutions included several special banks, particularly the Hypothec Bank of Japan, but, as noted earlier (in Part One) they have been converted into commercial banks; co-operative financial institutions therefore now play the most important part in this sphere.

Co-operative financial institutions fall into three groups: those for agriculture, those for forestry and those for fishery. Each is organised at three levels: at the bottom are unit co-operatives operating in their own local communes, that is, cities, towns and villages; next come credit federations of these unit co-operatives, which are organised in each prefecture: finally there is the Central Co-operative Bank of Agriculture and Forestry.

To supplement these co-operatives there is a system of governmental finance – the so-called institutional finance – such as direct lending of Treasury Funds through the Agriculture, Forestry and Fishery Finance Corporation, credit guarantees, reinsurance and interest subsidies. Formerly, direct fiscal disbursements, such as Treasury subsidies and public works expenditure, were the most important form of financial assistance to these sectors of the economy; since 1951, however, these have gradually been curtailed, so that the emphasis of policy has shifted to more indirect measures, such as institutional finance and other forms of financial assistance. Moreover, since 1961, when the Fundamental Law of Agriculture was enacted, the government has sought to modernise the structure of agriculture, forestry and fishery, so that the importance of institutional finance has further increased.

At present institutional finance takes the following form: (1) finance of new settlers, to whom the Treasury lends directly through a special account; (2) finance of agricultural improvements (local authorities lend to such projects their own funds together with Treasury subsidies); (3) finance of these industries by the Agriculture, Forestry and Fishery Finance Corporation, the source of its funds being the Treasury; (4) interest subsidies by the government and the local authorities to private financial institutions (chiefly of the co-operative type), which have made loans for agricultural modernisation or for relief in case of natural disasters, as well as credit guarantees by credit guarantee associations; and (5) credit guarantees, by the Credit Guarantee for Finance of New Settlers Associations, for private financial institutions, which have made loans to new settlers, and credit guarantees by the Livestock Industry Promotion Corporation. The most important of these facilities are the institutional finance provided by the Agriculture, Forestry and Fishery Finance Corporation, a government financial institution, and facilities for the finance of agricultural modernisation, provided mostly by co-operative-type financial institutions.

Ordinary financial institutions, such as commercial banks, also finance these industries, but mainly they lend to relatively large-scale undertakings, which are rather exceptional in these sectors. The proportion of such lending to the total of their loans, advances and discounts is also extremely small. At the end of 1969 only 1·1 per cent of the total lending of commercial banks had been made to these categories of industry, whereas the corresponding ratio of mutual loans and savings banks and of credit associations was 2 per cent.

Table 17.1 shows the recent trends in the relative shares of various financial institutions in total lending to agriculture, forestry and fishery. In agricultural finance three-quarters are provided by co-operative financial institutions. With the contribution of government financial institutions they account for more than 90 per cent of total lending to these industries. In lending to forestry and fishery, in contrast, the relative weight of co-operatives is rather small, while that of ordinary financial institutions is as much as 40 per cent. This is because they lend to large-scale enterprises in these fields. As the absolute amounts of lending to these two industries are much

TABLE 17.1

Relative Shares of Various Financial Institutions in Lending to Agriculture, Forestry and Fishery (end of March 1970)

(percentages)

	Agri-culture	*Forestry*	*Fishery*	*Total*
Co-operative Financial Institutions	77	21	45	69
Government Financial Institutions	17	45	12	18
Ordinary Financial Institutions	6	34	43	13
Total	100	100	100	100

SOURCE: Central Co-operative Bank of Agriculture and Forestry, *Statistics of Finance of Agriculture and Forestry, 1970.*

smaller than those to agriculture, however, co-operative and government financial institutions account for more than 80 per cent of the total lending to the three sectors. Institutional finance has grown remarkably (Table 17.2), but lending by co-operative financial institutions as a whole has recently tended to level off.

2. AGRICULTURAL FINANCIAL INSTITUTIONS

(1) *Agricultural Co-operatives*

A. General Survey

Co-operative organisations in agricultural villages have a long history. Their prototype can be found in the 'mujin' associations of the feudal period. They acquired a legal and systematic form, however, only after the enactment of the Industrial Co-operative Law of 1900. The present agricultural co-operatives have been organised under the Agricultural Co-operatives Law of 1947, the aim of which was to reorganise the agricultural societies, which were war-time control agencies, into democratic co-operatives. They are the basic units of the pyramid of co-operatives institutions for agricultural finance, which has the Central Co-operative Bank of Agriculture and Forestry at its apex, and the prefectural credit federations of agricultural co-operatives in the middle tier.

An agricultural co-operative is a body corporate on partnership principles. It is run according to the voluntary decisions of the members, i.e. farmers. It can engage in a variety of business such as credit, purchase, sale, public utility and mutual aid. Credit activities are of outstanding importance. There are, however, co-operatives specialising in sales or in

TABLE 17.2

Outstanding Amounts of Institutional Financing of Agriculture, Forestry and Fishery

(hundred million yen)

End of the Fiscal Year	*1965*	*1966*	*1967*	*1968*	*1969*
Financing by Treasury Fund					
Loans by Agriculture, Forestry and Fishery Finance Corporation	4,561	5,393	6,255	7,335	8,590
Loans to New Settlers	338	368	391	415	417
Loans for Improvement of Agriculture	83	104	140	188	235
Total	4,982	5,865	6,786	7,938	9,242
Financing by Private Funds					
Loans for Modernisation of Agriculture	1,611	2,037	2,461	2,880	3,530[a]
Loans for Relief of Natural Disasters	178	289[a]	350[a]	357[a]	258[a]
Guarantee of Debt for Promotion of Livestock Industry	19	16	16	14	15
Loans to New Settlers for Improvement of Agricultural Undertakings	19	16	12	10	9
Guarantee of Debt of New Settlers	34	39	52	70	82
Guarantee of Debt of Small Fishermen	158	195	267	346	442
Total	2,019	2,592	3,158	3,677	4,336
Grand Total	7,001	8,457	9,944	11,615	13,578

[a] End of December of the year.

SOURCE: Ministry of Agriculture and Forestry, *Statistics of Finance of Agriculture and Forestry*.

the development of specific kinds of agricultural products and which do not engage in credit business. Only those co-operatives with financial functions, therefore, belong to the hierarchical organisations of co-operative financial institutions. Most of these, however, are multi-purpose, and engage in business other than credit, such as sales. In this respect they differ markedly from other types of financial institutions.

The number of agricultural co-operatives has gradually decreased as a result of liquidations and mergers under the Law for Promoting Mergers between Agricultural Co-operatives of 1961. Even so, there is one in every town and village. At the end of 1969 the number of agricultural co-operatives engaged in credit business was 6087. They have six million members representing roughly 90 per cent of all farm households. In recent years, however, more and more farmers either have come to engage in ancillary business or jobs, or have deserted agriculture altogether, so that the characteristics of their membership have changed. Moreover, agricultural co-operatives have come to earn more and more income from other sources than agriculture proper, and are therefore gradually losing their agricultural character. This tendency is particularly noticeable with agricultural co-operatives in city suburbs, many of which have all but discarded their proper function of lending to agriculture, and are being more and more assimilated to credit associations. This poses a problem of the proper *modus operandi* of the hierarchy of co-operatives as a whole.

B. Credit Business

Agricultural co-operatives are permitted to receive deposits and instalment savings from their members, and to make loans to them for business or personal needs. To ensure sound management the Ordinance for Standards of Financial Management of Agricultural Co-operatives prescribes standard ratios of payment reserves and of lendings, and proper methods of employment of idle resources.

Agricultural co-operatives have an important role as savings institutions in agricultural villages. Under the pre-harvest rice sales contract system the government purchases unlimited amounts of rice from the farmers at their request. A similar system is practised for wheat and barley. As will be explained later, payments for these purchases are made through the transfer savings accounts of the hierarchy of agricultural co-operatives, so that the money remains largely in farmers' savings accounts. Farmers' incomes from their ancillary occupations and from land sales are also important sources of funds for agricultural co-operatives. As agricultural land is being converted for other uses all over the country as a result of the establishment of 'new industrial cities' and of the development of tourism, the increase in deposits from land sales is now not confined to co-operatives in city suburbs.

Lending is another important activity of agricultural co-operatives. Up to 1965 some 60 per cent of total lending used to be short-term. Since then, however, farms have tended to be increasingly self-financed and to find their own short-term capital because both farmers' deposits and their income from other sources have increased. Thus, the proportion of short-term lending is gradually falling. On the other hand, there has been a notable increase in long-term loans, particularly for agricultural modernisation; the relative weight of such lending in recent years has exceeded 50 per cent. The ratio of total lending to total deposits, however, is still below 50 per cent, if we exclude agency loans of funds on the account of the Agriculture, Forestry and Fishery Finance Corporation. Thus, money absorbed by the co-operatives is not fully returned to agriculture, although the proportion returned is gradually rising.

By a notification under the Temporary Money Rates Adjustment Law the maximum deposit rate may be 0·1 per cent higher than the ceilings placed upon the corresponding deposit rates of banks, as is the case with deposit rates of credit associations and of credit co-operatives. Lending rates vary considerably from co-operative to co-operative, but are generally in the range of 7–11 per cent.

C. Recent Trends

A strong campaign was launched at the end of 1964 to increase deposits with agricultural co-operatives; this succeeded in raising them above 2000 billion yen. At the end of 1969 they amounted to 5301 billion yen, so that they multiplied by about 2·7 in five years. This spectacular expansion is, of course, primarily due to the growth in agricultural income following a succession of bumper crops and the raising of wholesale rice price, but deposits arising from incomes from other occupations, from ancillary businesses and from land sales have also grown. The increase has, however, tended to flatten out of late because farmers' expenditures have much increased as their consumption levels and their purchases of fixed assets — evident in their increased investment in improvements to their houses – have risen.

On the other hand, lending has multiplied by 2·8 during the past five years. In spite of this the amount outstanding is far smaller than that of deposits, more than 50 per cent of which are kept in liquid form; this 'surplus' may be employed in investment in securities or in deposits with other financial institutions. The bulk is deposited with institutions further up the pyramid of co-operative financial institutions.

TABLE 17.3

Principal Accounts of Agricultural Co-operatives

(hundred million yen)

End of the Year	*1965*	*1966*	*1967*	*1968*	*1969*	*1970*
Savings Deposits	24,326	29,859	36,539	43,145	53,010	61,867
(of which Fixed Savings Deposits)	(15,295)	(18,716)	(22,863)	(25,836)	(33,736)	(40,711)
Lending	9,883	12,087	15,216	19,077	23,713	29,284
(of which Short-term Lending)	(5,488)	(6,475)	(7,557)	(9,027)	(11,043)	(13,228)
Deposits with Other Financial Institutions	14,182	16,970	20,479	23,275	28,440	31,813
(of which Deposits with Affiliated Organisations)	(13,609)	(16,286)	(19,709)	(22,426)	(27,381)	(30,701)

NOTE: Agency loans on the account of the Agriculture, Forestry and Fishery Finance Corporations are not included in Lending.

SOURCE: Bank of Japan, *Economic Statistics Monthly*.

(2) *Credit Federations of Agricultural Co-operatives*

There are in all 46 credit federations of agricultural co-operatives, one for each prefecture. They are special corporations under the Agricultural Co-operatives Law. Their members are the unit agricultural co-operatives and the federations of co-operatives engaged in business other than credit. Unlike the unit co-operatives they are not authorised to engage concurrently in business other than credit. The principal business of the federations is receiving deposits from members and lending money to them.[1] They can also discount bills for members or guarantee their debts. They adjust regional deficits and surpluses of funds among members in order to support the financial activities of agricultural co-operatives.

Deposits with the credit federations have multiplied by about 2·4 during the past five years, due partly to rapid growth of deposits with unit co-operatives, which represent about 80 per cent of the total number of their members, and due partly to the rise in the proportion of the co-operatives' surplus funds lodged with the federations. Thus, the resources of the federations have increased substantially until the recent levelling-off of the rise in deposits; this has reflected the failure of funds deposited by unit co-operatives and by mutual-aid federations of agricultural co-operatives to grow further. On the other hand, lending by the federations has multiplied by 3·0 during the past five years, if we exclude their loans to other financial institutions. Nevertheless, lending represented only 41 per cent of their deposits at the end of March 1970. The remainder is employed in loans to or deposits with financial institutions, and in investments in securities. With this increase in their resources, however, they have developed a greater capacity to employ surplus funds on their own initiative: only about half the surplus is deposited with the Central Co-operative Bank of Agriculture and Forestry; this is a far lower proportion than in the case of unit co-operatives.

The principle that surplus funds should be concentrated in the hands of the Central Co-operative Bank of Agriculture and Forestry, which should then employ it, is thus not fully observed. Loans to financial institutions are formally a species of loans to non-members, but in truth they are a form of employment of surplus funds. They rose noticeably from the latter half of 1963, when money became tight and call loan rates rose. At the end of 1964 they represented as much as a quarter of total surplus funds. After 1965, however, monetary ease brought down call loan rates, so that the federations diverted their

[1] In addition to ordinary loans to members the credit federations make low-interest loans for specific purposes, which are defined in a 'prescription' (prescription loans). The latter loans may be made either by themselves or jointly with the mutual-aid federations of agricultural co-operatives.

surplus funds from this channel of employment to deposits with the Central Co-operative Bank (the proportion of the federations' surplus funds held as deposits with the Central Co-operative Bank was about 70 per cent at the end of 1965). This, however, somewhat inconvenienced the Central Co-operative Bank, which experienced difficulty in employing the funds, while the federations suffered from low yields on their high-cost money. Thus, the need to rationalise the co-operative financial system as a whole, and to increase its efficiency, became apparent.

TABLE 17.4

Principal Accounts of Credit Federations of Agricultural Co-operatives

(hundred million yen)

End of the Year	*1965*	*1966*	*1967*	*1968*	*1969*	*1970*
Savings Deposits	16,119	18,800	22,330	25,186	30,760	34,792
(of which Fixed Savings Deposits)	(14,002)	(16,659)	(19,583)	(22,221)	(26,900)	(30,611)
Lending	4,544	5,336	7,389	8,474	9,291	12,728
(of which Lending to Financial Institutions)	(1,150)	(1,426)	(2,141)	(1,590)	(1,536)	(1,496)
Deposits with Other Financial Institutions	9,914	10,362	11,111	12,278	16,094	15,648
(of which Deposits with Affiliated Organisations)	(9,144)	(9,619)	(10,348)	(11,496)	(15,180)	(14,683)

NOTE: Call Loans are included in 'Lending to Financial Institutions'.

SOURCE: Bank of Japan, *Economic Statistics Monthly*.

From the latter half of 1966 economic expansion again led to tight money, so that loans to financial institutions once more began to increase. The rise in call loan rates, however, was much less evident than in earlier periods of monetary restraint, partly because of debt management policy. Loans to financial institutions have thus not increased very much. The proportion of federations' surplus funds held as deposits with the Central Co-operative Bank money has, however, fallen because their deposits decreased while loans to borrowers other than financial institutions have increased.

(3) *National Mutual Insurance Federation of Agricultural Co-operatives*

As already mentioned, agricultural co-operatives are authorised to provide mutual-aid facilities. This is a kind of insurance scheme legalised by the Agricultural Co-operative Law of 1947 by which farmers can provide against unforeseen contingencies by mutual co-operation. Insurance against agricultural disasters, however, is provided by Agricultural Mutual-Aid Associations established under the Agricultural Disasters Compensation Law of the same year; membership in these is compulsory. The mutual-aid schemes of unit co-operatives include, therefore, long-term insurance, such as endowment insurance, house-reconstruction insurance and juvenile insurance, and short-term insurance, such as fire insurance, group fire insurance and automobile insurance (at the end of the fiscal year 1969 the outstanding amount of insurance contracts under the mutual-aid projects of agricultural co-operatives was 8913·2 billion yen for long-term insurance, 9582·4 billion yen for short-term insurance and 1410·2 billion yen for others).

These mutual-aid schemes are also organised into a hierarchy of three tiers. Insurance premiums are paid into agricultural co-operatives, which pay them, in turn, to prefectural mutual-aid federations of agricultural co-operatives for reinsurance. Part of the money received by prefectural federations is further paid into the National Mutual Insurance Federation of Agricultural Co-operatives for retrocession.

The funds of mutual-aid schemes are employed by the prefectural federations and the National Federation; most of the money, however, is employed by the former. Restrictions are imposed upon the methods of employment by a ministerial ordinance. These restrictions used to be more strict than those imposed upon private insurance; yields had accordingly been low. In May 1967, however, the restrictions were relaxed and the mutual-aid federations were authorised to make loans to private business.

At the end of March 1970 the prefectural federations employed 29 per cent of their funds in deposits and 31 per cent in investment in securities. Most of the deposits are made with agricultural financial institutions including the Central Co-operative Bank of Agriculture and Forestry and the credit federations of agricultural co-operatives. The prefectural federations also lend money to farmers in order to restore to them the money absorbed from agricultural villages. The loans are made either directly or through the agency of credit federations of agricultural co-operatives. The credit federations also lend money lodged by the mutual-aid federations to farmers. The amount of money thus returned to agriculture is increasing year by year, but at the end of March 1970 it was still only 14·7 billion yen. On the other hand, ordinary loans to business firms also increased rapidly, reaching 283·0 billion yen at the end of March 1970. We must, however, recall that this was a year of credit squeeze, which led to extraordinary increases in their loans to business firms.

The mutual-aid schemes have come to play an important role in agricultural credit, because their funds have rapidly increased and must seek employment.

3. FINANCIAL INSTITUTIONS FOR FISHERY

Fishery co-operatives were first established in 1886 for the purpose of re-organising existing associations of petty coastal fishermen on modern, legal principles. They have, however, gradually developed into organisations for economic purposes. The present fishery co-operatives are established under the Fisheries Co-operatives Law of 1948. They comprise fishery co-operatives, fishery production co-operatives and marine products-processing co-operatives.

Of these three types, only fishery and marine products-processing co-operatives can engage in credit business. The importance of credit business is not, however, as great for them as for agricultural co-operatives. Their main business consists of the purchase and sale of products, ice manufacturing, refrigeration and cold storage and other productive activities.

The number of co-operatives engaged in credit business was 1605 at the end of 1969. They are organised into Credit Federations of Fishery Co-operatives (34 at the end of 1969) and Credit Federation of Marine Products-Processing Co-operatives (1 at the end of 1969). These federations are not permitted to engage in business other than credit.

The principal financial activities of these unit co-operatives and their federations are the taking of deposits from their members and lending to them. At the end of 1969 the outstanding amount of deposits with unit co-operatives was 180·5 billion yen, while their lending amounted to 196·8 billion. Deposits with the federations amounted to 152·1 billion yen and their lending to 132·7 billion. Thus, credit business of fishery co-operatives is on a much smaller scale than that of agricultural co-operatives. Furthermore, in contrast to the latter, the deposits of which exceed their lending, fishery co-operatives and their federations, particularly unit co-operatives, are in over-lent positions, so that they are in debt to other financial institutions to the amount of 207·2 billion yen.

At the summit of the hierarchy of financial institutions for fishery is the Central Co-operative Bank of Agriculture and Forestry. The bank's lending to fishery organisations (164·5 billion yen at the end of 1969) was the biggest single item in its total lending to affiliated organisations (404·7 billion yen). Most of the lending is made directly to unit co-operatives, while agriculture is mostly accommodated via credit federations of agricultural co-operatives.

TABLE 17.5

Principal Accounts of the Central Co-operative Bank of Agriculture and Forestry

(hundred million yen)

End of the Year	*1965*	*1966*	*1967*	*1968*	*1969*	*1970*
Deposits	10,075	10,696	11,540	12,766	17,066	17,108
(of which Deposits by Affiliated Organisations)	(9,404)	(9,984)	(10,341)	(11,739)	(15,605)	(15,114)
(of which Fixed Deposits)	(8,523)	(8,873)	(8,170)	(9,881)	(11,289)	(11,195)
Debentures Issued	2,425	2,873	3,338	3,771	4,605	5,867
Lending	8,232	8,557	9,456	11,135	13,706	15,953
(of which Lending to Affiliated Organisations)	(1,846)	(2,103)	(2,733)	(3,263)	(4,047)	(5,374)
Call Loans	958	714	1,118	1,133	3,951	2,421

SOURCE: Ministry of Agriculture and Forestry, *Summary of Statistics of Finance of Agriculture and Forestry.*

4. FINANCIAL INSTITUTIONS FOR FORESTRY

About 40 per cent of Japan's forests are the property of the state or of local authorities. More than half of the remaining 60 per cent is parcelled out among petty farmers, who manage them as a subsidiary occupation. Co-operative associations of private owners of forests were first organised in 1907. At present, there are 3193 forestry co-operatives and 46 prefectural federations (at the end of March 1969). They are organised under the Forestry Law, but have a much narrower scope than agricultural and fishery co-operatives. They are not permitted to receive deposits, so that their credit business is limited to lending. At the end of March 1969 the outstanding lending of forestry co-operatives was only 73·5 billion yen (of which 44·6 billion was lent on account of the Agriculture, Forestry and Fishery Finance Corporation), while in this field their federations were virtually inactive. In contrast the Central Co-operative Bank's lending to forestry co-operatives has registered a marked increase every year (48·4 billion yen at the end of 1969).

5. CENTRAL CO-OPERATIVE BANK OF AGRICULTURE AND FORESTRY

(1) *General Survey*

The Central Co-operative Bank of Agriculture and Forestry is the successor to the Central Bank of Industrial Co-operatives which was established in 1923 as the central agency of industrial co-operatives. Subsequently, in 1938, fishery co-operatives and their federations became affiliated to the bank. In 1943, when forestry co-operatives and their federations were made subsidiary organisations of the bank, its name was changed to the present title. It now plays a pivotal role in the finance of the affiliated organisations.

The Central Co-operative Bank is a special corporation with limited liability under the Central Co-operative Bank of Agriculture and Forestry Law.[1] Its capital of 10 billion yen is

[1] In 1950 the then U.S. Aid Counterpart Fund (now the Industrial Investment Special Account) invested 2 billion yen in the Central Co-operative Bank under the

subscribed wholly by affiliated organisations in agriculture, forestry and fishery. At present the bank has 26 branches and 6 offices all over the country. Its resources are comparable with those of a city bank.

(2) *Business*

The business of the Central Co-operative Bank can be roughly classified into its main business and business entrusted under various laws.

A. Main Business

The bank's main business consists of receiving deposits, lending, domestic exchanges and the issue of Agriculture and Forestry Debentures. Through these functions it adjusts local surpluses and shortages of funds among affiliated organisations. It is also in constant touch with the outside financial market, and seeks to absorb funds from it when the affiliated organisations tend to be short of funds, or to employ funds in it when they are in surplus.

The Central Co-operative Bank can take deposits from affiliated organisations and public bodies designated in the Central Co-operative Bank of Agriculture and Forestry Law as well as from non-profit-making corporations. More than 90 per cent of its deposits come from the affiliated organisations, of which agricultural co-operatives and their federations are the most important. About 80 per cent of their deposits are time deposits with high-interest yields, because such deposits are outlets for their surplus funds. On deposits of credit federations of agricultural co-operatives, higher rates of interest are paid than on corresponding deposits in banks. (For instance, a rate of 6·0 per cent is given on time deposits of six months' maturity.) Moreover, a bounty is granted for deposits of

---

Law Concerning Debenture Issues of Banks. The investment was scheduled to be paid off in instalments extending over fifteen years – i.e. by the fiscal year 1964. After the fiscal year 1955, however, the bank's financial condition had improved sufficiently for the 2 billion yen to be completely redeemed by July 1959. Since then the Central Co-operative Bank's capital has been contributed wholly by private bodies.

affiliated organisations. Thus, the cost of funds to the bank is considerably higher than that to ordinary banks.

To obtain funds for medium- and long-term loans the bank can issue Agriculture and Forestry Debentures. Of these there are two varieties: interest-bearing and discount debentures. In principle, they are bearer securities. The maximum issue is twenty times the paid-up capital and reserves. More than 70 per cent of the interest-bearing debentures are bought by financial institutions, particularly city banks, while nearly 90 per cent of discount debentures are purchased by individuals.

Lending is, in principle, confined to affiliated organisations. When the bank has surplus funds, however, it can make loans to non-affiliated bodies subject to approval by the competent minister (in principle, these should consist of short-term lending only).

Lending to non-affiliated bodies may be broadly divided into the three categories of lending to corporations (i.e. agricultural, fishery and construction companies doing works necessary for the development of affiliated organisations), long- and short-term lending to related industries, and lending to financial institutions and call loans. Of these, short-term lending to related industries, such as animal husbandry, fertilisers, agricultural implements and food-processing, are the most important. The bank is influential in the short-term financial market, because it lends substantial amounts, particularly to city banks and to call loan dealers. Lending rates differ not only in respect of maturities, but also according to the borrowers: credit federations of agricultural co-operatives are charged lower rates than other affiliated organisations, while lending to non-affiliated organisations carry the highest rates of interest.

In addition, the bank organises its head office, branches and agents – credit federations of agricultural co-operatives – into a nationwide network of domestic exchanges for the convenience of its affiliated organisations.

B. Entrusted Business

The principal business entrusted to the Central Co-operative Bank is agency business for the Agriculture, Forestry and Fishery Finance Corporation and payments for foodstuffs purchased by the government. Agency loans on account of the Agriculture, Forestry and Fishery Finance Corporation have diminished since 1958, when the Corporation began to make direct loans. Payments for foodstuffs, on the other hand, remain an important business of the bank. The bank receives from the Foodstuff Control Special Account advance deposits of money for rice and other staple foodstuffs purchased by the government. The money is then paid to farmers. Although this business is executed by ordinary financial institutions as well, the bank and the affiliated co-operatives handle about 90 per cent of the total payments.

In the fiscal year 1969 the advance deposits of such money with the Central Co-operative Bank amounted to as much as 1157·2 billion yen. As most of the money is deposited with it from September to December of each year, during these months the bank and its affiliated organisations have huge surplus funds, which it employs in the money market, in which it is therefore very influential. In order to absorb such temporary surpluses from its portfolio the Bank of Japan has at such times sold bills to the Central Co-operative Bank. It has followed this practice since 1954.

(3) *Recent Trends*

Table 17·5 shows recent movements in the principal accounts of the Central Co-operative Bank. Deposits suddenly increased in 1965 and exceeded 1000 billion yen (an increase of 63 per cent compared with a year earlier). This resulted largely from slack monetary conditions, which induced the credit federations of agricultural co-operatives to switch their surplus funds from the outside market to deposits with the Central Co-operative Bank. Subsequently, however, the deposits ceased to rise so fast; this was because deposits with unit co-operatives ceased to grow rapidly while the credit federations again began to lend to the outside market. Debenture issues by the bank, however, have grown steadily until their outstanding amount reached 460·5 billion yen at the end of 1969.

On the other side of the accounts the outstanding amount of lending was 1370·6 billion yen at the end of 1969 (an increase of 23 per cent compared with the year earlier; in addition, there were agency loans of 111·0 billion yen for the account of the Agriculture, Forestry and Fishery Finance Corporation). Formerly, most of the lending used to be to affiliated organisations, but the relative importance of this has gradually declined; at the end of 1969 it amounted to 404·7 billion yen and accounted for only about 30 per cent of total lending. Thus, lending to non-affiliated bodies (965·9 billion yen) now represents the overwhelming proportion. This largely reflects the decrease in lending to agricultural organisations, particularly to credit federations of agricultural co-operatives, which constitute the majority of affiliated organisations. The tendency is for the credit federations and the co-operatives to accommodate their members without depending upon borrowing from the Central Co-operative Bank. In consequence the original idea of the Bank, to reinforce the financial efficiency of the co-operative organisations through their mutual lending and borrowing, has receded somewhat. It now seems as if its principal function is the employment of the surpluses of the affiliated organisations. As will be explained later, the overlapping of the fields of operation of the bank and of the Agriculture, Forestry and Fishery Finance Corporation poses another problem. It is for these reasons that reorganisation and rationalisation of the system of co-operative finance, the pivot of which is the bank, is now being considered.

6. AGRICULTURE, FORESTRY AND FISHERY FINANCE CORPORATION

The Agriculture, Forestry and Fishery Finance Corporation is a government financial institution which lends long-term at low-interest to farmers, foresters or fishermen; these borrowers need funds to maintain or increase productivity, but experience difficulties in borrowing from the Central Co-operative Bank or from other financial institutions.

In post-war years long-term lending by the government at low interest to agriculture, forestry and fishery was at first undertaken through the Reconstruction Finance Bank established in 1947. When this bank ceased to function they were made through the U.S. Aid Counterpart Fund Special Account. Then, from 1951 the newly established Japan Development

Bank took over the claims of these two institutions. At the same time the Agriculture, Forestry and Fishery Finance Special Account was established to function as the long-term financial institution for these industries. The special account was reorganised in 1953 into the Agriculture, Forestry and Fishery Finance Corporation under the Agriculture, Forestry and Fishery Finance Corporation Law. This corporation took over the Japan Development Bank's claims on the industries as well as those of the Central Co-operative Bank, which had arisen from loans made between September 1948 and March 1949 for reconstruction of agriculture, forestry and fishery.

The capital of the corporation is 168·2 billion yen (end of 1969), which has been subscribed entirely by the government (the General Account, the Industrial Investment Special Account and the Land Improvement Fund). Its other sources of funds include borrowing from the Trust Fund Bureau, the Post Office Life Insurance and Postal Annuity and the Industrial Investment Special Account (at the end of 1948 borrowing amounted to 526·5 billion yen), as well as proceeds from repayments of past loans.

The business of the Corporation is to lend at low-interest rates to farmers, foresters and fishermen (including those engaged in animal husbandry, sericulture and salt manufacture). In the first years of its existence, however, it furnished accommodation mainly to public works, such as land improvement, afforestation, improvement, construction or the restoration of forest roads or fishing-ports. Subsequently, its scope has been considerably enlarged. Since 1955 loans to new and existing owner-farmers have been added; these used to be the concern of the Special Account for Special Measures for Establishment of Owner Farmers. Other new activities include the following special loans: loans for facilities designated by the competent minister (1955), loans for improvement of dry field farming in cold districts of Hokkaido and loans for new construction of manufactories of glucose and other facilities (1958), loans for planting of fruit-trees and loans for milking facilities (1961), loans for structural improvements of enterprises in agriculture, forestry and fishery (1963) and, more recently, loans for the construction of multi-purpose facilities and loans for the modernisation of wholesale markets (1965). Thus, the corporation has gradually diversified. It has already been noted that the modernisation and structural improvement of agriculture, forestry and fishery have become important policy objectives, and these loans by the corporation have recently stressed their importance. Its lending has thus increased annually until the amount outstanding reached 817·5 billion yen at the end of 1969.

At first, lending was made wholly by agency loans through other financial institutions, but direct loans by the corporation were initiated in the fiscal year 1958. In the fiscal year 1967 direct loans accounted for 15 per cent of the total lending, while agency loans represented 85 per cent (of which 11 per cent were made through the Central Co-operative Bank, 6 per cent through country banks and 62 per cent through credit federations of agricultural co-operatives). The maximum interest rates on its lending are stipulated in the Agriculture, Forestry and Fishery Finance Corporation Law, but actual lending rates are fixed by its 'conditions of operation', which are subject to approval by the Minister of Agriculture and Forestry and the Minister of Finance. The rates naturally do not exceed the legal ceilings. At the end of 1969 they ranged from 9·0 to 9·75 per cent. As loan maturities are from ten to thirty years, while repayments start only three to twenty years after loans are made, their terms are much more favourable than those of comparable loans by private financial institutions.

7. CREDIT GUARANTEE AND CREDIT INSURANCE

The system of institutional finance includes various organisations for credit guarantee; these seek to reinforce the low credit standing of farmers, foresters and fishermen by guaranteeing their debt, thereby facilitating their borrowing from financial institutions. The principal organisations of this type are as follows:

(1) *Agricultural Credit Fund Associations and Agricultural Credit Insurance Association*

Agricultural Credit Fund Associations and the Agricultural Credit Insurance Association are special corporations under the

Agricultural Credit Guarantee and Insurance Law of 1961. A credit fund association is established in each prefecture. The capital is subscribed by farmers, agricultural co-operatives, their credit federations and local authorities. The associations guarantee debt and capital of members. Guarantees are given for funds borrowed for agricultural modernisation or for funds borrowed for the routine work or living expenses of farmers. Funds eligible for borrowing guarantees for agricultural modernisation may be borrowed from the Agricultural Credit Insurance Association. At the end of 1969 the outstanding amount of debt guaranteed was 241·6 billion yen.

The Agricultural Credit Insurance Association is a national organisation established by contributions from the prefectural agricultural credit fund associations and from the Central Co-operative Bank of Agriculture and Forestry. Its principal business is the insurance of debts guaranteed by the credit fund associations, the insurance of modernisation loans by the Central Co-operative Bank (the interest on which is subsidised by the government) and the grant of loans at low-interest rates to credit fund associations. To assist it to fulfil these functions, the government makes grants to it. At the end of the fiscal year 1969 thc outstanding amount of debts insured by the association was 55·1 billion yen.

(2) *New Settlers' Credit Guarantee Associations*

There are special organisations which provide loans for the agricultural operations of new settlers. They include prefectural credit guarantee associations for new settlers (established by contributions from new settlers' agricultural co-operatives, their prefectural federations and prefectural authorities) and the Central New Settlers' Credit Guarantee Association (established by contributions from prefectural credit-guarantee associations for new settlers, the National Federation of New Settlers' Agricultural Co-operatives and the government). These were founded in 1953 under the Credit Guarantee for New Settlers Law. The outstanding amount of debt guaranteed by them was 6·4 billion yen at the end of April 1970.

(3) *Fishery Credit Guarantee Corporation*

The Fishery Credit Guarantee Corporation was established under the Small Fishers' Credit Guarantee Law of 1952. Its function is to guarantee debts of small fishermen, in order to facilitate their borrowing from financial institutions funds necessary for their operations. Its capital is contributed by fishery co-operatives, their federations and fishery production co-operatives. The capital provides the funds necessary for its credit guarantees, which are reinsured by the government. At the end of the fiscal year 1969 the outstanding amount of guaranteed debt was 43·9 billion yen.

(4) *Others*

There are other kinds of credit-guarantee associations. The Livestock Industry Promotion Corporation guarantees debts of dairy farmers and gives interest subsidies to financial institutions which have lent money to specific undertakings for promotion of dairy farming; the Forestry Credit Fund guarantees the obligations of foresters, in order to facilitate loans to them. The Sericulture Fund Association guarantees the debts of silkworm farmers. Although the operations of these associations are restricted to their special fields, the first two have recently been very active.

CHAPTER 18

INSURANCE COMPANIES

I. CHARACTERISTICS AND DEVELOPMENT OF INSURANCE BUSINESS

The business of insurance companies is to enter into insurance contracts with those who wish to provide for such contingencies as death or fire. They receive premiums and pay out money on the occurrence of the particular contingencies covered by the contracts. Insurance companies cannot, therefore, be regarded as financial institutions *per se*, like banks. They are, however, important participants in the money and capital markets, because they must accumulate insurance premiums to build up funds to meet policy claims, and they must meanwhile employ these funds in loans and investments. Thus, their financial functions are a necessary consequence of their proper business of insurance.

There are two kinds of insurance: life insurance and property (non-life) insurance. In Japan a company may not engage in both kinds of businesses at the same time. Life-insurance companies are a kind of long-term financial institution, because the ability to make accurate estimates of death ratios and the extension of contracts over long periods makes possible the employment of their funds on a stable and long-term basis. In contrast, non-life insurance is for unpredictable accidents, and contract periods are usually less than one year. Thus, such insurance funds must be employed in short-term loans and investments. Non-life-insurance companies are therefore essentially short-term financial institutions.

As mentioned in Part One, private insurance business has a history of steady progress from the early Meiji era, when a system modelled on European and American experience had been introduced. The Pacific War, however, dealt them a heavy blow, and defeat deprived life-insurance companies of their overseas assets. War-time emergency relief arrangements were discontinued, and post-war inflation made it difficult for them to acquire new contracts. Non-life-insurance companies fared no better: damage by air-raids, the sinking of a vast number of ships and the discontinuance of war-time reliefs adversely affected them.

Life-insurance companies, however, gradually recovered from the blows. Fresh companies were established under the Law for

TABLE 18.1

Business Condition of Insurance Companies

(hundred million yen)

	Life Insurance		*Non-Life Insurance*	
End of Fiscal Year	*Policy Value*	*Assets in Employment*	*Policy Value*	*Assets in Employment*
1960	69,971	7,435	153,969	1,895
1961	88,981	9,426	191,313	2,184
1962	114,453	11,739	228,829	2,525
1963	149,004	14,568	274,992	3,026
1964	194,928	18,009	346,416	3,624
1965	244,173	22,219	435,406	4,090
1966	304,445	27,128	667,946	4,904
1967	382,431	32,780	1,036,354	5,885
1968	474,242	39,688	1,551,326	6,957
1969	601,835	48,225	2,203,904	8,808
1970[a]	749,384	55,227	—	11,252

[a] End of December.

SOURCE: Bank of Japan, *Economic Statistics Annual*.

Reorganisation and Readjustment of Financial Institutions, and they entered into mutual agreements on various aspects of their operations (conventional rates of premiums and of dividends); new types of insurance were started, and, above all, the inflation was contained. Since the early 1960s in particular they have developed spectacularly with the rapid growth of the economy. In recent years this rapid development has made the existing conventions appear somewhat of an obstruction to their rationalisation. Thus, life-insurance companies are now gradually easing the terms of the agreements on rates of premiums and dividends, so that free competition may enable each company to operate in its own unique way.

Non-life-insurance companies have also made marked progress, because with the reconstruction and development of the economy the number and the value of factories and other productive facilities on which insurance is effected have increased, while disasters rarely occur.

Because of these developments the importance of insurance companies in the financial market has continued to increase. At the end of 1969 the total resources of insurance companies, both life and property, represented about 5 per cent of the resources of all financial institutions (see Table 8.2, pp. 114–15). The percentage is still smaller, however, than that of pre-war years: in 1934–6 life-insurance companies alone accounted for more than 10 per cent of the resources of all financial institutions and their relative importance was next only to that of banks. Thus, they have not yet regained their pre-war significance, but, if we take only long-term loans for fixed investment and investment in securities (in particular, shares) insurance companies have of late come to occupy an important share of the total, as is shown in Tables 18.2 and 18.3, so that they are now important providers of industrial funds.

TABLE 18.2

Relative Share of Insurance Companies in the Supply (Net Increase) of Funds for Fixed Investment in Plant and Equipment of Industries (Percentages of the Total Supply by Private Financial Institutions)

(percentages)

Fiscal Year	*1962*	*1963*	*1964*	*1965*	*1966*	*1967*	*1968*	*1969*
Life Insurance	12·6	10·7	13·9	10·0	7·8	9·3	10·8	10·0
Non-Life Insurance	0·2	—	0·6	0·5	0·3	0·4	0·6	1·0
Sub-Total	12·8	10·7	14·5	10·5	8·1	9·7	11·4	11·0
All Banks	36·7	44·8	44·2	44·8	46·3	44·9	44·2	46·6
Trust Banks	30·9	27·3	29·6	20·5	18·0	21·1	21·2	18·9
Mutual Loans and Savings Banks	9·7	6·9	1·9	11·3	12·2	9·9	9·3	8·7
Credit Associations	7·6	7·7	5·7	9·3	11·6	10·5	10·2	11·3
Others	2·3	2·6	4·1	3·6	3·8	3·9	3·7	3·5
Total	100·0	100·0	100·0	100·0	100·0	100·0	100·0	100·0

SOURCE: The Japan Development Bank, *Monthly Report*.

TABLE 18.3

The Amount of Shares Held by Insurance Companies

(hundred million yen)

End of the Year	*1963*	*1964*	*1965*	*1966*	*1967*	*1968*	*1969*	*1970*
Life Insurance	3,113	3,733	4,371	6,350	8,010	8,997	9,948	11,278
Non-Life Insurance	1,262	1,468	1,527	1,778	2,114	2,505	2,977	3,541
Sub-Total	4,375	5,201	5,898	8,128	10,124	11,502	12,925	14,819
All Banks	4,844	5,761	6,122	7,506	9,318	11,346	12,743	14,786
(of which City Banks)	(3,186)	(3,857)	(3,887)	(4,518)	(5,436)	(6,730)	(7,719)	(8,986)
Mutual Loans and Savings Banks	189	230	251	294	345	290	317	368
Credit Associations	99	102	175	243	256	253	287	341

SOURCE: Bank of Japan, *Economic Statistics Annual.*

As has been stated in Chapter 17, it may be recalled that the agricultural co-operatives had started their own mutual-aid schemes in post-war years. Further, the government engages in various kinds of insurance business. One is the Post Office Life Insurance, which was instituted in 1916 for the benefit of the low-income groups. The average contract is small, but its popularity compares well with that of private life insurance. The government also provides various types of social insurance and insurance for the furtherance of economic policy. The former includes health insurance, welfare pension insurance, workmen's accident compensation insurance, unemployment insurance and seamen's insurance, while the latter comprises agricultural mutual-relief insurance, forest-fire insurance, export insurance, fishing-boats insurance, small-business credit insurance and so on. Most of these insurance projects have either been started since the war or have developed significantly since then. They differ from private commercial insurance either in being compulsory or in that the government subsidises them. The reserves and surplus funds of these government insurance schemes are deposited with the Trust Fund Bureau and are its major source of funds, as will be explained later (see Chapter 22).

2. LIFE-INSURANCE COMPANIES

(1) *Organisation*

There are at present, 20 life-insurance companies in Japan,[1] Legally, they are either mutual companies (16 companies) or joint-stock companies (4 companies). In a mutual company policy-holders automatically become partners, and can participate in management through general meetings; all the profits are divided amongst policy-holders, but, on the other hand, policy moneys may be reduced should the company's business conditions deteriorate. In these respects they differ from joint-stock companies. The latter, too, however, divide some of the profits amongst policy-holders, while a reduction of policy moneys has never in fact been made by mutual companies. Thus, the two types of companies are almost identical in their practical operations.

The establishment of an insurance company requires approval by the Minister of Finance under the Insurance Business Law. The requirements are that the capital or the endowment of the company should be more than 30 million yen, whether it is organised on joint-stock or mutual principles. A mutual company, moreover, should have more than 100 partners.

(2) *Business*

Roughly speaking there are three kinds of life insurance: mortality insurance, by which policy money is paid upon the death of the insured person; adult or endowment insurance, by which policy money is paid when the insured person has reached a certain agreed age (the purpose of such insurance may be to secure marriage expenses or tuition and other fees for education); and mixed insurance (old-age insurance), which combines the advantages of the above two types, and by which

[1] There are also eleven foreign insurance companies operating in Japan (end of 1968). All of them are, however, American companies, which engage only in dollar contracts of life insurance for foreigners.

the policy money is paid either upon the death of the insured or upon the expiry of the insurance contract. Most life insurance has hitherto consisted of the last-mentioned variety. From about 1960, however, various new types of life insurance have been started, embodying new ideas of the respective companies: some fit the need to secure the family income of the insured, while others aim to guarantee income after retirement. From the viewpoint of the insured a distinction can be made between individual and group insurance: by the latter-type business firms insure the welfare of their employees as a group. Group insurance has made striking progress in post-war years, until it came to represent 19 per cent of the total outstanding amount of life-insurance contracts at the end of 1969.

Premiums are the chief source of life-insurance companies' income. They are composed of two parts: net premiums and additional premiums. As the overall frequency of accidents (projected death-rate) can fairly accurately be worked out in life insurance, it is possible to make calculations so as to equate the sum of insurance premiums with the amount of insurance money to be paid. As the accumulated premiums are employed in loans and securities investments until insurance money has to be paid, however, the anticipated earnings from such employment should be deducted from the sum of premiums. Net premiums are thus calculated from expected death-rates and from the rate of anticipated earnings (which was estimated at 4 per cent at the end of 1969) in such a way that their sum, together with employment earnings, should be enough to cover the expected payment of insurance money. Additional premiums, on the other hand, cover the expenses of the insurance company, such as those involved in the conclusion of contracts or in the collection of premiums. Premium rates and alterations in them are subject to the approval of the Minister of Finance.

A proportion of the collected premiums, amounting to some 90 per cent of assets, is accumulated for policy-holders (reserves for policy-holders). They are classified into a liability reserves, which provide for future payments of insurance money; payments reserves, which are for the payment of insurance money for accidents which have already taken place; and dividend reserves to provide for the division of profits and other reserves. Liability reserves are the most important. The manner in which these are accumulated is subject to the approval of the Minister of Finance.

The assets of life-insurance companies are a kind of trusted property in that they are built up from the accumulation of small sums collected from innumerable policy-holders, to whom the money is eventually repaid. To protect policy-holders by ensuring that assets are employed safely, strict legal regulations are imposed:

A. Securities for investment are limited to domestic and foreign government bonds, local bonds, government-guaranteed debentures, industrial debentures, shares and beneficiary certificates of loan trusts or money in trust. Holdings of shares are, however, restricted to less than 30 per cent of the total assets.
B. Loans are restricted to those on the security of the above-mentioned kinds of bonds, debentures and certificates, or of real property or of going concerns (loans on any one type of security should be less than 5 per cent of total assets), loans to public bodies, loans to policy-holders under insurance contracts, or call loans. Loans to one person may not exceed 10 per cent of the total assets. If the loans are made to a joint-stock company, the sum of loans on the security of the company's shares or debentures and the holdings of such securities may not exceed 10 per cent of the total assets of the insurance company.
C. Deposits should not be made with other financial institutions than banks, mutual loans and savings banks, credit associations or post offices. Deposits with a bank should be aggregated with the amount of holdings by the insurance company of the bank's shares and debentures and with loans to the bank on these securities: the sum may not exceed 10 per cent of the company's total assets. Money in trust and insurance policies in trust with one and the same trust bank should also be less than 10 per cent of the total assets.
D. Acquisition of real property may not exceed 20 per cent of the total assets.
E. If an insurance company wants to employ its assets in

ways other than those listed above, it must obtain the approval of the Minister of Finance.

Thus, the employment of insurance companies' assets is closely circumscribed by law. Loans and investments in securities were in pre-war years and have been since the war the main outlets. While investment in securities was the most important method of employment in pre-war years and during the war, loans have represented the bulk of assets employed in recent years. The relative importance of investments in securities and loans has therefore been reversed. (See Table 18.5).

TABLE 18.4

The Outstanding Amount of Life-Insurance Policies, by Type

(hundred million yen)

End of the Fiscal Year	*Mortality and Mixed Insurance*	*Endowment Insurance*	*Group Insurance*	*Total (Includes Annuity Insurance)*
1963	120,136	7,945	20,925	149,006
1964	158,346	9,359	27,223	195,104
1965	200,217	10,828	33,218	244,452
1966	249,516	12,445	42,685	304,857
1967	311,567	14,497	56,813	383,120
1968	381,425	15,199	78,474	475,371
1969	473,951	15,858	113,483	603,590

SOURCE: Ministry of Finance, *Annual Report on Finance of the Banking Bureau.*

Maximum interest rates are fixed for short-term loans by mutual agreement among members of the Life Insurance Association (8·5 per cent), but rates of interest on long-term loans are left to the discretion of the insurance companies. They are, on the whole, at about the same level as those of long-term credit banks.

The profits of life-insurance companies arise from three sources. First, there are earning-differential profits, consisting of the difference between actual and anticipated earnings from employment of the assets. Second, mortality-differential profits, arising from the difference between anticipated and actual death-rates. Third, cost differential profits arise from the difference between additional premiums and actual expenses. With mutual companies more than 90 per cent of such surpluses are set aside to add to the policy-holders' dividend reserves,

TABLE 18.5

Composition of Assets of Life-Insurance Companies

End of the Fiscal Year	*1935*		*1964*		*1967*		*1969*		*1970*[a]	
	million yen	*Percentages*	*hundred million yen*	*Percentages*	*hundred million yen*	*Percentages*	*hundred million yen*	*Percentages*	*hundred million yen*	*Percentages*
Cash and Deposits	287	11·4	233	1·3	388	1·2	539	1·1	202	0·4
Loans	626	25·0	11,338	62·3	18,912	57·3	30,513	62·8	37,052	66·5
Call Loans	—	—	171	0·9	316	0·9	349	0·7	317	0·6
Securities	1,429	57·0	4,272	23·5	9,774	29·6	12,383	25·5	12,596	22·6
(of which Shares)	(553)	(22·0)	(3,759)	(20·7)	(8,050)	(24·4)	(10,182)	(21·0)	(11,278)	(20·2)
Others	167	6·6	2,187	12·0	3,626	11·0	4,814	9·9	5,532	9·9
Total of Assets	2,509	100·0	18,201	100·0	33,016	100·0	48,598	100·0	55,699	100·0

[a] End of calendar year.

SOURCE: Bank of Japan, *Economic Statistics Annual*.

and are eventually divided amongst them. Joint-stock companies earmark dividends for policy-holders at about the same rate as the mutual companies' dividend rate before the computation of their profits.

In order to sell life insurance the companies maintain a huge army of canvassers (1,688,000 persons at the end of March 1970) who are either their employees or agents on a commission basis. In order to maintain order amongst so many canvassers, to protect the interests of policy-holders and to contribute to the healthy development of insurance business, the Law Concerning Preservation of Order in Selling of Insurance Contracts was promulgated in 1948; this requires canvassers to be registered with the competent authorities, and prohibits unjust or unfair methods of canvassing.

(3) *Recent Trends*

As remarked earlier, the business of life-insurance companies has grown steadily with economic expansion and the rise in personal income, as is reflected in the increased amounts of contracts outstanding and in insurance premiums. Accordingly, the volume of their assets has grown rapidly, until it reached 4823·0 billion yen at the end of the fiscal year 1969, 2·7 times their level five years earlier (see Table 18.1).

As Table 18.5 shows, loans accounted for 63·2 per cent of total assets at the end of 1969, while securities represented 26·1 per cent. Thus, loans and securities together were equivalent to almost 90 per cent of the total.

Most of the loans are for the finance of fixed investment in plant and equipment of various branches of industry. During the fiscal year 1964 the relative share of life-insurance companies in the total supply (net increase) of funds for fixed investment by all private financial institutions was 14 per cent. The percentage was next only to that of banking and trust accounts of all banks. After 1965, however, easy money and stagnation in fixed-investment led life-insurance companies to invest more in securities. Thus, in the fiscal year 1967 their relative share fell below that of credit associations and of mutual loans and savings banks (see Table 18.2). Their main borrowers are shown in Table 18.6. A salient feature is that more than 20 per cent of their loans are made to priority industries, such as electricity and steel, and to the Housing Loan Corporation.

TABLE 18.6

Principal Borrowers from Life-Insurance Companies

(percentages)

End of the Fiscal Year	*1962*	*1963*	*1964*	*1965*	*1966*	*1967*	*1968*	*1969*
Electricity	14·6	13·0	10·7	8·5	7·6	6·3	5·3	4·1
Iron and Steel	11·3	11·0	10·3	10·0	10·1	10·3	10·9	9·8
Shipping	2·6	1·9	1·3	0·9	0·8	1·1	1·3	1·1
Coal	0·5	0·5	0·5	0·4	0·5	0·5	—	—
Synthetic Chemical	6·6	7·0	7·5	7·8	7·1	6·4	8·3	7·7
Housing Loan Corporation	11·5	11·3	10·5	10·9	11·7	11·4	9·3	8·6
Others	52·9	55·3	59·2	61·5	62·2	64·0	64·9	68·7
Total	100·0	100·0	100·0	100·0	100·0	100·0	100·0	100·0

SOURCE: Life Insurance Association, *Monthly Statistics of Life Insurance.*

More than 80 per cent of their securities are shares. Thus, as institutional investors they carry great weight in the stock market. Their relative weight is surpassed only by the securities investment trusts and by banks as a whole.

3. NON-LIFE-INSURANCE COMPANIES

(1) *Organisation*

There are at present twenty-one non-life-insurance companies, of which nineteen are organised upon joint-stock principles, while two are mutual companies. They have to meet huge claims promptly, once an accident occurs. The periods of insurance contracts are short, while the risk factor is high. In order to provide for such contingencies they must have capital (or, in the case of mutual companies, endowments) considerably larger than that of life-insurance companies. All are engaged in fire, marine and transportation insurance. In addition, new types of contracts, such as automobile insurance, have been developed. Foreign non-life insurance companies also operate in Japan (there were thirty-three at the end of 1969), but they deal mainly with foreigners or foreign firms domiciled in Japan. Their scale of operation, moreover, is insignificant, because their premiums account for less than 4 per cent of total insurance premiums.

As in the case of life-insurance companies, non-life-insurance companies are subject to governmental supervision of various aspects of their business, including their establishment, under the Insurance Business Law and other laws.

(2) *Business*

In contrast to life-insurance companies, which chiefly deal with households, property-insurance companies are concerned mainly with business firms wishing to insure against unpredictable disasters. Non-life-insurance facilities in Japan include fire, marine, transportation, and new types of miscellaneous insurance. The relative importance of each group is shown in Table 18.7. The relative share of fire insurance, which used to account for more than 70 per cent of the total amount of non-life-insurance contracts outstanding, has declined rapidly and in the fiscal year 1967 its relative share fell to less than 40 per cent. On the other hand, the amount of new types of insurance contracts outstanding has strikingly increased each year, until at the end of the fiscal year 1967 it represented more than half of total non-life insurance. These new types of insurance include more than twenty varieties, such as automobile, automobile liability, accident, burglary, aviation, credit, storm and flood, animal, atomic energy, and other insurance.

Insurance premiums, as with life insurance, consist of net and additional premiums; net premiums are calculated on the basis of the probability of accident and the probable degree of damage, whereas additional premiums cover the company's expenses. As the probability of accidents is very difficult to determine, the computation of premium rates for fire, marine, transportation, automobile, accident, and other insurance are made by the Fire Marine Insurance Rating Association, and by the Automobile Insurance Rating Association, which operate under their respective laws. If the premium rates calculated are sanctioned by the Minister of Finance they are adopted by the companies as approved rates. Premiums on other kinds of insurance are either decided independently by the companies (free rates), or by mutual agreement among companies (agreed rates). As an insurance contract may be for too large an amount to be met by an individual company, there is wide resort to arrangements to spread risks, such as mutual reinsurance (reinsurance with the government in the case of automobile liability insurance), co-insurance and insurance pools.

As with life insurance, a proportion of the income from premiums is set aside as policy-holders' reserves, the bulk of which is liability reserves. A peculiarity of non-life-insurance companies is that they accumulate extraordinary risk reserves in order to provide for unanticipated catastrophes. In contrast to life insurance, premiums are usually not refunded at the expiry of the contract term, although with some types of fire insurance some of the premiums are repaid if no accident occurs during the contract period.

Employment of assets is subject to roughly the same legal regulations as with life insurance, although loans on the security of ships are permitted for companies engaged in maritime insurance. The liquidity of assets, however, is a special concern with non-life-insurance companies, because they insure against unpredictable disasters, thus resembling short-term financial institutions. Their short-term lending rates are subject to control under agreements between members of the Fire and Marine Insurance Association of Japan. The agreed rates are about the same as those of life-insurance companies.

The sale of insurance contracts is undertaken mostly by agents, who are subject to regulations under the Law Concerning Preservation of Order in Selling of Insurance Contracts, in the same way as life-insurance canvassers; for instance, they must be registered with the authorities (there were 181,000 agents at the end of March 1970).

(3) *Recent Trends*

The outstanding amount of non-life-insurance contracts and the income from premiums have steadily increased year by year, until at the end of 1969 the total assets of the 21 non-life-insurance companies amounted to 1080·5 billion yen (which was one-fifth of the total assets of life-insurance companies); in short they were 2·6 times as great as five years previously. As is shown in Table 18.8, nearly 50 per cent of their assets are employed in investment in securities (mostly shares) and in bank deposits, because liquidity is their prime concern. The proportion of shares is declining, but their absolute amount remains close to one-third of those held by life-insurance companies.

In contrast to life-insurance companies, loans have represented only about 17 per cent of total assets in recent years. The main borrowers are merchant firms, and manufacturing and marine companies. As non-life-insurance companies are closely linked with shipping through their marine-insurance business, loans on ships account for more than one-seventh of the total.

TABLE 18.7

The Outstanding Amount of Non-Life-Insurance Policies, by Type

End of the Fiscal Year	*1959*	*Percentage of the Total*	*1963*	*Percentage of the Total*	*1967*	*Percentage of the Total*	*1969*	*Percentage of the Total*
Fire	104,078	79·3	209,822	75·7	395,024	38·6	556,722	25·6
Marine	12,891	9·8	23,130	8·4	38,537	3·8	52,732	2·4
Transportation	6,519	5·0	10,478	3·8	14,879	1·5	27,019	1·2
New Types	7,708	5·9	33,597	12·1	574,398	56·1	1,541,482	70·8
(of which Automobile)	(4,957)	(3·8)	(17,826)	(6·4)	(440,435)	(43·1)	(1,186,501)	(54·5)
(„ „ Accident)	(1,120)	(0·9)	(3,654)	(1·3)	(77,094)	(7·5)	(246,916)	(11·3)
(„ „ Automobile Liability)	(348)	(0·3)	(5,018)	(1·8)	(23,030)	(2·3)	(31,066)	(1·4)
Total	131,196	100·0	277,027	100·0	1,022,838	100·0	2,177,955	100·0
(of which reinsured)	(36,192)		(73,380)		(172,009)		(298,679)	

SOURCE: *Insurance Year Book.*

TABLE 18.8

Composition of Assets of Non-Life-Insurance Companies

End of the Fiscal Year	*1935* million yen	*1935* Percentage of the Total	*1964* hundred million yen	*1964* Percentage of the Total	*1967* hundred million yen	*1967* Percentage of the Total	*1969* hundred million yen	*1969* Percentage of the Total	*1970*[a] hundred million yen	*1970*[a] Percentage of the Total
Cash and Deposits	130	26·5	788	18·9	1,402	19·8	1,886	17·5	2,154	15·9
Loans	24	4·9	645	15·5	731	10·4	1,943	18·0	3,367	24·9
Call Loans	—	—	128	3·1	314	4·4	510	4·7	651	4·8
Securities	251	51·1	1,691	40·6	2,949	41·7	3,860	35·7	4,376	32·3
(of which Shares)	(125)	(25·5)	(1,454)	(34·9)	(2,193)	(31·0)	(3,085)	(28·5)	(3,541)	(26·2)
Others	86	17·5	911	21·9	1,678	23·7	2,606	24·1	2,987	22·1
Total of Assets	491	100·0	4,163	100·0	7,074	100·0	10,805	100·0	13,535	100·0

[a] End of calendar year.

SOURCE: Bank of Japan, *Economic Statistics Annual*.

CHAPTER 19

CALL LOAN DEALERS

1. GENERAL SURVEY

The day-to-day operations of financial institutions may make some of them temporarily short of money, while others will find themselves with a temporary glut. Such short-term shortages and surpluses must be adjusted by mutual lending and borrowing if financial markets are to function smoothly. This may be accomplished by direct transactions, but dealing is done largely through the intermediary of specialised brokers in the short-term financial market, which consists of specialised markets, such as the call loan market, the government short-term paper market, the discount market and the foreign exchange market. As will be explained later (Part Four, Chapter 23), the call loan market is well developed in Japan, but the market for government short-term paper does not exist, while the discount market is still in an embryonic stage. The scale of the foreign exchange market is also small.

Call loan dealers are specialised intermediaries in the short-term financial market, their principal business being dealings in call money. Legally they are regulated by the Law Concerning Regulations of Receiving of Capital Subscription, Deposits and Interest on Deposits. In this respect they do not differ from ordinary money-lenders, but the supervisory authority of the Minister of Finance over ordinary money-lenders under the law is delegated to prefectural governors by the Ordinance Concerning Delegation of Authority in regard to Registration and Investigation of Money-Lending, while lenders of or dealers in call money, who are designated by the Minister of Finance, are not controlled by the ordinance. At present there are six call loan dealers designated by the Minister of Finance: Ueda Call Money Co., Tokyo Call

Money Co., Yamane Call Money Co., Nippon Discount and Call Money Co., Yagi Call Money Co., and Nagoya Call Money Co.

2. BUSINESS

In general the business of various financial institutions is defined in the relevant laws, but that of call loan dealers is not regulated by any law. Their articles of association generally provide, however, that they confine themselves to the following business:

(1) *Call Loan Transactions*

In pre-war years call loan dealers were mostly engaged in simple brokerage transactions connecting the supply of and the demand for call money. At present they deal on their own account: that is, they negotiate with lenders or borrowers as principals.

When a transaction is concluded the call loan dealer receives money from the lender in exchange for a promissory note and the collateral security, and the money is then transferred to the borrower in exchange for his promissory note and the collateral security.

(2) *Bill-Discounting*

It was originally intended to establish a bill-discount market on the model of advanced countries of the West, and the call loan market was to serve as an adjunct to it. The discount market has, however, hardly developed, because Japanese banks have been reluctant to divulge their transactions to other banks. Thus, bill-discounting by call loan dealers is negligible.

(3) *Buying and Selling of Securities*

As mentioned above, the market for government short-term paper does not exist in Japan, while that for public bonds and debentures is not well-developed. Thus, there is little buying and selling of securities by call loan dealers.

(4) *Foreign Exchange Dealings*

In 1952, when the foreign exchange market was reopened, some call loan dealers commenced to operate as foreign exchange brokers. At present, the articles of association of five of the six call loan dealers list foreign exchange transactions as their business, but four only of the five companies actually are engaged in this activity.[1] Call loan dealers are of considerable importance in the foreign exchange market, but as the market itself is small, their transactions do not in fact amount to much.

Thus, call loan dealers engage in a variety of business, but dealings in call loans represent the overwhelming bulk of their operations. Their other lines of business are trifling, as can be seen from their principal accounts shown in Table 19·1.

3. RELATIONSHIP WITH THE BANK OF JAPAN

The Bank of Japan undertakes transactions with call loan dealers; these transactions assist the functioning of the call loan market, thus contributing to the efficient utilisation of funds. The Bank is in constant touch with dealers to help its own monetary operations.

(1) *Current Accounts*

All call loan dealers have current accounts with the Bank of Japan, and they settle their call money transactions with cheques drawn on them.

(2) *Domestic Exchange (Transfer) Transactions*

Call loan dealers transfer funds between their offices in different localities by utilising the transfer facilities between the Bank of

[1] In the foreign exchange market foreign exchange brokers are defined as those firms engaged in the intermediary business between sellers and buyers of foreign exchange. In addition to the four call loan dealers, there are three specialised brokers.

TABLE 19.1

Principal Accounts of Call Loan Dealers

(hundred million yen)

End of the Year	1966		1967		1968		1969		1970	
ASSETS										
Call Loans	7,844	(92·5)	10,463	(93·5)	9,970	(84·6)	14,996	(84·1)	19,173	(93·6)
Cash and Deposits	62	(0·7)	37	(0·3)	14	(0·1)	4	(—)	16	(0·1)
Securities	29	(0·3)	32	(0·3)	1,017	(8·6)	1,804	(10·1)	25	(0·1)
Others	547	(6·5)	656	(5·9)	784	(6·7)	1,041	(5·8)	1,275	(6·2)
Total	8,482	(100·0)	11,188	(100·0)	11,785	(100·0)	17,845	(100·0)	20,489	(100·0)
LIABILITIES										
Call Money Borrowed	7,474	(88·1)	10,118	(90·4)	9,852	(83·6)	15,464	(86·7)	18,169	(88·7)
Borrowing	399	(4·7)	341	(3·0)	1,060	(9·0)	1,230	(6·9)	904	(4·4)
Capital	4	(0·1)	4	(—)	4	(—)	4	(—)	4	(—)
Others	605	(7·1)	725	(6·6)	869	(7·4)	1,147	(6·4)	1,412	(6·9)

SOURCE: Bank of Japan.

Japan offices. Call money markets in different places are thereby closely linked, and this enhances efficiency in the use of funds.

(3) *Loans and Discounts*

The Bank of Japan provides ordinary lending and makes margin transaction loans to call loan dealers. Ordinary lending is granted if it considers that conditions in the call loan market justify it. Lending is done in the form either of bill-discounting or of advances on collateral security. Margin transaction loans are made when dealers run short of funds through supplying too much money to securities companies for the finance of margin transactions. The amounts of such loans are limited to the actual amounts of their lending to the securities companies.

(4) *Purchase and Sale of Government Short-term Bills*

Since January 1966 the Bank has actively sold to or bought from call loan dealers short-term government bills, in order to regulate the supply of money in the call loan market.

CHAPTER 20

SECURITIES COMPANIES

1. GENERAL SURVEY

Securities companies are defined in the Securities Transaction Law (effective in 1948) as companies which are not banks, trust companies,[1] or other financial institutions designated in ordinances, but which engage in (1) the purchase and sale of securities; (2) intermediation or agency business of purchase and sale of securities; (3) intermediation or brokerage business on stock exchanges of purchase and sale of securities; (4) underwriting; (5) flotation; or (6) handling of public offerings of securities. Article 65 of the Securities Transaction Law prohibits banks, trust companies and other financial institutions from engaging in the above-mentioned types of business.[2] Thus, most security business is now handled by these companies, which play a leading role in the market.

It is, however, only during post-war years that they have come to play such an important part in the Japanese securities market. In pre-war years the majority of shares in large companies were subscribed for and held by firms in the same business groups. The underwriting of industrial debentures was virtually a monopoly of banks and trust companies. Most securities companies were, under the circumstances, mere stock-jobbers specialising in speculative dealings in shares. After the war, however, shares held by Zaibatsu companies were offered *en bloc* to the public. On the other hand, the Securities

[1] Trust companies are companies which engage in trust business under the Trust Business Law. More precisely they are trust banks and commercial banks with trust accounts.

[2] Banks are, however, permitted to buy or sell securities for the accounts of customers who have instructed them in writing to do so. Banks, trust companies or other financial institutions are allowed to purchase or to sell securities for their own investment purposes or for the accounts of the trusters under trust contracts.

Transaction Law of 1948 prohibited speculative term transactions, which had been predominant in the stock exchanges, so that spot transactions became the standard method. This law also forbade banks and trust companies to underwrite issues of industrial debentures. Thus, extensive changes have been brought about in the business of securities companies, which have come to deal in earnest with ordinary investors. The flotation of new shares and debentures has also become their concern. Further, securities investment trusts have been started under the Securities Investment Trust Law of 1951. These trusts are all managed by their affiliates.

These changes prepared the ground for the spectacular development of the securities market during 1955–64, when the high growth of the economy engendered a large-scale stock-exchange boom. The boom was so precipitate, however, that the reaction was severe: the market was plunged into a deep depression from 1963 to 1965. The securities companies, therefore, experienced severe strains. Thus, the Securities Transaction Law was partially amended in May 1965. Formerly, registration with the authorities was a sufficient condition for the establishment of a securities company, but it now became necessary to have a licence for this purpose; the minimum amount of capital was also raised. Thus, more vigorous regulation has been applied to them.

By April 1968 the licensing system was in full operation, and 277 securities companies (with 1858 offices) had obtained licences. The number was less than half of that of 1963. At present the breakdown of the licensed companies is as follows: 148 regular members of the eight stock exchanges in the country, 104 non-members, 20 floor brokers intermediating in transactions between members of the same stock exchange and 6 special members, who act as brokers in dealings between members of different stock exchanges. Of these, the four biggest companies, Nomura, Nikko, Yamaichi and Daiwa, surpass the others in capital, number of offices and employees, turnover, underwriting of shares and debentures and in the outstanding amount of securities investment trust operated by their affiliates.

2. BUSINESS

A securities company requires a licence for each of the following four categories of business: purchase and sale of securities for own accounts (dealers' business), purchase and sale of securities for customers' accounts (brokers' business), underwriting of new issues and their subsequent sale to the public (underwriters' business), and public offerings of securities (distributors' business). Licensed companies may deal in shares, certificates of pre-emptive rights to new shares, government bonds, local bonds, public corporation debentures, bank debentures, industrial debentures, beneficiary certificates of securities investment trusts and so on.

(1) *Purchase and Sale of Securities*

Securities companies buy or sell securities either for their own accounts or for customers' accounts. In the former case the profits consist of the differences between buying and selling prices, while brokerage is naturally the source of income in the latter case. Most securities companies in Japan engage in both types of business, but brokerage is relatively more important.

By type of security, shares predominate in total turnover; in recent years the proportion has been as high as 70 per cent. In contrast, purchases and sales of government bonds, local bonds, public corporation debentures, bank debentures, industrial debentures and others are much smaller, though recently they have tended to increase; one reason is the resumption, since February 1966, of dealings in public bonds and debentures on the stock exchanges, which had been discounted since March 1962.

The rate of brokerage charged to ordinary customers who buy or sell securities through the securities companies is fixed by the rules of the stock exchanges. For instance, the Tokyo Stock Exchange stipulates that the brokerage is 1 yen 70 sen per share for purchases of 1000 shares of 100 yen each.

(2) *Issuing Business*

The issuing business of securities companies includes the underwriting and public offering of newly issued securities. By underwriting an issue a securities company contracts to purchase the whole or a part of the newly issued securities from the issuer for the purpose of resale, or to take up the unsold portion of the new shares. On the other hand, securities companies are not obliged to take up the unsold portion when they handle public offerings; they are commissioned by the issuers or the underwriters to receive subscriptions to newly issued securities or to sell existing securities.

In Japan new shares are usually allotted to shareholders or to friends of the issuing company at par or as bonus shares. Issues by public offering or by underwriting through securities companies remain extremely rare.

In contrast, issues of bonds and debentures, such as long-term government bonds, government-guaranteed debentures and industrial debentures, are mostly underwritten by securities companies, banks and other financial institutions. Individuals are not important as final purchasers of these securities; financial institutions predominate, although the underwriting share of securities companies is only about 10 per cent of the issues of long-term government bonds, for the underwriting syndicate consists also of banks, insurance companies and others. As has already been pointed out, however, banks and other financial institutions are prohibited from underwriting the issue of industrial debentures. Thus, the flotation and underwriting of the debentures are undertaken by the so-called 'six regular members' including the four biggest securities companies. Nevertheless, large-scale purchasers, such as commercial, trust and long-term banks,[1] make arrangements in advance to take up the new issues.

The securities companies earn underwriting, flotation and sales commissions from such business.

[1] These financial institutions have a large say in the issue market, as they are trustees of debentures. (See Part Four, Chapter 25, pp. 426 ff.)

(3) *Ancillary Business*

In addition to the above-mentioned business, securities companies perform various services, including safe custody of securities, loans on securities and their intermediation, agency service for transfer of securities and so on. The acceptance of securities on deposit for use in the companies' business has been discontinued since April 1968. These loans, mostly of discount bank debentures, were made by customers of securities companies, which paid fees to borrow securities to be utilised as collateral against the borrowing of call money.

3. RECENT TRENDS

As dealings in shares represent the overwhelming bulk of the turn-over of the securities companies in Japan, their business results are intimately related to the vicissitudes of the share market.

Since the war, particularly since 1955, there has been a marked upwards tendency in share prices; this reflects the high growth rate of the economy.

Between 1956 and 1961 the share price index (the old index of average prices on the Tokyo Stock Exchange) rose from 485·33 to 1548·94. The number of shares traded on the country's stock exchanges increased from 10·6 billion to 48·3 billion, and their value from 1300 billion yen to 9800 billion. With this development the securities companies grew rapidly. Their total paid-up capital multiplied from 12 billion yen to 73·4 billion, while their offices increased from 1844 to 2802 and their employees from 28,000 to 83,000.

The rapid development of the securities companies may be explained by the persistence of a bull market in shares, reflecting the rapid growth of the economy. Moreover, corporate firms have frequently increased their capital to secure funds for investment; they have therefore maintained dividend rates at high levels. These circumstances made for rising share prices. Furthermore, the growth of stock investment trusts contributed significantly to the expansion of the share market; they could absorb money from the general public because the unit of investment was small, and yet capital gains could be expected just as from direct investments in shares.

The rapid development of the securities companies, however, suffered a setback after the middle of 1961, when share prices reached a peak and then began to fall rapidly. This fall, in turn, quickly damped the enthusiasm of ordinary investors and the stock market sank into a prolonged depression from 1963 to 1965. The share price index (the old index of average prices on the Tokyo Stock Exchange), which had reached 1829·74 in July 1961, fell as low as 1020·49 in July 1965. The value of shares traded on stock exchanges, which had been roughly 10,000 billion yen a year during 1961–2, decreased to 4800 billion in 1964 and 5800 billion in 1965. Consequently, securities companies were extremely hard hit: their profits deteriorated particularly during fiscal years 1963–5. Even some of the major securities companies fell into financial difficulties because of the fall in the price of the shares they held.

To remedy this situation the Joint Securities Co. Ltd of Japan was established in January 1964 by joint subscription of private financial institutions, including city banks, long-term credit banks and securities companies; its present capital is 30 billion yen. Its purpose was the purchase of redundant shares in order to stabilise the market and thereby to contribute to the sound development of the capital market. In addition to its capital it received joint loans from city banks and from the Securities Finance Company of Japan. With these funds it bought spot shares from stock exchange members. Then, in January 1965, the Securities Holding Association of Japan was formed to purchase redundant shares in order to improve demand–supply relationships, and to strengthen the securities companies, in order to revitalise the capital market. This is a voluntary association under civil law and was established by stock exchange members, chiefly of Tokyo and Osaka. Its resources consist of borrowing from the Securities Finance Company of Japan which are used to purchase shares from stock investment trusts and in buying (with resale condition) shares held by its members, the securities companies. A further step to strengthen markets was taken in May 1965, when the financial difficulties of some securities companies were brought to a head by increased cancellations of contracts for deposit of securities for employment; the Bank of Japan now made special loans to the Yamaichi Securities Company, under Article 25 of the Bank of Japan Law, to avert a credit crisis.

These were essentially emergency measures to deal with the depression of the securities market. More radical longer-term measures were, however, adopted at the same time both by the authorities and by the securities companies themselves. A partial amendment was made to the Securities Transactions Law in May 1965 in order to rationalise the methods of doing business and to strengthen the securities companies: this amendment required such companies to be licensed, reformed the system of margin transactions, abolished or reduced the permissible extent of depositing of securities for employment, and prohibited cross-transactions.[1] Securities companies themselves sought to rationalise by cutting their branch networks and numbers of employees, and by amalgamations among themselves.

These steps made for the gradual revival of the securities market from the middle of 1965, and by 1968 a considerable boom had developed. Shares held by the Joint Securities Company of Japan and by the Securities Holding Association of Japan were therefore gradually released after 1966, and their borrowings were substantially reduced. The Securities Holding Association, having sold all its holdings of shares, was dissolved in January 1969, and the profits realised were used to establish the Capital Market Promotion Foundation. The securities companies have also experienced a considerable recovery; after 1966 they were making profits and, in September of 1969, had completely repaid their special borrowings from the Bank.

APPENDIX: SECURITIES INVESTMENT TRUSTS

Securities investment trusts in Japan were started in 1937 on the model of unit trusts in the U.K. A fresh start was made after the war, in June 1951, when the Securities Investment Trust Law was enacted. According to the law, these are 'trusts, of which the purpose is to employ the trusted property in

[1] See for details Part Four, Chapter 25, pp. 426 ff.

investment in securities in accordance with the instructions of the trusters and the beneficiary rights of which are divided among a number of unspecified persons'. Beneficiary certificates are sold to ordinary investors (beneficiaries) by the securities investment management companies (trusters), which are affiliates of securities companies. The proceeds are trusted to trust banks or to banks with trust accounts (trustees), which employ the property in investment in securities in conformity with the trusters' directions. Profits from employment (profits from purchase and sale of securities, dividends and interests) accrue to the beneficiaries. Thus, securities investment trusts in Japan are contractual trusts composed of trusters, trustees and beneficiaries.[1]

At first, the securities companies themselves were the trusters, but in order to secure the independent employment of trusted properties, investment trust business has been separated from ordinary securities business since 1960. It has been entrusted to securities investment management companies, which are separate entities from securities companies. They require licences from the Minister of Finance, which are issued on condition that they are joint-stock companies with a capital of more than 50 million yen and that they have adequate qualifications to engage in the trust business. Although the trust business and the securities businesses have thus been separated, the sale of beneficiary certificates and trading of securities for purposes of investment by the trusts are conducted mostly by the parent securities companies. Thus, there are close connections between the management companies and the securities companies. In addition, there are four securities investment trust sales companies (affiliates of management companies), which specialise in the purchase and sale of beneficiary certificates.

There are two types of securities investment trusts: stock investment trusts, which started in 1951 under the Securities Investment Trust Law, and bond investment trusts, which were first established in January 1961. The trusted properties of

[1] Securities investment trusts can be classified into contractual and corporate trusts. With the latter, a special company for securities investment is established and the investors can become beneficiaries by becoming shareholders in it. In the U.S.A. and the U.K. corporate-type trusts predominate.

the former consist largely of shares in joint-stock companies; the remainder is invested in public bonds, debentures and other securities, in designated money in trust and in call loans.

Securities investment trusts differ from money in trust or loan trusts in providing no guarantee of the principal. For this reason there are severe restrictions upon the employment of trusted property. For instance, the Securities Investment Trust Law stipulates that 'The truster companies should act faithfully to serve the best interests of the beneficiaries, when they issue instructions about the employment of trusted property'. Other clauses in the law impose restraints upon their operations, on their articles of association, and upon agreements among the management companies; they are also subject to administrative guidance by the Ministry of Finance. For example, their establishment is subject to the Ministry's approval; the underwriting of securities or the making of loans with the trust property is prohibited; and criteria are laid down concerning the shares, bonds and debentures to be purchased by investment trusts. Limitations are also imposed upon the maximum holding of any one share, bond or debenture (in the case of shares this is less than 10 per cent of the total amount outstanding, and in the case of bonds and debentures, less than 30 per cent of the outstanding amount at par).

As the units of stock investment trusts are small, and as the beneficiaries can participate in capital gains, they have rapidly become popular with the rise in share prices, and have attracted money from the public; the outstanding amount of principal increased from 136·9 billion to 1130·7 billion yen between 1957 and 1962. Thereafter, however, it ceased to grow because of the depression in share markets. After 1964 the amount outstanding actually began to decline because of increased cancellations. This led to extensions of maturities by some unit trusts by one year. Some were redeemed at prices below par, for the first time since the war. In contrast, bond investment trusts grew steadily from their commencement in 1961, although at one time there were large-scale cancellations in reaction to initially excessive sales.

(1) *Stock Investment Trusts*

Stock investment trusts are operated by their management companies (9 companies), which are established by securities companies as subsidiaries. There are two types of stock investment trusts: unit trusts and open-end trusts.

A. Unit Trusts

Beneficiary certificates of units trusts are usually sold once a month. The monthly proceeds form one unit of trust property. Thus, trust properties originating from different months are administered and employed separately. The face value of a beneficiary certificate is 10,000 yen and the trust period is five years; settlements are made once a year. The principle is that the beneficiaries hold the certificates till maturity, but, if they want to encash them in the middle of the term they can request the securities companies designated by the trusters to purchase the certificates at stated prices. The trust periods can be extended or shortened by agreement between the truster and the trustee, subject to approval by the Minister of Finance, if such a step is held to accord with the best interests of the beneficiaries. The decision can be made either before or after the maturities of the trusts.

B. Open-end Trusts

With this type of trust the amount of a unit of trust property is fixed in advance, and the beneficiary certificates are sold from time to time until the amount is reached. The minimum unit of trading is 10 certificates; initially they are sold at a par of 1000 yen, but subsequently they are sold at current prices (standard prices). Trust terms are indeterminate: unless the trusts are wholly cancelled, they continue to exist. The certificates are freely bought and sold at any time; certificates purchased by securities companies are usually resold. Settlements are made twice a year.

(2) *Bond Investment Trusts*

Bond investment trusts are similarly operated by their management companies (5 companies), which are affiliates of securities companies. They are a kind of open-end trust in that the amount of trust property can be increased by selling beneficiary certificates even after the trusts have been started. They differ, however, from stock investment trusts of this type in that the increase in trust property can be made only once a year, on the day following the settlement, whereas beneficiary certificates of stock investment trusts can be sold whenever there is a demand for them. The management companies have twelve trust properties, the settlements of which fall in different months of the year, so that certificates are sold every month. Sales are in blocks of 10,000 units or their multiples (the value of a unit is one yen) at their nominal prices.

TABLE 20.1

The Scale of Business of Securities Companies (1969 Business Year)

	The Four Biggest Companies	*Other Member Companies (151 companies)*	*Non-Member Companies (166 companies)*	*Total (321 companies)*
Capital (hundred million yen)	428 (35·1)	449 (36·8)	342 (28·1)	1,219 (100·0)
Number of Offices	338 (18·3)	1,194 (64·8)	312 (16·9)	1,844 (100·0)
Number of Employees (hundred)	225 (36·1)	341 (54·6)	58 (9·3)	624 (100·0)
Amount of Securities Traded (hundred million yen)	227,628 (54·9)	175,905 (42·4)	11,322 (2·7)	414,855 (100·0)
of which Amount of Shares (,, ,, ,,)	159,923 (50·8)	146,476 (46·6)	8,146 (2·6)	314,545 (100·0)
Underwritings, Floating and Public Offering	20,445 (68·0)	8,288 (27·6)	1,333 (4·4)	30,066 (100·0)

NOTES:

1. Figures in parentheses are percentages of totals.
2. A 'business year' commences in October of the preceding year and ends in September of the year named.

SOURCE: Ministry of Finance, *Annual Report of the Securities Bureau of the Ministry of Finance, 1969*.

TABLE 20.2

Numbers of Licences Issued to Securities Companies, by Category (end of 1970)

Category of Licences	*Regular Members*	*Non-Members*	*Floor Brokers and Special Members*	*Total*
Classes 1, 2, 3, 4	55	—	—	55
„ 1, 2, 4	89	96	—	185
„ 1, 2	—	—	2	2
„ 1, 3, 4	—	4	—	4
„ 1, 4	—	1	—	1
Class 1	—	1	—	1
„ 2	2	—	20	22
Total	146	102	22	270

NOTE: Categories of licences are as follows:
Class 1. Trading for own account.
Class 2. Trading for customers' accounts.
Class 3. Flotation of securities with underwriting contracts.
Class 4. Handling of Public offerings of securities.

SOURCE: Ministry of Finance, *Annual Report of the Securities Bureau of the Ministry of Finance, 1970.*

TABLE 20.3

Principal Indices of Trading in Shares

Years	Old Index of Average Prices on the Tokyo Stock Exchange (First Section)	Average Yields (of Shares Listed on the First Section of Tokyo Stock Exchange)	Trading on All Stock Exchanges: Sales Volume	Trading on All Stock Exchanges: Sales Value	Total Value of Shares Listed on All Stock Exchanges at Current Prices: Numbers of Shares	Total Value of Shares Listed on All Stock Exchanges at Current Prices: Value of Shares
	Yearly Averages (1946=100)	Yearly Averages %	During the Year (hundred million shares)	During the Year (hundred million yen)	End of the Year (hundred million shares)	End of the Year (hundred million yen)
1956	485·33	6·68	106	13,405	146	17,047
1957	535·57	7·14	120	15,787	192	17,456
1958	571·97	6·66	178	23,904	222	24,091
1959	821·52	4·54	318	55,889	258	39,289
1960	1,116·62	3·93	433	93,343	335	56,435
1961	1,548·94	3·24	483	98,072	500	64,297
1962	1,419·44	3·86	530	98,933	621	80,029
1963	1,440·61	4·24	591	82,335	715	77,175
1964	1,262·88	5·69	418	48,295	816	76,943
1965	1,203·16	5·92	505	57,830	834	88,045
1966	1,479·16	4·44	520	75,706	863	97,370
1967	1,412·01	4·74	422	62,814	917	96,392
1968	1,544·81	4·36	657	117,341	977	131,338
1969	1,956·36	3·37	689	186,748	1,070	190,302
1970	2,193·21	3·52	571	120,303	1,144	162,355

SOURCE: Tokyo Stock Exchange, *Statistical Yearbook of the Tokyo Stock Exchange.*

TABLE 20.4

Changes in the Numbers of Securities Companies

End of Year	*Number of Companies*	*Number of Offices*	*Number of Employees (hundred)*	*Capital (hundred million yen)*
1956	669	1,844	275	120
1957	591	1,902	293	190
1958	561	1,984	318	196
1959	542	2,230	394	292
1960	553	2,530	571	368
1961	588	2,802	829	734
1962	598	2,928	951	775
1963	593	2,912	960	944
1964	532	2,542	807	1,263
1965	429	2,119	661	1,254
1966	404	2,042	644	1,218
1967	312	1,877	609	1,207
1968	277	1,850	606	1,202
1969	274	1,842	623	1,219

SOURCE: Tokyo Stock Exchange, *Statistical Yearbook of the Tokyo Stock Exchange.*

TABLE 20.5

Income and Profits of All Securities Companies

(hundred million yen)

Business Year	*Total Income*	*Income from Dealers' Business*	*Income from Brokers' Business*	*Income from Underwriters' Business*	*Other Income*	*Net Profits*
1959	918	191	481	59	187	134
1960	1,389	242	803	84	260	243
1961	2,073	384	1,028	168	493	250
1962	2,119	335	977	167	640	121
1963	2,271	213	1,192	254	612	26
1964	1,657	123	582	239	713	−264
1965	1,538	149	594	206	589	−117
1966	1,902	266	943	211	482	208
1967	1,744	190	793	282	179	69
1968	2,473	175	1,402	311	585	287
1969	3,207	241	1,766	372	828	411

SOURCE: Ministry of Finance, *Annual Report of the Securities Bureau of the Ministry of Finance.*

TABLE 20.6

Principal Accounts of Securities Companies (247 Companies) (at the end of 1970)

Assets		*Liabilities*	
Cash and Deposits	1,825	Short-Term Borrowing	4,742
Short-Term Lending and Advances	833	(of which Borrowing from Banks)	(1,514)
Loans on Margin Transactions	3,972	(of which Borrowing from Securities Finance Companies on Margin Transactions)	(1,936)
Securities Owned	1,559	Deposits	718
(of which Shares)	(801)	Borrowing on Margin Transactions	733
Customers' Securities	7,428	Securities Borrowed	2,207
Investment in Securities	506	Guarantee Money Borrowed	5,738
		Long-Term Borrowing	389
		Capital	1,025

SOURCE: Bank of Japan, *Economic Statistics Monthly.*

TABLE 20.7

Outstanding Amounts of Funds of Securities Investment Trusts

(hundred million yen)

End of the Year	*Stock Investment Trusts*		*Bond Investment Trusts*	*Total*
	Unit Trusts	*Open-End Trusts*		
1956	666	12	—	677
1957	1,164	205	—	1,369
1958	1,818	279	—	2,097
1959	2,650	650	—	3,301
1960	4,261	1,781	—	6,042
1961	6,774	3,494	1,560	11,829
1962	7,508	3,799	1,327	12,633
1963	8,833	2,871	1,715	13,419
1964	8,442	3,173	2,090	13,706
1965	7,498	2,166	2,196	11,859
1966	6,105	1,903	2,320	10,328
1967	4,734	1,971	2,752	9,457
1968	3,343	1,811	3,726	8,880
1969	3,313	2,288	4,892	10,493
1970	3,883	3,434	5,836	13,153

SOURCE: Bank of Japan, *Economic Statistics Annual.*

TABLE 20.8

Employment of Assets of Securities Investment Trusts

(hundred million yen)

End of the Year	*1961*		*1964*		*1967*		*1968*		*1969*		*1970*	
STOCK INVESTMENT TRUSTS												
Shares	7,996	(71·9)	9,229	(81·3)	3,545	(54·5)	3,326	(62·0)	3,968	(62·7)	4,102	(58·7)
Public Bonds and Debentures	1,707	(15·4)	619	(5·5)	1,342	(20·7)	1,028	(19·2)	786	(12·4)	822	(11·8)
Call Loans	1,198	(10·8)	1,261	(11·1)	1,547	(23·8)	946	(17·6)	1,448	(22·9)	2,015	(28·8)
Others	214	(1·9)	246	(2·1)	66	(1·0)	62	(1·2)	126	(2·0)	52	(0·7)
Total	11,115	(100·0)	11,355	(100·0)	6,500	(100·0)	5,362	(100·0)	6,328	(100·0)	6,991	(100·0)
BOND INVESTMENT TRUSTS												
Public Bonds and Debentures	1,450	(88·7)	1,717	(79·0)	2,633	(92·4)	3,518	(91·2)	4,606	(90·9)	5,579	(92·2)
Call Loans	150	(9·2)	411	(18·9)	161	(5·7)	268	(6·9)	371	(7·3)	350	(5·8)
Others	34	(2·1)	45	(2·1)	55	(1·9)	74	(1·9)	92	(1·8)	123	(2·0)
Total	1,634	(100·0)	2,173	(100·0)	2,849	(100·0)	3,860	(100·0)	5,069	(100·0)	6,052	(100·0)

NOTES:

1. Figures in parentheses are percentages of totals.
2. Shares, bonds and debentures are appraised at book values.

SOURCE: Bank of Japan, *Economic Statistics Annual*.

CHAPTER 21

SECURITIES FINANCE COMPANIES

I. MARGIN TRANSACTIONS AND THE SECURITIES FINANCE COMPANIES

In pre-war years futures transactions were the predominant form of stock-exchange dealing, so that share markets had a strongly speculative character. Since the war, however, only spot transactions have been permitted, and stock exchanges have been reorganised accordingly. Members of stock exchanges, i.e. securities companies, must pay cash for shares; they receive the shares on settling day, i.e. the fourth day after the contract. Sellers must deliver on settling day, when they receive payment. Thus, transactions between members are settled by cash payments and deliverance of actual shares. Customers of securities companies can, however, either make (or demand) spot payments or ask them to defer settlements up to six months, provided that they lodge certain sums of guarantee money (the margin) within three days from the conclusion of contracts. Thus, the securities companies in effect extend credit to their customers and finance their purchases and sales of shares. Such transactions are generally called margin transactions. By this method, customers require a smaller capital to deal in shares, while a speculative element is introduced into the market and facilitates transactions and fair prices. Margin transactions were started in June 1951 on the American model. Although the customers can defer settlement of transactions by recourse to this margin facility, the securities companies themselves cannot do so, as dealing between them on the stock exchanges must be on spot terms. A prerequisite for the smooth working of margin transactions is, therefore, that markets or institutions exist, which lend the companies the money or shares necessary for making stock exchange settlements. In Japan, however, banks and other financial institutions, unlike their counterparts in the United States, do not usually lend money for share purchase on the security of shares, nor do they lend shares on the security of the proceeds from the sale of shares. Thus, the demand of stock exchange members for money or for shares in connection with margin transactions is met mainly by the securities finance companies, which are financial institutions peculiar to Japan. They lend money to buying members on the security of the purchased shares, while sellers can borrow shares from them on the security of the sales proceeds. Thus, they may make loans both of money and of shares on the same issue at the same time, so that if loans of money and those of shares were of equal amounts, they need make no delivery either of money or of shares; the money lent would return to them through the sellers as security for the shares lent, which would return to them via the buyers. In such a case, therefore, it suffices for them to make book transfers. For the same reason when the loans of money and of shares differ in amount only the difference needs to be financed.

Nine securities finance companies were founded in late 1949 and early 1950 in towns having stock exchanges; this was a measure to improve the depressed condition of the share market. At first, their principal business was the so-called 'loan transactions', by which they made direct loans of money and shares to the customers of securities companies through the intermediary of the latter. Since June 1951, however, when the current system of margin transactions was established, they have come to play pivotal roles in it. With this development they became subject to the Law for the Control of Money Lending. In view of their important economic functions a section entitled Securities Finance Companies was added to the Securities Transaction Law in August 1955, by which they are now regulated. At the same time the nine securities finance companies were reduced by mergers into three: Japan Securities Finance Company (Tokyo), Osaka Securities Finance Company, and Chubu Securities Finance Company (Nagoya). The other companies became branches of these three.

2. BUSINESS

The principal business of the securities finance companies, which are licensed by the Minister of Finance, is defined in the Securities Transaction Law as 'the business of lending money or securities necessary for settlement of margin transactions to members of the stock exchanges through their clearing systems'. These are the so-called margin loan transactions. The law also permits them to engage in other business subject to the approval of the Minister of Finance, provided that this does not interfere with their main business. They therefore make loans of money to securities companies or to their customers, keep securities in safe custody and engage in other business.

(1) *Margin Loan Transactions*

Only the regular members of stock exchanges can borrow money or shares necessary for margin transactions. The shares which may be bought or sold in this way are determined by the head offices or branches of the securities finance companies. A member wishing to use the facility must lodge guarantee money with them before settling day, in addition to the collateral security (to which reference will be made later). The guarantee money is the margin money provided by the customer of the securities companies; securities may be used as substitutes for guarantee money.

The securities finance companies keep accounts for individual members in respect of their applications for loans of money or shares: the accounts are kept for each share and for each member. The loans are made on settling days by the delivery *en bloc* of the money or shares to the clearing departments of the stock exchanges. In exchange they receive the proceeds of the sale of shares (collateral money for loans of shares) or the shares purchased with the loaned money. The money or the shares received serve as collateral security for their loans. A characteristic of margin loan transactions is that they make use of the stock exchange clearing system. The size of loans depends on the prices of the shares on the days of applications for loans. Share prices fluctuate subsequently, however; the differences between their valuations on the contract days and those at the current prices are settled daily in cash (the so-called 'renewal differences'). When share prices rise the loans of money are increased, while more collateral money is collected from the borrowers of shares. The reverse happens in the case of price-falls: part repayments of the loans are demanded, while a part of the collateral money for loans of shares is returned to borrowers. Thus, with variations in the current valuations of shares lent or held as collateral security, the total credit extended by the finance companies changes, so that the collateral values of the securities are maintained. For this, daily revaluation of the shares is necessary.

In principle loans are made for one day, but are renewed daily unless borrowers give notice of repayment. The securities finance companies charge interest on loans to buyers of shares from the day the loan is made until it is repaid, while they pay to the borrowers of shares (sellers) interest on the collateral money for loans of shares. Ceilings are imposed upon these interest rates, subject to the approval of the Minister of Finance, although rates vary, within the ceilings, with market conditions.

When applications for loans of particular shares exceed those for loans of money to purchase such shares, shares deposited by bulls as collateral security for their borrowing of money would be inadequate to meet the need of bears. Such a deficiency must be met by borrowing shares from securities companies or from other sources. The securities finance companies, therefore, charge backwardation fees on shares lent to those selling them (the maximum for such fees is two yen *per diem* per share). The fees are distributed to the bulls and to the lenders of shares; the backwardation serves to adjust demand and supply by reducing the demand for loans of shares and by stimulating that for loans of money.

(2) *Other Loans*

In addition to margin loan transactions the securities finance companies make loans on securities (ordinary loans) and loans to stags in the same way as other financial institutions. These loans are made in the form of loans on notes, with maturities that are usually of one to two months, but renewals are possible under special circumstances.

A. Ordinary Loans

Relatively short-term loans on securities are made to members of stock exchanges, and to customers introduced by members, for the purchase of shares or for other purposes.

B. Loans of Subscription Money

Shareholders of listed companies, to whom new shares have been allotted, can borrow the money for subscription from the securities finance companies on the security of these shares.

C. Short-term Loans of Settlement Money

Members wishing to obtain the proceeds of share sales before settling days can borrow the money on the security of the shares; the loan is very short, usually for two to three days.

D. Loans on Public Bonds or Corporate Debentures

This form of loan was started in February 1960 in order to facilitate the negotiation of public bonds and corporate debentures and thus to encourage ordinary investors to take them up. Securities companies wishing to purchase outstanding bonds or debentures from their customers, and ordinary investors wishing to buy them from the securities companies, can obtain temporary accommodation from the securities finance companies.

E. Finance of Dealings in Public Bonds or Corporate Debentures

This form of loan was formerly styled 'finance on the security of bonds and debentures' (the so-called 'finance of underwriting'). Loans were made to the securities companies, which had temporarily to hold the newly issued but unsubscribed bonds and debentures under underwriting contracts, or which had purchased outstanding bonds or debentures in order to facilitate the flotation of new securities. In November 1968 the system was enlarged to include all loans to members on bonds and debentures eligible as collateral security at the Bank of Japan. The name was accordingly changed to the present one.

F. Loans to Stags

Members who have sold shares to be issued on condition that settlements will be made on the days of issue can borrow money from the securities finance companies on the security of such shares until settling days.

3. SOURCES OF FUNDS

In addition to their own capital the securities finance companies raise money for the above-mentioned business by borrowing from the call loan market, city banks and the Bank of Japan. Borrowing from the call loan market and from the city banks represents by far the greater part of their resources. Call money is usually used to finance margin loan transactions, and borrowing from banks is employed in ordinary and other loans.

(1) *Call Money*

The securities finance companies borrow from the call loan market on the security of bank and other debentures in their portfolios. They can also borrow from the market on the security of 'call loan transactions collateral receipts'. These receipts are issued by stock exchanges, when the finance companies lodge with them the shares which they have received as collateral for their margin loans. These transactions are governed by the Regulation for Call Loan Transactions Collateral Receipts, which came into force in 1951, when margin transactions were started.[1] The regulation stipulates that call loan dealers who require funds because of their lending to securities finance companies can borrow from the Bank of Japan on the security of promissory notes issued by the finance companies in their favour. These notes are known as 'call loan notes' and are issued on the security of collateral receipts, and the Bank recognises them as eligible security for advances.

[1] The regulation was established by the stock exchanges and the securities finance companies after consultation with the Bank of Japan.

This system makes it possible to raise money for margin transactions in the call loan market.

(2) *Borrowing*

Most of the money borrowed comes from city banks, which make joint loans to the finance companies under loan syndicate contracts. The form adopted is loans on notes secured by shares which the finance companies have received as collateral for ordinary and other loans. In addition, as already mentioned, the finance companies can borrow from the Bank of Japan in order to make loans to finance underwriting. Outstanding borrowing increased rapidly in 1964 and 1965, when they lent heavily to the Joint Securities Co. and to the Japan Securities Holding Association; of late, however, it has been decreasing because the two institutions have repaid their borrowing.

4. REGULATIONS OF MARGIN TRANSACTIONS

In order to prevent speculative excesses in margin transactions the securities finance companies can impose the following requirements:[1]

(1) *Alterations of Terms of Margin Loan Transactions*

The securities finance companies can forestall speculative excesses in margin transactions by changing the terms – that is, the interest rates on the loans, the margin money rate and the collateral value of substitute securities for margin money. These alterations are, however, subject to approval by the Minister of Finance under the Securities Transaction Law. The Minister can also direct them to alter the terms if he considers that current terms do not accord with general economic conditions; before issuing such a directive, however, the Minister must notify the finance companies of his intentions and undertake appropriate inquiries. Further, the Minister must disclose his reasons for this step.

[1] See Chapter 25 for regulations of margins transactions by bodies other than securities finance companies.

(2) *Additional Collateral and Additional Interest*

The securities finance companies can charge additional interest or demand additional collateral for loans in order to regulate the volume of margin transactions.

A. Credit Lines for Individual Members

A credit line may be fixed in advance for each member. If loans to a member exceed this, additional collateral is required, while additional interest may be charged if market conditions seem to warrant this.

B. Adjustment by Type of Shares

If outstanding loans on one kind of share are excessive, additional collateral may be required, after consultation with the stock exchanges. Restrictions may also be imposed on loans.

TABLE 21.1

Interest Rates of the Japan Securities Finance Co. Ltd (May 1970)

(percentages)

	Ceilings Authorised by the Minister of Finance		*Actual Rates*
Margin Loan Transactions			
Loans of Money	10·0		8·0
Loans of Shares	6·5		4·25
Ordinary Loans			
to Members	11·5		8·25
to Members' Customers	12·5		9·25
Loans of Subscription Money			
to Members	11·5 (both)		8·25
to Members' Customers			9·0
Short-Term Loans of Settlement Money			
Members Only	11·0		8·75
Loans on Public Bonds or Corporate Debentures			
to Members	11·5 (both)	Members: Secured Government Securities	7·0
		Members: Other Secured Bonds and Debentures	7·5
to Members' Customers			8·5
Finance of Dealings in Public Bonds or Corporate Debentures			
Members Only	11·5		6·75
Loans to Stags			
Members Only	11·0		8·75

SOURCE: Bank of Japan.

TABLE 21.2

Principal Accounts of Securities Finance Companies

(hundred million yen)

End of the Year	*1955*	*1958*	*1961*	*1964*	*1967*	*1968*	*1969*	*1970*
ASSETS								
Cash and Deposits	1	3	5	10	12	15	28	36
Call Loans	—	15	15	—	—	—	27	—
Loans	118	445	717	1,739	2,978	2,392	3,581	2,665
(of which Margin Loans)	(78)	(374)	(566)	(465)	(562)	(1,860)	(2,688)	(1,653)
LIABILITIES								
Borrowing	67	149	186	1,312	2,416	447	715	782
Call Money	33	266	414	284	373	1,646	2,390	1,478
Guarantee Money	2	4	7	1	—	110	151	5
Collateral Money for Loans of Shares	10	27	104	110	164	124	160	191
Capitals	10	10	18	34	34	34	34	34

SOURCE: Bank of Japan, *Economic Statistics Annual.*

CHAPTER 22

GOVERNMENT FINANCIAL INSTITUTIONS

I. DEVELOPMENT AND CHARACTERISTICS OF TREASURY LOANS AND INVESTMENTS

In Japan the government, as well as private financial institutions, is engaged in extensive financial activities, which greatly affect the overall flow of savings and investment. Considerable funds are absorbed annually by the government through post office savings and various state insurance schemes. These funds are the principal source for the government's financial activities in making loans to private businesses and in subscribing for their shares and debentures. Such activities are usually described as Treasury loans and investments.

The post office savings system has a long history, but it is largely since the Second World War that Treasury loans and investments have come to play an important role in the national economy. In the post-war reconstruction period huge amounts of Treasury funds were released to the private sector, mainly through the Reconstruction Finance Bank (1946–9) and the U.S. Aid Counterpart Fund (1949–53). The money materially assisted the rebuilding of basic industries, such as iron and steel, coal, electricity and shipping. For a few years after 1952 about 30 per cent of funds for fixed investment in plant and equipment of private industries were supplied by the Treasury (Table 22.1). Thus, the primary function of Treasury loans and investments in this period was to make good the shortfall of private funds.

Thereafter, with progress in reconstruction, most big firms became able to raise the bulk of their needs from private financial institutions and from the capital market, so that the relative importance of Treasury loans and investments gradually declined after reaching a peak in 1955. However, they have come to play vital roles in the finance of small business, which has lagged far behind big business; in the finance of public construction, such as roads, harbours, transport and housing; and in the finance of exports.

TABLE 22.1

Proportion of Treasury Money in Private Industrial Funds Raised

(hundred million yen)

	Private Industrial Funds			*of which Funds for Fixed Investment in Plant and Equipment*		
Years	*Total Amount Raised* (A)	*of which Treasury Money* (B)	(B)/(A) × 100 (C)	*Total Amount Raised* (D)	*of which Treasury Money* (E)	(E)/(D) × 100 (F)
			%			%
1952	10,213	958	9·4	2,989	933	31·2
1954	6,120	1,164	19·0	3,176	940	29·6
1956	14,166	1,036	7·3	4,304	744	17·3
1958	16,311	1,590	9·7	7,242	1,326	18·3
1960	29,272	2,187	7·5	13,538	1,764	13·0
1961	41,716	2,298	5·5	20,655	1,830	8·9
1962	42,039	3,011	7·2	17,520	2,197	12·5
1963	57,273	2,961	5·2	19,968	2,328	11·7
1964	50,941	4,141	8·1	21,089	2,801	13·3
1965	48,645	4,202	8·6	18,888	2,938	15·6
1966	55,420	5,326	9·6	18,664	3,670	19·7
1967	70,615	5,818	8·2	27,113	4,099	15·1
1968	74,344	7,893	10·6	34,058	6,010	17·6
1969	103,224	8,890	8·6	46,806	6,422	13·7
1970	126,259	10,144	8·0	56,614	7,001	12·4

NOTE: Treasury money is the sum of loans and discounts of government financial institutions and of special accounts for financial purposes.

SOURCE: Bank of Japan, *Economic Statistics Annual.*

Loans to and investments in small businesses, agriculture, forestry and fishery, housing construction and so on, are broadly matters of social policy, whereas loans to and investments in basic industries largely reflect industrial policy. Thus, Treasury loans and investments nowadays supplement those of private financial institutions. The relative importance of loans and investments in the maintenance of the social substructure has been rising annually, reaching 56 per cent of total (projected) Treasury loans and investments in the fiscal year 1970. This is because private financial institutions are largely unable to operate in these fields, for the loans are mostly for small amounts and long terms, while the collateral offered by borrowers generally has a low credit rating. The rapid development of Japanese industry has, however, created a pressing need for the reinforcement and expansion of the infrastructure, such as roads, harbours and communications. Although such investment promises ample long-run returns for the economy, their construction requires enormous amounts of money, which will be recouped only over a very long period. Such construction cannot, therefore, be wholly financed from private sources, so that Treasury money must fill the gap. Of such social capital projects, communication and transportation facilities occupy an intermediate zone between the public and private sectors. As they can be remunerative as private business undertakings, they are the most appropriate objects of Treasury loans and investments.

Furthermore, in recent years the relative share in exports of the heavy and chemical industries has risen; exports on credit terms, of ships, plants and machinery have greatly increased. Private institutions cannot entirely finance such exports, because credit is extended over a number of years, while interest rates must be on a level with international rates; consequently most of these exports are financed by the Treasury.

For these reasons, growth in Treasury loans and investments for social capital and for the infrastructure of industry, and for export promotion, has far outstripped that for the finance of basic industries during the last decade (see Table 22.2).

This clearly reflects the shift in emphasis of the Treasury's financial activities from being 'quantitative' props of private finance to 'qualitative' crutches for it. This change is reasonable in an economy where industrial activity is carried on mainly by private enterprise. The role of Treasury loans and investments in financing projects, which private financial institutions find difficulty in accommodating, is expected to become more important in the context of a policy of balanced economic development.

TABLE 22.2

Break-down by Purposes of Treasury Loans and Investments

(hundred million yen)

Fiscal Years	1955 (Actual)		1960 (Actual)		1965 (Actual)		1970 (Projected)		1971 (Programme)		1971/1955
		Per-centages of the Total		*Per-centages of the Total*		*Per-centages of the Total*		*Per-centages of the Total*		*Per-centages of the Total*	*Growth Multiple*
Substructure for Living	1,355	45·2	2,904	46·4	8,964	50·5	20,179	56·3	24,748	57·8	18·3
1. Housing	415	13·9	789	12·6	2,552	14·4	6,896	19·3	8,654	20·2	20·9
2. Improvement of Living Environment	230	7·7	569	9·1	2,035	11·4	4,168	11·6	5,199	12·1	22·6
3. Welfare Facilities	64	2·1	109	1·8	585	3·3	1,017	2·8	1,183	2·8	18·5
4. Educational Facilities	136	4·5	214	3·4	472	2·7	790	2·2	964	2·2	7·1
5. Small Businesses	244	8·1	784	12·5	2,285	12·9	5,523	15·4	6,584	15·4	27·0
6. Agriculture, Forestry and Fisheries	266	8·9	439	7·0	1,035	5·8	1,785	5·0	2,164	5·1	8·1
Infrastructure for Industries	962	32·1	2,024	32·4	5,706	32·1	9,792	27·4	11,567	27·0	12·0
7. Land Preservation, Rehabilitation of Damage by Disasters	231	7·7	401	6·4	686	3·8	560	1·6	617	1·4	2·7
8. Highways	110	3·7	272	4·4	1,415	8·0	3,078	8·6	3,508	8·2	31·9
9. Transport and Communication	366	12·2	915	14·6	2,467	13·9	4,723	13·2	5,651	13·2	15·4
10. Regional Development	255	8·5	436	7·0	1,138	6·4	1,431	4·0	1,791	4·2	7·0
Important Industries	681	22·7	1,323	21·2	3,094	17·4	5,828	16·3	6,489	15·2	9·5
11. Basic Industries	471	15·7	838	13·4	1,575	8·9	2,028	5·7	2,299	5·4	4·9
12. Promotion of Exports	210	7·0	485	7·8	1,519	8·5	3,800	10·6	4,190	9·8	20·0
Total	2,998	100·0	6,251	100·0	17,764	100·0	35·799	100·0	42,804	100·0	14·3

SOURCE: Ministry of Finance, *Monthly Statistics of Public Finance and Banking* and *Statistics of Public Finance.*

It is said that Treasury loans and investments can be conveniently used as anti-cyclical weapons, because their scale is more amenable to change than that of ordinary fiscal expenditures. Obligatory or continuing disbursements absorb much of the budgets of the General Account, while Treasury loans and investments can more easily be varied in the light of prevailing economic conditions. Moreover, plans for the employment of these funds can be altered at any time, and the timing of their payment can be accelerated or delayed at will. Thus, they are appropriate contra-cyclical policy instruments.

For instance, the amount of Treasury loans and investments for the fiscal year 1954 was reduced, because 1953–4 were years of monetary restraint. In 1957 and 1961, when measures were taken to improve the balance of payments, part of the payments under Treasury loans and investments plans was deferred, in order to prompt private industry to reduce its investment. More recently, in 1965, when a reflationary policy was followed, their scale was expanded and payments were accelerated. In the credit squeeze of 1967 a part of the payments was deferred, while at the same time the issue of government-guaranteed debentures was reduced. With the increased issue of government bonds and the increased scale of public finance since 1965, flexible administration of Treasury loans and investments has gained in importance, because they are an important part of the mix of fiscal and monetary policies.

As noted above, however, the shift of emphasis to public and social objectives has tended to diminish flexibility in determining their size, and this loss of flexibility detracts from their usefulness as an anti-cyclical policy weapon, particularly for purposes of restraint.

2. MECHANISM OF TREASURY LOANS AND INVESTMENTS

The government's loans and investments are governed by their annual programmes.[1] It is since 1953 that the annual pro-

[1] Treasury loans and investment programmes do not cover the whole of the government's financial activities. There are certain kinds of expenditures of the General Account, which serve the same purposes as those of the Treasury loans and investments. Further, as will be explained later, short-term loans of the Trust Fund Bureau with maturities of less than one year are not included in the pro-

grammes of Treasury loans and investments have come to be formulated as at present. The programme is drawn up for each fiscal year together with the annual budget and on the same basis, although the approval of the Diet is not required. Its scale and influence on the national economy are comparable with those of the budget of the General Account (for instance, for the fiscal year 1968, the former amounted to 2699·0 billion yen, while the latter was 5818·5 billion yen). For this reason, the Treasury loans and investments programme is, for practical purposes, treated as a component of the budget: their allocation plans are explained in speeches on budgetary policy. The Explanation of the Budget discloses their details, which are discussed in the Diet in connection with the budget.

The sources of funds for Treasury loans and investments are twofold: the 'Treasury fund' and 'borrowings and bonds issued for public subscription'. Their programme also shows the break-down of loans and investments by type of borrower and of recipients of investments: special accounts, public corporations, local authorities, special companies and so on. Thus, it is possible to see at a glance the kind of loans and investments made, with what funds, and from what sources. To elucidate further, the uses of funds will now be discussed.

(1) *Sources of Funds*

The chief source of funds for Treasury loans and investments is Treasury funds (they accounted for 84 per cent of the total for the fiscal year 1969). Treasury funds consist of funds of the Trust Fund Bureau, the Post Office Life Insurance, and the Industrial Investment Special Account; the Trust Fund Bureau funds represent the bulk (84 per cent of the total). As will be explained later, the surplus funds of postal savings, welfare annuity funds and of various special accounts are concentrated in the hands of the Trust Fund Bureau, the resources of which exceed 11,880 billion yen at the end of fiscal year 1969. This amount is roughly equal to the total funds of country banks. Post Office Life Insurance funds consist of reserves of Post Office

---

grammes. However, these do not amount to much. It may safely be said that the government's financial activities are almost completely governed by these programmes.

Life Insurance and of Postal Annuity; these amounted to 2600 billion yen at the end of the fiscal year 1969, and they thus are a relatively important source of funds for Treasury loans and investments. The Industrial Investments Special Account has taken over the assets of the former U.S. Aid Counterpart Fund Special Account; in addition, money is transferred to it from the General Account, and at the end of the fiscal year 1969 its assets were nearly 1100 billion yen.

The second source of funds is money raised by bond and debenture issues and by borrowing. More precisely, bond and debenture issues are made up of: (1) the flotation of local bonds for public subscription (issued to the public with the approval of the appropriate authorities); (2) the flotation of government-guaranteed debentures by public corporations, such as Japan National Railways, the Japan Telegraph and Telephone Corporation, the Housing Corporation and other government agencies; (3) borrowings are those from private financial institutions and from external sources, such as the World Bank, which has lent money to the Highway Corporation. Money raised by the issue of foreign currency bonds by the Industrial Investment Special Account is included in this category (Table 22.3).

(2) *Borrowers and Recipients of Investments*

The borrowers and recipients of investment are as follows: special accounts of the government, such as postal services; public corporations, such as National Railways, Telegraph and Telephone, Housing, Highway, Water Resources Development and Pension Welfare Service; government financial institutions, such as the Japan Development Bank, Export and Import Bank of Japan, Housing Loan Corporation, People's Finance Corporation and Small Business Finance Corporation; and special companies, such as Electric Power Development Company, Japan Petroleum Exploration Company and Japan Airlines Company. Purchases of local bonds and loans to the Government of Ryukyu are also made under the Treasury loans and investments programme (Table 22.4).

Loans to and investments in government financial institutions are made so that they can supply funds to the private sector.

TABLE 22.3

Sources of Funds for Treasury Loans and Investments

(hundred million yen)

Fiscal Year	1955 (Actual)		1960 (Actual)		1965 (Actual)		1970 (Revised Appropriation)		1971 (Original Appropriation)	
		Per-centages of the Total		*Per-centages of the Total*		*Per-centages of the Total*		*Per-centages of the Total*		*Per-centages of the Total*
Trust Fund Bureau	1,529	51·0	3,471	55·5	11,872	66·8	25,440	71·0	31,334	73·2
(of which Postal Savings)	(820)	(27·4)	(1,506)	(24·1)	(4,645)	(26·1)	(11,300)	(31·6)	(13,500)	(31·5)
(,, ,, Welfare Annuity)	(314)	(10·5)	(918)	(14·7)	(3,244)	(18·3)	(7,731)	(21·6)	(9,466)	(22·1)
(,, ,, National Pension)	(—)	(—)	(—)	(—)	(453)	(2·6)	(1,496)	(4·2)	(1,949)	(4·6)
Post Office Life Insurance	482	16·1	1,199	19·2	1,095	6·2	3,930	11·0	4,950	11·6
Industrial Investment Special Account	180	6·0	398	6·4	430	2·4	1,035	2·9	853	2·0
Others	291	9·7	—	—	—	—	—	—	—	—
Sub-total	2,482	82·8	5,068	81·1	13,397	75·4	30,405	84·9	37,137	86·8
Bond and Debenture Issues for Public Subscription and Borrowing	516	17·2	1,081	17·3	4,150	23·4	5,394	15·1	5,667	13·2
Foreign Currency Debenture Issues and Others	—	—	102	1·6	217	1·2				
Total	2,998	100·0	6,251	100·0	17,764	100·0	35,799	100·0	42,804	100·0

SOURCE: Ministry of Finance, *Monthly Statistics of Public Finance and Banking* and *Statistics of Public Finance*.

TABLE 22.4

Recipients of Treasury Loans and Investments

(hundred million yen)

Fiscal Years	*1955 (Actual)*		*1960 (Actual)*		*1965 (Actual)*		*1970 (Revised Appropriation)*		*1971 (Original Appropriation)*	
		Percentages of the Total		*Percentages of the Total*		*Percentages of the Total*		*Percentages of the Total*		*Percentages of the Total*
Special Accounts	45	1·5	95	1·5	263	1·5	371	1·0	435	1·0
National Railways and Telegraph and Telephone Public Corporations	315	10·5	796	12·7	2,064	11·6	3,600	10·1	4,374	10·2
Government Banks	385	12·9	915	14·7	2,886	16·2	12,026	33·6	14,061	32·9
Public Finance Corporations	585	19·5	1,490	23·8	4,719	26·6	4,415	12·3	4,837	11·3
Other Public Corporations	160	5·3	692	11·1	3,516	19·8	8,938	25·0	11,444	26·7
Local Authorities	1,176	39·2	1,676	26·8	3,764	21·2	6,006	16·8	7,106	16·6
Special Companies	303	10·1	587	9·4	552	3·1	392	1·1	442	1·0
Government of Ryukyu	—	—	—	—	—	—	51	0·1	105	0·3
Bank Debentures	29	1·0	—	—	—	—	—	—	—	—
Total	2,998	100·0	6,251	100·0	17,764	100·0	35,799	100·0	42,804	100·0

SOURCE: Ministry of Finance, *Monthly Statistics of Public Finance and Banking* and *Statistics of Public Finance*.

They represented 45 per cent of total Treasury loans and investments in the fiscal year 1970. Funds are also supplied to the private sector through public corporations, such as the Overseas Economic Co-operation Fund, and other financial agencies of the government as well as through the Central Bank for Commercial and Industrial Co-operatives, which is one of the government-affiliated special companies. If we include the money supplied through these corporations, government-affiliated agencies and special companies, about 50 per cent of the funds of Treasury loans and investments are provided to the private sector through various government financial institutions. This indirect method of financing the private sector is adopted to secure a more efficient utilisation of funds: government financial institutions are run on a self-balancing basis, so that sound credit management may be ensured.

Money is either lent or invested. Money raised by debenture issues to the public and by borrowings from private institutions can be used only for making loans. Funds of the Trust Fund Bureau and of Post Office Life Insurance, the source of which is personal savings, can also be employed only in loans. On the other hand, although money raised by the issue of foreign currency bonds can only be loaned out, funds of the Industrial Investment Special Account can be used for making either loans or investments; in recent years they have been almost exclusively invested.

Thus, the government is engaged in extensive financial activities with funds collected through postal savings and insurance or raised by bond and debenture issues to the public. The government in itself is, so to speak, a gigantic financial institution. We shall now describe its financial activities and the functions of various government financial institutions.

3. FINANCIAL SPECIAL ACCOUNTS

There are at present four special accounts for government financial operations: Trust Fund Bureau Special Account, Industrial Investment Special Account, Finance of New Settlers Special Account and City Development Fund Special Account.[1]

[1] The Economic Aid Funds Special Account and the Funds Accruing from

In addition to these, one of the insurance special accounts, that is, Post Office, Life Insurance and Postal Annuity Special Account, is engaged in lending and investing activities.

(1) *Trust Fund Bureau*

A. General Survey

The Trust Fund Bureau receives on deposit the small savings of individuals, which are collected through postal savings accounts and welfare annuity premiums, as well as the surplus funds and reserves of various special accounts of the government. The money is then loaned out to government financial institutions, public corporations, local authorities and so on. It is thus a kind of state-operated bank and plays a leading role as an executive organ for Treasury loans and investments. As has been mentioned (in Part One), it is a successor to the Deposit Bureau of the Ministry of Finance, which has a long history. The Deposit Bureau was transformed into the Trust Fund Bureau under the Trust Fund Bureau Fund Law of 1951. This change was accompanied by substantial alteration in the methods for the employment of funds; the foundation was thus laid of the current system of the Bureau. At the same time the Deposit Bureau of the Ministry of Finance Special Account was transformed into the Trust Fund Bureau Special Account under the Trust Fund Bureau Special Account Law of the same year. The special account was established to separate the Bureau's revenues (interest on loans and so on) and expenditures (interest on deposits, managerial costs and so on) from those of the General Account.

B. Sources of Funds

The resources of the Bureau consist of deposits, such as those received from postal savings account, and of the accumulated surpluses of the Trust Fund Bureau Special Account. All postal savings, excluding the reserves necessary for daily withdrawals, and all reserves (surpluses up to the preceding

---

Purchases of U.S. Agricultural Commodities Special Account were incorporated with the Industrial Investment Special Account in the 1968 fiscal year, while the Small Business Development Financing Special Account was merged with the Small Business Promotion Corporation in the same year.

year) of special accounts, except for the Post Office Life Insurance and Postal Annuity Special Account, must be deposited with the Trust Fund Bureau. Similarly, current surpluses of the special accounts cannot be employed other than in deposits with the bureau, although investment in government bonds by the Debt Consolidation Fund Special Account is an exception to the rule. Treasury surplus funds can also be lodged with the bureau. At the end of the fiscal year 1969 the resources of the bureau amounted to 11,896·3 billion yen; their composition is shown in Table 22.5. Small savings of individuals, such as postal savings, welfare insurance premiums and contributions to national pensions, account for over 80 per cent of the total, of which postal savings represent the bulk. Postal savings are absorbed through some 20,000 post offices scattered over the country; interest rates on them are stipulated in an ordinance under the Postal Savings Law: 3·6 per cent for ordinary postal savings and 4·25–5·75 per cent for savings certificates, the precise rate depending upon the maturity. The maximum deposit per person is 1 million yen. At the end of the fiscal year 1969 the outstanding amount of postal savings (excluding postal transfers) was 6034 billion yen, of which 29 per cent was ordinary deposits and 67 per cent savings certificates. Welfare insurance comprises the reserves of government-operated welfare annuity schemes and others (Table 22.5).

These deposits, which are the chief source of the bureau's funds have maturities of more than one month; the lowest deposit rate is 2 per cent for one to three months, while the highest is 6 per cent for deposits of over seven years. Since the fiscal year 1961, special interest (0·5 per cent at present) has been paid on deposits of over seven years, in addition to the legal interest. The break-down by maturity of these deposits reveals that more than 90 per cent of them have terms of more than seven years, deposits of postal savings, the most important source of funds, having such maturities.

Each year's increment in deposits with the bureau and repayments of past loans, as well as defrayals from accumulated reserves, determine the amount of funds which the bureau can contribute to the Treasury loans and investments programme in that year.

TABLE 22.5

Outstanding Amounts of Resources of Trust Fund Bureau

(hundred million yen)

End of the Fiscal Year	*1955*		*1960*		*1965*		*1966*		*1967*		*1968*		*1969*		*1970*	
		Percentages of the Total		*Percentages of the Total*		*Percentages of the Total*		*Percentages of the Total*		*Percentages of the Total*		*Percentages of the Total*		*Percentages of the Total*		*Percentages of the Total*
Postal and Postal Transfer Savings	5,335	59·2	11,176	53·8	26,732	52·9	32,671	52·4	40,634	52·3	50,487	52·4	62,555	52·6	76,757	52·5
Post Office Life-Insurance and Postal Annuity	1,289	14·3	1,418	6·8	898	1·8	1,437	2·3	1,509	2·0	2,165	2·3	2,635	2·2	3,501	2·4
Welfare Insurance	1,420	15·8	4,504	21·7	14,061	27·8	18,198	29·2	22,222	28·6	28,395	29·5	34,878	29·3	43,435	29·7
Surplus of Treasury Accounts	50	0·6	400	1·9	—	—	—	—	—	—	—	—	—	—	—	—
Deposits of National Pension Special Account	—	—	—	—	1,884	3·7	2,400	3·8	3,191	4·1	4,189	4·4	5,486	4·6	7,172	4·9
Deposits of Others	852	9·4	3,056	14·7	6,423	12·7	7,117	11·4	8,393	10·8	10,393	10·8	12,719	10·7	14,718	10·1
Sub-total of Deposits	8,946	99·3	20,554	98·9	49,999	98·9	61,823	99·1	75,959	97·8	95,629	99·3	118,273	99·4	145,583	99·5
Others	66	0·7	227	1·1	540	1·1	559	0·9	1,700	2·2	649	0·7	690	0·6	715	0·5
Total	9,012	100·0	20,781	100·0	50,539	100·0	62,382	100·0	77,649	100·0	96,278	100·0	118,963	100·0	146,297	100·0

SOURCE: Bank of Japan, *Economic Statistics Annual*.

C. Employment of Funds

The bureau's funds must be employed in safe and profitable ways which are at the same time conducive to the promotion of public welfare. The Trust Fund Bureau Council was set up to determine the methods of and conditions for the employment of funds.[1] The Trust Fund Bureau Fund Law permits only the following outlets for the Bureau's funds: (1) loans to the government or to local authorities or investments in government or local bonds; (2) loans to special corporations, such as government-affiliated institutions and public corporations, or investment in debentures issued by them; (3) loans to the Electric Power Development Company or investment in its debentures; (4) investment in limited amounts of bank debentures. At the end of the fiscal year 1969 the loan rates were 6·5 per cent for most loans to special accounts, government-affiliated institutions, local authorities and special corporations, such as public corporations; and 7·0 per cent for loans to Teito (Metropolitan) Rapid Transit Authority and the Hokkaido and Tohoku Development Corporation. Investment in bonds and debentures is made on the same terms as those for public subscription.

Table 22.6 shows the recent employment of the funds: about 80 per cent are employed in loans to government-affiliated institutions and to local authorities, while securities represent only about 20 per cent in spite of the increase in holdings of long-term government bonds in recent years. Short-term loans and investments of less than one year are not included in the Treasury loans and investments programme. Furthermore, approval of the Trust Fund Bureau Council is not required for: (1) purchase of bank and other debentures which mature within one year or of which resale within one year is the condition of purchase; (2) loans repayable within the same fiscal year; or (3) bridging-loans in anticipation of long-term loans (or of the issue of long-term bonds or debentures).

[1] The Trust Fund Bureau Council is composed of less than seven members, appointed by the Prime Minister, who are 'men of experience and learning'. Under them are a few specialist members who are either men of experience and learning or are representatives of the government departments concerned. In addition, six secretaries are seconded from the government departments concerned.

TABLE 22.6

Employment of Trust Fund Bureau Funds

(hundred million yen)

End of the Fiscal Year	*1955*		*1960*		*1965*		*1966*		*1967*		*1968*		*1969*		*1970*	
		Percentages of the Total		*Percentages of the Total*		*Percentages of the Total*		*Percentages of the Total*		*Percentages of the Total*		*Percentages of the Total*		*Percentages of the Total*		*Percentages of the Total*
SECURITIES																
Long-Term Government Bonds	142	1·6	828	4·0	887	1·8	887	1·5	6,287	8·1	4,879	5·1	5,302	4·5	11,125	2·6
Government Short-Term Bills	304	3·4	2,275	10·9	4,112	8·1	5,964	10·1	2,812	3·6	5,116	5·3	7,377	6·2	6,030	10·6
Corporate Debentures	1,380	15·3	1,927	9·3	2,694	5·3	2,591	4·4	5,119	6·6	10,013	10·4	15,333	12·9	19,112	11·8
(of which Bank Debentures)	(1,354)	(15·0)	(1,674)	(8·1)	(557)	(1·1)	(362)	(0·6)	(1,038)	(1·3)	(1,261)	(1·3)	(2,427)	(2·0)	(2,981)	(2·4)
Local Bonds	3	—	—	—	—	—	—	—	—	—	—	—	—	—	—	—
Sub-Total	1,829	20·3	5,030	24·2	7,693	15·2	9,442	16·0	14,218	18·3	20,008	20·8	28,012	23·6	36,267	25·0
LOANS																
General and Special Accounts	197	2·2	420	2·0	1,985	3·9	2,238	3·8	2,908	3·7	3,545	3·7	3,990	3·3	5,046	3·4
Local Authorities	3,646	40·5	4,789	23·0	10,403	20·6	13,074	22·1	15,189	19·6	17,338	18·0	19,644	16·5	22,487	15·3
Government Agencies	3,013	33·4	7,929	38·2	23,442	46·4	26,621	45·1	35,842	46·2	43,768	45·5	53,150	44·7	65,366	44·7
Others	300	3·3	2,601	12·5	7,012	13·9	7,655	13·0	9,418	12·1	11,504	11·9	14,036	11·8	17,079	11·7
Sub-Total	7,156	79·4	15,739	75·7	42,842	84·8	49,588	84·0	63,357	81·6	76,155	79·1	90,820	76·3	109,898	75·1
Cash, etc.	27	0·3	12	0·1	4	—	6	—	74	0·1	115	0·1	131	0·1	132	0·1
Total	9,012	100·0	20,781	100·0	50,539	100·0	59,036	100·0	77,649	100·0	96,278	100·0	118,963	100·0	146,297	100·0

The Trust Fund Bureau now undertakes the purchase and sale of bank debentures with private financial institutions dealing with small businesses in order to assist in the financing of such businesses. These operations do not have to be considered by the Trust Fund Bureau Council because of the considerations mentioned above.

(2) *Post Office Life-Insurance and Postal Annuity Special Account*

This special account was set up to manage Post Office Life-Insurance and Postal Annuity Schemes.[1] During the war it was decided that its reserves should be lodged with the Deposit Bureau; after its transformation into the Trust Fund Bureau they were deposited with the bureau and employed by it. Since the fiscal year 1953, however, the special account has again been independent of the Trust Fund Bureau.

Similar restrictions to those applied to loans and investments of the money of the Trust Fund Bureau are imposed upon the employment of its reserves. The special account can, however, make direct loans to policy-holders. After deductions for loans to policy-holders, the special account's surpluses in the preceding year and the repayments proceeds of past loans go to swell the resources of the Treasury loans and investment programme. The importance of these Post Office Life-Insurance Funds as a source of money for the programme is second only to that of the funds of the Trust Fund Bureau; their outstanding amount was 2100 billion yen at the end of the fiscal year 1969. As may be seen from Table 22.7, they have mostly been employed (61 per cent) in loans to local authorities and to government-affiliated organisations.

As in the case of the employment of money held by the Trust Fund Bureau the more important questions about policy and the terms on which funds are employed are considered by the

[1] Post Office Life Insurance is run by the state. Its characteristics are that the insurance money is smaller (the current maximum is 2 million yen) and that procedures for the conclusion of contracts and payments of insurance money are simpler than those of private life insurance. There are three varieties: life, old-age and family insurance. Postal annuity is a kind of pure endowment insurance. The object is to promote the welfare of, and to stabilise the lives of, the aged and of their families, who belong to the lower income groups. These premiums are as low as possible, so that it is a non-profit-making scheme. Both schemes have existed for about forty years.

TABLE 22.7

Outstanding Resources and Assets of the Post Office Life-Insurance and Postal Annuity Funds

(hundred million yen)

End of the Fiscal Year	*1955*		*1960*		*1965*		*1966*		*1967*		*1968*		*1969*	
		Percent-ages of the Total		*Percent-ages of the Total*		*Percent-ages of the Total*		*Percent-ages of the Total*		*Percent-ages of the Total*		*Percent-ages of the Total*		*Percent-ages of the Total*
ASSETS														
Securities														
Government Bonds	129	4·8	338	4·5	298	2·4	304	2·1	358	2·2	558	3·0	330	1·6
Local Bonds	5	0·2	2	—	40	0·3	52	0·4	68	0·4	102	0·5	135	0·6
Public Corporation Debentures	—	—	265	3·6	2,821	22·4	3,374	23·7	4,233	26·3	4,551	24·5	5,493	25·4
Sub-Total	134	5·0	605	8·1	3,159	25·1	3,730	26·2	4,660	28·9	5,211	28·0	5,958	27·6
Loans														
Postal Services	5	0·2	159	2·1	253	2·0	272	1·9	306	1·9	366	2·0	424	2·0
Local Authorities	1,188	44·4	2,709	36·3	5,081	40·3	5,397	37·9	5,824	36·2	6,354	34·2	6,906	31·9
Policy-holders	164	6·2	532	7·1	739	5·9	800	5·6	841	5·2	929	5·0	1,037	4·8
Government Agencies	30	1·1	1,879	25·2	2,201	17·5	2,329	16·3	2,546	15·8	3,115	16·7	4,122	19·1
Sub-Total	1,387	51·9	5,279	70·7	8,274	65·7	8,798	61·7	9,517	59·1	10,764	57·9	12,493	57·8
Deposits with Trust Fund Bureau	1,148	42·9	1,578	21·2	1,107	8·8	1,623	11·4	1,313	8·2	1,862	10·0	2,373	11·0
Others	5	0·2	—	—	51	0·4	108	0·7	605	3·8	753	4·1	780	3·6
Total	2,674	100·0	7,462	100·0	12,591	100·0	14,259	100·0	16,095	100·0	18,590	100·0	21,606	100·0
SOURCES OF FUNDS														
Reserves of Insurance and Annuity Contracts	2,632	98·4	7,131	95·6	12,069	95·9	13,887	97·4	15,450	96·0	17,792	95·7	21,078	97·6
Surpluses	42	1·6	331	4·4	522	4·1	372	2·6	645	4·0	798	4·3	528	2·4
(For Reference)														
For Accounts of Post Office Life	2,608	97·5	7,329	98·2	12,382	98·3	14,035	98·4	15,868	98·6	18,373	98·8	21,393	99·0

[rust Fund Bureau Council (at present the standard lending ate is 6·5 per cent, the same as that of the Trust Fund Bureau). [emporary surpluses can, however, be employed within ertain limits without the Council's approval.

3) *Industrial Investment Special Account*

[his special account was established in 1953 as the successor o the U.S. Aid Counterpart Fund Special Account to make nvestments for economic reconstruction, industrial develop-nent and the promotion of foreign trade.

From its start to the fiscal year 1955 the special account nade loans and investments to the Japan Development Bank, he Export–Import Bank of Japan and to the Electric Power Development Company. The expansion of basic industries and he promotion of foreign trade were its principal aims. Since he fiscal year 1956, the importance of the General Account as he supplier of funds for the Treasury loans and investments programme has gradually dwindled. The special account has argely taken over the function of the General Account in this espect and has begun to finance public corporations and pecial companies, mainly, in recent years as an investor in hem. This for the following reasons: government financial nstitutions and public corporations have recently required nore money, but, as they make loans at specially reduced ates of interest, they need non- or low-interest-bearing money. [he funds of the Trust Fund Bureau and of the Post Office Life nsurance cannot meet their requirements, because the cost of heir funds is not zero. Consequently, investment in government inancial institutions and in public corporations has recently levolved solely upon the Industrial Investment Special Ac-count, which can muster costless funds (although the General Account makes investments which are not included in the [reasury loans and investments programme).

The initial capital of the special account amounted to 348·1 billion yen, of which 229·4 billion consisted of assets aken over from the U.S. Aid Counterpart Fund Special Account, while 118·7 billion came from the General Account, which had invested this sum in the Japan Development Bank and in the Export–Import Bank of Japan. Thereafter, it took

TABLE 22.8

Outstanding Resources of the Industrial Investment Special Account

(hundred million yen)

End of the Fiscal Year	*1955*		*1960*		*1965*		*1966*		*1967*		*1968*		*1969*	
		Percentages of the Total		*Percentages of the Total*		*Percentages of the Total*		*Percentages of the Total*		*Percentages of the Total*		*Percentages of the Total*		*Percentages of the Total*
CAPITAL														
Taken over from the U.S. Aid Counterpart Fund	2,294	56·3	2,294	39·3	2,294	27·5	2,294	26·2	2,294	24·3	2,294	21·7	2,294	20·3
Taken over from the General Account	1,187	29·1	1,187	20·3	1,187	14·2	1,187	13·5	1,187	12·5	1,187	11·2	1,187	10·5
Taken over from the Strategic Materials Import Fund	23	0·6	23	0·4	23	0·3	23	0·3	23	0·2	—	—	23	0·2
Proceeds from Sale of Special Commodities	—	—	123	2·1	196	2·3	196	2·2	196	2·1	196	1·9	196	1·7
Transferred from the General Account	—	—	820	14·1	2,829	33·9	3,274	37·4	3,893	41·2	4,489	42·4	5,270	46·5
Capital Reduction in Connection with Liabilities to the U.S., etc.	—	—	—	—	−1,824	−21·9	−1,824	−20·8	−1,824	−19·3	−1,824	−17·2	−1,824	−16·1
Others	—	—	—	—	—	—	—	—	—	—	164	1·5	142	1·3
Sub-Total	3,504	86·0	4,447	76·2	4,705	56·3	5,150	58·8	5,769	61·0	6,506	61·5	7,288	64·3

Proceeds from Issues of Foreign Currency Bonds	141	3·5	108	1·8	357	4·3	348	4·0	431	4·6	472	4·5	484	4·3
Liabilities in Connection with U.S. Aid to Japan	—	—	—	—	1,350	16·2	1,225	14·0	1,096	11·6	965	9·1	830	7·3
Reserves	285	7·0	1,116	19·1	1,836	22·0	1,938	22·1	2,036	21·5	2,156	20·4	2,300	20·3
Current Profits	143	3·5	168	2·9	103	1·2	97	1·1	121	1·3	121	1·1	78	0·7
Others	—	—	—	—	—	—	—	—	—	—	359	3·4	355	3·1
Total	4,074	100·0	5,839	100·0	8,351	100·0	8,758	100·0	9,453	100·0	10,579	100·0	11,335	100·0

SOURCE: Ministry of Finance, *Monthly Statistics of Public Finance and Banking.*

over the assets of the Strategic Materials Import Fund Special Account and received funds from the Proceeds from Sale of Special Commodities Special Account as well as from the General Account. Further, in the fiscal year 1968, it absorbed the Economic Aid Funds Special Account and the Funds Accruing from Purchase of U.S. Agricultural Commodities Special Account. At the end of the fiscal year 1969 its capital amounted to 728·8 billion yen. The principal sources of funds for new investments for the special account are repayments of past loans from capital; interest income; and dividends from and redemption of investments in government-affiliated organisations. They differ, however, from the resources of the Trust Fund Bureau and of the Post Office Life Insurance in that steady growth cannot be expected of them, while postal savings and annuities increase annually. These sources of funds are therefore inadequate to meet the growing requirements for capital, so that large amounts of money have been transferred annually from the General Account in recent years (Table 22.8).

In addition to the above-mentioned sources of funds the special account can issue bonds: in 1953 14·2 billion yen of Special Tax Reduction Bonds were issued by the account, but they had all been redeemed by the end of the fiscal year 1958, and since then no bonds of this type have been issued. Foreign-currency bonds have been issued five times since February 1959, in the U.S.A., Switzerland and West Germany (the proceeds were 10·6 billion yen in 1958, 13·8 billion yen in 1963, 17·9 billion yen in 1964, 8·9 billion yen in 1967 and 5·0 billion yen in 1968 – all fiscal years).

At the end of the fiscal year 1969 the outstanding assets of the special account were 1135·6 billion yen, of which investments represented 91 per cent. Only the proceeds from issues of foreign-currency bonds can be employed in making loans, so that they accounted for only about 4 per cent of the total funds (although since the fiscal year 1968 its capacity for loans has been further increased, because it has absorbed the Funds Accruing from Purchases of U.S. Agricultural Commodities Special Account and has taken over its assets, which can be employed in making loans) (Table 22.9).

(hundred million yen)

End of the Fiscal Year	*1955*	*Percentages of the Total*	*1960*	*Percentages of the Total*	*1965*	*Percentages of the Total*	*1966*	*Percentages of the Total*	*1967*	*Percentages of the Total*	*1968*	*Percentages of the Total*	*1969*	*Percentages of the Total*
LOANS														
Japan Development Bank	732	18·0	504	8·6	375	4·5	323	3·7	352	3·7	348	3·3	292	2·6
Export–Import Bank of Japan	30	0·7	—	—	—	—	—	—	—	—	—	—	—	—
Agriculture, Forestry and Fishery Finance Corp.	29	0·7	17	0·3	3	—	—	—	—	—	—	—	—	—
Electric Power Development Co.	—	—	107	1·9	77	0·9	69	0·8	61	0·6	389	3·7	392	3·5
Japan Highway Public Corp.	—	—	—	—	187	2·3	187	2·1	187	2·0	187	1·8	187	1·6
General Account	60	1·5	60	1·0	—	—	—	—	—	—	—	—	—	—
Others	—	—	—	—	—	—	—	—	—	—	120	1·1	111	1·0
Sub-Total	851	20·9	688	11·8	642	7·7	579	6·6	600	6·3	1,044	9·9	982	8·7
CAPITAL SUBSCRIPTIONS														
Japan Development Bank	2,340	57·4	2,340	40·1	2,340	28·1	2,340	26·7	2,340	24·8	2,340	22·1	2,340	20·6
Export–Import Bank of Japan	340	8·4	583	10·0	1,758	21·0	2,128	24·3	2,608	27·6	3,088	29·2	3,723	32·9
Public Finance Corporations	147	3·6	679	11·6	1,885	22·5	1,893	21·6	1,901	20·1	1,911	18·1	1,918	16·9
(of which Agriculture, Forestry and Fishery Finance Corp.)	(66)	(1·6)	(366)	(6·3)	(1,118)	(13·4)	(1,118)	(12·8)	(1,118)	(11·8)	(1,118)	(10·6)	(1,118)	(9·9)
Other Public Corporations and Special Companies	330	8·1	1,115	19·1	1,678	20·1	1,784	20·4	1,957	20·7	2,174	20·5	2,345	20·7
(of which Electric Power Development Co.)	(330)	(8·1)	(600)	(10·3)	(625)	(7·5)	(645)	(7·4)	(645)	(6·8)	(645)	(6·1)	(593)	(5·2)
Sub-Total	3,157	77·5	4,717	80·8	7,661	91·7	8,145	93·0	8,806	93·2	9,513	89·9	10,326	91·1
PREFERENCE SHARES	35	0·9	7	0·1	—	—	—	—	—	—	—	—	—	—
TREASURY FUND	31	0·7	427	7·3	48	0·6	34	0·4	45	0·5	20	0·2	25	0·2
ADDITIONS TO REDEMPTION FUND OF FOREIGN-CURRENCY BONDS	—	—	—	—	—	—	—	—	2	—	—	2	2	—
Total	4,074	100·0	5,839	100·0	8,351	100·0	8,758	100·0	9,453	100·0	10,579	100·0	11,335	100·0

SOURCE: Ministry of Finance, *Monthly Statistics of Public Finance and Banking.*

(4) *Other Financial Special Accounts*

A. Finance of New Settlers Special Account

The special account was established in 1947 under the Finance of New Settlers Law. Its source of funds are borrowing from the Trust Fund Bureau and repayments of past loans. Loans are made to new settlers or to corporate bodies organised by them. They can be made only for the following purposes: (1) purchase of agricultural implements or machinery or installation of agricultural facilities; (2) promotion and stabilisation of farming for new settlers, experiencing fluctuations in their business; (3) assistance when damage results from extraordinary calamities.

The funds of the special account had been drawn from the General Account until the fiscal year 1954, but thereafter borrowings from the Trust Fund Bureau constituted its major resources (the maximum limit of such borrowings was 3·8 billion yen in 1968). Its loan rates (3·65–5·5 per cent), however, are lower than the interest payable on borrowing from the Trust Fund Bureau (6·5 per cent), so that the General Account subsidises the special account. In addition, the account can issue bonds.

At the end of the fiscal year 1969 the resources of the account amounted to 49·1 billion yen (of which borrowings were 35·3 billion, bonds outstanding 3·1 billion and transference from the General Account 8·9 billion), while its loans totalled 41·5 billion yen.

B. City Development Fund Special Account

This special account was established in the fiscal year 1966. Its purpose is to lend money to enable local authorities to purchase land from factories which are going to move away from big cities; to assist the authorities to use the space far more efficiently; or to enable them to buy land for the construction of important municipal facilities, such as trunk roads. At the end of the fiscal year 1967 its resources consisted of transfers from the General Account to the extent of 1·0 billion yen and of borrowing from the Trust Fund Bureau to the amount of 4·0 billion yen, while outstanding loans amounted to 4·8 billion yen.

4. GOVERNMENT FINANCIAL INSTITUTIONS

There are, at present, two government banks and nine financial public corporations: Japan Development Bank; Export–Import Bank of Japan; People's Finance Corporation; Housing Loan Corporation; Small Business Finance Corporation; Agriculture, Forestry and Fishery Finance Corporation; Hokkaido and Tohoku Development Corporation; Local Public Enterprise Finance Corporation; Small Business Credit Insurance Corporation; Medical Care Facilities Finance Corporation and Personal Services Finance Corporation. All of these are public corporations, their capital being subscribed entirely by the government. There is, however, a significant difference between government banks and finance corporations in respect of their organisation and their managerial autonomy. On the whole, banks enjoy relatively greater autonomy; for instance, the governor, vice-governor and auditors of banks are appointed by the government, but their directors can be nominated by the governor, while approval of the competent ministers is required for the nomination of a director of a public finance corporation. Their operations are also subject to differing degrees of governmental control: details of banks' operations such as business or financing projects, are left to their discretion, whereas public finance corporations must obtain the approval of the appropriate ministers for their quarterly plans of business and financing.

Such differences between banks and public finance corporations stem from differences in their natures: government banks are akin to ordinary financial institutions in that they mainly deal with modern big businesses, while public finance corporations chiefly make loans to particular branches of the economy, such as small businesses, agriculture, house construction and individuals, so that they are more concerned with social policy objectives. Thus, government banks might, if uncontrolled, come into competition with private financial institutions. The laws governing the banks, therefore, explicitly provide that they must be run 'so as not to compete with banks or other financial institutions'.

In addition, there are the Overseas Economic Co-operation Fund and various other government-affiliated agencies, the

TABLE 22.10

Principal Accounts of Government Financial Institutions (end of 1970)

(hundred million yen)

	Capital				Borrowings						
		General Account	*Industrial Investment Special Account*	*Others*		*Trust Fund Bureau*	*Post Office Life Insurance and Postal Annuity*	*Industrial Investment Special Account*	*Others*	*Debentures*	*Loans*
BANKS											
Japan Development Bank	2,340	—	2,340	—	12,313	12,064	—	249	—	287	17,051
Export–Import Bank of Japan	4,453	—	4,453	—	10,783	10,783	—	—	—	—	15,220
Sub-Total	6,793	—	6,793	—	23,096	22,847	—	249	—	287	32,271
PUBLIC FINANCE CORPORATIONS											
People's Finance Corporation	200	200	—	—	6,681	6,282	399	—	—	—	7,089
Housing Loan Corporation	972	322	545	105	9,550	8,604	946	—	—	34	10,697
Agriculture, Forestry and Fishery Finance Corp.	1,703	520	1,118	65	7,843	7,405	438	0	—	—	9,554
Small Business Finance Corporation	252	160	92	—	6,129	5,561	568	—	—	2,058	8,952
Hokkaido & Tohoku Development Corp.	75	—	75	—	174	117	57	0	—	1,481	1,846
Local Public Enterprise Finance Corp.	37	—	37	—	—	—	—	—	—	4,194	4,162
Small Business Credit Insurance Corp.	687	629	58	—	—	—	—	—	—	—	635
Medical Care Facilities Finance Corp.	115	115	—	—	1,279	1,279	—	—	—	—	1,433

AGENCIES

Total	14,974	4,032	9,167	1,775	61,196	58,351	2,408	249	188	8,539	84,903

NOTES:

Japan Development Bank: Borrowings and Loans in Foreign Currency are deducted from borrowing and loans.

Housing Loan Corporation: 'Others' of the capital account are 10·0 billion yen, subscribed by the U.S. Aid Counterpart Fund and 0·5 billion yen subscribed by the Housing Loan Insurance Fund.

Agriculture, Forestry and Fishery Finance Corporation: 'Others' of the capital account are subscriptions by Special Foundations.

Government-affiliated Financial Agencies: These include two public corporations with financial functions (Maritime Credit Corporation and Petroleum Development Corporation) and nine government-affiliated agencies (Coal Mining Damages Corporation – formerly Fund for Compensation of Mineral Damages and Rehabilitation of Mineral Damages Corporation – Coal Mining Industry Rationalisation Corporation, Employment Promotion Project Corporation, Pension Welfare Service Corporation, Agency for Redevelopment of Coal Mining Areas, Metallic Minerals Exploration Agency, Japan Emigration Service, Public Nuisance Prevention Corporation and Small Business Promotion Corporation).

SOURCE: Bank of Japan, *Economic Statistics Monthly*, etc.

functions of which are roughly the same as those of government banks and public finance corporations.

The outstanding loans of these government financial institutions amounted to about 8,500 billion yen at the end of 1970, which was equal to about 10 per cent of the total loans, advances and discounts of all financial institutions (83,400 billion yen). Of this 8,500 billion, 38 per cent was lent by the two government banks, while 54 per cent were lent by the nine public finance corporations. 70 per cent of their resources was raised by borrowing from the Trust Fund Bureau and others, while 10 per cent was raised by debenture issues and 20 per cent by contributions from the General Account, the Industrial Investment Special Account aad other government accounts (Table 22.10).

A description will now be given of the functions of the government financial institutions. The Small Business Finance Corporation, People's Finance Corporation and Small Business Credit Insurance Corporation have already been described in relation to small business finance (Chapter 16), while the Agriculture, Forestry and Fishery Finance Corporation has been explained in the chapter on the finance of agriculture, forestry and fishery (Chapter 17). These institutions will, therefore, be omitted.

(1) *Japan Development Bank*

A. General Survey

The Japan Development Bank is a public corporation under a Public Law of 1951. Its purpose is to supplement or assist private financial institutions by supplying long-term funds to promote economic reconstruction and industrial development.

The initial capital of the bank was 10 billion yen (subscribed by the U.S. Aid Counterpart Fund). Subsequently, it took over the claims of the Reconstruction Finance Bank (78·7 billion yen) and those of the U.S. Aid Counterpart Fund (134·5 billion yen); on the other hand, 2·6 billion yen were transferred to the Agriculture, Forestry and Fishery Finance Corporation and 12·0 billion yen to the Small Business Finance Corporation. With contributions from the General Account the capital reached 234·0 billion yen in October 1955 (the whole amount is now treated as subscriptions by the Industrial Investment Special Account). In addition to its capital the bank can raise funds by borrowing from the government or from overseas banks, or by issuing foreign-currency debentures. These borrowings and flotations should not exceed five times the sum of capital and reserves. At the end of the fiscal year 1970 borrowing from the government amounted to 1231·3 billion yen (1200·4 billion from the Trust Fund Bureau, 24·9 billion from the Industrial Investment Special Account), that from overseas banks to 49·4 billion yen (borrowed from the International Bank for Reconstruction and Development and lent to domestic borrowers), and the outstanding foreign-currency debentures to 28·7 billion yen.

The Development Bank is now the biggest of the government's financial institutions. Beside the head office (Tokyo) it has seven branches situated in big cities, two domestic offices and three overseas resident offices.

B. Business

The Japan Development Bank is engaged in the following business.

(A) LOANS OF DEVELOPMENT FUND. The bank lends money for the purchase, improvement or repair of facilities and equipment for economic reconstruction or for industrial development, as well as money for the reclamation of land to be used by undertakings engaged in the above activities, provided that private financial institutions have difficulty in supplying such funds. This is the most important business of the bank. The maturities of such loans are, in principle, from 1 to 10 years (up to 30 years, if necessary); the basic rate on loans is altered from time to time according to general financial conditions, especially the lending rates of ordinary banks. At the end of 1970 the rate was 8·5 per cent. In the majority of cases loans are made jointly with private banks.

(B) LOANS OF REPAYMENT FUND AND TRANSFER OF CLAIMS. The bank lends money necessary for the repayment of development loans by private financial institutions, or takes over responsibility for their credits. The terms of such loans are the same as those of development loans (in the case of transfer of claims the interest rate is determined by reference to that of

TABLE 22.11

Principal Accounts of the Japan Development Bank

(hundred million yen)

End of the Year	*1955*	*1960*	*1965*	*1966*	*1967*	*1968*	*1969*	*1970*
Capital	2,340	2,340	2,340	2,340	2,340	2,340	2,340	2,340
Borrowing from the Government	1,205	2,436	5,546	6,505	7,612	9,133	10,642	12,313
(of which from the Trust Fund Bureau)	(455)	(1,900)	(5,148)	(6,164)	(7,327)	(8,772)	(10,338)	(12,064)
(,, ,, Industrial Investment Special Account)	(716)	(516)	(388)	(335)	(279)	(361)	(304)	(249)
(,, ,, Economic Aid Funds Special Account)	(34)	(20)	(10)	(6)	(6)	(0)	(—)	(—)
Borrowing in Foreign Currency	145	911	845	766	700	631	567	494
Outstanding Foreign Currency Debentures	0	0	336	321	306	288	267	287
Loans	3,743	5,380	9,273	10,546	11,799	13,430	15,043	17,051
Loans in Foreign Currency	123	911	845	766	700	631	567	494
Securities	76	50	50	23	34	15	46	25

SOURCE: Bank of Japan, *Economic Statistics Annual.*

TABLE 22.12

Outstanding Loans of the Japan Development Bank, by Industry

(hundred million yen)

End of the Year	*1955*		*1960*		*1965*		*1966*		*1967*		*1968*		*1969*		*1970*	
		Percentages of the Total		*Percentages of the Total*		*Percentages of the Total*		*Percentages of the Total*		*Percentages of the Total*		*Percentages of the Total*		*Percentages of the Total*		*Percentages of the Total*
Electricity	1,837	49·1	2,747	51·1	3,348	36·1	3,047	28·9	3,518	29·8	3,511	26·1	3,587	23·8	3,625	21·3
Transport	1,204	32·2	1,757	32·7	3,167	34·2	3,855	36·6	4,561	38·7	5,423	40·4	6,251	41·6	7,347	43·1
(of which Shipping)	(1,187)	(31·7)	(1,703)	(31·7)	(2,865)	(30·9)	(3,432)	(32·5)	(3,966)	(33·6)	(4,640)	(34·5)	(5,279)	(35·1)	(6,065)	(35·6)
Mining	364	9·7	322	6·0	790	8·5	916	8·7	1,007	8·5	1,113	8·3	1,076	7·2	1,023	6·0
Chemical and Allied	69	1·8	230	4·3	546	5·9	623	5·9	661	5·6	785	5·8	893	5·9	1,057	6·2
Machinery	31	0·8	96	1·8	391	4·2	372	3·5	445	3·8	564	4·2	641	4·3	739	4·3
Others	238	6·4	228	4·1	1,031	11·1	1,733	16·4	1,607	13·6	2,034	15·2	2,595	17·2	3,260	19·1
Total	3,743	100·0	5,380	100·0	9,273	100·0	10,546	100·0	11,799	100·0	13,430	100·0	15,043	100·0	17,051	100·0

SOURCE: Bank of Japan.

the original loan). Both these types of loans are rarely made now.

(C) SUBSCRIPTION FOR CORPORATE DEBENTURES. The bank may subscribe for debentures issued to raise funds for development or for repayment of development loans, provided securities companies experience difficulty in subscribing for or underwriting them. The bank does not now engage in this business.

(D) GUARANTEE OF DEBTS. The bank guarantees debts resulting from the raising of development funds. At present, only foreign-currency borrowing from the Export–Import Bank of the United States and other overseas banks is guaranteed by the Japan Development Bank. The basic rate of commission for guarantees is now 0·3 per cent per annum.

C. Recent Trends

Table 22.11 shows recent movements in the principal accounts of the bank. At the end of 1969 its outstanding lending was more than 1500 billion yen, which was comparable to the amount of lending by a medium-sized city bank. In the first years of its establishment, loans to basic industries, such as electric power, shipping and mining, predominated. Though loans to such industries still figure large in the accounts, the relative importance of lending to chemical and machine industries and to regional developments is rising, while the proportion of loans to the electric power industry has experienced a relative setback (Table 22.12).

(2) *Export–Import Bank of Japan*

A. General Survey

The Export-Import Bank of Japan was established in 1950 to supplement or to encourage ordinary financial institutions through the finance of foreign trade and by overseas investments, and thus to promote economic relationships, mainly trade, with foreign countries. At first, export financing was its sole business and the title of the bank was the Export Bank of of Japan. Since the fiscal year 1952 it has engaged in import finance as well, and the name was changed to its present title – the Export–Import Bank of Japan. The scope of its business has since then gradually widened in the financing of overseas investment from August 1955; direct loans to foreign governments and others from May 1957; and refinancing from March 1954. The bank now plays an important role in the supply of long- and medium-term funds for the finance of exports, particularly of plant exports, and for overseas investment. At the same time it is the principal channel of Japanese funds for aid to underdeveloped countries.

In April 1970 its capital amounted to 445·3 billion yen (subscribed entirely by the Industrial Investment Special Account). Other sources of funds are borrowing from the government, and in foreign currency from overseas banks. It can borrow from these sources up to three times the sum of its capital and reserves. Borrowing (entirely from the Trust Fund Bureau) amounted to 1078·3 billion yen at the end of 1970, while foreign currency borrowing was nil.

B. Business

The Export–Import Bank of Japan is engaged in the following business.

(A) FINANCE OF EXPORTS AND OF TECHNOLOGICAL ASSISTANCE. The bank supplies funds to finance the export of plant and equipment manufactured in Japan (including ships and rolling-stock), and for the provision of technological assistance to foreign countries. The finance is made in the form of loans to domestic manufacturers, discount of bills for private loans to foreign governments or corporations (yen loans), and so on.

The most important business of the bank is loans to domestic manufacturers for the finance of exports on extended terms of plant and equipment, such as ships and rolling-stock. These account for over half of the bank's outstanding lending.

(B) FINANCE OF IMPORTS. The bank lends to importers for advance payment on important commodities, in the form either of loans to domestic traders or of discount of bills held by banks. The outstanding amount, however, is only 3 per cent of the bank's total lending.

(C) FINANCE OF OVERSEAS INVESTMENT. The bank lends money necessary for making overseas investment, for example for fixed investment or subscription to the capital of foreign corporations. Money may also be lent to foreign governments wishing to subscribe for shares of foreign corporations under joint Japanese and foreign management. Such loans are increasing with the growth of overseas investment by Japan, most notably in loans of funds for subscription to joint Japanese–foreign ventures.

(D) FINANCE OF OVERSEAS UNDERTAKINGS. Domestic enterprises may borrow from the bank funds for fixed investment and long-term working capital for their overseas undertakings, but few loans of this nature are in fact made.

(E) DEVELOPMENT LOANS TO FOREIGN GOVERNMENTS. Foreign governments developing important materials and products and importing most of the plant and equipment from Japan, may borrow from the bank to finance the imports.

(F) REFINANCE. When a foreign country experiences a deterioration in its balance of payments and is therefore unable to pay for plant and equipment imported from Japan, the bank will provide finance for making settlements with the government, government-affiliated institutions or banks of the country.

(G) GUARANTEE OF DEBTS. Instead of making loans the bank may guarantee debts of those domestic enterprises or banks which are entitled to obtain accommodation in the categories mentioned above.

Loans to domestic enterprises to finance exports or imports are, in principle, made jointly with commercial banks, because the bank's purpose is to supplement the activities of private financial institutions. The bank's 'condition of operation' stipulates that it should not contribute more than 70 per cent of the amount of joint loans. At the end of 1968 the lending rates to domestic firms were as follows: 4–7 per cent for finance of exports, 4·5–7·5 per cent for finance of imports and more than 4·5 per cent for finance of overseas investments and undertakings. Interest rates are determined separately for each loan to foreign governments. The maturity of loans for export or import finance is, in principle, less than 8 years (up to 15 years in exceptional cases), while for loans for overseas investments and undertakings it is less than 10 years (20 years in exceptional cases). The maturity of loans to foreign governments is fixed afresh for each loan, and is usually 15–18 years.

The commission rate for guarantee of debts is more than 0·5 per cent (more than 0·3 per cent for debt guarantee of yen loans).

C. Recent Trends

TABLE 22.13

Principal Accounts of the Export–Import Bank of Japan

(hundred million yen)

End of the Year	*1955*	*1960*	*1965*	*1966*	*1967*	*1968*	*1969*	*1970*
Capital	350	583	1,758	2,128	2,558	3,088	3,723	4,453
Borrowing	120	747	3,347	4,404	5,890	7,238	8,759	10,783
Loans, Advances and Discounts	392	1,254	5,145	6,593	8,506	10,363	12,470	15,220
Securities	38	40	48	27	24	31	50	46
Guarantee of Debts	0	68	119	174	283	385	419	420

SOURCE: Bank of Japan, *Economic Statistics Annual.*

Table 22.13 shows recent movements in the principal accounts of the Export–Import Bank of Japan. Its most important lending activity is the finance of plant exports on extended terms, which accounted for about 80 per cent of its outstanding lending at the end of 1969. The finance of exports of ships on such terms represents the bulk of this, or 49 per cent of the bank's total lendings.

In recent years, with the rapid economic growth of underdeveloped countries, plant exports to them have substantially increased, with a corresponding expansion in direct loans, such as yen or refinance loans (Table 22.14). By area, loans to Asian countries accounted for 42 per cent of total loans granted during the fiscal year 1969, while 20 per cent was made to European countries and 27 per cent to African countries.

(3) *Housing Loan Corporation*

This finance corporation was formed in 1950 in order to finance residential building provided that private financial institutions experience difficulty in supplying funds.

At the end of 1970 the capital of the corporation was 97·2 billion yen (of which 32·2 billion were subscribed by the General Account, 54·5 billion by the Industrial Investment

TABLE 22.14

Outstanding Amounts of Loans, Advances and Discounts of the Export–Import Bank of Japan, by uses of the Loan Proceeds

(hundred million yen)

End of the Year	*1955*		*1960*		*1965*		*1966*		*1967*		*1968*		*1969*		*1970*	
		Percent-ages of the Total %		*Percent-ages of the Total* %		*Percent-ages of the Total* %		*Percent-ages of the Total* %		*Percent-ages of the Total* %		*Percent-ages of the Total* %		*Percent-ages of the Total* %		*Percent-ages of the Total* %
Finance of Exports	384	98·0	1,003	80·0	3,727	72·4	4,692	71·2	5,867	69·0	7,221	69·7	8,910	71·4	10,835	71·2
(of which Ships)	(250)	(63·8)	(543)	(43·3)	(2,244)	(43·6)	(2,966)	(45·0)	(3,970)	(46·7)	(4,751)	(45·8)	(5,794)	(46·5)	(6,872)	(45·2)
(,, ,, Rolling-stock)	(47)	(12·0)	(67)	(5·3)	(199)	(3·9)	(142)	(2·2)	(172)	(2·0)	(227)	(2·2)	(249)	(2·0)	(231)	(1·5)
(,, ,, Textile Machinery)	(64)	(16·3)	(74)	(5·9)	(261)	(5·1)	(342)	(5·2)	(341)	(4·0)	(365)	(3·5)	(423)	(3·4)	(560)	(3·7)
Finance of Imports	0	0	20	1·6	41	0·8	54	0·8	75	0·9	81	0·8	157	1·3	381	2·5
Finance of Overseas Investment	8	2·0	231	18·4	485	9·4	538	8·2	621	7·3	680	6·5	737	5·9	1,045	6·9
Direct Loans	0	0	0	0	892	17·4	1,309	19·8	1,943	22·8	2,381	23·0	2,666	21·4	2,959	19·4
Total	392	100·0	1,254	100·0	5,145	100·0	6,593	100·0	8,506	100·0	10,363	100·0	12,470	100·0	15,220	100·0

NOTES:

1. Lending to finance exports does not include yen loans, but includes loans for technical assistance or for development works.
2. Finance of overseas investments includes loans to overseas undertakings.
3. Direct loans include yen loans and refinance loans.

SOURCE: Ministry of Finance, *Monthly Statistics of Public Finance and Banking.*

Special Account, 10·0 billion by the U.S. Aid Counterpart Fund and 0·5 billion by the Housing Loan Insurance Fund). Its other sources of funds include borrowing from the government (955·0 billion yen, of which 860·7 billion were borrowed from the Trust Fund Bureau and 94·6 from the Post Office Life Insurance and Postal Annuity) and issues of Housing Loan Corporation Housing Land Debentures, which have been authorised by the competent minister since the fiscal year 1963 (the outstanding amount at the end of 1970 was 3·4 billion yen; interest rates are 4·5 per cent and 5·0 per cent for debentures of three and five years' maturity respectively).

The corporation's activities include: (1) loans for house-building (building of the borrower's own house, improvement of houses in agricultural, mountainous or fishing villages, building of houses to let, reconstruction of houses damaged or destroyed by natural disasters or construction of multi-story fireproof buildings); (2) loans to develop housing sites; (3) loans for construction of related facilities; and (4) loan insurance to facilitate housing loans of private financial institutions. At the end of 1970 outstanding loans amounted to 1069·7 billion yen, of which about 70 per cent, or 755·1 billion yen, consisted of loans to ordinary individuals for constructing their own houses. The terms of loans differ according to the type of loan: interest rates range from 5·5 to 7·5 per cent, while maturities are from 5 to 50 years; the proportion of loans to the total amount required for building varies from 55 to 90 per cent (mostly in the range of 75–80 per cent). The outstanding amount of loan insurance was 42·9 billion yen at the end of the fiscal year 1970. Insurance premiums are gradually being reduced and from April 1970 the rate of premiums is 0·45 per cent per annum.

As many as 2,430,000 houses were built with funds lent by the corporation from its start to the fiscal year 1970. During the fiscal year 1969 it was planned to build 590,000 houses with government funds. The corporation was to supply funds to construct 246,000 houses (in addition, 78,000 were to be built for the Japan Housing Corporation). Thus, the corporation plays an important part under the government's aegis in house-building plans.

The corporation has its head office in Tokyo and 12 branches and one office in various places of the country. With the approval of the competent minister, part of its business is entrusted to private financial institutions (643 institutions) and to local authorities (prefectures and six big cities).

(4) *Hokkaido and Tohoku Development Corporation*

The corporation was established in 1956 as the Hokkaido Development Corporation under the Hokkaido Development Corporation Law. Its initial aim was to supplement and to encourage private financial institutions and private investment by providing long-term funds for the industrial development of Hokkaido, and thus to contribute to the overall development of the national economy. Subsequently, its field of operation was extended to the Tohoku district, and it was renamed the Hokkaido and Tohoku Development Corporation in 1957.

The resources of the corporation consist of its capital (7·5 billion yen at the end of the fiscal year 1969, subscribed by the Industrial Investment Special Account); borrowing from the government (17·4 billion yen at the end of the fiscal year 1970, of which 11·7 billion yen was borrowed from the Trust Fund Bureau, 5·7 billion yen from the Post Office Life Insurance and Postal Annuity and 60 million yen from the Industrial Investment Special Account); and the issue of Hokkaido and Tohoku Development Debentures (48·1 billion yen at the end of the fiscal year 1970), the outstanding amount of which should not exceed 20 times the capital.

The corporation makes loans to, invests in or guarantees debts of enterprises engaged in development undertakings[1] in Hokkaido and Tohoku (Aomori, Iwate, Miyagi, Akita, Yamagata, Fukushima and Niigata).

Loans are made to companies with capital of more than 10 million yen, which are engaged in development under-

[1] 1. Industries which make use of large amounts of coal, combustible natural gas or other undeveloped mineral resources.

2. Industries which mainly process products of agriculture, forestry, animal husbandry or fishery.

3. Mining and smelting.

4. Transport and communication which contribute to the promotion and development of industry.

5. Reclamation of land to be used by enterprises which contribute to industrial development and promotion.

6. Other undertakings designated by the competent minister.

takings in Hokkaido or Tohoku districts. They are, in principle, made jointly with ordinary financial institutions. The corporation cannot contribute more than 70 per cent of the money needed for fixed investment and not more than 50 per cent of money for working capital (which is needed in relation to the corporation's loans for fixed investment or to its subscriptions to capital). In principle, loans should be for sums exceeding 10 million yen. The basic loan rate is 8·3 per cent, but a special rate of 7·7 per cent is charged on loans to projects which contribute particularly to industrial development. The maturities are 1–10 years for loans for fixed investment, while for loans for working capital they are 1–5 years. The corporation can subscribe for shares of companies with a capital of more than 100 million yen (the amount may include subscriptions by the corporation). The funds raised by capital issues should be used for the acquisition of equipment or for the reclamation of land, and the corporation should not subscribe for more than 50 per cent of an issue. Debt guarantees may be given for companies with a capital of more than 10 million yen, and the maximum limit is 80 per cent of the outstanding obligations. The commission rate for guarantees is less than 2 per cent. Up to now, however, no guarantee of debt has been made. The sum of subscriptions for capital and debt guarantees should not exceed the company's capital.

At the end of the fiscal year 1971 outstanding loans and investments were 186·4 billion yen (184·6 billion for loans and 1·8 billion for investments), of which 91·6 billion were for Hokkaido and 94·8 billion for Tohoku. By industry, loans to paper and pulp industry, to chemical industry and to mining and refining stand out.

(5) *Local Public Enterprise Finance Corporation*

The corporation was set up in 1957 to assist the sound development of local public enterprises by subscribing to bonds of local authorities responsible for such enterprises, and which need stable and low-cost funds for them.

The capital of the corporation was 3·7 billion yen (subscribed by the Industrial Investment Special Account) at the end of the fiscal year 1970, but its biggest source of funds is the issue of

Local Public Enterprise Debentures. They are either offered to the public through the securities market (in which case they are government-guaranteed) or purchased directly by public bodies, such as local public servants' mutual benefit associations (in which case they are not guaranteed by the government). The latter variety of debentures has been issued since the 1962 fiscal year. At the end of the fiscal year 1970, outstanding debentures amounted to 419·4 billion yen, of which 239·9 billion had been floated in the market. In addition, subject to the approval of the competent minister, the corporation may borrow from financial institutions to bridge the period to the actual issue of debentures (such borrowing is short-term).

Local public enterprises are defined as local-authority undertakings, the expenses of which are covered largely by income from their operations. Thus, loans are made to waterworks, waterworks for industry, transport, electricity, gas, maintenance of harbours, hospitals, market-places, slaughterhouses, sightseeing facilities, toll road, car parks, land reclamation for regional development, sewage disposal and so on. The maturity of loans should be 5–23 years. The basic loan rate is 7·6 per cent, but it is variable in the light of financial conditions. There is a minimum rate, however, given by the issuers' cost on Local Public Enterprise Debentures (at present most long-term loans carry interest at 6·7 per cent).

At the end of the fiscal year 1970 outstanding loans came to 416·2 billion yen (all of which consisted of long-term loans). Besides these, there were 22·7 billion yen of agency loans for for the account of the Agriculture, Forestry and Fishery Finance Corporation outstanding.

(6) *Medical Care Facilities Finance Corporation*

The corporation was established in 1960 to assist the spread and advancement of medical care by making low-interest long-term loans to establish or improve private hospitals and clinics if they experience difficulty in obtaining accommodation from private financial institutions.

Its sources of funds are its capital (11·5 billion yen at the end of the fiscal year 1970, which was subscribed by the General Account) and borrowing from the government (127·9 billion yen at the end of the fiscal year 1970, borrowed entirely from the Trust Fund Bureau).

The corporation lends funds to establish, to improve or to run hospitals, clinics, pharmacies or maternity hospitals managed by individuals, medical corporations, public-service corporations, social welfare corporations, educational corporations and so on. Maturities are from 1 to 25 years for loans for new construction, while the basic loan rate is 6·5 per cent. For loans to extend or to rebuild facilities maturities are less than 20 years and the loan rate is between 6·5 and 7·0 per cent. For loans to purchase machinery maturities should not exceed five years, and the loan rate is 8·2 per cent. For long-term working capital, loans should be for less than three years, while the interest rate is 8·2 per cent.

At the end of the fiscal year 1970 outstanding loans amounted to 143·3 billion yen, of which 124·6 billion were lent through the agency of other financial institutions (230 institutions).

(7) *Personal Services Finance Corporation*

The corporation was founded in 1967 to facilitate the improvement and promotion of public sanitation. It makes loans to raise the level of hygiene or to modernise undertakings concerned with the public health or with the daily life of the population, provided ordinary financial institutions have difficulty in lending such money.

The sources of funds of the corporation are its capital (1·0 billion yen at the end of 1970, subscribed entirely by the General Account) and borrowing from the government (108·0 billion yen at the end of 1970, from the Trust Fund Bureau).

Its sphere is the provision of funds for fixed investment in plant and equipment, and for working capital (as well as money for joint purchases by associations) to undertakings concerned with public sanitation (companies with less than 50 employees) or to associations of such undertakings.

Terms for loans are as follows: the maximum amount does not usually exceed 10 million yen in the case of loans to private or joint-stock enterprises, while the maximum amount of loans to their association are, in principle, less than 30 million yen: the basic interest rate is 8·2 per cent, but a lower rate of 6·5–7·7 per cent is applied to special loans for specific types of fixed investment in plant and equipment; maturities are less than 10 years for fixed investment (less than 7 years in most instances) and less than five years for working capital. For the time being, the loans are made through the agency of the People's Finance Corporation, the Small Business Finance Corporation and the Central Bank for Commercial and Industrial Co-operatives.

At the end of 1970 the outstanding amount of the loans was 122·9 billion yen.

(8) *Overseas Economic Co-operation Fund*

A. General Survey

The fund is a special corporation established in March 1961 for the purpose of promoting economic collaboration with foreign countries in developing regions of South-East Asia and other areas; it facilitates the supply of funds for their economic stabilisation and industrial development, if such funds are difficult to obtain from the Export–Import Bank of Japan or from ordinary financial institutions.

Originally aid for the development of South-East Asian countries was given indirectly by the finance of exports on extended terms by the Export–Import Bank. Later, however, it became necessary for Japan to take a more active part in economic co-operation, so that the fund was set up as an entity distinct from the Export–Import Bank.

Its initial capital was 5·4 billion yen, which it took over from the South-East Asian Development Fund of the Export–Import Bank of Japan (the 5·4 billion yen consisted of subscriptions by the General Account and of reserves accumulated from income). The General Account has subsequently added to its subscriptions and at the end of 1970 the fund's capital amounted to 79·3 billion yen. In addition, the fund can borrow money or issue Overseas Economic Co-operation Debentures up to the sum of its capital and reserves. At the end of 1970 its borrowing amounted to 57·0 billion yen (from the Trust Fund Bureau), but no debentures were outstanding.

B. Business

The business of the fund is described below.

(A) FINANCE OF PROJECTS FOR DEVELOPMENT. The fund makes loans to undertakings concerned with the industrial growth of developing countries, and which are considered to be particularly important for promoting economic relations with Japan.

(B) SUBSCRIPTIONS. The fund may supply money for the above-mentioned purposes by subscribing for the capital of undertakings if there are special circumstances hindering the availability of loans for the uninterrupted completion of development works.

(C) LOANS OF FUNDS FOR EXPLORATION. The fund lends money for preparatory explorations for development works, or for experimental works in connection with them.

(D) LOANS OF FUNDS FOR ECONOMIC STABILISATION. The fund lends to foreign governments for the import of Japanese goods which are urgently required to stabilise the economies of developing countries.

Thus, the fund's loans and investments are made for industrial development or economic stabilisation in developing countries. These loans and investments are, however, at times indistinguishable in nature from those of the Export–Import Bank, which provides funds to promote foreign trade, although the fund makes loans and investments on uneconomic terms.

The terms of loans are determined by their likely contribution to industrial development, the prospect of completing the works, their profitability, the use of the loan proceeds and other factors. In the past interest rates have usually

TABLE 22.15

Principal Accounts of the Overseas Economic Co-operation Fund

(hundred million yen)

End of the Year	*1961*	*1965*	*1966*	*1967*	*1968*	*1969*	*1970*
Capital	104	169	254	309	389	539	793
Borrowing	0	0	0	10	185	406	570
Loans	3	121	194	310	578	931	1,344
Capital Subscriptions	4	15	15	42	47	50	51
Securities	80	65	85	17	10	30	39

SOURCE: Bank of Japan.

been in the range of 3·0–6·5 per cent, while loan maturities have been mostly from three to 20 years.

C. Recent Trends

Table 22.15 shows recent movements in the principal accounts of the fund. By area, most of its loans and investments have been made to Asia; the next important region is Latin America. The break-down by industry of loans to and investments in Japanese enterprises shows that about half have been made to manufacturing industries, particularly to the foodstuffs industry, followed by those to the public utilities industry (maintenance of canals, water-supply, micro-wave facilities, hydro-electricity, agricultural irrigation and so on), agriculture, forestry and fishery, and mining. In addition direct loans have been made to the Republic of Korea, Republic of China (Taiwan), Malaysia and so on.

(9) *Government-affiliated Financial Agencies*

The principal agencies are as follows:

A. Pension Welfare Service Corporation

Reserves of welfare insurance, seamen's insurance and national pensions are deposited with the Trust Fund Bureau, which employs them in Treasury loans and investments. These schemes differ from systems for voluntary savings, such as postal savings, in that they are compulsory and that their reserves are accumulated from insurance premiums. About a quarter of the annual increments in the reserves is, therefore, restored to the insured in the form of loans for building houses, hospitals and other facilities for public welfare and health.

The Pension Welfare Service Corporation is a governmental corporation (under the authority of the Minister of Health and Welfare), which was established in 1961 under the Pension Welfare Service Corporation Law for the purposes of managing such loans. The corporation has no capital and its chief source of funds is borrowings from the Trust Fund Bureau. Although it is legally entitled to issue Pension Welfare Service Corporation Debentures, none has yet been issued. The outstanding amount of the borrowing was 292·9 billion yen at the end of 1970.

Loan rates range from 5·5 to 7·0 per cent, while the loan periods are from 15 to 25 years (repayments are deferred for six months to two years). Outstanding loans were 297·3 billion yen at the end of 1970, and the corporation was the biggest lender among government-affiliated agencies.

B. Employment Promotion Projects Corporation

This is a governmental corporation (under the authority of the Minister of Labour) which was founded in 1961 under the Employment Promotion Projects Corporation Law. It took over the assets and business of the Labour Welfare Corporation and of the Displaced Coal Miners' Relief Association. Its purpose is to contribute to the welfare of workers and to the development of the economy by helping them to find suitable jobs: it assists workers to acquire or to improve their skills, promotes inter-regional movement of labour and undertakes other activities to help them to find employment. Its business includes loans to promote employment, the source of funds for which is borrowing from the Trust Fund Bureau under the Treasury loans and investments programme; such loans include those for the construction of housing quarters for workers, for the establishment of welfare facilities, and for establishing facilities for technical training by private enterprises. Interest rates on such loans are 6·5–7·0 per cent, while maturities are from five to 30 years.

Its capital was 115·7 billion yen at the end of 1970 (of which 114·7 billion was contributed by the Unemployment Insurance Special Account), while its borrowing totalled 56·5 billion and loans 56·2 billion yen. The law authorises the corporation to issue Employment Promotion Projects Debentures, but none has so far been issued.

C. Coal Mining Industry Rationalisation Corporation

This is a governmental corporation (under the authority of the Minister of International Trade and Industry) which was established in 1960 under the Temporary Measures for Rationalisation of Coal Mining Law. Its business is to make loans for fixed investment in plant and equipment for the modernisation and reorganisation of coal pits. The loan rates are usually under 6·5 per cent for periods of less than eight years (repayments are deferred for less than three years).

At the end of 1970 the capital of the corporation was 60·5 billion yen (of which 30·3 billion was subscribed by the General Account and 30·2 billion by the Special Account for Measures for Coal Mining), while its borrowing (from the Trust Fund Bureau) totalled 40·0 billion and its loans 80·7 billion. The law authorises the corporation to issue Coal Mining Rationalisation Debentures, but they have not so far been issued.

D. Metallic Minerals Exploration Agency

The agency is a governmental corporation (under the authority of the Minister of International Trade and Industry), which was founded in 1963 under the Metallic Minerals Exploration Agency Law.[1] Its purpose is to contribute to a stable and cheap supply of metallic minerals by lending money for prospecting and by assisting, e.g., geological surveys for the development of metallic mineral resources. The loan rate is 7·5 per cent, while the period of the loan is usually less than six years (repayments are deferred for less than a year).

The capital amounted to 2·1 billion yen (subscribed by the Industrial Investment Special Account) at the end of 1970, while its borrowing (from the Trust Fund Bureau) was 9·1 billion and its loans 10·7 billion. It is authorised to issue Metallic Minerals Exploration Debentures, but they have not yet been issued.

E. The Agency for Redevelopment of Coal Mining Areas

This is a governmental corporation (under the authority of the Minister of International Trade and Industry), which was set up in 1962 under the Agency for Redevelopment of Coal Mining Areas Law. The agency is concerned with the development of industry and mining in coal-mining districts which have been particularly hard hit by the depression in the coal industry. Its business included loans to mine-owners and industrialists, who are expected to contribute to the development of such areas. Loans may be made to finance fixed investment in plant and equipment or for working capital, and the agency may itself invest in such undertakings. The terms of loans are as follows:

[1] At first, the title was the Financing Agency for Metallic Minerals Prospecting, but the name was changed to the present one in 1964.

the loan rate is 6·5 per cent, while maturities are less than ten years for loans for fixed investments (repayments are deferred for less than three years), and less than five years for loans for working capital (repayments are deferred for less than a year).

At the end of 1970 the capital was 21·1 billion yen (of which 8·4 billion was contributed by the General Account and 12·8 billion by the Special Account for Measures for Coal Mining), while its borrowing (from the Trust Fund Bureau) amounted to 25·0 billion and loans to 39·2 billion. The law authorises the agency to issue Redevelopment of Coal Mining Areas Debentures, but none has yet been issued.

F. Coal Mining Damages Corporation

This is a governmental corporation (under the authority of the Minister of International Trade and Industry), established under the Temporary Measures for Compensation of Coal Mining Damage Law, and was organised in 1968 as successor to the Mining Damages Fund (established in 1963). At the same time the Rehabilitation of Mineral Damages Corporation was abolished and its business was taken over by the new corporation.

The interest rates on loans for compensation is 3·5 per cent, and that on loans for prevention of damages is 6·5 per cent; the periods of the loans are less than eight years (repayments are deferred for less than three years). At the end of 1970 the capital was 4·7 billion yen (of which 1·0 billion was subscribed by the General Account and 3·7 billion by the Special Account for Measures for Coal Mining), while its borrowing (from the Trust Fund Bureau) totalled 5·7 billion and loans 12·2 billion. Coal Mining Damages Debentures have not so far been issued.

G. Environmental Pollution Prevention Corporation

This is a government agency (under the joint authority of the Minister of Health and Welfare and of the Minister of International Trade and Industry) which was founded in 1965 under the Public Nuisance Prevention Corporation Law. Its purpose is to encourage the sound development of industries and the improvement of environmental conditions by making loans for facilities to prevent public nuisances, such as air or water pollution, which are caused by concentrations of factories. Loans are also made to rehabilitate sites, to construct buildings for joint operations of factories, or to establish facilities for the prevention of public nuisances.

Loan rates range from 6·0 to 7·0 per cent, while maturities are from 10 to 20 years (repayments are deferred for 1–3 years). At the end of 1970 the capital was 300 million yen, while borrowing (from the Trust Fund Bureau) amounted to 30·1 billion and loans to 10·9 billion. Public Nuisance Prevention Debentures have so far not been issued.

H. Small Business Promotion Corporation

This is a governmental corporation (under the authority of the Minister of International Trade and Industry) which was established in 1967 under the Small Business Promotion Corporation Law. With the establishment of the corporation the Small Business Development Financing Special Account and the Small Business Guidance Centre were abolished and their business taken over by the corporation. It seeks to contribute to the expansion of small enterprises by organising comprehensive schemes for their development, such as advice on their business, and the provision of loans. It also undertakes projects such as instruction in managerial rationalisation or in the improvement of techniques.

Loans are, in principle, made jointly with prefectural authorities. Interest rates on most loans are 2·6 per cent, for periods from 12 to 15 years (repayments are deferred for less than 2 to 3 years). At the end of 1970 the corporation's capital was 86·9 billion yen (subscribed by the General Account) and its borrowing (from prefectural authorities and from ordinary financial institutions) amounted to 16·7 billion yen, while the outstanding amount of Small Business Promotion Debentures was 25·9 billion yen. Loans totalled 111·0 billion yen.

I. Japan Emigration Service

The Japan Emigration Service is a governmental corporation (under the authority of the Minister of Foreign Affairs) established in 1963 under the Japan Emigration Service Law. At the same time the Japan Emigration Promotion Company was abolished, its business being taken over by the new corporation. Its purpose is to ensure the efficient operation of arrangements for overseas emigration, such as the provision of assistance and advice to emigrants, both before they depart and subsequently.

Terms of loans are as follows: the interest rate is about 5 per cent and the period of loans for fixed investment is less than eight years (repayments are deferred for less than four years), while for loans for working capital it is less than one and a half years. At the end of 1970 the capital amounted to 5·9 billion yen (of which 0·5 billion was subscribed by the General Account and 5·4 billion by the Industrial Investment Special Account); its borrowings (from the Trust Fund Bureau) were nil, and its loans amounted to 28·7 billion. It is authorised by the law to issue Japan Emigration Service Debentures, but none has been issued.

FIG. 22. *Mechanism of Treasury loans and investments*

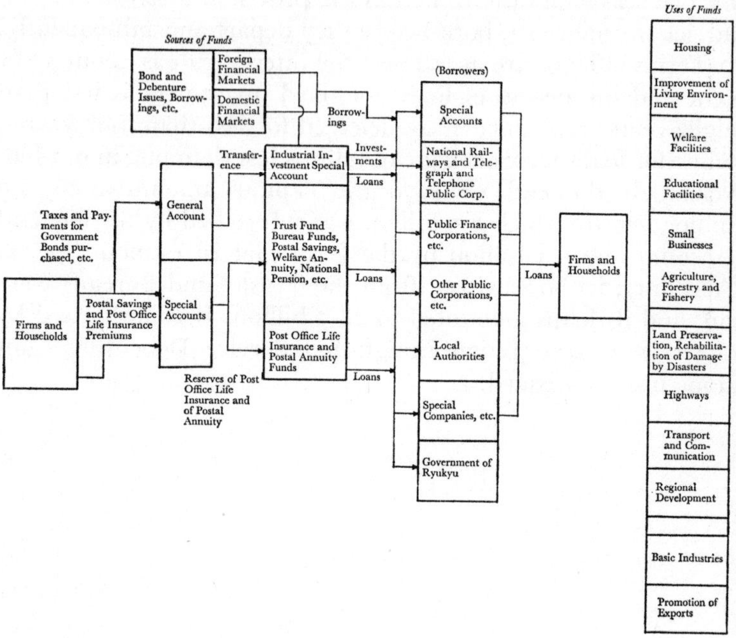

PART FOUR

Money and Capital Markets

CHAPTER 23

THE CALL LOAN MARKET

I. CHARACTERISTICS

Dealings in short-term funds in Japan were started in the first decade of the present century on the model of the British and American money markets. In Japan, however, a bill market similar to that of the London discount market has not evolved, but the call loan market has developed none the less to become the main component of the money market. The call loan market is a market in which financial institutions lend or borrow very short-term funds; to the lender it is an outlet for temporarily idle money, while to the borrower it is a source of funds to meet temporary shortages. The market is useful in ensuring the smooth functioning of the financial market in the wider sense, because it enables financial institutions to exchange temporarily idle funds among themselves, and thus contributes to the more efficient use of money. For this reason the call market is the most sensitive indicator of ease or tightness in the financial market in general, so that movements in it are an important index of financial conditions.

There are call loan markets in three places: Tokyo, Osaka and Nagoya. Table 23.1 shows the volume of funds outstanding in these markets, which has gradually increased and is now quite substantial. Nevertheless, numerous anomalies persist in the market. Call loan funds are by their nature temporary surpluses of financial institutions; they should therefore be short-term, at low interest and secure, but in practice the bulk of the funds in the market do not reflect these principles.

First, borrowers, particularly city banks with chronically over-lent positions, have a strong demand for long-term, stable money. In post-war years, therefore, the bulk of market transactions have been for unconditional or over-the-month money,

TABLE 23.1

Outstanding Amounts of Call Loans in the Market

(hundred million yen)

End of the Year	*Tokyo*	*Osaka and Nagoya*	*Total*
1953	222	60	282
1958	1,222	291	1,513
1963	5,063	1,716	6,779
1964	8,053	2,736	10,789
1965	5,975	2,115	8,091
1966	5,769	1,706	7,474
1967	7,504	2,614	10,118
1968	7,447	2,405	9,852
1969	11,263	4,200	15,464
1970	13,870	4,299	18,169

SOURCE: Bank of Japan, *Economic Statistics Annual.*

whereas in pre-war years overnight money used to represent the greater part of the market's funds. Nowadays, financial institutions sometimes directly negotiate loans of call money among themselves (this is usually referred to as 'bilateral call money'). Moreover, what are described as 'loans to financial institutions'[1] are in fact akin to call loans. Bilateral money and loans to financial institutions are now considerable in amount: they are often negotiated between financial institutions having special ties with each other, such as parents and subordinates. This, too, reflects the demand for long-term and stable money.

Second, interest rates on call loans have often exceeded the Bank rate or even the long-term interest rate, particularly during the high growth period of 1955–64. Such extraordinarily high levels of call loan rates are due primarily to the strong demand for money from city banks, which have been over-lent. Thus, there has consistently been a lenders' market. Particularly during credit squeeze call loan rates rose to remarkable heights. While it is undeniable that the jerking-up in this way of call loan rates has greatly influenced the costs of funds to financial institutions and their lending attitudes, and has strengthened the efficacy of the monetary policy, it has also given rise to a number of evils: for instance, lender financial

[1] Since 1959 the Ministry of Finance has advised banks and others to make separate accounts of call money with maturities of over one month or without reliable security under the head of 'loans to (borrowings from) financial institutions'.

institutions have come to regard the call loan market as a safe and profitable outlet for their funds, and they have become rather chary of holding government short-term bills, bonds or debentures.

These anomalies were largely corrected during the monetary ease of 1965 and 1966. Even so, a number of problems remain. Several attempts have been made to restrict the market to dealings in purely short-term money and to bring rates down to more 'normal' levels; but, as the irregularity is deeply rooted in the structural peculiarities of the financial market in Japan, it is difficult to eliminate such phenomena completely.

2. MARKET TRANSACTIONS

(1) *Participants in the Market*

The call loan market is composed of financial institutions, who figure either as lenders or borrowers, and of call loan dealers who are specialised intermediaries.

As has been stated (Part Three, Chapter 19), call loan dealers play vital roles in the market. They borrow temporarily idle money of financial institutions which they lend to institutions temporarily short of funds. Although they make such transactions on their own accounts their functions are more or less similar to those of brokers, who simply connect lenders with borrowers.

Some financial institutions tend habitually to be lenders, while others tend persistently to be borrowers of call loans (see Table 23.2). The principal lenders in the market are country banks, trust banks, the National Federation of Credit Associations, credit associations, Central Co-operative Bank of Agriculture and Forestry, credit federations of agricultural co-operatives and insurance companies. The most important borrowers are city banks, which are in a chronically over-loaned state. They absorb the overwhelming bulk of the market's resources and in recent years they have been tapping more than 80 per cent of its resources. Securities companies also borrowed heavily in the market between 1955 and 1964 when the securities market was booming, and at one time their borrowing represented more than 30 per cent of the total amount of call loans outstanding. In recent years, however, they have borrowed much less in the market, because of the slump in the securities market from 1963 to 1965, and also because the authorities have been persuading the securities companies to strengthen themselves by adopting sounder business policies.

TABLE 23.2

Percentage Shares of Various Financial Institutions in the Supply of and Demand for Call Loans (Average Amount Outstanding during December of each year)

Years	*1956*	*1958*	*1960*	*1962*	*1964*	*1966*	*1968*	*1970*
BORROWERS								
City Banks	63·2	64·3	55·2	55·8	80·5	82·0	81·2	88·2
Country Banks	5·5	4·1	2·3	2·1	2·4	4·9	1·7	0·7
Trust Banks	10·0	3·2	4·7	4·3	2·7	2·6	2·3	1·3
Long-Term Credit Banks		7·0	1·6	4·8	1·7	0·1	—	0·9
Securities Companies	21·3	9·0	25·0	21·6	9·5	4·0	1·5	0·6
Others		12·4	11·2	11·4	3·2	6·4	13·3	8·3
Total	100·0	100·0	100·0	100·0	100·0	100·0	100·0	100·0
LENDERS								
City Banks	17·2	14·9	2·9	0·5	0·1	0·2	0·1	—
Country Banks	26·5	26·5	23·3	22·1	11·5	13·1	17·7	17·8
Trust Banks	13·3	17·3	29·5	30·2	18·7	28·1	17·1	21·4
Long-Term Credit Banks	4·6	2·4	2·0	2·1	1·9	7·1	2·7	0·5
Mutual Loans and Savings Banks	1·4	2·2	2·4	3·3	3·2	2·8	3·3	4·7
National Federation of Credit Associations,	7·5	9·5	15·4	20·1	18·1	12·0	15·2	18·1
Central Co-operative Bank of Agriculture and Forestry, Credit Associations of Agricultural Co-operatives	6·4	12·0	9·2	11·4	31·4	18·4	26·3	22·6
Securities Companies	4·2	3·6	5·0	1·1	3·4	2·6	5·4	4·8
Insurance Companies	14·7	8·0	5·2	3·5	5·1	10·9	6·6	7·4
Others	4·2	3·6	5·1	5·7	6·6	4·8	5·6	2·7
Total	100·0	100·0	100·0	100·0	100·0	100·0	100·0	100·0

SOURCE: Bank of Japan, *Economic Statistics Annual.*

(2) *Types of Call Loans*

Call loans are the temporarily surplus funds of financial institutions which are borrowed by other financial institutions temporarily short of money. They must therefore be repayable at short notice, and should in principle be of short maturity; but they vary from those with extremely short maturities to those with relatively long maturities. For this reason they are classified into the following categories according to maturity:

Half-day money. This is subdivided into morning money and afternoon money: morning money must be repaid the day the money is borrowed by the time of the bill-clearing (one o'clock in the afternoon on weekdays and half-past eleven on Saturdays in Tokyo), while afternoon money is lent and repaid some time between the bill-clearing and the end of business. As these loans are settled within the same day, they do not appear in the statistics of the outstanding amount of call loans.

Overnight money. The loan is made for one day only, and must be repaid by the time of bill-clearing next day. Sometimes, a condition is attached to the loan that it must be repaid in the morning. In this case the money is referred to as 'overnight money repayable in the morning'.

Unconditional money. The repayment is deferred for two days (i.e. the day of the contract and the next day), but thereafter the money is repayable at one day's notice from either the borrower or the lender. In recent years the habit has grown of notifying 'undecided' to the borrower (or the borrower may notify 'undecided' to the lender), in which case the lender may demand the repayment on the day following the notification, if necessary.

Over-the-month money. A certain day of the next month is designated as the settling day.

The breakdown by maturity of outstanding call loans (Table 23.3) shows that their average terms are lengthening because of the circumstances mentioned above; demand is strong for long-term money, such as the over-the-month money.

(3) *Collateral Security*

As call loans form a part of the liquid assets of lenders they must be secured by reliable and easily realisable collateral,

TABLE 23.3

Percentage Composition of Call Loans by Maturity (Average Outstanding Amount for Lenders during December of each year)

Years	*1956*	*1958*	*1960*	*1962*	*1964*	*1966*	*1967*	*1968*	*1969*	*1970*
Overnight Money	13·0	5·0	6·6	2·4	0·5	0·3	0·3	0·2	—	—
Unconditional Money	62·2	66·5	69·6	58·3	37·9	33·6	28·8	26·4	21·4	14·7
Money due within the Month	10·6	10·8	14·4	15·3	30·1	36·8	36·2	32·8	38·5	39·1
Over-the-month Money	14·2	17·7	9·4	24·0	31·5	29·3	34·7	40·6	40·1	46·2
Total	100·0	100·0	100·0	100·0	100·0	100·0	100·0	100·0	100·0	100·0

NOTE: Money due within the month is over-the-month money, the maturity of which occurs during the month.

SOURCE: Bank of Japan, *Economic Statistics Annual.*

because, should the borrowers default, the collateral must be encashed at once in order to restore liquidity. Thus, in pre-war years it was a rule that call loans were secured by government bonds. In post-war years, however, there were virtually no issues of long-term government bonds until recently, so that the volume of call loans secured by government bonds has markedly declined. Instead, government-guaranteed debentures, prime local bonds, bank debentures, prime industrial debentures, bills eligible for rediscount at the Bank or for serving as collateral security for advances from the Bank as well as ordinary bills, are used for this purpose. In particular bank debentures and ordinary bills figure prominently as security. Call loan transactions collateral receipts may be used as security for borrowing by the securities finance companies.[1]

(4) *Call Loan Rates*

The interest rates for lenders of call loans are those usually referred to as 'call loan rates': the rates for the borrowers are

[1] For details, see Part Three, Chapter 21, 'Securities Finance Companies'.

higher, for the call loan dealers charge brokerage (0·1825–0·365 per cent).

It goes without saying that rates differ according to the maturities. Given the nature of the loans, rates should be low and should fluctuate in reflection of demand and supply relationships in the market. As has been mentioned, however, they are prone to jump to extraordinary heights. For some time after the war, therefore, the maximum rate on overnight money was subject to regulation under the Temporary Money Rates Adjustment Law, while other rates were controlled by the Bank of Japan. Subsequently, however, financial conditions gradually reverted to normality, so that the Bank ceased to control rates in August 1955, while regulations under the Temporary Money Rates Adjustment Law were abolished in May 1957. From July 1957 voluntary agreement among members of the National Federation of Bankers' Associations set a ceiling on rates, but the agreed maximum rate was geared to the Bank rate, so that it could not be flexibly adjusted. Moreover, only one maximum rate, regardless of the maturities of the loans, was imposed. Thus, the system did not always correspond with reality, and was abolished in September 1967.

(5) *Activity of the Call Loan Market*

The call loan market is an outlet for the temporary employment of the liquid funds of financial institutions and also provides them with a temporary source of such liquidity; it is therefore the most sensitive mirror of financial conditions, because it is readily affected by changes in the reserve positions of financial institutions. Such changes may be represented by variations in their cash reserves (cash on hand and deposits with the Bank of Japan). The total amount of financial institutions' cash reserves is determined directly by changes in the Treasury accounts with the public and in the outstanding amount of bank-notes issued. It must be noted that the balance of payments influences the Treasury accounts with the public (more precisely, yen receipts and disbursements of the Foreign Exchange Fund Special Account). The cash reserves of individual banks, however, are also affected by their clearing positions and balance of remittances. Each bank offsets the resulting increases or decreases of cash reserves first of all by lending or borrowing in the call loan market. The chronically over-lent city banks, however, cannot fully recoup their deficiencies of cash reserves in the call loan market, and have to replenish them by recourse to borrowings from the Bank.

TABLE 23.4

Variations of Call Loan Rates in Post-War Years (Tokyo, Interest Rates for Lenders)

(percentages)

Years	*Overnight Money*	*Unconditional Money*	*Over-the-month Money*
1947	2·92	3·65–4·38	4·02–4·75
1948	3·29–4·02	4·38–5·84	4·93–6·57
1949	4·02	5·66–6·75	6·57–7·67
1950	4·02	5·84–6·94	6·39–7·30
1951	4·02	6·94–7·12	7·30–8·21
1952	4·02	7·12–8·40	8·21–8·58
1953	4·02	7·30–8·21	7·85–8·40
1954	4·02	7·30–8·03	7·85–8·58
1955	4·02	5·84–8·03	6·57–8·58
1956	4·02	4·75–9·13	5·66–9·13
1957	4·02–21·54	6·57–21·90	8·40–21·90
1958	5·48–10·95	7·67–10·95	8·12–10·95
1959	5·11–9·13	7·30–9·13	7·05–9·13
1960	8·40	8·40	8·40
1961	8·03–8·40	8·03–8·76	8·03–8·76
1962	8·03–11·68	8·03–12·41	8·03–12·41
1963	6·57–8·03	6·94–8·40	8·40–12·05
1964	7·30–10·95	7·67–11·32	9·49–13·14
1965	5·48–8·03	5·84–8·40	6·57–9·49
1966	5·48	5·84	6·57
1967	5·48–6·94	5·84–7·30	6·57–8·03
1968	6·94–8·03	7·30–8·40	8·30–9·13
1969	6·57–8·25	6·94–8·50	8·03–9·25
1970	7·50–8·25	7·75–8·50	8·50–9·25

SOURCE: Bank of Japan, *Economic Statistics Annual.*

In these circumstances, then, the demand and supply relationships in the market are constantly changing. Market activity does not remain the same even in the course of a single day, not to mention the same month or the same year. For instance, bill and domestic remittance-clearing balances greatly affect a day's call loan transactions. Further, a regular monthly pattern is discernible: the market tightens at the beginning of the month, when tax receipts are transferred to the Treasury; on days when salaries are usually paid; and at the end of the month, when various settlements are concentrated. In the course of a year the market is influenced by seasonal variations in the demand for bank-notes and in the Treasury's accounts with the public. The circulation of bank-notes increases in March-April, when they are required for preparations for farming, for school entrance fees and other expenses, and for tourism; in June, when bonuses are paid, and at the year-end, when bonuses are also paid and settlements are made of commercial transactions. In contrast, at the beginning of the year bank-notes which have been issued at the preceding year-end return to the Bank. Treasury accounts with the public are also subject to seasonal variations, because of the seasonality of business activity and of institutional fiscal arrangements. In the first quarter of the fiscal year (April to June), a small surplus of payments over receipts usually develops and a small excess of receipts over payments is customary in the second quarter (July to September); during the third quarter (October to December) large net payments to the public are made by the government and then the trend is reversed in the fourth quarter (January to March), when large net payment is made by the public to the government. Increases in bank-notes in circulation and the excess of receipts over payments by the Treasury fund are factors making for tightness in the call loan market, whereas the return to the Bank of bank-notes from circulation and the Treasury fund's surplus of payments over receipts produce ease in the market.

Needless to say, demand for and supply of money in the market are greatly affected by business cycles. In the overheating phase of the cycle the call loan market tightens, because more cash is demanded for circulation to meet the requirements of the expanded economy, while in the Treasury fund an excess of receipts over payments develops; in particular, the balance in international payments goes into deficit, so that the Foreign Exchange Fund Special Account absorbs yen from the public. In the recession, on the other hand, the market eases, because the demand for cash dwindles and the government makes net payments to the public.

3. THE ROLE OF THE BANK OF JAPAN

As the call loan market plays a vital role in the smooth functioning of the whole financial market the Bank is in constant touch with it, and has endeavoured to foster its healthy development.

As explained earlier (see Part Three, Chapter 19), the Bank has direct transactions with call loan dealers when they are short of funds through having supplied too much money to the securities finance companies to finance their margin loan transactions; or, when market conditions necessitate such a step, the Bank makes advances to them or purchases government short-term bills from them. The Bank also indirectly influences the call loan market by having recourse to various policy weapons. For instance, during the third quarter of each fiscal year, when large payments are made for rice delivered to the government, the Bank tries to absorb the surplus funds of the Central Co-operative Bank of Agriculture and Forestry by selling to it bonds, debentures or bills from its portfolio, thereby preventing excessive ease from developing in the call loan market. Furthermore, the call loan market tightens when the Bank adopts policies of monetary restraint. The raising of Bank rate, the increase of reserve requirements under the reserve deposit system, the restriction of the Bank's advances, and its sales of bonds and debentures: these cause private financial institutions to seek to borrow from the market.

CHAPTER 24

THE FOREIGN EXCHANGE MARKET

I. CHARACTERISTICS AND DEVELOPMENT

In pre-war years foreign exchange dealings in Japan were conducted either through specialised dealers or directly between banks. Three banks – Yokohama Specie Bank, Bank of Taiwan and Bank of Chosen (Korea) – were the most important, but eventually other big banks began to participate in the market, so that there was a fairly active business.

Immediately after the war, however, the General Headquarters of the Allied Forces imposed thoroughgoing exchange control. At that time not even a par of exchange had been established. Later, in April 1949, the par was fixed at 360·00 yen to the U.S. dollar. The power of exchange control was then gradually transferred from G.H.Q. to the Foreign Exchange Control Board, a Japanese government agency. The board took over the Foreign Exchange Special Account (later renamed the Foreign Exchange Fund Special Account), which was established to concentrate and manage foreign exchange reserves. In December of the same year, moreover, the Foreign Exchange and Foreign Trade Control Law was enacted; together with the Law Concerning Foreign Investments, this regulated all the external transactions of Japan. At the time no foreign exchange market could exist, because foreign exchange was concentrated entirely in the authorities' hands and all transactions had to be done at the official rate. Strict controls on foreign currency dealings and on foreign trade were thus maintained long after the war, but they were gradually relaxed from June 1952, when foreign exchange banks were allowed to maintain open positions in U.S. dollars; previously they had had to sell any foreign exchange they might acquire to the authorities. After 1956 foreign exchange rates were gradually liberalised, thereby increasing market activity. In particular, in July 1960 non-residents' free yen accounts could be opened, while at the same time the system of yen exchanges was introduced. Then, in April 1963, the limits of the yen's fluctuations in terms of dollars were widened from 0·5 per cent to 0·75 per cent either side of the parity. Since then the market has developed considerably.

The scale of the market remains small, however, and a number of problems persist; for instance, foreign exchange banks in Japan are unable to raise sufficient resources to carry large amounts of foreign exchange because of the high cost of money and their tendency to be short of funds. On the other hand, there are substantial seasonal fluctuations in the demand for the supply of foreign exchange in connection with foreign trade. At one time buyers predominate, at other times sellers preponderate. Foreign exchange rates consequently press sometimes against the upper limit and do not come down, while at other times they come close to the lower limit and will not rise. With the widening since 1963 in the range of permissible fluctuations and with the equalising operations of the Foreign Exchange Fund Special Account the demand–supply imbalance has been considerably reduced. These operations cannot, however, completely obviate the imbalance because they are designed only to smooth extreme movements in the exchanges, and do not remove the fundamental instability. The foreign exchange market in Japan remains small so that exchange rates respond abruptly to seasonal pressures.

A further consideration is that Japanese banks have been chronically short of liquidity, so that interest rates have been at high levels. In spite of this, the spread between spot and forward rates has not accurately reflected interest-rate differentials between Japan and other nations. Large amounts of short-term foreign capital have therefore flowed in since the liberalisation of foreign exchange transactions. Some of the short-term capital is for the finance of Japan's imports such as money raised by discounting-bank acceptances, but as some, such as Euro-dollars, resembles hot money, there have been fears lest it be converted into yen and cause disturbances in the domestic financial market.

From April 1964 Japan has adhered to Article VIII of the International Monetary Fund Agreement; at the same time she became a member of the Organisation for Economic Co-operation and Development. Thus, in principle, Japan is prohibited from resorting to exchange controls. Instead, monetary policy has become the authorities' main tool in ensuring a sound balance of payments. For the same reason, official intervention in the exchange market has become more frequent than previously. It is therefore imperative to expand and strengthen the exchange market. It must, however, be pointed out that the shortage of bank liquidity and excessive competition among the banks hamper the accomplishment of this aim.

2. THE PRESENT STATE OF TRANSACTIONS

(1) *Outline of the Current Foreign Exchange System*

It is best to give a brief exposition of the current system of exchange control before describing foreign exchange dealings. This description is based upon the Foreign Exchange and Foreign Trade Control Law and upon a number of governmental and ministerial ordinances made under it.

A. Open Position Holding System

The system now in force in Japan is what is termed the 'open-position holding system'. In principle, only the government (Foreign Exchange Fund Special Account), the Bank of Japan and authorised foreign exchange banks may hold foreign exchange. Excluding trading firms and manufacturers engaged in the export of their own goods, ordinary enterprises and individuals (ordinary residents) must sell any foreign exchange which they have acquired by export, or in any other way, to foreign exchange banks, money-changers or post offices; the last two named must resell such foreign currency to foreign exchange banks.

Foreign exchange banks may hold *nostro* accounts in foreign currency with their correspondent banks, both domestic and foreign (some foreign exchange banks may hold such balances in domestic foreign exchange banks only). They may also open foreign currency deposit accounts or free yen deposit accounts for their correspondent banks or for their non-resident customers. Practically all foreign currency transactions, whether for current or for capital purposes, are settled through these accounts of foreign exchange banks. The foreign exchange banks adjust the resultant surpluses or deficiencies of foreign or yen currency by transactions in domestic or overseas exchange markets, or with the Foreign Exchange Fund Special Account.

There can be exceptions to the rule that ordinary business firms and individuals cannot hold foreign currency. Since January 1956, to facilitate their operations, some trading firms have been allowed to purchase and hold designated foreign currencies, within limits, from authorised foreign exchange banks. Further, as a step towards liberalising foreign exchange dealings, the introduction of the system of foreign currency deposits for trading firms permits them to retain U.S. dollars or sterling, the proceeds of their exports of goods or services, in account with authorised foreign exchange banks for up to 21 days; this money may be used in payment for their imports. And since February 1970 those manufacturers, engaged in the export of their own goods, who have foreign subsidiaries or branches are also allowed to purchase and hold designated foreign currencies within limits for the purpose of extending loans to those subsidiaries or branches and for making deposits with foreign financial institutions.

B. Designated Receivable Currencies and Currency Saleable to the Foreign Exchange Fund Special Account

The current foreign exchange control law of Japan permits traders and others to accept 16 foreign currencies in addition to the yen; these include U.S. dollars, sterling, Canadian dollars and Deutschmarks. No limitation is imposed upon the kind of currency to be used for foreign payments. The Foreign Exchange Fund Special Account, however, purchases only U.S. dollars, the most important international currency. The special account buys unlimited amounts of dollars from foreign exchange banks at a given rate. (An explanation is given on pp. 418–19 of Ministry of Finance purchasing and selling rates.) Currencies other than U.S. dollars are not directly saleable to the special account, but they are freely convertible into

U.S. dollars in overseas markets, so that indirectly they may be sold to the special account.

C. Foreign Exchange Fund Special Account

The Foreign Exchange Fund Special Account concentrates foreign currencies in its hands, and sells them to foreign exchange banks, which require them for payments to foreign countries for imports and other transactions. It also keeps account of receipts and payments in yen arising from such dealings. The yen necessary for buying foreign currency from the banks are raised by ways-and-means borrowings from the General Account (this is known as 'inventory financing', although it has not been employed in recent years), by transference to the account of Treasury surpluses, by the issue of government short-term bills (Foreign Exchange Fund Bills) and by selling to the Bank foreign currency not required for the day-to-day working of the special account. The special account does not limit itself to passive purchases and sales of foreign exchanges at the request of the banks, but it also actively intervenes in the market and sells or buys foreign exchange in order to offset violent fluctuations of exchange rates, which may reflect seasonal or temporary movements in the market. These are known as 'exchange equalisation operations' and are managed by the Bank of Japan. Most of the foreign currency held by the special account is either invested in foreign currency securities in the name of the Minister of Finance or deposited with American or British banks. A part however, is held in deposit accounts with Japanese banks, and these are commonly known as the Ministry of Finance (M.O.F.) Accounts. It should be noted that the Bank of Japan does not deal in foreign exchange with private institutions, but with banks, and in this it acts as the agent of the Minister of Finance. The Foreign Exchange Fund Special Account is the only customer with which the Bank has direct dealings in foreign exchange. The Bank's holding of foreign exchange constitutes the floor beneath which the country's official reserves are not expected to fall.

(2) *Parties to the Transactions in the Market*

The 'open-position' system permits foreign exchange banks, trading firms, and manufacturers conducting the export of their goods to hold foreign currency, within certain limits. As will be explained later, inter-bank exchange rates are subject to variations, so that there is room for exchange operations by banks. Thus, there is an exchange market among banks, and between them and their customers.

The foreign exchange market in the widest sense consists of foreign exchange banks, their customers, exchange brokers and the Foreign Exchange Fund Special Account (the business of which is managed by the Bank of Japan). Foreign exchange banks play a crucial role in the market (see Chapter 13). 'Customers' refers here to the bank's clients who buy from the banks foreign exchange required for foreign trade or other transactions, or who sell foreign currency receipts to the banks. Foreign exchange brokers are intermediaries between banks and are indispensable for the smooth working of the market; they are involved in over 90 per cent of dealings in the Tokyo and Osaka inter-bank exchange markets which constitute the foreign exchange market in the narrower sense. They are not, however, authorised to retain foreign exchange, so that they cannot become principals in transactions; they are running brokers with no part in the delivery either of foreign exchange or of cash. For some time after 1952, when the open-position holding system was adopted, such brokerage business was undertaken by call loan dealers as an ancillary function. Subsequently, however, the business has become more important with the expansion of Japan's foreign trade, together with the easing of exchange controls. At the end of 1969 seven exchange brokers, including three specialised brokers and four call loan dealers, were active. Another important participant in the market is the Foreign Exchange Fund Special Account, which intervenes through the exchange banks or through brokers.

Since July 1960 non-residents' free yen accounts and yen exchanges have been legalised and free yen has been traded in New York and London, though on a small scale. The turnover has, however, been increasing year by year.

(3) *Exchange Rates*[1]

As Japan is a member of the International Monetary Fund and the yen's par value is 360·00 yen to a U.S. dollar, all other exchange rates of the yen are fixed by reference to this parity.

Under I.M.F. rules spot exchange rates may vary up to 1 per cent either side of the parity, but there is no limitation on fluctuations in forward rates (Article IV, Section 3, Agreement of the International Monetary Fund). In Japan, for some time after the war, both spot and forward rates were pegged, but since 1954 variations in forward rates have been permitted, while the spot rate has been liable to fluctuations since 1956. As will be explained later, however, the Foreign Exchange Fund Special Account does not deal in spot foreign exchange with the banks at rates differing by more than 0·75 per cent from the par of exchange. When the rate is 0·75 per cent above parity the special account sells unlimited amounts of foreign currency to the banks, and when it is 0·75 per cent below it buys from them unlimited amounts. Market rates of exchange (inter-bank rate and the bankers' rate for customers) therefore cannot go beyond these official limits.

At this point it is appropriate to explain briefly the various exchange rates now quoted in Japan: basic rate, arbitrated rate, M.O.F. (Minister of Finance) rate, inter-bank rate (market rate), bankers' rate for customers and so on.

A. Basic and Arbitrated Rates of Foreign Exchange

The basic rate of exchange is the registered I.M.F. parity. It is fixed at 360·00 yen to a U.S. dollar by a Ministry of Finance Ordinance (December 1949) under Article 7, Sections 1 and 2, of the Foreign Exchange and Foreign Trade Control Law. The arbitrated rates are the parities of the yen with foreign currencies other than the U.S. dollar, which are indirectly calculated from the basic rate and the parities of foreign currencies to the U.S. dollar. The ordinance stipulates that the Minister of Finance should publish these rates at the head office of the Bank of Japan. The arbitrated rates of only 10 currencies are thus published: sterling, Deutschmarks, French francs, Italian lire, Belgian francs, Dutch guilders, Swedish kronor, Norwegian kroner, Danish kroner, Austrian schillings.

[1] See Postscript on p. 425.

B. M.O.F. (Minister of Finance) Rate

The M.O.F. rate is also known as the Minister of Finance exchange rate and is the rate at which the Foreign Exchange

TABLE 24.1

Ranges of Fluctuations in Various Spot Rates for U.S. Dollars

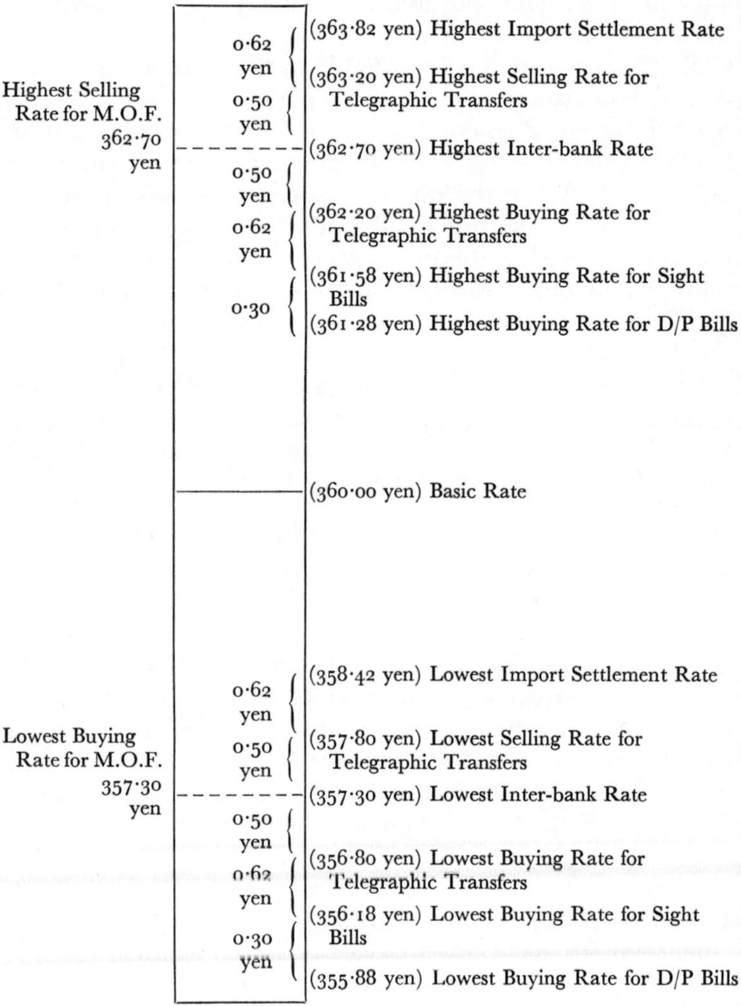

Fund Special Account (the agent of which is the Bank of Japan representing the Minister of Finance) deals in foreign exchange with authorised foreign exchange banks. At present only spot U.S. dollars may be sold to the special account. The Minister of Finance determines the rate under Article 2 of the Regulation Concerning Concentration of Foreign Exchange, etc., in the Hands of the Authorities. Since April 1963, when the margin for variations of spot exchange rates was widened, the M.O.F. rate has been within 0·75 per cent either side of parity; the highest rate is 362·70 yen to a dollar and the lowest 357·30 yen.

C. Inter-Bank Rate

The inter-bank rate (market rate) is the rate of exchange at which the authorised foreign exchange banks deal in foreign currency between themselves. No restriction is now imposed upon movements of either spot or forward inter-bank rates, although they were subject to various controls for some time after the war. Spot transactions in U.S. dollars do not however take place at rates beyond the upper or lower limits of the M.O.F. exchange rates, because the banks compare market rates with official rates; if the latter are more favourable to them, they can deal in dollars with the Foreign Exchange Fund Special Account. Further, brokerage (0·03 yen per dollar, charged to the buyer) must be taken into consideration, so that the ceiling for the market rate is 362·67 yen and the floor is 357·27 yen.

For currencies other than the U.S. dollar there are no such clear-cut limits to their variations. The spread of fluctuations of the principal currencies of western Europe is generally 0·7–0·75 per cent either side of their parities; the maximum range of movements of inter-bank rates for these in Japan is about 1·5 per cent either side of their arbitrated rates, because arbitrage takes place on the basis of market rates for these currencies and for U.S. dollars.

Forward rates can, on the other hand, vary freely in response to such factors as interest-rate differentials between Japan and other countries, demand and supply relationships peculiar to the forward market, and speculation.

D. Bankers' Rate for Customers

The bankers' rate for customers is sometimes referred to simply as the bankers' rate, and is the rate at which authorised foreign exchange banks buy or sell foreign currency for their clients. In contrast to the inter-bank rate, which is invariably the rate for telegraphic transfers, the bankers' rate for customers is a general term applied to a motley of exchange rates, including the buying and selling rates of telegraphic transfers, buying rate of sight bills, import settlement rate, buying rate of usance bills and buying rate of D/P bills (Documents on Payment). As telegraphic transfers are settled instantly by telegrams their rates do not include interest for the period needed to collect bills, so that they are a most accurate reflection of the market demand for and supply of foreign currencies. Interest rates are included in other exchange rates, because in such cases the transfer takes time.

Controls upon movements in bankers' rates for customers in respect of telegraphic transfers were lifted in April 1963; they can now be fixed freely by the banks. In practice their variations are determined by those of the inter-bank rate, because bankers' rates are fixed by adding to or subtracting from this the bankers' commission. By agreement among banks the commission is 0·50 yen per dollar. Thus, the bankers' highest selling rate of telegraphic transfers is 363·20 yen and the lowest is 357·80 yen, while the maximum buying rate is 362·20 yen and the minimum 356·80 yen.

The buying rate of sight bills is the rate at which banks buy sight export bills from customers; the import settlement rate is applied when their clients buy foreign currency required for settlement of import bills drawn on them. These rates are determined after allowing for interest for mailing days. For greater convenience the banks have agreed to apply the uniform rate of interest of 0·45 yen per dollar. Thus, the maximum sight bill buying rate is 361·75 yen and the minimum 356·35 yen, while the highest import settlement rate is 363·65 yen and the lowest 358·25 yen.

Buying rates for usance bills are those at which banks buy bills with usances such as 30, 60, 90, 120, or 150 days. They are reached by subtracting from the sight bill rate the interest for the relevant periods and also the bankers' commissions, and by allowing for the margin between spot and forward rates.

The buying rate for D/P bills is the rate at which banks purchase sight bills drawn without letters of credit. The banks

TABLE 24.2

Variations of Foreign Exchange Rates

(yen)

	U.S. Dollars			*Pound Sterling*		
End of the Year	*Basic Rate*	*Inter-Bank Rate*	*T.T. Selling Rate*	*Basic Rate*	*Inter-Bank Rate*	*T.T. Selling Rate*
1960	360·00	358·30	359·60	1008·00	1004·00	1008·20
1961	360·00	361·77	361·80	1008·00	1014·70	1016·00
1962	360·00	358·20	359·60	1008·00	1003·80	1007·80
1963	360·00	361·95	362·40	1008·00	1011·45	1013·50
1964	360·00	358·30	358·80	1008·00	998·90	1001·10
1965	360·00	360·90	361·40	1008·00	1011·45	1013·00
1966	360·00	362·47	362·90	1008·00	1011·26	1012·60
1967	360·00	361·91	362·20	864·00	870·60	871·60
1968	360·00	357·70	358·15	864·00	853·00	854·20
1969	360·00	357·80	358·05	864·00	858·00	859·70
End of Mar. 1970	360·00	357·53	358·10	864·00	860·90	861·80
End of June 1970	360·00	358·70	359·20	864·00	859·60	860·60
End of Sept. 1970	360·00	357·90	358·35	864·00	854·30	855·50
End of Dec. 1970	360·00	357·65	357·95	864·00	855·80	856·50

NOTES:

1. Inter-bank rates are the prevailing rates.
2. T.T. selling rates are the average rates of the 12 Class A authorised foreign exchange banks.

SOURCE: Bank of Japan, *Economic Statistics Annual.*

have agreed that the rate must be 0·30 yen lower than the buying rate of sight bills with letters of credit. Thus, the highest rate for such bills is 361·45 yen, while the lowest is 356·05 yen.

(4) *Foreign Exchange Operations of the Banks*

Foreign exchange banks play a vital role in the exchange market. Their transactions may be either passive or active: they may buy or sell foreign exchange at their customers' request, but the resultant imbalances in their positions and their holdings of yen and foreign currencies must be adjusted by active purchases or sales. The latter type of trading constitutes the bank's exchange operations, which are important to them in order both to ensure their smooth working and to avoid exchange risks. If the banks limit themselves to passive dealings with customers, their purchases may exceed their sales or vice versa; consequently, they may not achieve an optimum distribution of their resources between foreign and yen currency holdings. Eventually they might be unable to meet their clients' demands, and, moreover, they would be exposed to risks through exchange-rate fluctuations. Thus, the banks have to resort to exchange operations in order to adjust their exchange positions and to correct any disproportion in their holdings of domestic and foreign currency.

Exchange operations in U.S. dollars differ somewhat from those involving other currencies. Open positions in U.S. dollars may be liquidated either by inter-bank dealings or by transactions with the Foreign Exchange Fund Special Account. As the inter-bank rate is usually more favourable to the banks than the M.O.F. rate because of the equalising operations of the Bank of Japan, the banks resort, as a rule, to inter-bank transactions. Other currencies are not saleable to the special account, so that exchange operations involving them are limited to inter-bank trading. As the domestic market is too narrow for these currencies most of the operations are conducted in overseas markets.

Controls on open positions of authorised foreign exchange banks have been relaxed since September 1960. Limits are now imposed upon the maximum amount of the net open positions of the several banks in all foreign currencies. Hitherto, Japanese banks have tended to have over-sold positions. This is because they were eager to borrow low-interest foreign funds in order to convert them into yen.[1] Recently, however, the international short-loan fund market has tightened thanks largely to the stronger measures taken by the U.S. to improve her balance of

[1] After the summer of 1960 exchange liberalisation made rapid progress, so that Japanese banks were able to borrow excessively large amounts of foreign short-term funds. In June 1962, therefore, the system of foreign currency reserves was introduced in order to restrict short-term borrowing and their foreign currency holdings.

payments. Thus, banks have ceased to borrow abroad, while their customers have brought to them more export bills,[1] reflecting the growth of Japan's exports. The net open positions of banks have, therefore, become long ones.

(5) *Market Transactions*

The foreign exchange market in the narrower sense exists in Tokyo and Osaka, although the Osaka market is rather insignificant; only about 10 per cent of total turnover is negotiated there, as banks operate mainly in the Tokyo market. Business is usually transacted through exchange brokers. Dealings can be classified into spot, forward and swap transactions.

Spot transactions. In spot transactions delivery of and payment for foreign exchange ought in theory to take place simultaneously on the conclusion of the contract, but in Japan they include both 'value today' and 'value tomorrow' transactions.

Forward transactions. In forward transactions advance contracts are concluded to effect delivery of and payment for foreign exchange on some future dates or over certain periods in the future. Most contracts are for periods of less than six months.

Swap transactions. In swap transactions the purchase or sale of spot exchange is made at the same time as sale or purchase of forward exchange.

Dealings in the foreign exchange market have steadily increased year by year with the growth of Japan's foreign trade and with liberalisation of foreign exchange transactions. This has been particularly outstanding during recent years (see Table 24.3, p. 424).

[1] The System of Loans against Export Usance Bills was altered to the System of Loans against Foreign Exchange Assets in September 1961. Under this system the Bank of Japan makes yen loans on the security of export usance bills purchased by the exchange banks. The export bills are, however, left in the hands of the banks as their assets, so that their spot positions remain over-bought. They have, therefore, to cover by selling forward, so that forward rates tend to be depressed. In order to remedy this situation, the Bank instituted the System of Purchase of Foreign Exchange Bills in December 1965: the Bank purchases bills in U.S. dollars, which are drawn by the exchange banks on themselves upon the security of the export usance bills, denominated in foreign currency, in their possession.

TABLE 24.3

Turnover of Foreign Exchange in the Inter-Bank Markets (Tokyo and Osaka)

U.S. DOLLARS ($ m.)	*1960*	*1963*	*1965*	*1966*	*1967*	*1968*	*1969*	*1970*
Spot	330	1,310	2,163	1,962	2,149	3,109	4,258	4,845
Forward	318	1,083	1,844	1,885	1,806	2,636	2,926	4,241
Swap	48	511	829	677	618	727	1,229	2,611
Total	696	2,904	4,836	4,524	4,573	6,472	8,413	11,697
POUND STERLING (£ m.)								
Spot	59	75	88	101	95	68	50	31
Forward	21	9	14	13	14	5	1	2
Swap	3	1	4	4	12	1	0·6	0·2
Total	83	85	106	118	121	74	52	33

SOURCE: Bank of Japan.

As the banks have come to rely more and more upon the services of exchange brokers few direct transactions take place between banks. Most of the currency traded consists of U.S. dollars, and dealings in sterling are small. Other currencies are rarely negotiated in the market. Small amounts of Deutschmarks, Swiss francs, French francs, Dutch guilders and so on are sometimes offered and purchased.

3. THE BANK OF JAPAN AND THE FOREIGN EXCHANGE MARKET

Under the current system of exchange controls in Japan foreign exchange is in principle concentrated in the Foreign Exchange Fund Special Account, and the Bank of Japan does not directly deal with private institutions on its own account. The Bank is, however, entrusted by the government with licensing under the exchange control law; it is also a custodian of the Special Account's foreign currencies and acts as the agent of the Minister of Finance in their employment. Thus, the Bank plays an important role in the market, first by selling and buying foreign exchange for the special account, and, second, by giving guidance on the exchange positions of banks.

POSTSCRIPT

RECENT DEVELOPMENTS IN THE JAPANESE FOREIGN EXCHANGE MARKET

The U.S. announcement of its new economic policy on 15 August 1971 brought about a drastic change in international monetary conditions. For its part, Japan decided on 27 August to suspend temporarily the limits on the margins within which the yen was allowed to fluctuate. Following this step the spot rate for the U.S. dollar on the Tokyo exchange market was quoted at around ¥340, or 5 to 6 per cent below parity (by the I.M.F. formula). Subsequently, it continued to edge downwards, to reach the level of ¥322, some 12 per cent below parity, towards the middle of December. Meanwhile, all the countries concerned strove to resolve existing international monetary difficulties, primarily through discussions at meetings of Ministers and Central Bank Governors of the ten countries participating in the General Arrangements to Borrow ('The Group of Ten'). Japan sought a solution to the problem of establishing a new parity through the widely desired multilateral realignment of parities. Eventually, on 19 December, the new basic exchange rate of the yen in terms of the U.S. dollar was fixed at ¥308, or 16·88 per cent (by the I.M.F. formula) above the old parity.[1]

[1] Developments in foreign-exchange markets and in Japan's exchange-rate policy since December 1971 have further modified the account given in this chapter, and have been such as to render nugatory an attempt to provide an up-to-date description.

CHAPTER 25

THE SECURITIES MARKET

I. CHARACTERISTICS

The securities market is an abstract concept, covering the whole process from the issue of new securities to their acquisition by investors, as well as dealings in existing securities. Thus, it comprises the new issue market and the market for trading in existing securities, that is, the stock exchanges.

In the new issue market the newly created securities are offered to the public for subscription; this is known as the 'market flotation of securities'. Investors are thereby provided with more investment outlets.

On the stock exchanges, on the other hand, investors and securities companies purchase or sell existing securities among themselves. The exchanges thereby serve the useful purposes of forming reasonable prices for securities by the free interplay of demand and supply and of making them known to the public. As investors can encash the securities by selling them in the market, it ensures their liquidity or negotiability.

There is a close interrelationship between the issue market and the market for old securities; both are indispensable for the smooth functioning of the market as a whole. Because securities are easily realisable when necessary at reasonable prices on stock exchanges, investment in them is facilitated and the issue market can grow. Conversely, without development of the issue market, stock-exchange dealings cannot increase.

The history of the securities market in Japan dates back to the early years of the Meiji era, but in pre-war years the issue market was poorly developed. Its growth was impeded by the existence of giant holding companies and by direct subsidisation of industry by the government. The result was an asymmetric development of the share market, in which active dealings were made for speculative purposes. The securities market could not therefore properly perform its original function of mobilising industrial funds, and, in consequence, the credit standing of securities companies was low.

For some time after the war stock exchanges remained closed, but they reopened in May 1949, when various improvements were made in their organisation and in dealing methods. Stock exchanges have been reorganised on partnership principles; term transactions have been prohibited; members of stock exchanges have been forbidden to deal in listed shares in places other than stock exchanges, although there are some exceptions to the rule. These measures, together with the dissolution of the Zaibatsu, the diversification of share-holdings and the growth of the economy, made for a rapid development of the market. An outstanding feature of the post-war market has been the popularisation of investment in shares. This tendency has been further promoted by the growth of investment trusts, which were started in 1951. With the boom in the share market, unlisted shares also began to be actively traded in it. Thus, second divisions were opened in stock exchanges in 1961. The market has thus achieved rapid development in post-war years and its importance in the supply of industrial funds has accordingly increased gradually. The development of the market for bonds and shares has, however, lagged far behind that of the share market. Moreover, the share market itself suffered a sharp setback from 1963 to 1965 (see Part Three, Chapter 20, 'Securities Companies'). Although improvements and reorganisations are under way in the market as a result of the crisis, the Japanese securities market is still far from perfect.

First, the scale of the issue market is still too small. Excessive indirect financing, which is responsible for the distorted financial structure of Japan, has its roots in this circumstance. Thus, in the supply of industrial funds, loans by banks and other financial institutions account for about half of the total, while the relative importance of share issues and of industrial debentures is much smaller. Moreover, the amounts and issue terms of new securities are not always determined by agreement among the parties concerned with due regard to market conditions. This is particularly true of the issue of bonds and debentures, the terms of which have been insufficiently flexible. Furthermore, the market for existing bonds and debentures is not well developed, so that investment in them is not very profitable; they are mainly absorbed, therefore, by financial institutions, few subscriptions being made by ordinary investors or by business firms.

TABLE 25.1

Net Supply of Industrial Funds (Increase and Decrease)

(million yen for 1934–6, hundred million yen for other years)

Years	*Outside Capital*				
	Shares	*Industrial Debentures*	*Loans and Discounts*	*Total*	*Own Capital*
Averages of 1934–1936	999 (80·4)	6 (0·5)	237 (19·1)	1,243 (100·0)	
1956	1,774 (12·5)	575 (4·1)	11,815 (83·4)	14,165 (100·0)	10,002
1957	2,856 (15·9)	523 (2·9)	14,602 (81·2)	17,982 (100·0)	13,632
1958	2,328 (14·3)	576 (3·5)	13,405 (82·2)	16,310 (100·0)	13,105
1959	2,350 (11·2)	1,447 (6·8)	17,254 (82·0)	21,051 (100·0)	14,936
1960	4,719 (16·1)	1,528 (5·2)	23,025 (78·7)	29,272 (100·0)	22,007
1961	9,285 (22·3)	3,857 (9·2)	28,573 (68·5)	41,716 (100·0)	26,479
1962	7,978 (19·0)	1,331 (3·1)	32,728 (77·9)	42,038 (100·0)	28,773
1963	5,894 (10·3)	1,636 (2·8)	49,742 (86·9)	57,273 (100·0)	31,986
1964	7,913 (15·5)	1,540 (3·0)	41,486 (81·5)	50,940 (100·0)	39,746
1965	2,626 (5·3)	2,193 (4·4)	44,892 (90·3)	49,712 (100·0)	40,753
1966	3,351 (6·0)	2,252 (4·0)	50,458 (90·0)	56,061 (100·0)	51,189
1967	3,323 (4·7)	2,780 (4·0)	64,306 (91·3)	70,409 (100·0)	65,857
1968	4,914 (6·6)	1,594 (2·1)	67,835 (91·3)	74,344 (100·0)	82,400
1969	7,544 (7·3)	2,988 (2·9)	92,691 (89·8)	103,224 (100·0)	98,313
1970	10,029 (8·0)	3,589 (2·8)	112,640 (89·2)	126,259 (100·0)	. .

SOURCE: Bank of Japan, *Economic Statistics Annual.*

The second problem is that the market for existing bonds and debentures is underdeveloped in contrast to the market for shares. On the stock exchanges dealings in bonds and debentures which had been suspended since March 1962, were restarted in February 1966, in order to encourage the development of the market. Turnover and the number of listed stocks are both, however, much smaller than for shares. It goes without saying that this state of affairs is due to the inactivity of the issue

Outstanding Amounts of Securities

(hundred million yen)

End of the Year	*1953*	*1958*	*1963*	*1965 (Financial Year)*	*1966 (Financial Year)*	*1967 (Financial Year)*	*1968 (Financial Year)*	*1969 (Financial Year)*
Government Short-term Bills	1,750	5,180	6,167	7,082	8,099	11,973	15,742	18,137
	(9·9)	(11·6)	(5·0)	(4·2)	(4·1)	(5·2)	(5·9)	(6·1)
Long-term Government Bonds	3,635	3,265	3,099	5,281	12,599	19,600	25,010	29,585
	(20·5)	(7·3)	(2·5)	(3·1)	(6·3)	(8·4)	(9·5)	(10·0)
Local Bonds	150	1,116	2,874	5,495	7,692	10,017	11,740	13,518
	(0·8)	(2·5)	(2·3)	(3·2)	(3·9)	(4·3)	(4·4)	(4·5)
Public Corporation Debentures	176	1,964	10,886	22,615	30,423	38,893	46,959	54,938
	(1·0)	(4·4)	(8·7)	(13·4)	(15·3)	(16·8)	(17·8)	(18·4)
Bank Debentures	2,500	6,317	19,066	30,230	36,135	41,942	48,146	54,803
	(14·1)	(14·2)	(15·3)	(17·9)	(18·2)	(18·1)	(18·2)	(18·4)
Industrial Debentures	1,824	3,950	13,751	18,130	20,174	22,175	24,857	27,571
	(10·3)	(8·8)	(11·0)	(10·7)	(10·1)	(9·6)	(9·4)	(9·2)
Shares	6,938	20,781	55,339	69,009	73,542	77,995	82,639	88,756
	(39·1)	(46·5)	(44·5)	(40·8)	(37·0)	(33·6)	(31·3)	(29·7)
Investment Trust Beneficiary Certificates	764	2,100	13,273	11,303	10,082	9,256	9,132	11,150
	(4·3)	(4·7)	(10·7)	(6·7)	(5·1)	(4·0)	(3·5)	(3·7)
Total (A)	17,737	44,673	124,455	169,145	198,746	231,851	264,225	298,458
	(100·0)	(100·0)	(100·0)	(100·0)	(100·0)	(100·0)	(100·0)	(100·0)
Gross National Product (B)	69,654	113,416	236,279	313,492	367,011	431,167	527,803	627,206
(A)/(B), %	25·5	39·4	52·7	54·0	54·2	53·8	50·0	47·6

NOTE: Figures in parentheses are percentages of totals.

SOURCE: Bank of Japan, *Flow of Funds Accounts*.

market in those securities, the fixing of subscribers' yields at low levels, and the small amounts of bonds and debentures held by ordinary investors or business firms.

As is shown in Table 25.2, the outstanding amount of securities has been increasing annually. Its ratio to the gross national product was 25 per cent at the end of 1953, but it is now above 47 per cent. Its composition has undergone considerable changes in the process. In the post-war years, after the enforcement of the Dodge Line, balanced budgets were maintained and no long-term government bonds, other than delivery bonds, were issued until January 1966. From that date, however, large amounts of long-term bonds began to be issued and their relative weight in the total amount of securities outstanding is rapidly going up. The relative proportion of local bonds and of public corporation debentures is also growing year by year. In contrast the relative weight of shares and investment trust beneficiary certificates has been declining since 1962, when the share market faced a slump; it had been increasing until then.

2. THE NEW ISSUE MARKET

(1) *Organisation*

The main parties in the new issue market are the issuers of securities and their subscribers, but intermediaries facilitate the flotation of securities by undertaking the issue business or by acting as brokers between the parties. These intermediaries include the following institutions.

A. Underwriters

Underwriters take up the whole or part of the newly issued securities in order to sell them to the public, and they undertake to purchase any unsold portion thereof. The Securities Transaction Law provides that in principle only securities companies may engage in this business, but the underwriting of issues of government bonds, local bonds and government-guaranteed debentures is an exception; financial institutions, including banks and trust companies, can underwrite the flotation of such securities.

B. Sub-Underwriters

Sub-underwriters take up the whole or a part of the new securities already underwritten by other institutions and they undertake to absorb any unsold portion thereof. At present, only minor securities companies act in this capacity, their functions being simply to act as agents in receiving subscriptions from the public.

C. Trustees

There are two distinct varieties of trustees: offering and mortgage trustees. The former are entrusted by issuers to undertake the business of bonds and debentures; the latter administer mortgage property for debenture-holders. Only banks or trust companies can become offering trustees, while authorisation by the competent authorities is required for acting as mortgage trustees. In most instances, however, the same banks or trust companies perform both functions for given issuers.

(2) *The Issue Market for Given Issuers*

The following kinds of bonds and debentures are now issued in Japan: government bills and bonds, local bonds, public corporation debentures, bank debentures and industrial debentures.

Government securities are divided into long-term government bonds and government short-term bills. When, in January 1966, government bonds were floated for the first time in many years it was to make good the fiscal deficit of the fiscal year 1965. Subsequently, 'construction bonds' under Article 4 of the Fiscal Law have been issued each year. Government bonds are floated in the following manner: contracts for underwriting and for delegation of the business of offering the new securities are concluded between the Bank of Japan, the government's agent for the national debt, and the underwriting syndicate (composed of city banks, country banks, long-term credit banks, trust banks, mutual loans and savings banks, credit associations, Central Co-operative Bank of Agriculture and Forestry, life-insurance companies and securities companies). The syndicate undertakes the work involved in publicly offering the securities, and underwrites the issue and agrees to take up any unsold portion. Private individuals can, however, subscribe for new government bonds only through the intermediary of securities companies in the syndicate. Government short-term bills include Treasury Bills, Foreign Exchange Fund Bills, Foodstuffs Control Bills and others. The principle is that they are offered to the public, but in practice most are purchased by the Bank of Japan, because banks are short of liquidity and interest rates on these securities are low, so that few subscriptions come from private individuals and institutions.

Local bonds are issued by local authorities. They are either sold to the public through the underwriting securities companies or financial institutions, or are directly placed with financial or other institutions having special connections with the issuing bodies.

Government-guaranteed debentures are akin to government bonds in character. They are issued by government-affiliated organisations, public corporations and companies established under special laws, such as the Japan Northeastern Development Company or the Japan Air Lines Company. The government ensures the redemption of their principal and the payment of interest. Not all debentures issued by these semi-governmental agencies carry such guarantees. For instance, debentures allotted to telephone subscribers by the Japan Telegraph and Telephone Public Corporation and those allotted by the Japan National Railways to their affiliates and users do not carry government guarantee. Government-guaranteed debentures are floated by the so-called contract system: banks are entrusted by issuers to make public offerings, but the issues are managed by securities companies. Unsold portions of new securities are underwritten jointly by the banks and the securities companies.

Industrial debentures are issued by ordinary business firms. They are floated by various methods, but in most instances the contract system is adopted as in the case of government-guaranteed debentures. There is, however, a shade of difference. Financial institutions, including banks, are forbidden to underwrite the issue of industrial debentures, so that the underwriting syndicates are organised by the six 'regular member' securities companies, which include the four biggest companies.

TABLE 25·3

Holdings of Bonds and Debentures (end of March 1970)

(hundred million yen)

	Government Short-term Bills	*Long-Term Government Bonds*	*Local Bonds*	*Public Corporation Debentures*	*Bank Debentures*	*Industrial Debentures*	*Total*	*Total: Percentages to Total*	*Shares (For Reference)*
Financial Institutions	8,216	19,670	12,838	23,095	27,026	25,049	115,894	58·5	32,115
(of which All Banks)	(—)	(6,797)	(9,151)	(11,197)	(14,219)	(18,679)	(60,043)	(30·3)	(12,977)
(,, ,, Financial Institutions for Small Businesses)	(—)	(694)	(615)	(1,994)	(7,194)	(1,803)	(12,300)	(6·2)	(651)
(of which Financial Institutions for Agriculture, Forestry and Fishery)	(—)	(398)	(2,771)	(5,586)	(4,382)	(3,995)	(17,132)	(8·6)	(226)
(of which Insurance Companies)	(—)	(710)	(301)	(550)	(830)	(422)	(2,813)	(1·4)	(13,246)
Public Sector	9,519	5,772	135	16,064	4,054	706	36,250	18·3	1,093
(of which Government)	(8,891)	(5,772)	(135)	(16,064)	(4,054)	(706)	(35,622)	(18·0)	(1,093)
Corporate Businesses	282	166	232	6,380	3,600	395	11,055	5·6	23,743
Individuals	120	3,521	313	9,399	20,123	1,421	34,897	17·6	39,737
Total	18,137	29,129	13,518	54,938	54,803	27,571	198,096	100·0	96,688

SOURCE: Bank of Japan, *Flow of Funds Accounts*.

Bank debentures are issued by financial institutions. They are either interest-bearing or discount debentures. At present they are issued by the long-term credit banks, the Central Bank for Commercial and Industrial Co-operatives, the Central Co-operative Bank of Agriculture and Forestry and the Bank of Tokyo – the specialised foreign exchange bank. Their flotation is managed by the issuing institutions themselves, but the receipt of subscriptions and public offerings are handled also by the securities companies.

Banks and other financial institutions are the most important subscribers to these various types of bonds and debentures (see Table 25.3). Most of the long-term government bonds, local bonds and government-guaranteed debentures are absorbed directly by financial institutions, particularly banks, few being purchased by ordinary individuals and business firms; government short-term bills, as noted already, are purchased almost entirely by the Bank of Japan. Although financial institutions are prohibited from underwriting the issues of industrial debentures and interest-bearing bank debentures, it is customary for allotments of new securities to be made in advance to large subscribers – that is, to banks and other financial institutions. Bank discount debentures are, however, bought by individuals to a large extent, because their maturity is only one year and their unit face value is small.

Thus, financial institutions, particularly banks, exert a strong influence on the bond issue market. The market is therefore fairly sensitive to changes in financial conditions; in periods of financial stringency the market tends to tighten because of squeezes on bank liquidity. In spite of this, the volume and terms of bond issues have not always responded flexibly to changes in market demand–supply relationships; this, together with diversification of subscribers and improvements in the mechanism of underwriting, constitute important problems to be solved in the future.

(3) *Issue Market for Shares*

Shares may be issued by rights issues, by allotments to friends of the companies or by public offerings. By the former two methods new shares are issued to specific persons, such as shareholders or those who have special connections with the issuers. Allotments may be made gratis, or against payment of subscription money, or by a combination of the two. New shares are sold by the last method to the public. They may be sold either by the issuers themselves or indirectly through the underwriting securities companies.

Issues by public offerings are made at current prices, so that the issuing companies can obtain premiums above the face values; this method is attractive to business firms, and, indeed, there are arguments that this method is desirable in order to strengthen them. On the other hand, existing shareholders would suffer losses if new shares are offered to the public instead of being allotted to them. There is a further disadvantage, by this method of raising capital, in the possible increase in the number of unstable shareholders. For these reasons public offerings are rare in Japan: they have been made largely to dispose of forfeited shares or of odd-lot shares. Thus, in most cases, new shares are allotted to shareholders.

3. MARKET FOR EXISTING SECURITIES

Securities may be bought and sold both on and outside stock exchanges. In pre-war years dealings on stock exchanges were mostly speculative, so that spot transactions of shares and bonds were made largely over the counter of securities companies. After the war, however, transactions other than those on spot terms were prohibited on stock exchanges. Moreover, over-the-counter transactions in listed shares are forbidden. This is in order to form fair prices and also to facilitate dealings. The post-war share market has therefore been dominated by stock exchanges.

(1) *Dealings on Stock Exchanges*

Stock exchanges are composed of juridical persons on partnership principles, the purpose of which is to open and maintain markets for trading in securities. Only securities companies can become members of stock exchanges. Decisions are made by resolutions of the general meeting of the members; the executive organ is the board of directors, the chairman of which represents the stock exchange concerned and presides over its business. At present, there are eight stock exchanges: Tokyo, Osaka, Nagoya, Kyoto, Hiroshima, Fukuoka, Niigata and Sapporo. Their relative sizes can best be gauged from their turnover. The Tokyo Exchange accounts for about 70 per cent of total turnover, both in value and in number of shares; in effect, it is the central market for shares. The Osaka Exchange is the central trading place in the Kansai (Western) district. The total trading on these two markets represents more than 90 per cent of the total turnover of all stock exchanges in Japan (see Table 25.5).

Securities that are traded on the stock exchanges are termed 'listed securities'. Each exchange establishes its own regulations for securities-listing, on the basis of which, and subject to approval by the Minister of Finance, the stock exchange designates the shares and other securities to be listed. For instance, the criteria of the Tokyo Stock Exchange for screening shares to be listed take account of paid-up capital, number of shareholders, degree of dispersal of shareholdings, length of time the company has been in existence, and dividend rate. At the end of 1969, 1330 shares were listed in Tokyo (of which 727 were traded in the First Section, while 603 were listed in the Second Section). Eighty-three types of bonds and debentures were listed, of which 14 were government bonds, 1 was a local bond, 2 were government-guaranteed debentures, 3 were interest-bearing bank debentures, 38 were Telegraph and Telephone debentures, 23 were industrial debentures and 2 were special debentures.

The market for bonds and debentures was virtually non-existent for ten years after the war, but from April 1956 stock exchange dealings in some bonds and debentures were started in Tokyo and Osaka (and in Nagoya from 1961). There were only nominal transactions, however, and from March 1962 stock exchange dealings in bonds and debentures were discontinued; only Telegraph and Telephone debentures continued to be traded. In 1965, however – the year of monetary ease – the demand for bonds and debentures strengthened. In August of that year, therefore, over-the-counter market prices of bonds and debentures began to be published. Then, in February 1966, when government bond issues were started, stock exchange dealings in bonds and debentures were resumed in Tokyo and Osaka; the purpose was to foster the development of the bond market.

TABLE 25.4

Terms of Issues of Bonds and Debentures (in March 1971)

	Nominal Interest Rates %	*Issues Price (yen)*	*Maturities*	*Subscribers' Yields* %
Government Short-term Bills (Discount)	5·625	99·07	60 days	5·677
Long-term Government Bonds (6·5%)	6·5	97·60	7 years	7·011
Local Bonds	7·5	98·50	7 ,,	7·831
Government-guaranteed Debentures	7·0	98·00	7 ,,	7·434
Discount Bank Debentures	5·83	94·15	1 year	6·213
Interest-bearing Bank Debentures	7·5	99·50	5 years	7·638
Industrial Debentures (A)	7·6	98·00	7 ,,	8·046
(A')	7·6	97·50	7 ,,	8·161
(B)	7·6	97·25	7 ,,	8·218
(C)	7·8	97·50	7 ,,	8·366
(D)	7·8	97·00	7 ,,	8·483

NOTE: Bank of Tokyo Debentures are not included in interest-bearing bank debentures.

SOURCE: Bank of Japan.

In contrast to the bond market the share market is highly developed, with prices determined by the free interplay of demand and supply. The turnover is large and is not inferior to that of share markets in the principal countries of the world. As has been pointed out, however, the recent slump has revealed a number of underlying defects in the market, and therefore a strengthening of it is desirable (see Chapter 20).

Dealings on Japanese stock exchanges are supposed to be spot, but there may be a time-lag between the contract and settlement. There are the following varieties of spot transactions:

TABLE 25.5

Principal Statistics of Listed Shares on Stock Exchanges of Japan (end of February 1971)

Number of Companies	1,581	
Number of Names of Shares	1,708	
Number of Shares Issued	120,574	million shares
Amount of Capital	68,458	hundred million yen
Total Amount of Current Prices of Shares	186,993	hundred million yen
Number of Shares Sold (During 1970)	57,099	million shares
(of which sold on Tokyo Stock Exchange)	(42,753)	,,
(of which sold on Osaka Stock Exchange)	(11,778)	,,
Value of Shares Sold (During 1970)	120,302	hundred million yen
(of which sold on Tokyo Stock Exchange)	(91,525)	,,
(of which sold on Osaka Stock Exchange)	(23,973)	,,

SOURCE: Tokyo Stock Exchange, *Statistical Yearbook of Tokyo Stock Exchange.*

A. Ordinary Transactions

Settlement is made on the fourth day from the contract date. More than 99 per cent of dealings on the Tokyo Stock Exchange are made in this way.

B. Same-day-Settlement Transactions

Settlement is made on the day of contract. Recourse is had to this method when cash or securities are urgently required.

C. Specified-date Transactions

Settlement is made within 15 days from the contract date. This facility is utilised when the transactions are between distant places.

D. When-issued Transactions

These are dealings in pre-emptive rights to new shares. Trading starts from the day when the issue of new shares has been decided; settlement takes place on a prearranged day after the issue of share certificates.

(2) *Over-the-counter Market*

Unlisted or odd-lot shares are traded outside the stock exchanges. They are personally negotiated at the counter of individual securities companies, and such dealings are known as over-the-counter transactions. With the post-war boom in the share market dealings in unlisted shares rapidly increased, and it became essential to organise trading in them; hence, the Second Sections were opened in the Tokyo, Osaka and Nagoya Stock Exchanges in October 1961. The over-the-counter market in unlisted shares is now on a much smaller scale than that of the regular market.

Over-the-counter transactions of bonds and debentures are, on the other hand, much more active than stock exchange transactions in them, because trading in listed bonds and debentures outside the exchanges is not prohibited; their prices, however, should not deviate far from their current quotations on the stock exchanges. Over-the-counter prices of bonds and debentures are published once a week.

4. REGULATION OF THE SECURITIES MARKET

It is desirable to ensure that the securities market functions more efficiently, and it is also imperative to protect investors. Fairness must therefore be maintained in the issue of and trading in securities; obstacles to their smooth negotiation must be removed. The Securities Transaction Law was accordingly enacted in 1948 to control, together with governmental ordinances made under it, the securities market in Japan. In addition, it is subject to administrative guidance by the Ministry of Finance, to the intervention of the Bank of Japan, and to the voluntary regulations of the stock exchanges and other organisations.

As previously noted, the securities investment trusts are regulated by the Securities Investment Trust Law of 1951 (see Chapter 20, 'Securities Companies').

(1) *Regulation by the Securities Transaction Law*

Various controls are imposed upon issuers of securities, securities companies, stock exchanges, securities finance companies and so on by the Securities Transaction Law and by the ordinances made under it. Several alterations have been made in these regulations since the enforcement of the law in 1948; in particular, in May 1965, the law was partly amended (with effect from 1 October of that year) and the ordinances were also revised and new ones were promulgated. The purpose was to strengthen and to perfect the controls of the securities market, because the market's slump from 1964 to 1965 and the attendant failures of securities companies revealed deficiencies in the existing regulations.

A. Regulations for Issuers of Securities

When public offerings are made of shares or industrial debentures with a total face value exceeding 50 million yen, or when a public sale is made of securities with a total face value exceeding 10 million yen,[1] their issuers must file a report with the Minister of Finance; this must state the purpose, the trade name, the capital, important matters relating to the business and accounts and the names of the officers or promoters of the issuing company as well as matters relative to the securities concerned. Only then may the securities be offered or sold to the public, and the issuing company must then draw up a prospectus. Moreover, it must submit a securities report to the Minister of Finance every business year. The contents of these prospectuses and securities reports are similar to those submitted at the time of the public offering or sale. If the securities are listed on the stock exchanges, these reports are submitted to the stock exchanges as well. These papers are available to the public for inspection at the Ministry of Finance, at the head office or branch offices of the issuing company or at the stock exchanges. When the amounts of the securities to be offered or sold to the public are less than 50 million yen, but exceed 1 million yen, the issuer must notify the Minister of Finance.

B. Regulation of Securities Companies

Previously a securities company could be established simply by registering with the Ministry of Finance, provided it met certain conditions, but since the amendment to the Securities

[1] The Securities Transaction Law defines 'public offering' as the act of inviting the public to subscribe for securities to be issued on uniform terms, while 'public sale' is defined as the act of soliciting the public to purchase already issued securities on uniform conditions.

Transaction Law a securities company has been required to obtain a licence from the Minister of Finance for each of the four branches of the business: purchase and sale of securities for own account (dealers' business), purchase and sale of securities for customers' accounts (brokers' business), underwriting of issues and public offerings of securities (underwriters' business), and public sales of securities (distributors' business). (This regulation has been in effect since April 1968.) The licence is granted after the Minister has given due consideration to the adequacy of the petitioning company's financial basis, its profits prospects, its knowledge, experience and credit standing in relation to the requirements for operating securities business in a sound, just and accurate manner. In addition, securities companies require permission from the Minister of Finance for changes in their trade names, capital and methods of business, and also for the establishment of branches or other offices, for mergers and for engaging in business other than securities business. Their salesmen must now also be registered with the authorities, while formerly it sufficed merely to report their names. Moreover, the securities companies concerned must clearly specify the extent of business delegated to them.

The minimum amount of capital of securities companies is specified, according to the type of licence held, conditions of business and location of offices. For instance, the minimum capital for securities companies engaged in underwriting business is as follows: (1) 3·0 billion yen for companies which act as main underwriters, but which engage in other business as well; (2) 1·0 billion yen for those companies which act as main underwriters but which do not engage in business other than underwriting; (3) 0·2 billion yen for other underwriters. The minimum capital for other types of securities companies is as follows: 30 million yen for members of stock exchanges (100 million yen for members of the Tokyo and Osaka Stock Exchanges and 50 million yen for members of the Nagoya Stock Exchange) and 20 million yen for non-members (30 million yen for those with offices in special wards of the Tokyo metropolis or in the city of Osaka). Controls are also imposed upon the assets and accounts of securities companies, which are obliged to maintain financial soundness. For instance, liabilities should not exceed ten times the net worth.

Margin transactions are also regulated by the authorities. Securities companies must receive deposits of money from their customers within three days of the conclusion of contracts for margin transactions or of such transactions as may be specified by ordinances of the Ministry of Finance (only when-issued transactions are so specified). Money thus deposited in respect of margin transactions is termed 'collateral margin money', the ratio of which to the total amount of transaction is fixed by the Minister of Finance, who determines it by reference to prevailing market conditions. The minimum ratio is, however, 30 per cent and the minimum amount is 150,000 yen. Securities, the assessment rate of which is also altered with market conditions, may be substituted for collateral margin money.

In addition, securities companies, their officers and executives are required to transact business in a sound and fair manner. For example, they are prohibited from offering specific advice or special benefits or to promise to compensate losses when they sell securities to their customers. They are also forbidden to make false or misleading advertisements, and they must not purchase or sell securities by utilising their privileged positions.

C. Regulation of Stock Exchanges

The Securities Transaction Law provides for the establishment, organisation, membership, administration and supervision of stock exchanges. Various regulations are also made to facilitate dealings and to prevent speculative excesses.

D. Regulation of Securities Finance Companies

Securities finance companies require licences from the Minister of Finance in the same manner as securities companies and stock exchanges. When they fix or alter the terms or methods of their loans of money or shares they must obtain the Minister's approval.

(2) *Administrative Guidance of the Ministry of Finance*

The Ministry of Finance is the competent authority in matters relating to securities; its operations, such as licensing, registration, approval and inspection are based on the Securities Transaction Law and on ordinances made under it. It also gives administrative guidance to the securities companies, for instance, in regard to rationalisation of their managements and transactions. In this way it is hoped to further the broader aims of the legislation.

(3) *Intervention in the Securities Market by the Bank of Japan*

The Bank of Japan Law stipulates that the regulation of the terms of loans by financial institutions to securities companies is the province of the Policy Board of the Bank, but there is no clause elaborating this point, so the provision is only nominal.

The Bank is in direct contact with the securities market when it makes loans to call loan dealers on the security of call loan notes; these are issued by securities finance companies in favour of dealers when they borrow money from the latter on the security of call loan transactions collateral receipts (see Part Three, Chapter 21). The names of shares, on which the securities finance companies can request stock exchanges to issue collateral receipts, are settled by consultation among the Bank, the securities finance companies and the stock exchanges. The assessment rate of shares used for collaterals is also fixed by consultation among these bodies. The evaluation of call loan notes as security for loans from the Bank is decided by the Bank, which, moreover, is always watching variations in the amounts of money demanded by the securities finance companies, and, if necessary, advises them to restrain their borrowing from the call loan market. Further, the Bank has lent money to the Japan Securities Finance Company, to support the latter's loans on bonds and debentures. The Bank also made special loans to some securities companies during the slump in the securities market in 1964 and 1965. The loans were made under Article 25 of the Bank of Japan Law, the purpose being to prevent a financial panic. The Bank influences the volume of bond and debenture flotations through its guidance of the trustee banks for their issues. It must also be remembered that the Bank treats first-class bonds and debentures as eligible collateral security against its loans on notes. The Bank also undertakes market operations in government bonds and government-guaranteed debentures, which naturally influence markets.

(4) *Other Regulations*

In order to ensure fair dealing the stock exchanges impose their own voluntary regulations. For instance, when excessively speculative dealings in short shares occur, such transactions may be placed under the direct supervision of the stock exchanges. Restrictions are also imposed upon the daily ranges of individual share prices, except for those of specially designated shares. When it becomes necessary to curb corners in shares the stock exchanges can request members to submit reports on trading in such shares. As already noted, stock exchanges establish criteria for selecting shares to be listed, in connection with which they examine the eligibility of listed shares from time to time. This, too, is important for maintaining fair trading. It may be added that from October 1967, cross-transactions – that is, the marrying by a member of a stock exchange of purchases and sales of the same amounts of given shares on the same day – have been prohibited.

The securities finance companies can also restrain unsound transactions by altering the terms of margin loan transactions, for example, by demanding additional security for their loans (see Part Three, Chapter 21, 'Securities Finance Companies').

In addition, security dealers' associations organised under the Securities Transaction Law (there are at present ten associations) have formulated voluntary rules to prevent unfair trading and to harmonise trading practices.

INDEX

References to tables, figures and footnotes are given in brackets after the relevant page number(s), T indicating a table, F a figure and FN a footnote.

)ATE